# Strategic Innovation

C000146160

The creative aspect of strategy is the central focus of this book. Through a selection of case studies, the editors show how creativity fits into the general context of the manager's role in the firm, and the firm within its industry.

The key role of the 'strategic innovator' is to create new strategies which alter the 'rules of the game'. Some of the cases explore the competitive dynamics of innovative firms, and how they use their competencies and capabilities to change the patterns of competition in the industry. Others explore how the managers in companies put together the efforts of those around them to effect innovation in their own firms. Companies discussed include IKEA, Ariston, JVC, Benetton and Honda.

In tune with the emerging dynamic resource-based theory of the firm, central to the new strategy courses, this collection of key case studies is targeted at MBA students as well as senior executives on short courses.

**Charles Baden-Fuller** is Centenary Professor of Strategic Management at City University Business School. **Martyn Pitt** is lecturer in Strategic Management and Marketing at the University of Bath.

# Strategic Innovation

An international casebook on
strategic management

Edited by Charles Baden-Fuller and
Martyn Pitt

London and New York

First published 1996
by Routledge
11 New Fetter Lane, London EC4P 4EE

Simultaneously published in the USA and Canada
by Routledge
29 West 35th Street, New York, NY 10001

Typeset in Garamond by
Datix International Limited, Bungay, Suffolk
Printed and bound in Great Britain by
T J Press (Padstow) Ltd, Padstow, Cornwall

*British Library Cataloguing in Publication Data*
A catalogue record for this book is available from the British Library

*Library of Congress Cataloguing in Publication Data*
A catalogue record for this book has been requested

ISBN 0–415–12869–2 (hbk)
ISBN 0–415–12870–6 (pbk)

# Contents

# Figures

# Tables

# Contributors

**Charles Baden-Fuller**, City University Business School, London
**Joshua Bamfield**, Nene College, Northampton
**Carlo Boschetti**, University of Bologna, Italy
**Charlotte Butler**, INSEAD-CEDEP, France
**Roland Calori**, Groupe ESC Lyons, France
**Derek Channon**, Imperial College, London University
**Chong Ju Choi**, City University Business School, London
**Bo Eriksen**, University of Odense, Denmark
**Sumantra Ghoshal**, INSEAD-CEDEP, France
**Peter Golder**, City University Business School, London
**Robert Grant**, Georgetown University, Washington DC
**Chris Holland**, Manchester Business School
**François-Xavier Huard**, INSEAD-CEDEP, France
**Jens Krag**, University of Odense, Denmark
**Geoff Lockett**, University of Leeds
**Gianni Lorenzoni**, University of Bologna, Italy
**Andrew Mair**, Birkbeck College, University of London
**Børge Obel**, University of Odense, Denmark
**Martyn Pitt**, University of Bath
**Mikael Søndergaard**, University of Odense, Denmark
**John Stopford**, London Business School
**David Williams**, Bournemouth University

# Introduction

This book is addressed to practising and aspiring managers who want to stretch their understanding of strategy. It is our ambition that teachers in universities and institutes of higher learning will use this book for MBA and excecutive students, as well as the more advanced undergraduate level. The cases are stretching, relevant and fun.

Our cases are rich and complex, without being overly lengthy. In comparison to many cases used in business schools, we aim to step closer to real life which is necessary, because strategizing is a complex and difficult task. Often the data are unclear, the manager is prisoner of history, and the choice of possible actions is crucially dependent on the resources and people potentially available. We try to show these constraints realistically, and the cases in this book have been selected because they are the outcome of extensive detailed research. In general, the various writers have had close contact with the organizations, have met and interviewed many managers, and have watched events over an extended period of time – from many months to years. For example, the Richardson and Edwards cases involved more than thirty interviews over a period of three years, as well as extensive contacts with others in the industry. In the Benetton case, the writer travelled several countries, using longitudinal research of both primary and secondary sources. Such care in building cases is the hallmark of this book.

Good managers need to learn about strategy and strategizing in an international setting. This task has many facets, one of which is the study of actions of other managers through carefully constructed case histories. Our cases allow practising and aspiring managers to appreciate a breadth of situations from a variety of industries, countries and contexts, which is very difficult to gain from first-hand experience. For those who have worked as managers, our cases should trigger new thoughts, forcing the reader to rethink what he or she has already learnt. Our cases also provide an excellent medium for understanding theory, and seeing how theory translates into practice. Because most of our authors are well known for their contributions to theory, our cases have been carefully constructed to allow the reader to refine and create theory from the data they have around them.

Whilst there are very many styles of writing a case, two stand out. There are those which present a problem for students to solve, and there are those which document important change processes in companies revealing how managers think and act. Our cases have elements of both, but an emphasis on the latter. There are opportunities to define the strategic problem (a critical element of good management thinking), and there are detailed insightful data for learning about how strategy is conceived and executed inside a variety of organizations.

Our choice of companies has been guided by many criteria. We resisted the temptation to claim that our cases are 'excellent companies'. As the follow up of *In Search of Excellence* showed, continued success is precarious. In this book, we chose organizations which are known to have been rule-breakers, exemplars and challengers of the status quo. Some of our organizations are famous and have achieved success for a long period of time: Benetton, Swatch, IKEA, Samsung, JVC, and Honda are obvious examples. Others are only famous in their sectors, such as Richardson, Edwards, and Amtsparkassen. A few are much less established in the public eye. When choosing the cases for this book, we make no judgement about the sustainability of future success; on the contrary we expect that success will be hard to sustain.

## CONTEXT, PROCESS AND CONTENT

In real life, strategy formulation is rarely separated from implementation. The history of the individual and that of the organization are inextricably linked, and both colour diagnosis and action. Whilst there is clearly a place for discussions of formulation which is separate from implementation, our cases do not do this – we seek to explore how these factors interact.

In all our cases, we have tried to give a *context*. In some instances, we have found it necessary to go back several years to give a flavour of how situations arose and how people thought about their surroundings. In addition, we have tried to explain the industry setting. We have typically found that industry analysis, apparently so clear in some text books looks quite different inside organizations. Often there is considerable disagreement about matters such as: market definition, market size, share of competitors and relative cost positions. In addition, managers do not always readily agree about the entry barriers or even the names of the potential entrants. Because of this, in some of our cases, there is an absence of agreed hard data in these economic factors, a reflection of the reality of those working in the business. The existence of these ambiguities couples with softer data, feel and impressions are made evident, and it is with such information that managers have to work. Absence of tables should not delude the reader or teacher into thinking that economic or technical analysis is not possible; in all cases, there is considerable scope for using analytical tools and techniques.

Most of our cases pay detailed and extensive attention to the managerial *process*. How were things done? Who acted when? What did people think? When answering these questions, we reconstruct internal and external history. We go into considerable detail explaining how some initiatives were started and stalled, and how others were carried to successful conclusions. Capturing successes and failures within organizations is vital for learning. Our case-writers usually made repeated visits to the organizations to gain their stories, and were sometimes there when critical matters were debated and decisions made. Of course, all our stories are partial, but in almost every case they have been discussed with the firm's management.

What people and organizations do, that is, the *content* of their actions, is often critically important. Most of the achievements of our organizations are highly technical, and quite subtle, and one should not underestimate the true innovations they produced. The new I.T. system, the new production methods, the successful marketing campaign, are nearly always the consequences of sophisticated understanding. In general, we have not gone into these achievements in detail, but readers who are experts will be able to gauge these successes. In class discussions, teachers are encouraged to explore the magnitude of the achievements.

Content goes further than technical content, it also covers economic achievements. We have selected cases where the traditional economic rules have been broken. Many of our firms have reversed a trend of seemingly inevitable decline. Others have delivered growth and profitability in the most unpromising circumstances. Others have achieved much in the face of much larger and more powerful competitors.

In short, context, process and content are all intertwined in our cases, to varying degrees. It is for this reasons that we believe that our cases are exciting and challenging. We do not present 'problems' for the clever student to guess solutions which might not be capable of implementation, but rather descriptions and subtleties for active and aspiring managers to appreciate.

## INTERNATIONAL

Our case book is unambiguously international – a reflection of the fact that most firms face international competition. This is most obviously true for those operating in Europe where both manufacturing and services are subject to international competition. Even utilities, which used to be a sacred ground for domestic firms are facing foreign competition.

Internationalism can exhibit itself in many ways. Firms can differ in the location of their operations and their ownership; this is most obvious in our case book because it describes firms from nine countries in Europe, Asia and the Americas. Firms can be involved in competing against foreign firms, in exports and imports, or in both of these by organizing and co-ordinating a transnational empire. Almost all of the firms in this book import and export, most are true multinationals. Notable here are Ariston, Benetton, Cartier, Honda, IKEA, Motorola, JVC, Salomon, Samsung, and Swatch. Internationalism can be exhibited because firms are involved in international joint ventures, mergers, acquisitions, and informal alliances. Once again, there are many examples, with specific emphasis given to these activities in the Ariston, Benetton and Motorola cases.

There is another important dimension to international competition, that of the differences in strategic approach among international firms. Firms from other countries often play by different rules; their resources are different, their costs bases are different, they bring new skills and different technologies. They perceive things differently. Sometimes this makes them less efficient, often it makes them more effective. We believe that courses on international business benefit from having cases which explore these dimensions. To capture this, we have not only chosen a span of the cases which is international, but authorship is international too. Although all the cases are written in English, many authors are local to the company. Thus Samsung is written by a Korean, Benetton by an Italian, Ariston-Indesit by another Italian, Cartier by a Frenchman, Salomon by another Frenchman, and Amtsparkassen by a Dane. This is important, for by using local writers, new perspectives are brought to the class room, and we are better able to see and understand organizations through the eyes of those who work there.

## TEACHING AND USING THIS BOOK

Why should a teacher use this book? We have suggested in the paragraphs above that our book contains cases which are relevant to those who wish to teach strategy and international business at a higher level than introductory, and wish to use stretching material. In addition, the book will be attractive to those who wish to use cases which are research based.

How should this book be used? It is not necessary to have a companion text, the book can stand alone. We have provided two strong introductory chapters which suggest themes, and items for discussion. In addition, there is a short editorial for each case, which introduces some of the issues and highlights topics for discussion. Reading these, the teacher can judge the range of possible uses for the cases. Thus Benetton can be used to discuss international alliances, the networked organization, how organizations can manage rapid growth, as well as providing a challenge to the idea of maturity. Some cases bring in very topical issues such as the strategic use of Information Technology (Motorola and Direct Line), some look at issues such as mergers (Ariston). All in all, there is a great richness here. Teachers will also be pleased to know that a set of teaching notes is in preparation.

We know that many strategy and international business management teachers have their own set of readings, which they prefer to use in accompaniment to a book of this kind. For them, they need no text book. But, if the teacher wishes to use a companion text, which book should he or she use? There are a number of possibilities, and they include: C. Baden-Fuller and J. M. Stopford, *Rejuvenating the Mature Business* (Routledge, 1995). R. Grant, author of one of the cases, has also produced a text, *Contemporary Strategy Analysis* (Blackwell, 1995). De Wit and Meyer's book *Strategy: Process, Content, Context* (West, 1994) contains a set of readings which teachers may also find valuable.

We note that Baden-Fuller and Stopford's book has the merit of having *strategy as a creative process* as its central theme. Rejuvenating mature businesses, they argue requires firms to break the mould of their own past and that of the industry. In addition, extensive mention is made to three cases in the book: Benetton, Richardson and Edwards, as well as more limited references to Ariston Merloni and Honda. In the table below, we note how particular cases can be matched to particular chapters, but we emphasise that there is considerable flexibility. Indeed, we mention many cases more than once for this reason.

## Possible course layout using Baden-Fuller and Stopford:

| Chapter | Title | Possible case/alternatives |
| --- | --- | --- |
| 1 | Maturity is a state of mind | Swatch, Pyrochem, Direct Line |
| 2 | The firm matters more than the industry | Cartier, Richardson, JVC |
| 3 | Strategic innovation | Direct Line, IKEA, Honda, Motorola |
| 4 | Creative scope | Amtssparekassen, Swatch, Cartier |
| 5 | The entrepreneurial organization | Edwards High Vacuum, Pyrochem, Salomon, Benetton |
| 6 | The crescendo model | Edwards High Vacuum, Woolworth, Ariston-Indesit |
| 7 | Reduce complexity and start initiatives | Richardson, Motorola, Woolworth |
| 8 | Shape the collective effort | Benetton, Honda, JVC, Ariston-Indesit |
| 9 | Maintaining momentum | Samsung, IKEA, Salomon |

Our selection of tried and tested cases should be exciting for both teachers and students. We know from experience that undergraduate and MBA students engage for an hour to an hour and a half on the issues raised in each case. This makes them ideal for most courses. We also know that many cases are very successful with more senior managers, and that they identify very clearly with the issues raised. When asked to compare the actions of the subjects in the case with the activities of their own organizations, we have enjoyed discussions of up to three hours. More important, the executives have universally acclaimed the enjoyment and learning. We believe that you, like us will also have good experience using this book.

# Acknowledgements

We gratefully acknowledge the help of Peter McNamara and Neil Thomson, who carefully read and annotated the cases in this book, and who encouraged and inspired us with many good ideas. We also acknowledge the assistance of Xavier Boza, who in the early stages was vital in contacting potential authors and making suggestions for our selection of cases. Rosemary Nixon, Business Editor at Routledge, was an inspiration encouraging us to press ahead. In addition to our thanks, our authors also acknowledge their many sources of help from colleagues and companies, and we would like to add our thanks to theirs. Without the patience of many executives, this book could not be written. Lastly, we have tried to check all the copyrights, and hope that there are no oversights.

# Part I

# The nature of innovating strategic management

# Chapter 1

# Positional choices and competence upgrading[1]

## *The editors*

## INTRODUCTION

Ensuring success is a creative process. Creativity is not the only factor of importance, it needs to be used judiciously – for in business, as in life, those who succeed are also focused, energetic, persistent and brave. By using the combination of factors, which includes creativity, managers not only confront the changes taking place in their environments, but also take charge of the change to lead their businesses, and ultimately their circumstances. The creative aspect of strategy is the centre of attention of this book, and through case studies we show how creativity fits into the general context of the manager's role in the firm, and the firm in its industry.[2]

The importance of creativity in strategy has been long recognized. For example, almost everyone knows the story of how Ford at the beginning of the century used the novel strategy of mass production and mass marketing to create in a very short time one of the world's most successful companies.[3] That mass production had been developed in other industries is not so well known, but it is indisputable that Ford advanced it to a fine art in the field of automobiles. With standardization and creative design in all areas of the firm, including purchasing, production, marketing and distribution, Ford's novel strategy resulted in the Model T, which was an attractive product at low cost and modest prices. Nowadays the phrase 'You can have it any colour, so long as it is black', is used to suggest an absence of creativity, but then it was the opposite, for it aptly captured one aspect of Ford's novelty: standardized mass production in an industry that ignored costs and relied on every car being custom-built to different specifications. Ford's creativity brought fortunes, but the firm began to be troubled ten years later because of its inability to change its strategy again. Sloan, at General Motors, built a team that learned from Ford, and became most successful.[4]

The heart of creating and sustaining success is the ability to generate effective and innovative strategies. The need to devote resources to research and development activities in general is recognized by most organizations (although some may contract out the work). Most effort will be devoted to new or better designs, processes, products and marketing. Without innovation, existing product portfolios will slowly die, processes will be outmoded, advertising lose its credibility and the source of sustained profitability dry up. For this reason, those who work in organizations often find themselves exhorted to be more creative. But, if product innovation is to be really successful and process innovation is to show its true worth, there must be new strategies to help and to encourage them. The creativity will be apparent because the new strategy will typically break some established norm or rule and challenge accepted thinking about how the organization as a whole should behave.

Our view of strategy is in contrast to that image which often exists in the minds of managers. They often act as though strategy choices, patterns and directions should be unchanging and somehow constant in this sea of change. They seem to believe that rules and laws can guide one to make enduring choices.[5] Thus we are told choose good not bad industries,[6] and that success can be achieved only if one has a high share of the market.[7] Such thinking, we suggest, constrains options. Our purpose is to show, through our case studies, that successful organizations can push back the boundaries of accepted thinking about the rules of success. It is not just emerging, growing industries that provide opportunities; mature industries offer equally exciting potential. In the same way, small share firms can also achieve outstanding success.

Finally, a new strategy has to be one that can be executed. We recognize that implementation is *not* an issue which can be relegated to a side line, for strategy lies in the detail. Good strategy, like much of that which is good, is a subtle combination of the perfect command of detail and the ability to have a grand vision. Detail is vital, for without attention to detail, things go wrong; imagination in overall scope is critical too, or there is no impact.

## KEY THEMES

In the opening chapters we will explore with a new emphasis four important themes in strategic management: positioning, resourcing, corporate entrepreneurship (which includes leadership) and the incentive reward system. Our emphasis will suggest that effective strategy contains two aspects: creativity or innovation in the conception and a high standard of implementation. We will suggest that good strategy goes beyond effective market positions and the deployment of existing resources back to the basics of corporate entrepreneurship and flow of rewards. For organizations to create and sustain success, a complete system has to be built which allows development and maintains itself.

'What business are we in?' is one of the oldest and more important strategy questions. Choosing the right sector, and segment in that sector, has long been seen as an important component of firm success. We provocatively propose that there are no *intrinsically* good or bad sectors, or good or bad segments. The challenge for organizations is to understand and exploit their markets, and this may require them to be creative about positioning to achieve success. Sometimes, seemingly unattractive industries and sectors are the best place for investment of time, energy and resources. Sometimes, old segments can be successfully approached in new and novel ways, combining new thoughts with old customers. And, of course, sometimes the novelty can also be expressed in firms discovering and creating new markets.

Many managers are heard to say, 'Our key assets are our people, knowledge, systems and routines.' The newly emerging framework of the resource-based theory of the firm makes explicit that hidden routines, capabilities, skills and knowledge are the core to competitive advantage. A firm that is rich in these assets can successfully tackle markets whose profitability eludes others. But even those firms that are not so rich can be successful if they are creative about how they deploy their existing resources. This ability to see in new ways allows organizations to adopt new approaches to markets and to tackle seemingly impossible tasks in creative and profitable ways. There is more; whereas many traditional strategy books emphasize fitting current resources to current markets, the entrepreneurial firm is one step ahead creating resources to fit tomorrow's markets.

Some leaders are heard to remark that 'Corporate entrepreneurship is central to building tomorrow's skills, capabilities and competencies.' In this and the next chapter we examine some of the issues surrounding entrepreneurship, and explore the process by which organizations build tomorrow's critical resources faster and more effectively than their rivals. This suggests that the process of building is not just the work of managers at the top, but should pervade the whole organization. It is a process that emphasizes teamwork, ambition, experimentation and learning to challenge accepted practices of both the firm and its surrounding industry.

Corporate entrepreneurship is more than an activity of teams; it is complemented by leadership. Leadership is an activity that does not occur just at the top of the organization, but almost everywhere. Through the case studies in the book, we probe the important aspects of those leading and working in organizations: imagining, guiding, planning, realizing and learning. All these activities are revealed through what people say and do, and are therefore part of corporate entrepreneurship.

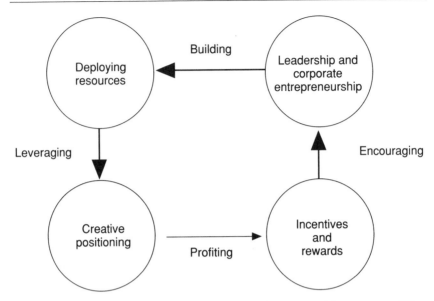

*Figure 1.1* Connecting resources and positions to achieve competitive success via entrepreneurship and creative thinking

To close the loop, we mention the importance of constructing the reward and incentive structures that both encourage the process and distribute the profits and other spoils of success. The extensive literature on corporate governance deals mainly with the problem of financial rewards to shareholders. It is becoming increasingly apparent that capital is not as scarce as other resources such as leadership skills and knowledge. Successful firms will die if there is no reward to the large group of people and factors that also contribute to success. The human factors need both financial and non-financial rewards, which can include an exciting place to work and the association with innovation and success. For the firm to remain an effective dynamic system there needs to be a reward and incentive system that is congruent to the needs of those who supply the scarce inputs and which feeds on the successes.

In Figure 1.1, we portray the four ideas mentioned above: creative positioning, deployment of resources, corporate entrepreneurship (including leadership), and incentives (including the division of the spoils) and we connect these with encouraging, building and leveraging. We place positions and resources on the left side of the diagram, because they are associated with the rational analytical side of thinking. In contrast, entrepreneurial behaviour and reward systems are placed on the right side, because they are associated with the softer side of the process. Our diagram seeks to suggest that the effective firm balances the soft and the hard sides, and that both are equally important and inextricably inter-twined. Reality is more complicated, and there are feedback loops. For example, entrepreneurship and leadership are critical in making good positioning choices. However, our diagram shows the simple basic model, with the key important directions of thought.

Although we present a holistic closed system, where successful managing is balancing a complex system, we propose to analyse each part separately, recognizing that history and interdependencies are also important.

## ENTREPRENEURIAL ATTITUDES TO INDUSTRY SECTOR

It is possibilities, informed but not constrained by history, that should guide the entrepreneurial organization in understanding the potential of its markets. In selecting the cases in this book, we were keen to show how firms can be successful in a wide variety of settings, and to give a flavour of the ways they surmount their challenges.

The video-recorder (VHS) case illustrates that high growth industries are both exciting and demanding. It is shown here that even the innovative giant Sony, which has an enviable track record, can get it wrong. Matsushita was able to push its video product using a combination of factors. One was the use of 'open standards'; a positioning of its product quite differently in respect of the competition. By surrendering control over the technology, it induced others to copy and promote its product package, ultimately to good effect. This case is rich with many lessons, but one is clear: making money in high growth environments is not always easy and requires creativity.

Not all firms are in a position to invest in high technology, fast-moving industries. Indeed, many would like to consider the possibilities of more mature markets. We suggest that lower growth 'mature' markets offer just as great a chance of rewards as those which appear to be glamorous and profitable. Our reasoning is simple. In general, glamorous high growth industries are typically populated by more imaginative and more creative businesses. They create an environment which attracts custom, raises the industry revenues and makes the industry attractive. But creative and innovative businesses are also more fiercely competitive. Winning may be difficult, as the pace of change may be rapid and the minimum standards high. In contrast, many less profitable industries are populated by sleepy uncreative businesses which fail to innovate, and the potential for success by a creative newcomer may be greater and the demands of the competition may be less exacting.

In this case book there are many examples of firms being successful and profitable in mature markets. When Direct Line entered the motor vehicle insurance market, traditional wisdom based on simplistic historic analysis would have suggested that the possibilities were severely limited. The market appeared to have limited profits potential. The industry was quite fragmented, with some large players who were unable to dominate. Moreover, the situation seemed to have little promise. For years, motor insurance had been beset with rising risks, matched by rising premiums, a fragmented set of suppliers and a regulatory environment that did not assure profitability. Direct Line proposed selling motor insurance direct to the customer over the telephone, avoiding the traditional broker or agent arrangement of distribution. Direct Line was not the first company to take this approach for some of Lloyd's syndicates had sold policies directly but Direct Line's approach was novel in its combination of elements and vigour. It matched a new array of skills and resources in the areas of marketing, IT and access to capital to carry out its own insurance. In a very few years it had changed the rules of the game, creating profits for itself and forcing rivals to follow.

In most sectors, industry decline in demand is the signal of lost competitiveness. In the automobile industry, the sales of European and US producers have been static in recent years because of locally changing conditions and better, stronger foreign competition. Their decline was not caused by a decline in the product demand, for the global market for cars is booming, with rapid expansion in developing and former communist countries. In the Honda case, we show how the mind-set and approach of this famous Japanese firm helped reshape the industry.

Strategies for declining markets have been examined by several writers, and these typically emphasize the importance of predicting the speed of decline and the exit game.[8] Harrigan and Baden-Fuller have shown that declining demand can be managed beneficially, and result in high profits for some of the players. Declining demand for the product is rare, and in the final analysis it forces the business to create new competencies to serve related markets; this is not disastrous. Many horse and buggy carriage-builders have evolved into highly successful motor car service stations and farm equipment dealers.

Most mature markets are not declining, and the fortunes of the firm can be revived with better products and services. Many managers of mature firms realize that transformation is possible if there are new products, new processes, new service delivery systems and new strategies. The Richardson case provides a vivid example of the possibilities that can be created in a declining industry. British kitchen knives were under threat from many quarters, of which one was a decline in consumption due to more eating out, and another was the threat of Eastern competition. The case shows how rethinking and repositioning helped stimulate new demand by selling knives as gifts and fashion items, and was part of

| Sectors exhibiting unfavourable characteristics | Well-established industries | Fast-growing emerging sectors |
| --- | --- | --- |
| Direct Line (car insurance) | Amtssparekassen (Danish banking) | JVC (video-recorders) |
| Benetton (European textile manufacturing) | Ariston (domestic appliances) | Motorola (electronics) |
| Richardson (UK cutlery) | Cartier (high class jewellery) | Pyrochem (fire-retardant paint) |
| Swatch (Swiss watches) | Edwards (high vacuum pumps) | Samsung (electronics) |
| Woolworths | Honda (motor cars) | |
| | IKEA (furniture retailing) | |

Figure 1.2 Classifying the case studies by the basic attractiveness of the sector

the process of rejuvenation allowing the firm to capture a position of industry leadership, in sales and profitability.

Figure 1.2 shows how the cases in this book can be grouped into firms in growing and challenging sectors, traditional sectors and unpromising sectors. As can be seen, we have tried to produce examples in all kinds of environments to help the reader appreciate our ideas in a wide variety of contexts. Our choice of labels is not meant to be scientifically exact, although we argue that sectors such as the British cutlery industry are widely recognized as ones that seem most unattractive, and that video-recorders in the 1980s were obviously a challenging, potentially high growth industry. The point we wish to make is that there are possibilities in all kinds of industry situations.

It is necessary and appropriate to analyse the environmental forces facing the organization. This kind of analysis was developed by a long line of industrial economists starting with Bain and Mason, and has been launched most effectively in strategy by Michael Porter.[9] Specific issues which can be included are entry and exit barriers, the power of rivalry from close competitors, the power of suppliers and buyers, and the role of government regulations. This analysis indicates the hurdles that the firm faces, but our cases show how the forces need not be a constraint. Far from being a prisoner of their environments, firms can overcome them. Likewise, value chain analysis is vital. This kind of analysis, pioneered by McKinsey and popularized by Porter, helps firms understand their role in the value chain and the possibilities for creating value for their suppliers and customers as well as money for themselves.[10]

In the volume *Rejuvenating the Mature Business*, Baden-Fuller and

| Cases where firms redefined and re-made their markets | Cases where firms repositioned themselves in their markets or value chain |
| --- | --- |
| Benetton | Amtssparekassen |
| Cartier | Ariston-Indesit |
| IKEA | Edwards High Vacuum |
| JVC | Woolworths |
| Pyrochem | |
| Richardson | |
| Swatch | |

*Figure 1.3* Classifying the case studies by the degree of repositioning

Stopford examine at greater length why the industry need not be a constraint to the business. There it is argued that all industries offer opportunities for firms that are appropriately resourced. In high growth sectors, there are obviously possibilities for excellent returns, but there are also very high risks. The wrong choice of technology, product or market segment can result in a failure to make an acceptable return. In more mature sectors, the opportunities may seem more constrained, but they are still high. New approaches to traditional markets can, and do, yield exceptional profits, even in seemingly adverse environments. Here, it is important to realize that adverse circumstances are not a real constraint, but rather obstacles to be overcome. Indeed, the very adverse circumstances are likely to be the outcome of the failure of firms in the sector to be creative and innovative, rather than vice versa.

Our reasoning is not just based on a few case studies, but also has support from wider statistical work. For example, Rumelt in a study of the influence of sector choice on business unit profitability found little support for the proposition that adverse economic environments affect profitability; nor did he conclude that high growth sectors are necessarily more profitable.[11]

## CREATIVE AND EFFECTIVE POSITIONING

Successful entrepreneurial organizations do not just challenge conventional thinking about the industry sectors that they choose to compete in; many choose to compete by selecting, combining or creating segments in unusual ways. They realize that being successful requires an understanding of the dynamics of markets, and the ability to reposition the existing resources of the firm in a new way so that better value can be achieved (see Figure 1.3).

The Amtssparekassen case provides an excellent example of what can be achieved by repositioning. In the late 1980s, the Danish banking industry was experiencing a difficult time. Amtssparekassen decided to refocus its activities avoiding head-on competition with other banks, and exploiting its competencies and capabilities. It found profits in segments that the other banks ignored or handled badly.

The Swatch case shows both the decay of the old and the rise of the new in a sector which was traditionally focused on technology. Swatch was formed from the residue of a Swiss firm which made its reputation from accurate mechanical watches. It chose to battle with the Japanese and Far Eastern watchmakers on a different territory, that of watches as symbols of fun rather than as pieces of electronic or mechanical wizardry. By purchasing and developing the necessary skills it was able to carve out a new segment. Its success was attributable to its ability to pre-empt and even create a new market that had not been displayed before.

Segment choice encompasses position in the value chain and how parts of the chain are combined or unbundled. Edwards High Vacuum chose to focus on making component pumps in a sector where most rivals believed the conventional wisdom that systems not components was the way to make money. Pyrochem also broke the rules about how to distribute its fire retarding paint. It chose to target builders and architects, those who had direct influence on building design and construction, rather than the more technical routes of its rivals.

In understanding the source of success, managers and students should not be mistaken in the value they ascribe to market share. Market share can be acquired by delivering high value, or it can be acquired by reducing margins without delivering value. The former is truly a symbol of success, the latter not so. Market share can also be acquired by purchasing competitors. Where value is subsequently created, this is good, but where value is destroyed, it is not so. We make the point because we wish to show that repositioning, refocusing or creating is not just a question of market share numbers, but something more substantial. It is wrong to suggest that being number one or number two in an industry gives the business unique advantages and that by implication large market share can be a substitute for creative positioning.

We intentionally digress for a moment to explore this point more fully, to show that our cases are concerned with something quite fundamental. A false understanding about market share is widespread. It appears in many guises. At one extreme there are chief executives who say, 'We are only interested in industries where we hold a number one or number two position.' Such statements, if unaccompanied by an emphasis on innovation, will send out the wrong signal that high share will lead to success. At a more mundane level, managers are encouraged to write in their plans, 'We should dominate the industry and seek success by capturing a number one position.' Again, such statements are dangerous where the writer and reader believe that share is the source, not the measure of success.

In our book there are a number of cases which illustrate that absence of a large market share need not be a barrier to success. Pyrochem won a great share of the market, but the causal linkage of its success was from creative resourcing and positioning to high share, and not the other way around. Likewise for Benetton, Richardson, Salomon, Edwards and most other companies described in this book. These cases show that growing market share is not the panacea for an organization's ills, not even in mature, slow-growing markets.

The belief that gaining market share will lead to greater profitability comes from confusing cause and effect. Many successful businesses do have a large market share but the causality is usually from success to share, not the other way. Successful businesses often (but not always) grow because they have discovered an overwhelming source of competitive advantage, such as quality at low cost. Such advantages can be used to displace even the most entrenched incumbents.

Our cases raise some serious doubts about the validity of some past highly simplistic strategic paradigms based on the importance of scale and share. Barry Hedley and the Boston Consulting group are generally credited with first writing about the scale effects, which may exist in all industries, that could affect the choice of strategy.[12] In their work they examined the issue of the experience curve, and suggested that firms that had the largest cumulative output (typically but not always the largest market share player) would in general be more successful.[13] Buzzell and Gale are generally credited with the popularizing of the value of seeking market share as the route to success, although it too has many earlier antecedents.[14] They note that large market share can have a beneficial influence on profitability through many triggers. It can reduce costs on account of scale or experience effects, in production, service delivery, logistics and marketing. It may allow the firm to charge higher prices, because the service or product may seem intrinsically less risky to consumers, and entrants may be discouraged. Although they stress the importance of quality in the process, the simplistic view is often associated with their writings.

The statistical evidence supports our view that market share by itself cannot guarantee success. Schmalensee in his extensive study of more than four hundred firms in US manufacturing, found that less than 2 per cent of the variations in profitability between one business and another could be explained by differences in market share.[15] Market share effects appear to be relatively unimportant across a wide sample of industries.

| Cases emphasizing internal resource development | Cases emphasizing acquisition, borrowing or rapid resource formation |
|---|---|
| Amtssparekassen | Ariston-Indesit |
| Edwards | Benetton |
| IKEA | Cartier |
| JVC | Direct Line |
| Richardson | Motorola-Citibank |
| Salomon | Swatch |
| Woolworths | Samsung |

*Figure 1.4* Classifying the case studies by the resource creation process

## CREATING, COMBINING AND DEPLOYING RESOURCES

Many strategists are now arguing that it is the resources of the organization that are the key to long-term competitive advantage. Positions can be altered with relative ease in comparison to resources, and the identification, collecting and deployment of resources represent the harder challenge for the organization.

The cases in this book document firms with a creative attitude towards building and utilizing resources, and their actions challenge one of the strongest conventional thoughts in strategy. The challenge facing an organization can be analytically divided into three parts: exploiting existing resources more effectively; bringing in or borrowing new resources from others; and the process of creating resources from within. All organizations do all these things, but some are more obviously associated with one aspect. We name some examples in Figure 1.4.

The Woolworths case shows an organization reshaping existing resources to deploy them to greater effect. Woolworths was a nearly defunct organization, with a large number of retail outlets selling low priced, low margin goods, yielding an unacceptable return. At first sight it seems as though the company is poorly positioned, in the wrong market, with the wrong physical assets and the wrong image. Its new top managers found ways to release hidden energy in its assets to unlock value. They proved that there was a large residue of latent skills in the organization, which if reorganized and redirected could yield an effective and valuable return. By releasing and mobilizing talent and redirecting and refocusing the segment choice, they provide an excellent example of a business which was rejuvenated along the lines described by Baden-Fuller and Stopford.

The Edwards case is an excellent example of a firm building resources from within, over long periods of time, to create leading positions in its markets. In the 1970s Edwards was an almost defunct company, having trouble making money. It worked hard on building new competencies step by step, starting with effective production of a high quality pump, and then building the related competencies of marketing to new and growing segments in an increasing world market. Its steps to success have required it to redefine all the functions of the organization, and to redefine its scope and positions. After many years of hard work, it is now at the top of the world league.

Richardson is another example of what can be accomplished on even more limited resources. Richardson learned to build leading edge technology using its own engineers. In the late 1960s Richardson was a small cutlery firm located in Sheffield, England. It was not profitable, it had no famous brand name, it had no financial resources, and its share of the UK market was small, and that of the world market insignificant. In a little over two decades it has reached the number one world position in kitchen knives against competition from the Far East. Its resource base is now formidable, exhibiting excellence in production, marketing, new product design and innovation, and human resource management; and most of these resources were built in-house. It has demonstrated a capacity to renew and reconstruct from within.

The Benetton case shows how capabilities and competencies can be built rapidly by using outsiders. Benetton encourages its partners to develop special skills in many areas, especially in retailing and manufacturing. This has allowed the organization to avoid spreading its own resources too widely, and in its turn it has built some special core skills such as dyeing, fashion design, logistics and global systems management. Contrary to received wisdom, it has shown that core competencies do not need to lie inside the firm's legal boundaries.

The Ariston-Indesit case explores how resources are transferred and built in a merger. It shows that the process is dependent on function and geography, and how competencies have to be destroyed and skills unlearned, before new ones can be built. The Swatch, Direct Line and Cartier cases show how skills can be bought in to have a significant effect on an organization.

The resource-based theories of competitive advantage date back many years, when it was typically argued that firms had to match their resources to the markets they were in.[16] Then the resources were often seen as the physical and tangible resources. It was only recently that academics began to think more closely about resources, and integrate the theory into strategy thinking. At the simplest level of analysis, there is little new in saying that we should ensure that current resources are fitted to currently perceived market opportunities. It is more significant to point out that success can come by judicious addition of new resources, and that a poorly resourced firm can build wholly new capabilities and competencies to become successful. Moreover, when we think about how the resources are to be deployed, we need to recognize that the challenge is not to fill the markets as perceived today, but to recognize where markets will be tomorrow, and how we can shape and create those markets.

The modern resource theory emphasizes that hidden assets are critical. These ideas are usually attributed to the work of Penrose and Selznick, but it was left to more recent writers such as Barney, Teece, Pisano and Schuen to develop them further.[17] They stress the role of knowledge of products and processes, systems and reputation in determining the firm's long-run health. Basic resources such as land, buildings and capital are important, but not as critical. Because tangible resources can be traded, they may be critical to survival but paradoxically are not the source of the competitive advantage. It is the intangible resources which are the key. In the battles between organizations in markets it is those with superior intangible resources which appear to be at an advantage.

Being cash rich or asset rich is neither necessary nor sufficient for success. Robert Grant points out that many well-endowed firms find it difficult to exploit their resource bases.[18] It is the combining of resources through the skill base of the employees, the hidden routines, the systems, and the 'culture' of the business that leads to value creation. Its effect can be powerful. Many firms can perform better by utilizing these resources more effectively.

Making resources for tomorrow's challenges is as critical as utilizing more effectively what we have today. The literature on mergers and joint ventures has long argued that bringing together organizations with complementary skills and capabilities may be the way to create competitive advantage. Resources can also be built by purchasing the skill base through hiring key people or acquiring specific know-how. Although it is difficult to do this effectively, the ability to see how novel combinations can be used to create value is one of the features of dynamic competition.

Building resources, skills and capabilities for tomorrow's challenges is a very important part of creating sustainable competitive advantage. Many firms have become winners by building resources (consciously or unconsciously) to capture new markets. As Prahalad and Hamel point out, competencies such as Sony's ability to develop the skills for miniaturized electronics or Canon's ability to develop capabilities in optics, imaging and microprocessor controls have been the keys to those firms' success.[19] In another article, these two authors go on to talk about strategy as stretch; others have referred to it long before as a process of building talent and ability.[20]

Our rich case descriptions show the power of the resource-based view. It is not the absolute quantity of resources which matter, but rather the capacity to create them and then exploit them. The cases show that what the organization lacks can in many circumstances be built in time.

## CREATING COMPETENCIES THROUGH CORPORATE ENTREPRENEURSHIP AND LEADERSHIP

Where then is the longer-term source of competitive strength? We suggest that it lies in the capacity of the organization to be corporately entrepreneurial, and of its managers to show true leadership. With these two elements the organization can win, for it can build resources fastest at lowest cost. The next chapter examines much of the manager's agenda in more detail, but here we review a few key elements very briefly.

There is an extensive literature on corporate entrepreneurship, which has focused on how organizations build resources from within.[21] Much of this literature is fairly new, for only recently has the importance of creativity in larger organizations been more sincerely recognized. The themes of the literature can be grouped under five heads: a team orientation; the ability to have ambition beyond current resources; an experimental attitude; a desire to reconcile important dilemmas to create economic value; and an ability to learn and accumulate knowledge.

Without doubt, in every case in this book success came from effective teamwork and it is always evident that there was a great deal of orchestrated effective effort, not only in carrying out current tasks, but also in creating new combinations of resources and finding and creating new market opportunities. Team working is more than gang labour, and quite different from committees. It is the effective combining of differently talented individuals. The importance of team working in creating effective organizations has been explored extensively by Moss Kanter.[22] Katzenbach and Smith have explored more fully how such teamwork can be effectively organized.[23]

In all organizations we observe limited team working in single functions. Team working across functions is much more difficult, yet is observed either directly or indirectly in almost all the cases. Team working across hierarchical and functional boundaries is even rarer, but again holds significant value. We see evidence of this in the richer cases such as Richardson, Edward, and Pyrochem, to name a few. The cases show how effective team working was in harnessing energies and skill levels across the whole organization.

Some of our cases show a most unusual dimension of teamwork, namely across organizational or cultural boundaries (see Figure 1.5). Three cases stand out here. In Benetton there is extensive team working between retailers, agents and Benetton's factories. This kind of close co-

| Team working within a single simple company context | Team working across national boundaries | Team working across organizational boundaries |
| --- | --- | --- |
| Edwards | Ariston-Indesit | Benetton |
| Pyrochem | Benetton | Motorola-Citibank |
| Richardson | Honda | Samsung |
| Woolworths | IKEA | JVC |

*Figure 1.5* Case studies with rich examples of team working

operation is hard to achieve inside a single firm, and is almost unknown on the scale and scope described in this case. In Motorola-Citibank, we see a team at work stretching across an organizational boundary. Again, it is an extraordinary event for most firms. The Ariston-Indesit case also shows how conflicting cultures that come together in a merger can create a new and better organization. The case also describes the geographic tensions and creative management of the product, function and geography matrix.

A more extensive investigation of aspects of entrepreneurship and leadership is covered in the next chapter. Here we note in passing that each of the cases exhibits a strong sense of ambition among those who worked in the organization. Often this ambition started with some trigger, perhaps in the form of the arrival of a new chief executive, or the influence of a single person. He, or she, seems to have been critical in starting processes and having the ability to infect others with the same enthusiasm. There has been much recent writing on the role of mission statements and planning processes in creating a sense of purpose and enthusiasm. In this book we see that creation of a sense of purpose can also be achieved in other ways. In some cases there were plans, but often excitement was created by charisma and setting an example through personal action. There is no single best way.

From the earliest literature, the importance of an experimental orientation has been associated with entrepreneurship. Entrepreneurs are seen as rule breakers, experimenters and pushers back of the boundaries, the importance of which has been strongly stressed in the text above. It is therefore obvious that effective entrepreneurial firms exhibit this activity. Our cases show experimental activity in larger organizations and that bureaucracy and entrepreneurship can co-exist and thrive. Organizations which are able to cross this boundary of experimental behaviour within the hierarchy are associated with success. The reader should be cautious however. Not all experimental activity leads to success. Whilst not shown in this book, there are many examples of organizations being experimental and failing.

What kinds of experiments are important and are associated with success? We suggest that those that push back accepted thinking to create new value for customers or suppliers are those that the organization needs to adopt. The cheap kitchen knife that never needs sharpening (Richardson), the clothes that are affordable, which young people want to wear (Benetton), the fun but cheap watch (Swatch), the cost-effective ski equipment (Salomon), the cheaper insurance company that provides better service (Direct Line), the bank that is more reliable and less costly (Amtssparekassen). These are but a few examples of the stretching goals that our organizations realized.

Much has recently been made of the learning organization. In the learning organization progress is cumulative. We all know that individuals learn, but collective learning is far more difficult. Creating a cumulative sense of learning requires discipline, and sometimes it is necessary to inject outsiders, sometimes it can be achieved within. In all the cases there is fascinating evidence on learning being undertaken, often in a directed systematic manner.

Describing corporate entrepreneurship and leadership in such simple terms will do it some injustice, for as we show in the next chapter there are many complex features. But one point is borne out. All organizations which aim to improve performance need to exhibit these kinds of activities. Corporate entrepreneurship is not just confined to small organizations, nor to those that are entrants or even industry leaders. Rejuvenation requires it too. Moreover, as can be seen in the book, there are similar elements in all situations.

This leads us to two observations. One is that corporate entrepreneurship may be the heart of firm success, it may be the well-spring which drives the process of renewal, industry leadership and frame-breaking behaviour. Second, trying to create corporate entrepreneurship may be an effective goal for managers, and it may provide a good guide to what to aim for in the organization.

## REWARDS, INCENTIVES AND CORPORATE GOVERNANCE AND MANAGING THE REWARDS

How do we define success? More critically, how do those in an organization define success? In most Anglo-Saxon cultures successful strategy is measured by profitability. Yet this is clearly a limited view. Successful enterprises can give value to all their stakeholders, including employees and suppliers (see Figure 1.6). They avoid the trap of borrowing from Peter to pay Pauline, but rather create enough value for all.

Using this criterion, Benetton is very successful. Although Benetton does not earn a particularly high rate of return on capital for its shareholders, for its franchisees the returns are spectacular. There is not only

| Long-term shareholder behaviour | Value creating attitude towards employees | Value creating attitude towards suppliers and partners |
|---|---|---|
| Ariston | Edwards | Ariston |
| Benetton | Honda | Benetton |
| Cartier | IKEA | Cartier |
| Edwards | Pyrochem | Honda |
| IKEA | Richardson | JVC |
| JVC | Samsung | Motorola |
| Richardson | | |
| Salomon | | |

*Figure 1.6* Classifying the case studies by their emphasis on stakeholder benefits

a pay back to capital of about three years, but also the opportunity for a young person to become an entrepreneur. The agents make excellent money, and they are closely involved in choosing and shaping the fashion trends of Benetton. Although not described in the case study, it is not hard to imagine that the subcontractors do well also. For them there is constant growing demand for their services, they have long runs of garments in simple basic designs, which permit the use of highly capital-intensive processes. They are also closely associated with a successful business.

In several cases we have clear evidence of a long-term view by the suppliers of capital. The shareholders of Richardson asked for no dividends for many years, permitting the firm to reinvest its cash in growth. BOC group was quite generous towards Edwards; despite its long unsuccessful history, BOC too did not press for a quick return. Ariston is notable as a family firm that asks for only a modest return on its capital, in exchange for an opportunity to create a truly world-class business. Many of its employees speak openly of this as a motivating factor. We argue that there is evidence of such shareholder attitudes elsewhere too, and that in every case this long-term view has not meant that shareholders suffer in the long run. Foregoing dividends in the near term has typically yielded spectacular capital gains in the long run.

Many of our case studies show that management has tried to take a long-term view towards its employees. In all these cases, employees have not only had the pleasure of working for a growing profitable organization that provides some stability of work, but have seen other tangible benefits too. In Richardson, there has been a history of promotion from the very lowest levels. Kathy Sanchez and Denise Ogden became senior managers having started life on the shop floor. Of course there have been others brought in at much higher levels, including Gordon Bridge, the current Managing Director. Hamish Dean, at Pyrochem, was particularly keen to be loyal to his employees, although this brought about some extreme tensions when their goals conflicted with those of the organization. In Samsung, we find a most unusual paternalistic attitude towards the employees from a chairman who changes the hours of work to ensure that workers have a more extensive home life. In a country where loyalty has typically meant working late, this was a revolution. In Edwards, a truly Anglo-Saxon firm, there is a strong emphasis on training and personal development to help both the employees and the company.

In many cases, value is created for suppliers and partners. Despite the difficulties, Ariston persists and succeeds in trying to use the Indesit employees to create value for the whole merged enterprise. Cartier, Motorola, and Honda are all companies which utilize others and reciprocate. Benetton, already spoken of, provides perhaps the best example of the networking philosophy.

Whilst it was not the central purpose of the book to explore formally issues of corporate governance, the attitudes and actions of our firms raise questions about how managers should conduct themselves. Success is far more than a high return on capital today, it is creating benefits for all the stakeholders, who include the employees and suppliers. Our cases provide vivid illustrations that nurturing shareholders to take this long-term view can yield every party an excellent return.

## NOTES

1  We acknowledge the helpful comments of Peter McNamara and Neil Thomson.
2  The ideas in this chapter are developed further in C. Baden-Fuller and J. M. Stopford, *Rejuvenating the Mature Business* (London: Routledge, 1992).
3  See for instance D. Hounshell, *From the American System to Mass Production* (Baltimore, Mass.: Johns Hopkins Press, 1984).
4  A. Sloan, *My Years with General Motors* (Garden City, NY: Doubleday, 1963).
5  For a review, see H. Mintzberg, 'The design school: reconsidering the basic premises of strategic management', *Strategic Management Journal*, 11(3), 1990: 171–96.
6  For example, M. Porter, *Competitive Strategy* (New York: Free Press, 1980).
7  See for example R. D. Buzzell and B. T. Gale, *The PIMS Principles*, (New York: Free Press, 1987).
8  C. Baden-Fuller (ed.) *Managing Excess Capacity* (Oxford: Basil Blackwell, 1990), K. Harrigan, *Strategies for Declining Business* (Lexington, Mass.: Lexington Books, 1980).
9  In 1951 Joe Bain argued that some industries had features that made them inherently more profitable than others. His results were first published in the *Quarterly Journal of Economics* in August 1951 and they sparked off a mountain of further work and debate. For a strategist's interpretation, see Porter (1980).
10  See M. E. Porter, *Competitive Advantage* (New York: Free Press, 1985).

11  Richard Rumelt, 'How much does industry matter?', *Strategic Management Journal*, March, 1991. Using US data, he showed that the choice of industry explained at best 8.3 per cent of a business unit's profitability.

12  Boston Consulting Group, *Perspectives on Experience*, (Boston, Mass.: Boston Consulting Group, 1968).

13  The dynamics of entry and profitability under various scenarios to do with learning and experience effects has received much attention, including modelling by writers such as Spence (see for instance A. M. Spence, 'Entry capacity, investment and oligopolistic pricing', *Bell Journal of Economics*, 8, 1977: 534–44).

14  R. D. Buzzell and B. T. Gale, *The PIMS Principles*, (New York: Free Press, 1987). The antecedents come from industrial economics; see for instance F. M. Scherer, *Industrial Market Structure and Economic Performance* (Chicago, Ill.: Rand MacNally, 1973) for a review.

15  R. Schmalensee, 'Do markets differ much?', *American Economic Review*, 75, 1985: 341–51.

16  See for instance I. Ansoff, *Corporate Strategy* (New York: McGraw Hill, 1965).

17  J. Barney, 'Firms' resources and sustained competitive advantage', *Journal of Management*, 17(1), 1991: 99–120; E. Penrose, *The Theory of the Growth of the Firm* (New York: Wiley, 1959); P. Selznick, *Leadership in Administration: A Sociological Interpretation* (New York: Harper and Row, 1957); D. Teece, G. Pisano and A. Schuen, *Firm Capabilities, Resources and the Concept of Strategy*, Working Paper No. 90–8, University of California at Berkeley, December 1990.

18  R. Grant, 'The resource-based theory of competitive advantage', *California Management Review*, 33 (3), 1991: 114–34.

19  C. K. Prahalad and G. Hamel, 'The core competence of the corporation', *Harvard Business Review*, May–June, 1990: 79–91.

20  G. Hamel and C. K. Prahalad, 'Strategy as stretch and leverage', *Harvard Business Review*, March–June, 1993: 75–84.

21  For a recent review see J. M. Stopford and C. Baden-Fuller, 'Creating corporate entrepreneurship', *Strategic Management Journal*, 15, 1994.

22  R. M. Kanter, *The Change Masters: Innovation for Productivity in the American Corporation* (New York: Simon and Schuster, 1985).

23  J. R. Katzenbach and D. K. Smith, *The Wisdom of Teams: Creating the High Performance Organization* (Boston, Mass.: Harvard Business School Press, 1993).

# Chapter 2

# Strategic managerial processes

## *The editors*

## INTRODUCTION

The process of innovating strategic management comprises three essential, *interlocking* behaviours: envisioning, galvanizing, and doing (enacting). Visionary, creative thinking conceives potentialities for the firm and the outline of strategies to realize them. Galvanizing and motivating behaviours encourage and enable individuals to convert strategy concepts to detailed, actionable programmes that in turn achieve tangible outcomes (intended or otherwise). Outcomes generate new information on which learning and adapting can be based.

In the complex, modern firm there is a continuous dynamic among these behaviours. They are neither wholly separate, nor sequential, though descriptions often convey the impression that they are. No behaviour in isolation from the others will advance the firm significantly, but in conjunction they are a powerful force for transformational change. The nature of these behaviours is the theme of this chapter.

Perhaps it will be useful to apply the metaphor of a pool. When the pool is disturbed at some point, ripples on the surface of the pool radiate outward in concentric circles. Over time there can be numerous such disturbances at various locations. Suppose we think of organization behaviours in these terms. Over time a variety of initiatives emanate from creative, imaginizing cores, spreading ripples outwards. The pool symbolizes the organizational arena, whilst the ripples symbolize the innovating and interlocking behaviours in the organization (Figure 2.1). The frequency, location and timing of new initiatives (and their significance – represented by the size of the ripples they create) will obviously vary from firm to firm. The outcome, as on the surface of the pool, is a complex, dynamic and seemingly unpredictable flux. None the less, we can in principle seek to understand these complex dynamics by considering each systematically.

This is the challenge presented by the case studies in this book, and in

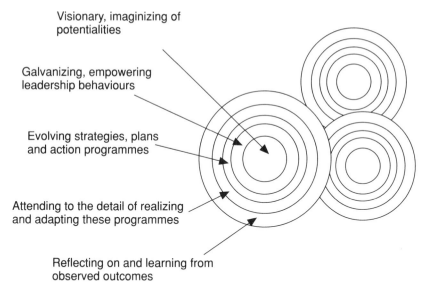

Visionary, imaginizing of
potentialities

Galvanizing, empowering
leadership behaviours

Evolving strategies, plans
and action programmes

Attending to the detail of realizing
and adapting these programmes

Reflecting on and learning from
observed outcomes

*Figure 2.1*  A model of strategic innovating behaviours

the world beyond. In this chapter we examine key behaviours under
four headings:

1 Visionary imaginizing of potentialities.
2 Galvanizing, empowering leadership behaviours.
3 Achieving desired results: attending to the detail of strategies.
4 Reflecting on and learning from observed outcomes.

## VISIONARY IMAGINIZING OF POTENTIALITIES

Many case studies of change in the firm and its competitive arena affirm
the importance of *intuitive judgements* in triggering the processes of
transformation.[1] Knowing what strategic issues the organization needs
to address – and will be rewarded for so doing – is arguably the most
difficult challenge senior executives face. It is a quality of effective
leadership and though it ought not to be confined to the chief executive, it
is a challenging responsibility that these individuals are typically well
aware of. It has variously been characterized as 'framing', 'problem
finding', and 'agenda building', for as one authority explained:

> In real world practice problems do not present themselves to the
> practitioner as givens. They must be constructed from the materials
> of problematic situations which are puzzling, troubling, and uncertain.
> In order to convert a problematic situation to a problem, a practitioner

must . . . make sense of an uncertain situation that initially makes no sense . . . When we set the problem, we select what we will treat as the 'things' of the situation, we set the boundaries of our attention to it, and we impose upon it a coherence which allows us to say what is wrong and in what direction the situation needs to be changed. Problem setting is a process in which, interactively, we name the things to which we will attend and frame the context in which we will attend to them.[2]

Notwithstanding the systematic analysis of issues one would expect in a modern corporation, constructing a relevant strategic agenda requires wisdom and judgement, grounded in relevant experience rather than narrow personal expertise. The evidence suggests that many successful corporations set and reset their strategic direction based on the visionary leadership of well-informed and focused individuals. In the early 1950s Eiji Toyoda and Taiichi Ohno concluded that mass production of automobiles in the American manner would not work for Toyota, still a comparatively small volume producer. Ohno challenged the conventional wisdom that machines required lengthy tooling changes before a different product could be made.[3] Drastic reductions in set up times became a key plank of the Toyota flexible production system. But the hardest part of the innovation, arguably, was to recognize that reducing set up times was a strategic problem worthy of attention.

Visionary reassessments of a situation can produce radical, transformational change. Such imaginative leadership has featured in all the companies described here at some stage of their development. Innovating companies like Pyrochem, Salomon and IKEA came into being because someone saw potential in a product or service concept that others had failed to see or had discounted the significance of. The VHS videorecorder became a reality because imaginative people saw the value of miniaturizing existing products and because other dedicated people refused to accept defeat when many attempts over more than a decade failed to achieve the result they believed was possible. In many, perhaps all, of the cases involving processes of rejuvenating, leaders envisioned a more attractive future that others did not – thus we are told that David Pitts at BOC persuaded Chairman Richard Giordano to support continued investment in Edwards High Vacuum, despite the latter's scepticism.

It is important for original ideas to be properly developed and to be seen to have merit before they receive critical evaluation: ideas 'with legs' still need their stamina to be developed before they meet the challenge of a marathon race! Even when the chief executive has originated an idea, premature and aggressive evaluation by colleagues will tend to emphasize aspects of the concept that are presently weak or infeasible given current knowledge, casting doubt on the wisdom of developing it or even causing it to be rejected. Thus, for example, had Edwin Land's conception of an instant picture camera been subjected to such a premature critique in technical or commercial terms, it would almost certainly have been killed off. People like Edwin Land and Peter Wood of Direct Line Insurance demonstrate not only imagination, but great powers of persuasion in convincing others to back them financially, and the determination to succeed when the going gets tough.

Of course, it sometimes helps *not* to have the preconceptions that accompany long experience. From the age of 20, Fred Smith who was later to found Federal Express 'knew' that a hub-and-spokes configuration was the ideal way to organize overnight mail and parcel distribution in the USA, whilst all the existing operators 'knew' it was wholly impractical. This intuitive sense of what will be practical and implementable is crucial to bold and effective strategic innovating.

In some cases, exemplified here by Amtssparekassen, Samsung and Woolworths, the visionary role calls for radical change when others in a similar position would have settled for incremental tinkering, on the basis that 'If it ain't broke, don't fix it.' In retrospect, visionaries who have advocated radical change often admit that they had little understanding of where the new direction would ultimately lead – only a profound conviction that it would be better than the alternative of continuing on the existing track. Moreover, they recognize the need for good fortune: an innovative product or strategy with great potential may fail miserably whilst another with seemingly less promise may succeed dramatically. This suggests the need for multiple ideas and experiments. Top executives at Benetton, Honda and other companies featured in this book understand this, and whilst they do not welcome failure, they do not regard the risks associated with new product failure as invalidating the need for creative, intuitive thinking.

Indeed, vision is not possible without imaginative and creative thinking. Novel business concepts, and ideas that help the firm to achieve similar results in new ways, are precious commodities. Much is known and hypothesized about the nature of creative thinking and how to encourage it.[4] Innovative ideas typically begin as a 'Gestalt', a loose, intuitive personal conception of a possibility whose detailed structure and significance come into focus only later. To use an analogy, the structure of the rose becomes apparent after we have recognized and admired the bloom. Examples abound of sudden insights from serendipitous, non-linear or lateral individual thinking. In 1980 Ernst Thomke, then president of Swiss watchmaker ETA for only two years and formerly a pharmaceuticals marketing executive, conceived the innovative product concept that was to become the Swatch. That same year

Richardson Sheffield launched the Laser knife, the first knife guaranteed not to need sharpening for twenty-five years, an idea actually conceived by a leading customer but adopted enthusiastically by Jerome Hahn and Bryan Upton.

Drawing analogies between situations known to the thinker can be fruitful. A situation as it is presently understood can be contrasted with an alternative possibility, experienced or idealized. Thus we see Masaru Ibuka's exhortation in Sony to produce a video-tape mechanism using a cassette no bigger than the ubiquitous paperback book. Peter Wood of Direct Line drew an analogy between firms selling tangible goods by telephone and the use of the same medium to sell insurance services. Anita Roddick, founder of the Body Shop, has admitted to acquiring her successful formula via the inspiration of travelling in parts of the world where natural products are commonly used as cosmetics.

Juxtaposing dissimilar, even seemingly opposing concepts can generate constructive paradoxes, meaning tensions or incongruities 'within the logic or rhythm of a process' or 'between economic realities'.[5] Thus Cartier juxtaposes its flair for publicity with maintaining a sense of mystery about the brand, exclusivity with global distribution; Honda Motors seeks to reconcile manual with mental labour, mass production with niche marketing, global coverage with sensitivity to local market priorities. Seeming oppositions highlight dilemmas for the firm to tackle and sometimes help turn perceived problems into perceived opportunities.[6] One way to understand this process is in terms of 'thinking the unthinkable', or simply 'Why not; why don't we . . .?'. For many years US car makers did not believe it was possible to make small cars with the interior space of much bigger ones, nor that US consumers would buy them even if made available. The Europeans thought and subsequently proved the first of these 'unthinkable' propositions, the Japanese the second. In the late 1950s, when those around him thought it was madness, Soichiro Honda conceived the possibility that people would buy cars made by a motorcycle company. Today, Honda Motors is equally renowned worldwide as a car and motorcycle maker.

Many commentators have also pointed to the creative stimulus of rich and varied metaphoric imagery both to (re)conceive situations and to share understandings with others.[7] This approach has proved its worth in the conception of new products and the interpretation of ambiguous situations.[8] Acknowledging a variety of sense-making metaphors helps the constructive exploration of different perceptions. For example, the parties in a proposed take-over will respond very differently to each other depending on whether the shared language portrays the dominant firm as *predator shark* or a *white knight*.

Although analogies and metaphors can be highly idiosyncratic and imperfect, the sharing and exploration of them are thought to be highly beneficial in the creative process. Though the germ of an idea may be personal, the influences of an enthusiastic and free-thinking team and their perceptions of the wider context in which the organization operates assist the processes of imaginizing and refining unusual ideas. The 'Walkman' personal stereo is said to have been conceived by Sony's chairman Masaru Ibuka as a consequence of wandering around the factory, talking to staff, observing the development of miniature tape recorders and headphones, and then envisioning these concepts fused into a new form of personal entertainment product.

However, many new ideas draw on years of relevant prior training and work experience, a factor that is easily overlooked after the event. Chester Carlson, the originator of xerography, was a physics graduate and later patent attorney. Robert Hocq was an experienced maker of inexpensive cigarette lighters long before he conceived of the association with Cartier that was to transform the fortunes of them both. Likewise, Jan Carlzon gained considerable experience in the travel industry before applying the service ideas he learned there as a source of competitive advantage for Scandinavian Airlines.

Carlzon's success exemplifies the application of a cognitive script, a mental template by means of which individuals make sense of unusual, or novel situations.[9] Scripts synthesize experience as coherent, prototypical or exemplary scenarios. Accordingly, they inform expectations of future events by facilitating inferences in the face of limited knowledge, and they guide and constrain future behaviour by encoding and legitimizing specific organizational roles. Whilst a script could be highly individualistic, in practice it is more likely to be recognized and shared by colleagues and associates with long experience of working together in and around the firm. Clearly, this may have negative as well as positive implications: for many years senior executives at Ford Motor Co. shared a complex automobile manufacturing script reinforcing their many assumptions about dedicated, hence rather inflexible assembly lines and their own place in a multilayer reporting hierarchy with Henry Ford at the apex. The dominance of this shared script made it possible for Ford to produce motor cars that the average person could afford, but it later made it extremely difficult for Ford executives to understand, much less respond to, more flexible and adaptive Japanese competition in the 1970s.

In novel and ambiguous situations personal sense-making evaluates the 'goodness of fit' of new observations with known and trusted situational scripts. Perceived absence of fit creates uncertainty. One response is to invoke a more abstract, generalized script. Another is *ad hoc*, essentially creative, reinterpretation of the script. An example is Schreiber's successful improvization on the traditional mass production script employed at GEC Hotpoint when he became chief executive. Yet another approach is to reject the conventional script in favour of a totally novel approach, arguably the principal contribution of IKEA's Ingvar Kamprad to the furniture industry. Similar arguments seem to apply to Amtssparekassen in its rejection of the conventional wisdom prevailing in the Danish banking industry.

Unfortunately, truly creative thinkers are often branded as mavericks by their colleagues and tolerated with reluctance, if at all. At best they may be viewed as inconsistent and unpredictable. This is clearly one reason why many radical ideas come to fruition only when promoted by independent-minded entrepreneurs, such as Hamish Dean of Pyrochem or François Salomon of the company that bears his name.

Yet creative thinking is a valuable commodity in large firms too. Precisely because senior executives have no monopoly on novel ideas, part of the wisdom they need is to be tolerant of counter-intuitive thinking by subordinates. Thus leaders have to be ready both to challenge conventional wisdom and to have their own entrenched assumptions challenged. Moreover, even when they doubt that such ideas can lead to valued outcomes, they need sometimes to put their own reputation on the line by endorsing them publicly in the firm. For example, despite some Board members of Woolworths remaining personally sceptical of the need for greater market focus, Operation Focus was a collective declaration by the Board members that was necessary to secure tangible actions in support of specialization by this so-called variety chain store. Moreover, this initiative was counter-intuitive in that it led Woolworths to reduce its total selling space in the high streets of the UK at a time when conventional retail thinking associated enhanced profit performance with increasing scale.

## GALVANIZING, EMPOWERING LEADERSHIP BEHAVIOURS

If a revitalization of the collective mind-set of a firm is to be achieved, leaders must foster an environment in which creative ideas are respected, treated sympathetically and *acted on*. This has on many occasions been said to explain the secret of 3M Corporation's extraordinary capacity to conceive and exploit new products. Leaders must exercise this galvanizing duty – to promote ideas with the potential for positive long-term strategic impact on the survival and success of the firm. Their crucial contribution is to enable a bridge between the idea and the organizational domain where ideas have to be realized and exploited – to make things happen.

The ability to communicate a new vision of future direction is a key trait of strategic leadership.[10] It requires personal courage, anticipation, tolerance of ambiguity and the ability to enthuse and inspire others.

Leaders require an appropriate blend of personal qualities including advanced political skills to convince others to act upon ideas that they feel have reached their time. A key stage is the almost evangelistic repetition or rehearsal of ideas,[11] sometimes for a very long time before they become widely shared and accepted. As Andrew Pettigrew commented:

> Visions with a simple yet ambiguous content, expressed in symbolic language . . . are not only likely to be potent consciousness raisers but also flexible enough to survive and thereby validate events. If visions are to be used by an entrepreneur as a potent mechanism for directing and influencing others the language contained within the vision is crucial . . . sometimes using metaphors and analogies to create fresh meanings. Words can provide energy and raise consciousness. The capacity to use the full power of words – to make words walk – I suspect is one of the unexplored characteristics of successful entrepreneurs.[12]

For an organization to proceed with a shared sense of purpose, the leadership role of communicating and representing ideas, and conveying a sense of excitement and direction is crucial and by no means limited to the chief executive. However, communication is a two-way process and those who follow must be responsive to and supportive of new ideas if innovative leadership is to be legitimized and the firm is to thrive. When this role is performed effectively, new ideas and relevant values diffuse rapidly to become shared organizational property. In the process they become developed, elaborated, and enhanced as others own new ideas and their implications. A good example is the ownership of and commitment to the John Lewis Partnership shown by its employees and the promotion of an innovating culture in IKEA by Ingvar Kamprad.

The logic of continuous improvement has led to convincing arguments for promoting an enabling corporate culture in which innovating at all levels is seen as natural behaviour. So called 'change champions' then have the freedom to create programmes and initiatives that encode desired directions for change.[13] The promotion of such a culture is an important enabling aspect of strategic leadership, because to create elegant conceptual strategies is of minimal significance for the firm if the advantage they confer in theory cannot be translated into concrete, desirable outcomes.

Much of the conventional strategy and change literatures portray organizational change as given, imposed from the top down. So people focus on how individuals and work groups can be encouraged to respond constructively to imposed change, rather than how they can be enabled to create continuous change and improvement. In some circumstances, notably when a sense of crisis prevails, incisive, directive leadership may be exactly what is needed. Then it takes courage to impose directions that others may see as bold, unduly optimistic, ill advised or downright dangerous. Interpreting situations as crises to which the firm must respond with conviction has undoubtedly been effective in particular cases.[14] Such behaviour can be said to have characterized the leadership at varying times in Amtssparekassen, Cartier, Edwards, Richardson, Swatch and Woolworths. Yet the secret of rejuvenating leadership is surely to avoid crisis and the need for imposition. Under favourable circumstances strategic innovating is and should be great fun, conducted in a light-hearted atmosphere some have termed playfulness. The early days of Apple Computer are a fine example.

However, when a CEO succeeds in fostering an enabling culture it is quite possible that he or she then loses the power to dictate directions. Particularly in ambiguous, fast-moving, even 'chaotic' innovating environments, it is difficult for any chief executive to feel comfortable. To succeed here requires senior managers to trust and to empower a very special kind of manager.[15] Such individuals possess many of the qualities we expect to find in entrepreneurs who set up their own firms. Sustaining their enthusiasm and loyalty is a substantial challenge for senior executives, one in which they frequently fail.[16]

Of central importance, the operating environment within the firm must confer adequate freedom for these people to experiment, allied to due reward and recognition when they succeed, and comparative tolerance of their well-intentioned failures.[17] It requires a blind corporate eye to be turned to quasi-deviant behaviour such as the diversion of slack resources to illicit experiments that, when successful, can be legitimized as properly budgeted development projects. In the late 1960s Soichiro Honda was personally committed to developing air-cooled engines, though many of his younger engineers favoured water cooling. They quietly continued with designs for the latter, despite Mr Honda's known disapproval. Ultimately there was a confrontation and Honda accepted the wisdom of his junior colleagues and the consequent reversal of his product policy. Tadashi Kume who was in favour of water cooling later became chief executive of the firm.[18] Likewise, 'The VHS Success Story' describes how a small team at JVC continued with video-recorder development even when this work was officially 'off the agenda'. Even when a particular initiative is not successful it may have valuable spin-offs that the adaptive firm can subsequently exploit.

Yet, whilst organizational mechanisms such as delegating to flexible task forces, eliminating overbearing formality, and encouraging informal, cross-functional, multilayer communication networks among professional staff[19] will generally motivate innovatively minded engineers and technologists, large organizations have obligations to many stakeholders that place limits on the senior executives' scope to permit excessively informal action. It is almost by definition problematic for personalized, pioneering enthusiasms and initiatives to be structured and institutionalized, as such innovative firms as the pharmaceutical giant Glaxo have discovered. Texas Instruments is another example of a corporation that has tried to institutionalize a very structured and codified approach to innovating. But when too much structuring and codification occurs, the perceived quality of the innovating environment as it is experienced by the innovators deteriorates. So for innovating to thrive, a paradoxical accommodation must be achieved between supervision and delegation. This phenomenon has been referred to as *loose-tight* management,[20] which in the best-run innovative firms manifests itself as a vibrant sense of dynamism, excitement and uncertainty.

## ACHIEVING DESIRED RESULTS: ATTENDING TO THE DETAIL OF STRATEGIES

The envisioning, galvanizing role of leadership must, however, be directed towards implementing intelligent strategies for achieving desirable results. Key aspects of strategic thinking have been discussed in Chapter 1. One view of strategy is that of identifying advantageous competitive market and/or industry positions to which the firm's finite resources are then directed,[21] in essence an ends- or goals-oriented view. Equally, it can be fruitful to view the firm as an array of knowledge-based competences to be deployed and enhanced systematically,[22] essentially a more dynamic and means-oriented view in which paths are perceived as more relevant than end points.

In the case studies in this book we see examples of both perspectives informing managerial choices, sometimes in conjunction. Thus Kamprad of IKEA endorsed a strategy that focused on market opportunity and achieving a dominant position in mass market furnishings, yet this strategy was realized by developing a tightly coupled set of distinctive competences in his firm. The evidence is that strategic innovators conceive and implement new rules of the game, creating an ever-changing environment to which competitors can only react. Strategies continually evolve and hence sources of advantage become upgraded over time. Any firm's know-how resides partly in the design of equipment and other fixed assets it currently deploys, but these are relatively easy for competitors to emulate, particularly when they can be acquired in the market-place, as Lee Kun-Hee, current chairman of Samsung, observed. By contrast, tacit and semi-codified know-how in the minds of key employees, especially those involved in R&D, constitutes an intangible strategic asset that firms should jealously protect.

Effective leaders determined to secure continual improvement in their firms' competitive performance characteristically contribute a sense of urgency and great attention to detail. Taiichi Ohno did not seek one-off changes in Toyota's production systems, he sought to implement a strategy of continuous improvement in work organization. This was galvanized by his instilling a sense of urgency among production workers and by invariably being well informed and in command of the details. In this environment, any failure to improve on past performance was construed as a personal affront. The evidence to this day is that Toyota pursues essentially the same strategy of continuous improvement, albeit in a less personalized fashion.

In this sense strategy can be regarded as a set of clearly defined and detailed steps along a winding path whose general direction is understood, even if its many twists and turns cannot be anticipated with confidence. Whilst it can be argued that this kind of strategy is more difficult to implement in western firms, a strong sense of obligation to one's colleagues, particularly in close-knit project teams at the cutting edge of strategic innovation, creates considerable commitment to the continuous improvement philosophy, as demonstrated by JVC when developing the VHS video-recorder system,[23] by Richardson in its continuous enhancement of the ever-sharp knife concept, and by Edwards in vacuum pump design.

Thus although being the first to pioneer a new direction may be a necessary element of strategic success, it is never sufficient alone. The evidence of successful strategic innovators the world over is that they attend — sometimes fanatically — to the detail of implementing their chosen strategies. Attention to detail is critical if firms that engage in the cost and risk of innovating are to appropriate a fair and adequate economic return for their efforts. More specifically, firms need to understand and anticipate what actions will be needed for the innovation to secure a strong 'appropriability regime' in which the firm sustains prices well above costs, and thus enjoys quasi-monopoly profits. In its early days Pyrochem saw that changes to the way its products were marketed and distributed held the key to preventing much bigger and resource-rich competitors taking away its markets. The Direct Line insurance business may have been built on an innovative idea in tune with motorists' needs, but its success derives very specifically from the firm's ability to implement a responsive and effective motor car insurance service covering not just buying insurance by telephone, but after sales service too, including very efficient administration of claims for accident repairs.

Swatch pioneered the watch as a fashion accessory, but it also worked relentlessly at the detail of its business to retain a dominant position in the face of a host of emulators. Richardson's success, too, has been built on a very good product, the stay-sharp Laser knife, but success hinged on a range of complementary factors in manufacturing and marketing.

The development of Cartier's prestigious brand and product portfolio, and the partnership between Motorola and Citibank to plan and control the former's global cash movements are very different, but equally valid examples of focused corporate attention over the long term to specific, highly significant aspects of global corporate strategy in the two firms. The move by Honda Motors into US manufacturing is also a classic instance of fanatical attention to detail.[24]

Whilst it is easy to advocate the need to anticipate the many detailed problems likely to arise as a strategy unfolds, this is unrealistic. For example, having acquired the bankrupt Indesit company, Ariston's executives become aware of how much detailed planning and careful execution of changes were needed if the integration of the two firms was to be successful. They began attending to a wide range of tasks and issues; success still did not always come quickly. None the less, Ariston persevered and today the combined firm is one of the most powerful in the industry. Similar observations can be made in respect of the earlier acquisition of Zanussi by Electrolux. In a very different environment, Apple Corporation has over the years confronted many problems and sometimes made mistakes, but its powerful brand name and unique, copyrighted operating system has given Apple executives comparative freedom to assess market developments and explore attractive and relevant options. Even though they still have to work with incomplete information, a strong exploitation regime extends the time available for strategists to make and revise decisions as markets evolve and needs clarify, despite the contrary external influences.

Especially in western firms, innovators with an optimistic, outgoing approach can be influenced more by prospective regret over lost opportunities than by fear of competitive failure. So executives tend to envision creating a strong appropriability regime through bold, competitively aggressive first-mover strategies. A poor understanding of the forthcoming regime, typically by failing to engage with the detailed imperatives of sustaining a position, creates the illusion that their firm controls the pace and direction of innovation and exploitation. This escalates their commitment to strategies which later prove unwise, and frequently leads to early commercial failure.[25] Whereas Pilkington first developed and then reflected carefully on how best to exploit its new float glass technology – which it did successfully through a licensing strategy – EMI used its early lead in diagnostic medical imaging to take on the industry giants such as GE of America head to head. Inadequate attention to the uncomfortable, but significant details of its strategic circumstances resulted in its rapid exit from this fast-growing, high technology arena. Several firms featured here, including the episode of Sony and VHS, also demonstrate that first moving is not always a winning formula. The concurrent RCA Selecta Vision videodisc project reinforces the point. Failure to attend to important strategic detail cost both firms dearly and in consequence they suffered a period of adversity before they were able to counter the damage arising from poor decisions.

In fact the VHS success story illustrates the difficulty for any firm to appropriate fully the rewards of a significant innovation. Despite making the early running, Sony made important and, as it turned out, incorrect assumptions about the adoption of its VCR standard. Thus it saw no need to be patient and assess the needs and interests of the other influential firms, as JVC did. So was JVC the ultimate winner? To be sure, it has done well, but its parent company Matsushita has arguably done much better. However, though Sony can be said to have lost face – important to a self-confident Japanese company – it has subsequently applied its VCR know-how very effectively to further successful design innovations based on the VHS concept.

A qualitatively different case is that of Philips of Holland which has a long history of underachieving returns to its innovating efforts. This observation is true not just in relation to its products, but would include its adoption of a complex matrix organization structure to ally internal knowledge of markets and technologies to enhance its responsiveness to customers' needs. This bold innovation proved counter-productive because it actually slowed decision-making, and it was abandoned at considerable cost. Yet Philips continues to produce imaginative and exciting consumer products such as CDi and Digital Compact Cassette that lesser firms would no longer have had the courage to proceed with.

A strong appropriability regime can also be supported by attending carefully to creating barriers deterring others from entering (or staying in) the market. Secrecy and obtaining patents and copyrights covering new processes and technical standards are obvious examples that can be converted into lucrative but restrictive licence agreements. The experience of key personnel is also very significant since it constitutes the main proprietary know-how of the firm. Employment contracts ('golden handcuffs') can be offered to key personnel to minimize the risk of this know-how going to competitors.

Strong brands and a reputation for benchmark levels of product design and performance that dictate the terms for continued success are further barriers to emulation. Cartier, Benetton, Mercedes, Richardson, Swatch and JVC have all set standards of performance others have had no choice but to follow, usually on unfavourable terms. Barriers to emulation are also created when the innovating firm accesses and exploits complementary assets and skills denied to competitors. Where such assets do not exist in the firm it may be possible to acquire them by taking over another firm or by entering some form of collaborative agreement. Thus Sony acquired CBS to add marketable 'software' to its extensive hardware portfolio. Benetton and IKEA, for example, are noted for their achievements in developing capable and responsive supply networks that others cannot readily emulate. Needless to say, most of the firms in this book have paid great attention to creating effective barriers to emulation.

We suggest that the successful strategic innovating firms are capable of great sensitivity to issues that others may overlook. They assess carefully the impact of innovative change on existing products and organizational routines and they try to avoid change that may hurt demand for current offerings and render expensive investments in plant and equipment prematurely obsolete. They think carefully about the opportunity and they also consider the opportunity cost it entails in terms of *not* pursuing other exciting projects. They exercise considerable patience in pursuit of due rewards, often over a period of time that involves several chief executives.[26] Conversely, they try to avoid unrealistic or imprudent innovations that could ultimately create an unwieldy portfolio of diverse products, technologies and capabilities with inadequate financial returns.

None the less, attention to detail evidently does not prevent the successful firms from responding opportunistically to emerging situations when they see this as consistent with the strategy in place. Edwards doubled manufacturing capacity in short order to respond to emerging demand for its products from the semiconductor industry. The Benetton family prides itself on the ability of the firm to respond constructively to changing fashion needs. Honda Motors is extraordinarily responsive to shifts in global demand for its products and has grown rapidly as a consequence.

## REFLECTING AND LEARNING

The preceding section emphasized attention to detail in the implementation of strategy. In consequence, we argue, strategic management is fundamentally a learning, adapting task. Long-run success means reflecting on the lessons of detail, and a capacity to draw lessons from unfolding experience. Adaptive learning implies a range of qualities such as striking a balance between focus and goal directedness on one hand, and the ability to respond decisively to emerging opportunities and to unanticipated threats on the other. Adaptiveness applies also to structures and styles of organizing. Adaptiveness implies patience, determination and resilience in the face of setbacks. This seems to characterize all the firms in our sample, especially those experiencing a process of rejuvenation.

In conditions of uncertainty – some would say unknowability – continued experimentation, or placing multiple, prudent 'bets' makes good sense – seeing what works and building on that. Flexibility and adaptiveness can therefore be equated with survival and hence strategic effectiveness, even if it means trading potential high returns for more modest, but certain ones. But flexibility is also – as instanced by lean production philosophy – a legitimate way to reduce investment in non-productive assets such as inventories and thereby enhance operating efficiency. This applies clearly in firms like Honda, Woolworths and IKEA.

Flexibility is an appropriate, perhaps the only, way to cope with unexpected adversity in the course of a firm's development. The Body Shop is well known as an environmentally conscious business, exemplified in its policy of minimal packaging and encouraging customers to reuse plastic bottles. This innovation was, according to founder Anita Roddick, a reaction to adversity, namely a lack of funds as a start-up business to commission fancy packaging and promotional materials. By the time the firm could afford these, recycling had become a respected feature of its operation, with which Roddick realized it would be wise to persist.

Precisely because it is an unpredictable, non-linear process, strategic innovating is challenging and risky. The more emphasis a firm places on innovating to sustain future competitive advantage, the harder it will be to develop without high uncertainty. Nor can the philosophy of continuous, adaptive improvement wholly eliminate the possibility of, or compensate for, the discontinuity arising from a massive technical breakthrough, especially one not anticipated in form or scale by any of the existing players. A large number of consumer electronics firms in the mid-1970s foresaw the emergence of pre-recorded video material for home entertainment, but few had much confidence to predict how the emerging industry would evolve, and of those who did, few did so accurately – indeed, in differing ways some leading names got it badly wrong.

During significant transitions it is necessary to reconcile notions that from the current frame of reference seem contrary or paradoxical, such as combining high quality and low cost, or high volume and variety.[27] Radical reframing means interpreting known facts in a new light, asking seemingly obvious but hitherto ignored questions such as 'how can we make a knife that never needs sharpening?'.[28] In the reframing process an obsolescent script (e.g. high volume equates with poor quality and inflexibility) is either unlearned in favour of a new Gestalt[29] or rejuvenated in line with the demands and potentialities of the changing situation. Whilst the incubation of ideas for change may be protracted, the actual substitution is typically quite sudden. Frame changes are emergent in character, manifesting few of the qualities one associates with deliberate planning. Thus transformational strategic management is characteristically a process of tolerating and ultimately reconciling – hence learning from – seemingly contrary ideas and prescriptions.

Consider Pilkington's new float process for making sheet glass in the late 1950s. It was a successful glass maker, by no means in crisis. If the new technology was successful, high quality (precise, flat surfaces and high optical clarity) would no longer be wholly the preserve of costly ground and polished plate glass. Quality would no longer command a price premium in the market-place. How could the innovator justify the risks and costs of commercializing this innovation? It chose to distance premium-priced plate glass from float glass and to license its new process to other manufacturers around the world – in effect *making the process the product*. For more than a decade this strategy was a principal source of revenue and market influence for Pilkington as the leading glass makers all adopted the float process.

A dilemma of crisis proportions faced the Swiss watchmakers in the early 1970s when the potential of inexpensive, but extremely accurate electronic watches was first appreciated. Unlike Pilkington the Swiss had a strategic position that appeared weak, since they had neither the know-how nor the capacity to mass produce the microchips on which the new timing technology was based. In hindsight, the Swiss (and the Japanese) interpreted the paradox of combining time-keeping accuracy with low cost much better than did the leading electronics companies. The latter made the watch an inexpensive commodity, a strategy that was ultimately without profit. The Swiss took their time, reflected and learned from the mistakes of others. Their designers adopted electronic components, but since these offered them no scope for competitive advantage they began to compete by redefining the quality of a watch in terms of style and fashionability, conveyed through its brand image, the design of the case and the choice of materials used.

As part of the experimental philosophy, strategists are advised to think *inclusively* rather than *exclusively*: instead of saying, because we will do X, we cannot do Y – an either/or choice – they should say, we can do X *and* Y concurrently, or X now and Y later, or X unless/until Y becomes more appropriate, all essentially and/both choices. Pilkington invested in a float glass plant *and* licensed the process to others. Over time it began to focus on making glass for specialist, high value-added applications *as well as* continuing as a bulk producer of sheet. Likewise, the leading producer of Swiss watches sees no inconsistency in maintaining a product portfolio that includes both the inexpensive fashion brand, Swatch, alongside the prestige brand, Omega, and electronic watches alongside mechanical ones.

These examples show that despite the best endeavours of strategic planners, innovations emerge in a competitive arena in a seemingly unpredictable manner whereby the innovator is not certain to reap the benefits, and where newcomers with access to relevant, novel technologies may sometimes disadvantage existing players. Transformational episodes have to be understood as part of a continuing evolutionary dynamic in a firm's innovative progress. As know-how becomes increasingly more significant than tangible assets as a source of advantage (being harder for competitors to emulate and assimilate), the logic of a continuous dynamic of innovating grows stronger, descriptively and prescriptively. Yet innovation even in the most dynamic firms proceeds irregularly and with an unpredictable rhythm.[30] A closer inspection of the 'fine grain' of innovation reveals the continuing development of a wide range of skills and capabilities. From time to time a myriad of small initiatives, by design or good luck, converge into a change that from a distance looks like a significant discontinuity. This is probably a good description of the development of the video home entertainment industry over two decades.

Change which affects the development of the individual firm can usefully be distinguished from that which affects the competitive arena as a whole. Clearly, there is much to be gained by learning from exemplar firms, by benchmarking of best practice (whether by competitors or others beyond the competitive sector), engaging in joint ventures, licensing new ideas and processes and by working closely with suppliers and competitors in a spirit of partnership rather than combat. But the learning process for the firm can still be imitative and painful, with perhaps only marginal impact on its competitors. The rejuvenation of Rover Cars was arguably of this form. In this sense we can describe rejuvenating as changing the 'rules of history' as they are understood by the firm's actors, not necessarily changing the 'rules of the competitive game' in any meaningful sense. On the other hand, whilst Rover may not have set new standards for motor manufacturing in the UK, it has contributed to a widespread recognition by other UK producers of what standards are necessary to remain competitive.

Even so, such innovating may have comparatively little impact on the broad arena of firm–customer relationships: implementing a new flexible production process does not significantly change the automobile or how it is used. But when strategic innovating impacts the firm and the competitive arena, including firm-customer relationships, this signifies the emergence of new strategies for competing. As their effectiveness becomes noted, emulation follows, albeit imperfectly, since firms' development paths tend to remain idiosyncratic. In retrospect the innovation becomes regarded after the event as an industry dematuring or 'architectural' change.[31]

## CONCLUDING REMARKS

In this chapter we have considered a range of issues germane to the management of the strategic innovating firm. We have stressed the need to think imaginatively, to encourage galvanizing leadership, to attend to the detail of imaginative and effective strategies so that the due returns to innovating are secured in practice, and to reflect on and learn from outcomes.

These ideas come alive when we consider them in particular contexts, hence the detailed case examples in this book. Readers are encouraged to understand fully the particular circumstances of the situations described. What issues were considered by the actors on each stage? What issues, if any, did they ignore and why? Probe beneath the surface explanations and ask penetrating questions. Consider what should happen subsequently and why. Only by so doing can you – both as a student of organizations and as a strategic innovator – hope to understand an organization in order to change it.

To this end we present a brief review of each case to set the scene and suggest a number of questions with which to begin your deliberations. These will not cover all the issues you may consider important. Try to project yourself into the situation described and develop insightful and exciting perspectives of your own. But remember that hindsight is a wonderful, if overrated faculty!

We wish you pleasurable and rewarding reading.

## NOTES

1 A classic work on intuition and judgement in management is G. Vickers, *The Art of Judgement* (London: Chapman & Hall, 1965). For a readable account of senior level behaviour see W. Agor, 'The logic of intuition: how top executives make important decisions', *Organizational Dynamics*, 14, Winter, 1986: 5–18. Finally, J.-C. Spender ties together the notion of managerial judgement and shared, industry-wide knowledge in his *Industry Recipes: the Nature and Sources of Managerial Judgement* (Oxford: Blackwell, 1989).

2 The quotation about defining the problem is from D. A. Schon, *The Reflective Practitioner* (New York: Basic Books, 1983) pp. 39–40. See also P. Arlin, 'Wisdom: the art of problem finding', in R. Sternberg, *Wisdom: Its Nature, Origins and Development* (Cambridge: CUP, 1990). Jane Dutton has written extensively on *strategic agenda-building*, e.g. J. E. Dutton, 'Understanding strategic agenda-building and its implications for managing change', in L. Pondy, R. Boland and H. Thomas, *Managing Ambiguity and Change* (Chichester: Wiley, 1988) and J. E. Dutton, 'The importance of organizational identity for strategic agenda-building', in J. Hendry, G. Johnson, and J. Newton, *Strategic Thinking: Leadership and the Management of Change* (Chichester: Wiley, 1993).

3 J. Womack, D. Jones and D. Roos, *The Machine that Changed the World* (New York: Rawson/Macmillan, 1990).

4 For a useful set of review articles on creativity see J. Henry (ed.) *Creative Management* (London: Sage, 1991). Also A. Koestler, *The Act of Creation* (London: Hutchinson, 1984).

5  The quotes come from P. Drucker, *Innovation and Entrepreneurship: Practice and Principles* (London: Heinemann, 1985). For a discussion of paradoxical thinking see R. Quinn and K. Cameron (eds) *Paradox and Transformation* (Cambridge, Mass.: Ballinger, 1988).

6  C. Hampden-Turner, *Charting the Corporate Mind* (Oxford: Blackwell, 1990) is a readable account exploring the resolution of paradoxical dilemmas in strategic thinking. For a more abstract treatment, see also Quinn and Cameron op. cit.

7  G. Lakoff and M. Johnson, *Metaphors We Live By* (Chicago, Ill.: University of Chicago Press, 1980).

8  A notable detailed discussion of how analogy works in an innovating context can be found in D. Schon, *Displacement of Concepts* (London: Tavistock, 1963).

9  Much of what has been written about scripts features in the psychology literature. Some sources more accessible to managers include R. Schank and R. Abelson, *Scripts, Plans, Goals and Understanding* (Hillsdale, NJ: Lawrence Erlbaum, 1977); D. Gioia and P. Poole, 'Scripts in organizational behavior', *Academy of Management Review*, 9(3), 1984: 449–59; and R. Lord and M. Kernan, 'Scripts as determinants of purposeful behavior in organizations', *Academy of Management Review*, 12(2), 1987: 265–77.

10 The leadership literature is enormous. For our purposes the following are well worth inspection: W. Bennis, 'The artform of leadership', in S. Shrivastva (ed.) *The Executive Mind* (San Francisco: Jossey Bass, 1983), pp. 15–24; G. Donaldson and J. Lorsch, *Decision Making at the Top: The Shaping of Strategic Direction* (New York: Basic Books, 1983); J. Harvey-Jones, *Making it Happen: Reflections on Leadership* (London: Collins, 1988); D. Hurst, J. Rush and R. White, 'Top management teams and organizational renewal', *Strategic Management Journal*, 10, 1989: 87–105; B. Leavy and D. Wilson, *Strategy and Leadership* (London: Routledge, 1994); and L. Smircich and G. Morgan, 'Leadership: the management of meaning', *Journal of Applied Behavioral Studies*, 18, 1982: 257–73.

11 This draws on a theatrical analogy. The theatrical or dramaturgical interpretation of managerial action has been expounded by I. Mangham and M. Overington, *Organizations as Theatre* (Chichester: Wiley, 1987) and by F. Westley and H. Mintzberg, 'Visionary leadership and strategic management', *Strategic Management Journal*, 10, 1989: 17–32.

12 A. Pettigrew, 'On studying organization cultures', *Administrative Science Quarterly*, 24, 1979: 570–81.

13 For broad-ranging treatments see for instance R. Kanter, *The Change Masters: Corporate Entrepreneurs at Work* (New York: Simon & Schuster, 1983) (and more recent works); R. Normann, *Management for Growth* (Chichester: Wiley, 1977); and C. Baden-Fuller and J. Stopford, *Rejuvenating the Mature Business: The Competitive Challenge* (London, Routledge, 1992).

14 e.g. A. Pettigrew, *The Awakening Giant: Continuity and Change in ICI* (Oxford: Basil Blackwell, 1985): M. Pitt, 'Crisis modes of strategic transformation: a new metaphor for managing technological innovation', in R. Loveridge and M. Pitt (eds) *The Strategic Management of Technological Innovation* (Chichester: Wiley, 1990).

15 See J. Quinn, 'Managing innovation: controlled chaos', *Harvard Business Review*, May/June, 1985: 73–84; I. Nonaka, 'Creating organizational order out of chaos: self-renewal in Japanese firms', *California Management Review*, Spring, 1988: 57–73; and M. Pitt, 'Crisis modes of strategic transformation:

a new metaphor for managing technological innovation', in R. Loveridge and M. Pitt (eds) *The Strategic Management of Technological Innovation* (Chichester: Wiley, 1990).

16  As witness Robert Noyce and others quitting Fairchild to found Intel, and the three Texas Instruments executives who quit to found Compaq. For a discussion of encouraging entrepreneurship in the firm see R. Burgelman, 'Corporate entrepreneurship and strategic management', *Management Science*, 29(12), 1983: 1349–64; R. Burgelman, 'Managing the new venture division: research findings and implications for strategic management', *Strategic Management Journal*, 6(1), 1985: 39–54; and Baden-Fuller and Stopford op. cit.

17  More specific discussions worth examining include R. Rosenfeld and J. Servo, 'Facilitiating innovation in large organizations', in M. West and J. Farr (eds) *Innovation and Creativity at Work* (Chichester: Wiley, 1990); P. Lorange, 'Strengthening organizational capacity to execute strategic change', in J. Pennings (ed.) *Organization Strategy and Change* (San Francisco: Jossey-Bass, 1985).

18  T. Sakiya, *Honda Motor: The Men, the Management, the Machines* (New York: Kodansha International, 1982).

19  J. Child and C. Smith, provide a detailed account of transformational change and how it was enabled in 'The context and process of organizational transformation: Cadbury Ltd. in its sector', *Journal of Management Studies*, 24(6), 1987: 565–93; also, for their discussion of 'prospector' type firms the ageing, but still pertinent work of R. Miles and C. Snow, *Organization Strategy, Structure and Process* (New York: McGraw Hill, 1978).

20  T. Peters and R. Waterman, *In Search of Excellence: Lessons from America's Best-run Companies* (New York: Harper and Row, 1982).

21  A concept typically associated with Porter; see M. Porter, *Competive Strategy* (New York: Free Press, 1980) and *Competitive Advantage* (New York: Free Press, 1985).

22  This idea has found expression in a variety of ways. See for example C. K. Prahalad and G. Hamel, 'The core competence of the corporation', *Harvard Business Review*, May–June, 1990: 79–91; I. Nonaka, 'The knowledge-creating company', *Harvard Business Review*, November–December, 1991: 96–104; and S. Winter, 'Knowledge and competence as strategic assets', in D. Teece (ed.) *The Competitive Challenge: Strategies for Industrial Innovation and Renewal* (Cambridge, Mass.: Ballinger, 1987).

23  In marked contrast to one competitor, RCA, which failed in the development of the Videodisc through lack of coherence: M. Graham, *The Business of Research: RCA and the Videodisc* (Cambridge: CUP, 1986).

24  See A. Mair, *Honda: The Global-Local Corporation* (London: Macmillan, 1994).

25  See D. Teece, 'Profiting from technological innovation: implications for integration, collaboration, licensing, and public policy', in D. Teece (ed.) *The Competitive Challenge: Strategies for Industrial Innovation and Renewal* (Cambridge, Mass.: Ballinger, 1987) for a theoretical review. R. Loveridge, 'Incremental innovation and appropriative learning styles in direct services', in R. Loveridge and M. Pitt (eds) *Strategic Management of Technological Innovation* (Chichester: Wiley, 1990), pp. 339–68 explores these issues in relation to a particular industry setting.

26  B. Leavy and D. Wilson, *Strategy and Leadership* (London: Routledge, 1994). Edwards High Vacuum also experienced a similar progression, needing several changes at senior executive level before transformational new directions were cemented.

27 See Baden-Fuller and Stopford (1992) op. cit.
28 Ibid.
29 The early chapters of M. McCaskey, *The Executive Challenge: Managing Change and Ambiguity* (Marshfield, Mass.: Pitman, 1982) offer a readable account of frame-breaking thinking. J. Bartunek, 'The dynamics of personal and organizational reframing', in R. Quinn and K. Cameron (eds) *Paradox and Transformation: Toward a Theory of Change in Organization and Management* (Cambridge, Mass.: Ballinger, 1988) provides a more theoretical account. The earlier work by B. Hedberg and S. Jonsson, 'Strategy making as a discontinuous process', *International Studies of Management and Organization*, 7(2), 1977, 88–109, and R. Mason and I. Mitroff, *Challenging Strategic Planning Assumptions* (New York: Wiley, 1981), offer contrasting perspectives.
30 For perspectives on adaptiveness see Baden-Fuller and Stopford op. cit. chapter 5. Also B. Chakravarthy, 'Adaptation: a promising metaphor for strategic management', *Academy of Management Review*, 7(1), 1982: 35–44. One can also regard adaptiveness as *learning*: P. De Geus, 'Planning as learning', *Harvard Business Review*, March/April, 1988: 70–4; D. Kolb, 'Problem management: learning from experience', in S. Shrivastva (ed.) *The Executive Mind: New Insights on Managerial Thought and Action*, (San Francisco: Jossey-Bass, 1983); D. Kolb, D. Lublin, J. Spoth and R. Baker, 'Strategic management development: experiential learning and managerial competencies', *Journal of Management Development*, 3(5), 1986: 13–24; and G. Morgan, *Riding the Waves of Change: Managerial Competencies for a Turbulent World* (San Francisco: Jossey-Bass, 1988).
31 K. Clarke, 'Investment in new technology and competitive advantage', in D. Teece (ed.) *The Competitive Challenge: Strategies for Industrial Innovation and Renewal* (Cambridge, Mass.: Ballinger, 1987).

# Part II

# The case studies

# Section 1

# Creative positioning

# Chapter 3

# The rise of the Swatch: revitalizing the Swiss watch industry

*Martyn Pitt*

## EDITORS' OVERVIEW

Is there anyone who has not heard of Swatch? Within two years of its 1983 launch 13 million units had been sold. By the end of the decade this figure had risen to a staggering 100 million, despite widespread competitive imitation.

Swatch's parent firm ETA was a traditional Swiss firm whose success had been based on making good quality mechanical watch movements. Hardly the firm to launch a disposable, fashion-oriented electronic watch, one might think. But technological innovation had already created reliable electronic timing devices, the cost of which had fallen from $US 200 + in 1972 to $US0.50 in 1984. Specific advances in production technology allowed the Swiss to overcome their apparent disadvantage as a high cost locality for watch assembly, enabling them to make the Swatch in large numbers at low unit cost.

Thereafter the success of Swatch was very much about the marketing approach used to exploit these advances for good financial return. Designs were changed twice a year, a most unusual strategy in the watch trade. Retail prices were low, but not rock bottom. Non-traditional channels of distribution were often used and promotional spending was high. Although ETA headquarters in Switzerland might have preferred a global approach to marketing, they respected the desire of Swatch's US and European managers to take account of significant differences in their consumers' attitudes and opinions. Not every local market initiative succeeded, but continuing product innovation into the 1990s has protected Swatch's unique position.

### Discussion questions

- Early attempts by US electronics firms to dominate the cheap watch market failed, in part due to severe competition from low-cost producers in Hong Kong and Taiwan. So why did Swatch succeed in this mass market despite its traditional high-cost, mechanical technology base? What advantages did its Swiss roots give Swatch and how were these exploited?

- Why was the US market seen to be so important? Was this a fair assessment?
- Why did the Swatch approach to product extension beyond watches during 1986–8 not succeed?
- What is the right balance between global and local approaches to strategy development? How can Swatch keep the initiative beyond the 1990s when facing persistent 'me-too' competition?
- 'Innovation in marketing contributes more than technological innovating to the commercial success of consumer products.' Discuss in the context of the Swiss watch industry.

### List of named characters

Dr Ernst Thomke, managing director of ETA, Swatch's parent company, later chief executive of the SMH group's watchmaking activities
Max Imgrüth, president Swatch Watch USA
Jacques Müller and Elmar Mock, Swatch product engineers
Franz Sprecher, independent marketing consultant
Kåthi Durrer and Jean Robert, collection designers

### Keywords

Technological innovation; low cost production; marketing innovation; appropriating returns; product line extensions; planned obsolescence; global-local strategies

## DECLINE OF THE SWISS INDUSTRY

Watchmaking came to Switzerland in the seventeenth century with the French Huguenots. By 1900 the industry was a complex and clumsy web of more than 2,000 firms, mostly small, family-owned and craft-oriented component makers. These firms supplied movement (*ébauches*) assemblers which then supplied the assemblers of finished watches.

Difficult trading conditions between the First and Second World Wars led to drastic protectionism by the Swiss government. It regulated competition by encouraging two large, loosely knit groupings: ASUAG with famous names like Longines and Rado, plus a leading movements making group, Ebauches SA, and SSIH with equally famous Omega and Tissot. Most Swiss watches, however, bore simply the legend 'Made in Switzerland' as their promise of quality.

Between 1930 and 1950 the structure of the Swiss industry was effectively frozen; restrictive practices discouraged innovation and cost reduction. Still, at its 1950 'high tide' Switzerland produced some two-thirds of the 40–45 million watches made annually. It exported 97 per cent of its output and its share of world markets was over 80 per cent by value. The Swiss dominated every price and quality segment, from jewel-encrusted gold watches to inexpensive children's pin (rather than jewel) lever watches. They monopolized imports into the USA where about half their output was sold. Other producers included the USA, Germany, France and to a lesser extent the UK and Japan. At that time all watches were mechanical, having over one hundred miniature moving parts powered by a flat, coiled mainspring.

In the 1950s the Swiss faced rapidly advancing competition. The Japanese firms Seiko and Citizen adopted mass production techniques learned from US car makers and attacked the Swiss in the medium price sector worldwide. In the $US30–100 price range the US Bulova Corporation competed strongly with watches made in the USA and at its Swiss factories. It also introduced the first battery-powered electronic watch, the Accutron, in 1960. This offered unprecedented, but costly accuracy via a patented tuning fork mechanism. Meanwhile, the upstart Timex Corporation was mass producing pin lever watches selling for under $US10 in drugstores and supported by massive TV advertising. By 1960 Timex claimed to sell one watch in three in America and enjoyed volume sales in Europe too. The Swiss share of 98 million units of world output fell to 43 per cent (East Germany 20 per cent, the USA 10 per cent, West Germany 8 per cent, Japan 7 per cent, France 6 per cent; others 6 per cent).

By 1970 world production had grown to 174 million units. Switzerland retained 42 per cent of unit volume, helped by exporting assembled pin lever movements to Hong Kong where they were put into locally made cases for resale in South East Asia. Swiss share of US imports had declined to 70 per cent as Japan doubled its share of world output and US firms sourced watches from low-cost plants in the Virgin Islands, a strategy denied the Swiss firms since their government prohibited the export of components. In the mid-1960s the Swiss began to dismantle such long-standing restrictive practices, precipitating integration and rationalization of the industry. US watch firms soon acquired Swiss firms as captive suppliers. Yet in 1970 there were still over one thousand Swiss firms, although eight accounted for three-quarters of exports.

## THE EMERGENCE OF THE ELECTRONIC WATCH

The 1960s began the race to make the affordable electronic watch. The Swiss were involved but sceptical. From 1962 Ebauches SA collaborated (unsuccessfully) to create a rival for the Accutron. In 1966 the Swiss Watch Federation encouraged R&D by the multinationals Brown Boveri, Landis & Gyr and Philips of Holland into *electronic* watches using integrated circuits and quartz crystal timing devices. Seiko of Japan launched the first (unreliable) quartz analogue watch (having a conventional face and hands) in 1970. Bulova launched a quartz model in 1971 priced at $US1,350, matched by the exclusive Swiss firm Piaget at $US2,900. Bulova then released a new model at $US395, paralleled by a Seiko range at similar prices. The US firm Hamilton launched the first fully electronic watch (no moving parts) called Pulsar at $US2,100. Soon after, it went bankrupt and was acquired by a Swiss consortium. In 1972 Ebauches SA launched a range of analogue and digital models retailing at under $US300 with components from the leading US semiconductor house, Texas Instruments. Timex launched its first electronic model at around $US125.

Thereafter the watch market grew dramatically as US chip makers National Semiconductor, Motorola, Texas Instruments and Hughes drove down the cost of components until cheap electronic watches could be sourced from low-cost assemblers in Hong Kong for under $US10 ex-factory. SSIH tried to compete by acquiring a leading pin lever manufacturing group in 1971. To add to the Swiss woes, the US dollar more than halved in value against the Swiss franc during the 1970s, making Swiss watches too expensive for many consumers. One response was to focus on supplying high quality watches under prestige brand names like Cartier, Gucci and Raymond Weil.

By 1980 the world market was around 300 million units, but the Swiss share was down to 18 per cent (29 per cent by value) and over 80 per cent of all watches retailed at under $US100. Of the Japanese output,

60 per cent was electronic, many with reliable and readable liquid crystal displays, whilst the Swiss had only 20 per cent. The entire Swiss industry struggled to make profits; employment fell from a 1970 peak of 76,000 to 44,000 and bankruptcies reduced the number of firms to 850. Between 1980 and 1984 a further 230 firms and 13,000 jobs were lost. Output plummeted to under 10 per cent of 400 million watches assembled worldwide. Over the decade to 1984 sales of Ebauches SA movements, two-thirds of which went into ASUAG-SSIH brands, dropped from 51 million to 32 million. This pair of Swiss watchmaking groups had to be rescued by the banks which orchestrated their merger in 1983. The new group called SMH was briefly the second largest worldwide manufacturer after Seiko.

## ENTER THE *SWATCH*MAKER

In 1978 Dr Ernst Thomke, aged 39, was headhunted from his marketing role in Beecham pharmaceuticals to be Managing Director of ETA, the largest firm in the Ebauches SA group. Thus he returned to ETA where he had served an apprenticeship in his teens. ETA was best known for its ultra-thin mechanical movements; in all it produced over one thousand variants. Thomke rationalized production, closing nine factories and reducing the number of models to about 250. Layers of management were cut out and a more innovative culture was actively encouraged. To improve morale, Thomke challenged his engineers to make the world's thinnest quartz analogue watch, a feat claimed earlier by Seiko. Project Delirium as it was known – because initially it seemed a crazy idea – bore fruit in 1979. To make it possible, some parts were bonded to the case, a world first, and a very thin battery was also commissioned. That year ASUAG sold 5,000 Delirium watches at an average price of $US4,700.

In 1981 ETA began marketing its movements outside ASUAG and Switzerland, even in Japan. But it was desperate for new products in the medium and low price range. Thomke decided to avoid the middle ground dominated by Japan, instead setting his team the target of making a quartz watch to retail for no more than SFr.50 (then $US25). Because the retail and wholesale watch trades expected mark-ups approaching 100 per cent, the target ex-factory price had to be at most a quarter of retail selling price. Given that Swiss manufacturing costs were typically 80–85 per cent of ex-factory price, this implied the need to *make* a watch for SFr.10. Thomke's initial cost ceiling was SFr.15, but he stipulated that the production methods must have the potential to halve the unit cost over time. If achieved, the new watch would be uniquely profitable, with a factory profit margin more than twice that achieved by Far Eastern firms.

But Thomke insisted that the watch also had to be of good quality, water- and shock-proof, as standardized as possible, with variations limited to the look of the case, dial, hands and strap. But other than battery replacement, it did not have to be repairable. If all this was achieved, Thomke thought ETA could sell 10 million units in three years, the minimum needed to offset declining sales of inexpensive mechanical watches.

Two young engineers, Jacques Müller and Elmar Mock, masterminded this low-cost 'Daughter of Delirium'. Their design took a much larger team to implement, and a series of radical innovations involving seven patents. The case was a precision plastic moulding onto which component sub-assemblies were mounted. The 51 parts included a new, low-cost miniature stepping motor. Sub-assemblies were held together by ultrasonic welds not screws. The face cover was also welded to the case, sealing the watch for good. The strap was attached via a patented hinge and the battery located in a chamber on the back. Final assembly was automated as far as possible. Because no rectification of faults was possible, high quality of assembly had to be designed in. The initial capital investment to make Swatch was $US12.5 million. Only 800 people were needed to produce 8 million watches in 1985, final assembly requiring just 130. For comparison 350 were needed to assemble 700,000 Omega watches. By 1986 production costs were reportedly under SFr.10 per unit.

Thomke believed the US market would be critical for success. ETA still had no marketing department so he asked Franz Sprecher, an independent consultant, for ideas. Working with New York advertising agency, McCann-Erickson, Sprecher coined the name Swatch. The team decided to downplay its technical prowess in favour of associating the name with a concept of fun, excitement and fashionability (and perhaps disposability) aimed at people between 18 and 30 who would be encouraged to buy two or three for different occasions.

The first test market was organized by the Swiss Watch Distribution Center at Dallas, Texas, department stores in December 1982. There were a dozen fairly conventional designs, each given a name, a practice that has persisted. Results were mixed, but Swatch was launched in Europe in March 1983 and was soon on its way to meeting its first year target of 70,000 units retailing at SFr.40 for the basic watch, SFr.45 for a watch with a second hand and SFr.50 for a calendar version (US prices: $25, $30 and $35). A second test market in New York and Dallas organized by a Swiss fashion design graduate, Max Imgrüth, who had worked in America, convinced ETA that the first designs were too staid to create real excitement. Zurich designers Jean Robert and Kåthi Durrer were invited to style two collections each year, as for fashion clothes. Imgrüth was appointed President of Swatch Watch USA to manage product promotion and distribution. By autumn 1984 a system was in place to pre-test 80–100 new designs to find the best for each new season's collection. The use of coloured plastics aided rapid style changes. Scented models were also experimented with, and they added a smaller model appealing particularly to women.

Swatch watches were sold in shop-in-shops in classy department stores, selected watch and jewellery stores, sports, gift and fashion boutiques. Advertising and promotional activities were intense and flamboyant, especially in the USA where advertising expenditure in 1985 was $US8 million on sales of $US45 million. Endorsement by celebrities was also a leading aspect of publicity. The German launch was accompanied by hanging a giant watch with a 10 metre diameter face from a Frankfurt skyscraper. Supplies were managed to actual demand, to discourage retail discounting. Where Swatches were displayed below list price, the US distributor is said to have spent almost $US1,000,000 buying them back. Retailers were warned about counterfeits, first seen in 1985. US sales of Swatch reached 100,000 in 1983 and by 1985 were 3.5 million.

A separate subsidiary of ETA, Swatch AG, was created in 1985 to implement a US initiative to create a complementary range of casual clothing and footwear, umbrellas, sunglasses, cigarette lighters, etc. They hoped to generate $US100 million of additional sales in 1986. This proved too ambitious and the accessories line was discontinued in 1988. Still, Swatch itself went from strength to strength: 12.5 million units were sold in 1986, a total of 26 million since launch. Dr Thomke was promoted to manage the entire SMH watch business which had been sold by the banks to private investors in 1985. Swatch now accounted for well over 80 per cent of SMH's total unit sales, by far its biggest selling brand and rapidly becoming its most important revenue earner. By the end of 1989 over 70 millions units had been sold worldwide in 450 styles since launch.

Despite widespread imitation throughout the 1990s, Swatch has stayed ahead by creative advertising, aggressive high profile promotion and continued product innovation. Designs remain eye-catching and sometimes outrageous. ETA introduced the 'PopSwatch', the Maxi Swatch, the Recco Reflector, Swatch wall clocks, telephones and chronographs, scuba watches, and in 1992 watches with radio pagers and an Olympics commemorative collection of nine models retailing at around $US450. There are even mechanical, self-winding Swatches priced 50 per cent above similar electronic styles. Industry commentators are generally agreed that the Swatch brand has created and sustained a substantial, wholly new market niche defined by an original/ authentic, classless fun-and-fashion concept with which it is uniquely associated.

## NOTE

1 © M. Pitt 1995.
   This case study has been written as a basis for class discussion rather than to illustrate effective or ineffective managerial or administrative behaviour.

   This case draws, *inter alia*, on data from a number of documentary sources. These include W. Dullforce 'Swatch comes to the rescue', *Financial Times*, 21 February 1985; W. Dullforce 'Revival of the fittest: how Swatch cut costs in time', *Financial Times*, 28 May 1986; F. Knickerbocker, *Note on the World Watch Industry in 1970* (Boston: Harvard Business School, 1972); W. Luetkens 'Fashion circus lifts exports', *Financial Times*, 28 April 1986; S. Nye and J.-P. Jeannet, *Tissot: Competing in the Global Watch Industry* (Lausanne: IMDI, 1985); C. Pinson and H.C. Kimball, *Swatch* (Fontainebleau: INSEAD-CEDEP, 1987); Swatch product catalogues; Swiss Watchmakers Federation, Geneva: Annual Reports various; R. Tredre 'A stop-watch whose fashion time has come', *Independent on Sunday*, 19 April 1992; A. Ullmann; *The Swatch* (Binghampton: State University of New York, 1991).

## Chapter 4

# Direct Line Insurance PLC: new approaches to the insurance market[1]

*Derek Channon*

## EDITORS' OVERVIEW

Direct Line is an insurance company. Founded in 1985, it has experienced explosive growth in the sale of motor vehicle policies. This case study describes the development of Direct Line up to early 1993. Whilst its focus is on motor insurance, it refers also to Direct Line's impending diversification into other forms of insurance provision, beginning in 1993.

In 1990 Direct Line was one of only three motor insurance companies awarded a top rating by the consumer magazine *Which?* for its speed and efficiency in claims handling. Furthermore, it was the only leading UK motor insurer that year to report net profits on its underwriting business. By 1992 Direct Line was one of the top five UK motor insurers, covering 4.5 per cent of all cars.

Direct Line is backed by The Royal Bank of Scotland. The concept of providing motor insurance services by telephone was proposed to the bank by Peter Wood, an entrepreneurial former insurance broker in 1984. Direct Line was trading within eight months with Wood as its chief executive. The arrangement allowed him to operate without interference from the parent company, and by 1992 Wood had become the UK's highest paid executive.

Direct Line accepts customers only by telephone, so it does not have to pay commissions to traditional brokerage channels, estimated to be 25–40 per cent of the value of premiums. It also differs from the majority of the industry in other respects. It accepts payments only via bank direct debit or credit card, for example. In addition to these innovations in customer contact, Direct Line employs powerful IT systems to control costs, to speed processing of quotations and claims, to facilitate market analysis, and to exploit marketing and product opportunities rapidly. IT provides management with timely information on past underwriting experience in general and also regarding specific customers. This enables it to maximize efficiency in dealing with claims, to ensure customer satisfaction, yet contain the costs of fraudulent claims.

The case outlines Direct Line's aggressive and high profile advertising and publicity strategies. The firm monitors the effects of its advertising on sales and corporate image. However, Direct Line focuses not only on the *generation* of new business but also on the successful *retention* of current customers, an endemic problem for the industry. It has achieved a customer retention rate of 85 per cent versus 50 per cent for the industry as a whole. It has achieved this considerable success by providing rapid and very competitive quotations, and in the quality of its after sales service. Senior management has been very committed to excellent after sales service, exemplified by providing 24-hour emergency telephone lines for clients in distress – such as after an accident – and optional rescue services for vehicle breakdown. The firm also emphasizes the need to give prompt approval for repair work to begin. All these services are enabled by the investment in information technology.

The case outlines the various aspects of the Direct Line 'formula' including systems and structures. The formula has, arguably, transformed the UK motor insurance market. Most of the large companies have either introduced a direct writing facility or are seriously considering doing so. Meanwhile, Direct Line has moved on, entering the market for home insurance and, with support from The Royal Bank of Scotland, the provision of mortgages to existing clients. The case closes with some financial exhibits and reflections on Direct Line's future prospects.

## Discussion questions

• How would you describe the Direct Line strategy? Why has Direct Line been so profitable if the industry is fundamentally unattractive – as many full line insurance companies have long perceived it to be?

• What are the main competitive advantages of Direct Line and why, in hindsight, was it right to develop a business based on them in the mid-1980s?

• What are Direct Line's core competences? Is information technology one of them?

• Looking beyond 1993 what are the principal competitive challenges which face Direct Line? Is its strategy sustainable or will it have to upgrade its competences in the foreseeable future as competitors seek to emulate the current 'formula'? If yes, how?

• How important has Peter Wood's contribution been to implementing the direct writing insurance concept? Is he a true innovator and leader in the insurance market or an opportunist? If for any reason he should leave, will Direct Line retain its strong position?

## List of named characters

Peter Wood, chief executive, Direct Line Insurance
Nikki de Jaeger, telesales operator, Direct Line Insurance
Clive Bannister, insurance specialist, Booz Allen Hamilton

## Keywords

Direct marketing; first moving; innovating; market dominance; related diversification; strategic use of information technology; excellence; distinctive competences; low cost operation; industry 'recipe' or 'formula'

## INTRODUCTION

'Too-to-to-toot toot toot toot toot tooo' the red telephone on wheels scooted across the car park to stop in front of a lady motorist who had just been involved in a minor auto accident. She picked up the phone to Direct Line to find to her delight that, unlike most insurers, immediate authorization could be given for her car to be repaired. The busy little red phone which had become the household symbol of Direct Line Insurance and features in all the company's literature and advertising, by 1992 was achieving widespread recognition as a symbol of low cost but personalized service to customers interested in purchasing motor and household insurance.

From its beginnings in 1985, Direct Line Insurance, in the year to September 1992, posted its sixth successive gain in gross premiums written to £213.2 million, an increase of 71.3 per cent on the previous year. Moreover, in a year when there was severe pressure on the motor insurance industry as traditional competitors made moves to diversify their delivery systems and regain market share, Direct Line still managed to achieve underwriting profits. Details of recent financial performance are shown in Tables 4.1, 4.2 and 4.3.

*Table 4.1* Direct Line Insurance: parent company revenue account 1989–
92 (£ million)

|  | 1989 | 1990 | 1991 | 1992 |
|---|---|---|---|---|
| Gross premiums | 66.0 | 84.1 | 124.4 | 213.2 |
| Reinsurance premiums | (1.6) | (1.8) | (3.3) | (4.0) |
| Net premiums written | 64.4 | 82.3 | 121.1 | 209.2 |
| Increase in unearned premium | (9.9) | (10.1 | (25.9) | (53.6) |
| Premiums earned | 54.5 | 72.2 | 95.2 | 155.6 |
| Investment income | 5.7 | 7.8 | 10.5 | 11.7 |
| Realized gains less losses on disposal of investments | (0.1) | — | — | — |
|  | 60.1 | 80.0 | 105.7 | 167.3 |
| Gross claims | 36.2 | 54.1 | 73.0 | 117.5 |
| Reinsurance recoveries | (0.5) | (4.4) | (4.6) | (2.3) |
| Net claims incurred | 35.7 | 49.7 | 68.4 | 115.2 |
| Expenses | 19.9 | 26.2 | 32.6 | 44.7 |
| Increase in deferred acquisition expenses | (0.5) | (0.5) | (2.5) | (5.4) |
|  | 55.1 | 75.4 | 98.5 | 154.5 |
| Underwriting result – transfer to consolidated profit and loss account | 5.0 | 4.6 | 7.2 | 12.8 |
|  | 60.1 | 80.0 | 105.7 | 167.3 |

*Source*: Annual Reports

*Table 4.2* Direct Line Insurance: consolidated profit and loss account
1989–92 (£ million)

|  | 1989 | 1990 | 1991 | 1992 |
|---|---|---|---|---|
| Investment income | 3.3 | 4.7 | 4.7 | 6.1 |
| Realized gains less losses on disposal of investments | (0.1) | — | — | — |
| Underwriting result | 5.0 | 4.6 | 7.2 | 12.8 |
| Other income | 1.5 | 1.3 | 2.4 | 4.0 |
|  | 9.7 | 10.6 | 14.3 | 22.9 |
| Other expenses | (1.8) | (1.3) | (0.6) | (1.8) |
| Profit before CEO bonus | 7.9 | 9.3 | 13.7 | 21.1 |
| Provision against investments charged (1989 released) | 0.2 | (0.2) | — | — |
| Bonus payable to CEO | — | — | (1.6) | (6.0) |
| Profit before taxation | 8.1 | 9.1 | 12.1 | 15.1 |
| Taxation | (3.2) | (3.3) | (3.1) | (4.4) |
| Profit after taxation | 4.9 | 5.8 | 9.0 | 10.7 |
| Dividend paid/proposed | (1.8) | (2.7) | (2.4) | (4.5) |
| Retained for the year | 3.1 | 3.1 | 6.6 | 6.2 |

*Source*: Annual Reports

Table 4.3 Direct Line Insurance: parent company and consolidated balance sheets year end 30 September 1989–92 (£ million)

| | Consolidated | | | | Parent company | | | |
|---|---|---|---|---|---|---|---|---|
| | 1989 | 1990 | 1991 | 1992 | 1989 | 1990 | 1991 | 1992 |
| **Fixed assets** | | | | | | | | |
| Tangible assets | 10.9 | 20.7 | 26.5 | 30.2 | 5.8 | 7.6 | 17.4 | 18.4 |
| Investments | 11.5 | 11.3 | 32.4 | 33.2 | 11.5 | 11.3 | 32.4 | 33.2 |
| Listed investments | 22.4 | 32.0 | 58.9 | 63.4 | 17.3 | 18.9 | 49.8 | 51.6 |
| Amounts paid in advance on new building | — | — | — | — | 10.3 | 10.0 | — | — |
| Deferred acquisition expenses | 2.8 | 3.3 | 12.9 | 18.3 | 2.8 | 3.3 | 12.9 | 18.3 |
| **Current assets** | | | | | | | | |
| Debtors | 11.0 | 18.0 | 24.1 | 28.4 | 9.7 | 16.9 | 22.8 | 27.1 |
| Short-term deposits and cash at bank | 73.7 | 84.5 | 109.5 | 194.2 | 63.9 | 80.0 | 109.3 | 194.2 |
| | 84.7 | 102.5 | 133.6 | 236.6 | 73.6 | 96.9 | 132.1 | 221.3 |
| Creditors: amounts falling due within one year | (8.7) | (12.3) | (15.3) | (27.2) | (5.2) | (8.1) | (8.2) | (15.3) |
| Net current assets | 76.0 | 90.2 | 118.3 | 195.4 | 68.4 | 88.8 | 209.0 | 206.0 |
| Creditors: amounts falling due after more than one year | (1.9) | (1.8) | (2.5) | (0.4) | — | — | — | — |
| **Provisions for liabilities and charges** | | | | | | | | |
| Defferred taxation | — | (0.5) | (0.4) | (0.4) | — | (0.2) | (0.3) | (0.3) |
| Insurance funds | (39.3) | (49.4) | (75.3) | (128.9) | (39.3) | (49.4) | (75.3) | (128.9) |
| Outstanding claims | (22.1) | (29.8) | (37.5) | (61.1) | (22.1) | (29.8) | (37.5) | (61.1) |
| Net assets | 37.9 | 44.0 | 74.4 | 86.3 | 37.1 | 41.6 | 73.5 | 75.6 |
| **Capital and reserves** | | | | | | | | |
| Called-up share capital | 35.0 | 38.0 | 62.0 | 67.0 | 35.0 | 38.0 | 62.0 | 67.0 |
| Profit and loss account | 1.3 | 4.6 | 15.6 | 21.8 | 0.5 | 2.2 | 14.7 | 21.1 |
| Investment reserve | (0.2) | (0.4) | 0.8 | 1.5 | (0.2) | (0.4) | 0.8 | 1.5 |
| Property revaluation reserve | 1.8 | 1.8 | (4.0) | (4.0) | 1.8 | 1.8 | (4.0) | (4.0) |
| Shareholders' funds | 37.9 | 44.0 | 74.4 | 86.3 | 37.1 | 41.6 | 73.5 | 85.6 |

Source: Annual Reports

## COMPANY HISTORY

In April 1985 Nikki de Jaeger, a telesales operator, sold Direct Line's first motor insurance policy and so started a revolution which was to transform the UK motor insurance market in a short time. Peter Wood, Direct Line's chief executive, believed that it was possible to develop a high quality but cheaper service to motorists than that offered by traditional insurance providers operating via brokers.

Peter Wood, a former employee of insurance brokers Alexander Howden, with a background in operations, approached The Royal Bank of Scotland, one of the leading British Clearing Banks and the premier institution in Scotland, to provide financial support and the benefit of the bank's assured reputation. With initial funding of £20 million to back the development of the necessary infrastructure and investment in comprehensive IT systems, the new company obtained Department of Trade and Industry approval to enter the insurance industry in January 1985, eight months after the venture had begun.

Direct Line became a subsidiary of the Royal Bank Group and Peter Wood sold his 25 per cent shareholding to the bank in return for an earnings formula based on the performance of Direct Line. In return, Wood was given a free hand to develop the business without central interference. In 1992, Wood was appointed to the board of The Royal Bank of Scotland Group.

This early period was spent in frantic development of the sophisticated communication and information systems behind Wood's idea. It was intended from the beginning to develop a direct telephone and mail distribution channel bypassing the brokerage route and thus saving the commission charged.

After the sale of the first policy there followed a period of test marketing prior to a national launch in September 1985. The business grew rapidly, driven by carefully monitored tactical press advertising and marketing to the customers of the Royal Bank. By 1992 Direct Line had grown dramatically and was the market leader in direct insurance with some 670,000 motor policy holders. This represented an increase of 89.9 per cent in premium income over 1991 while at the same time the company's expense ratio had reduced from 19.6 per cent to an industry low of 14.5 per cent. In a traditional broker-based insurance company around 38 per cent of total expenses are commission and a further 17 per cent relate to claims handling. In Direct Line some 12 per cent of expenses were variable. The remainder of the expense base was more or less fixed. Substantial scale economies would thus occur if volumes were increased to the point where capacity constraints occurred. Nevertheless, since much of Direct Line's fixed costs were based on computing and communication while labour costs were limited, substantial experience effects were possible.

In addition to its expense ratio advantage Direct Line had been highly successful in driving down its claims ratio to less than 70 per cent compared with an industry average of over 80 per cent. This reflected the superior risk profile of Direct Line's motor portfolio. In motor insurance Direct Line had become one of the leading participants with a national market share of 4.5 per cent and many analysts believed that the company would shortly become the leading motor insurer in the UK. Further, Direct Line enjoyed a customer retention rate of 85 per cent compared with the industry average of around 50 per cent.

In October 1988, adopting similar tactics to those used to develop the motor market, Direct Line launched its home insurance product and by 1992 had over 206,000 policies in place. Like the motor industry the split between structure and contents was some 60/40. Moreover, around 30 per cent of those with a household policy also had a motor policy with the group. Direct Line was also extremely careful when insuring properties with contents valued at over £40,000. Such properties were physically inspected and strict security requirements laid down before policies were enforced.

Growth also brought regional expansion with the opening of a sales and claims office in Glasgow, followed by the opening in June 1990 of a further regional centre in Manchester to service Northern England and Wales. The original Croydon office continued to service the southern parts of England and Wales but the company moved to a new, custom-built head office in Croydon in 1992. In November of the same year Direct Line opened a new regional office in Birmingham to service customers in the Midlands.

As planned, the company came into profit in its third full year of trading and further profit gains were made in subsequent years. Details of the growth of motor and home policy holders and in premium income are shown in Figure 4.1. Direct Line had not, however, achieved the same superior performance in its household business as it had in its motor business. The company's claims ratio had tended to be consistently higher than the industry average although these figures fluctuated substantially from year to year due to weather conditions, theft, subsidence and the like. In 1992 while the industry average claims ratio for all property was 61 per cent, Direct Line could only achieve 73.4 per cent.

While most insurers lose money in underwriting motor and household, they hope to recover their position from profits made from investments. As a result such investment portfolios usually consist of a mix of property, equities and fixed securities. By contrast, Direct Line was extremely conservative in its investment policy. Investments were therefore relatively liquid and risk-free, being held mainly in cash and deposits (£194 million at September 1992), government securities (£22 million) and owned occupied freehold properties (£18 million). Declining

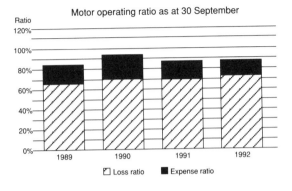

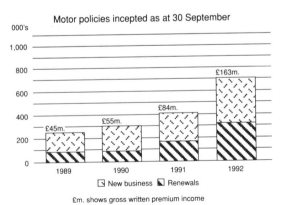

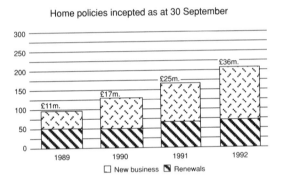

*Figure 4.1* Direct Line Insurance: growth in policies incepted, premium income and operating ratios, 1989–92

yields resulting from falling interest rates had therefore reduced investment income. However, the company argued that it did not wish to take risk on both sides of the balance sheet, in both insurance and investments, and hence its policy was to take only risk-free investments.

The dramatic success of Direct Line had spawned imitators. The nearest competitor was Churchill Insurance. This company, started by one of the co-founders of Direct Line and operating in a very similar manner, had been acquired by Winterthur, one of the leading Swiss insurers. Other recent 'direct writers' included Topdanmate from Denmark and Gan-Minster from France.

The main casualties of Direct Line's success, however, were the British composite insurers who historically had sold their policies through independent brokers. Direct Line, by bypassing the brokers, saved their commission which averaged 25–40 per cent of premiums written. The success of direct writing had spurred the composites to reply with a variety of strategies. Some had responded by tightening their links with those brokers who obtained the best quality business for them. Further, they had stopped accepting policies from brokers whose business produced higher than average claims. One problem in this strategy of broker selectivity had been the lack of sophisticated management information systems in many insurance companies which made it difficult for individual companies clearly to identify the source of specific segment/broker profits or losses.

Other companies had attempted to secure their channels of distribution by integrating forward into broking by acquiring interests in leading broking groups such as Swinton, AA Insurance Services and Hill House Hammond. Three companies – General Accident, Royal Insurance and Eagle Star – established their own direct writing operations between 1988 and 1990. However, these companies were anxious not to disturb their traditional broker-based channels and thus did not capitalize on the parent company's image by identifying closely with their subsidiaries. During 1991, for example, General Accident was faced with a brief boycott by brokers angered by its promotion of direct sales. The continued success of Direct Line and the other direct writers was forcing a change of attitude amongst the composites and greater recognition of the new channel seemed an essential strategy for the 1990s. 'They have to fish or cut bait. They have to choose one way or another,' stated one leading strategic management consultant, Clive Bannister, insurance specialist at Booz Allen Hamilton, 'If they continue to walk down the middle of the road they will get run over.'[2]

## THE UK MOTOR INSURANCE MARKET

Throughout the 1980s the UK motor market had been expanding slowly as a result of rising consumer affluence. The number of private cars and light goods vehicles expanded from 16.3 million in 1980 to 22.1 million in 1991. There had been a slight swing towards private cars in the late 1980s. This resulted from a decline in the attraction of 'company cars' due to the changes in tax treatment and a rise in the number of two-car families. This trend was expected to continue and even accelerate in the 1990s.

Premium income for motor insurers rose at a rate greater than GDP but claims tended to rise even faster. As a result most motor insurers made a loss on underwriting, endeavouring to make this up with investment profits. In 1991, of approximately 600 motor insurers in the UK, only Direct Line amongst the leaders made a net profit on underwriting alone. In addition, the industry had done little to reduce its expense ratios. This was partially due to the fact that nearly 40 per cent of expenses were related to commissions to intermediaries but also resulted from insurers failing to grapple with the issue. The largest motor insurer was the Norwich Union in terms of gross premium income written. Details of the leading insurers are shown in Table 4.4.

By the end of the 1980s there was a clear sign of a structural shift in the distribution system for motor insurance. The biggest intermediaries were beginning to market their product more actively. The Automobile Association, which had adopted a traditionally aggressive approach, was being followed by the leading banks, and most recently by leading brokers that had been acquired by insurance companies. These latter included Hill House Hammond acquired by Norwich Union and Swinton now owned by Sun Alliance. In addition, led by Direct Line, direct writing had expanded dramatically. The main insurers, although initially reluctant, had been forced to respond by offering their own direct writing alternatives despite their fear of alienating their traditional intermediaries. Finally, there had been a strong move to build direct business with affinity groups.

Direct writing was estimated by the Associations of British Insurers to account for around 13 per cent of private car motor premiums in 1991. However, this figure included business written directly by branches, direct mail operators and affinity group business. Actual figures for 1991 and 1992 for the leading direct writers are shown in Table 4.5. The leader by far was Direct Line, followed by TIS, a subsidiary of Royal Insurance, Churchill, a company created by former executives of Direct Line and now owned by Swiss giant Winterthur, and the direct subsidiaries of General Accident and Eagle Star. Direct writing was the fastest-growing delivery system for motor insurance.

## THE UK HOUSEHOLD INSURANCE MARKET

There are few accurate available statistics on the household insurance market. However, the basis for such insurance is house ownership. It

*Table 4.4* Leading insurance companies in the UK private car market 1991

| Company | Gross earned premium (£ million) | Market share % | No. of vehicles | Average claims | Operating ratio expenses | Total % |
|---|---|---|---|---|---|---|
| 1 Norwich Union | 330.1 | 8.3 | 1078 | 96.3 | 22.4 | 118.7 |
| 2 General Accident | 306.8 | 7.7 | 1302 | 84.3 | 29.1 | 113.5 |
| 3 Sun Alliance | 275.4 | 6.9 | 1692 | 84.4 | 30.1 | 114.5 |
| 4 Eagle Star | 258.2 | 6.5 | 925 | 80.2 | 28.3 | 108.5 |
| 5 GRE | 247.2 | 6.2 | 960 | 97.6 | 25.2 | 122.8 |
| 6 Royal Insurance | 219.6 | 5.5 | 1222 | 85.3 | 28.9 | 114.2 |
| 7 Cooperative | 156.6 | 3.9 | 660 | 92.2 | 25.0 | 117.2 |
| 8 AGF Insurance | 142.9 | 3.6 | 717 | 79.4 | 37.7 | 117.0 |
| 9 Commercial Union | 128.0 | 3.2 | 486 | 82.6 | 28.4 | 111.0 |
| 10 Cornhill | 121.4 | 3.0 | 542 | 82.7 | 25.8 | 108.5 |
| 17 Direct Line | 65.4 | 1.6 | 336 | 68.4 | 23.0 | 91.5 |

*Source:* Gerrard Vivian Gray financial analysts (London, 1992)

*Table 4.5* Market share of the direct response writers in the UK private motor industry

| | 1991 | | | 1992 | | |
|---|---|---|---|---|---|---|
| | Premium (£ million) | Market share % | No. of policies in force (,000) | Premium (£ million) | Market share % | No. of policies in force (,000) |
| Direct Line | 84 | 2.1 | 411 | 159 | 3.5 | 670 |
| Churchill | 35 | 0.9 | 179 | 70 | 1.5 | 300 |
| TIS (Royal) | 44 | 1.1 | 292 | 60 | 1.3 | 314 |
| GA 121 | 37* | 0.9 | 175 | 48* | 1.0 | 180 |
| Eagle Star Direct | 16* | 0.4 | 55 | 38* | 0.8 | 115 |
| Smaller operators | 15* | 0.4 | 75 | 30* | 0.7 | 125 |
| Total | 231* | 5.8 | 1,187 | 405* | 8.8 | 1,704 |

*Source*: Gerard Vivian Gray financial analysts (London, 1992)
*Note*: *Estimated figure

was estimated that there were some 23 million homes in the UK in the late 1980s, two-thirds of which were privately owned. On 75 per cent of houses either owner-occupied or privately rented there was a demand for structural insurance. A lower percentage of households had taken out contents insurance coverage.

Premium income growth proceeded steadily during the 1980s but claims grew rapidly in the early 1990s due to weather damage and dry weather leading to a sharp increase in subsidence claims. There were also substantial increases in claims for theft.

The sale of household insurance was concentrated in the hands of the building societies. The leading insurers were all linked to particular societies and the top seven insurers held some 59 per cent of the market in 1992. In addition, company agents held a 27 per cent market share and direct marketing operations had achieved a 9 per cent penetration by 1991, again led by Direct Line. Other direct writers were mainly at the entry phase of the market.

## THE DIRECT LINE APPROACH TO INSURANCE

The aim of Direct Line was to provide customers with high quality cover, backed by high standards of personal service at low prices. The company's research showed that this proposition was the opposite to the perception most people had of traditional insurance companies. Direct Line aimed to achieve this lower price, higher quality service by operating at lower cost not only by eliminating the role of the broker, but by the innovative use of technology.

## The use of advertising

Direct Line reaches its customers by the use of high profile advertising coupled with extensive direct marketing. In its early years this was largely via national press advertising. In 1990, however, Direct Line moved much of its advertising to television and introduced the red telephone on wheels responding to a number of motor and household insurance situations. Conceived by Peter Wood and his team, the TV campaign was awarded the BDMA Royal Mail Direct Marketing Award for the most innovative campaign of the year. Commenting on the success of the campaign, the originating agency, David Wilkins Advertising, stated:

> The lively use of the very simple device of the Red Phone has achieved a much greater level of enquiries than press alone. It also had to persuade a broader audience, which had perceived direct insurance operations as being 'fly by night' or financially unsound. The Red Phone has achieved the added benefit of making the method of response – the phone – virtually its own. It has become an immediately recognisable and memorable symbol for Direct Line.

As a result of the campaign, quotations from areas with TV support, compared with those without, were dramatically higher. Moreover, tracking data showed that awareness of Direct Line increased from 27 per cent to 46 per cent while perceptions of Direct Line as a forward-looking company rose from 20 per cent to 40 per cent, as a reputable company from 11 per cent to 26 per cent and for high quality service from 7 per cent to 15 per cent. The judges of the BDMA award described the results of the campaign as 'fantastic' (samples of Direct Line's literature are illustrated in Figure 4.2). The response rates to Direct Line advertisements were carefully monitored to identify their economic effectiveness. All potential customers seeking quotations were asked where they had heard of Direct Line. The number of quotations per advertisement, whether TV or press, was thus monitored as were conversion rates from quotations to policies, although this latter figure was also influenced by the telesales operators. Nevertheless, management was confident that it had a reasonable view of economic effectiveness of Direct Line advertising including advertising decay. This data was immediately available on Direct Line's sophisticated MIS system.

Direct Line backed up its advertising by the aggressive use of public relations with a view to seeking editorial coverage. Commenting on Direct Line's approach to home insurance for example, Peter Wood noted that having introduced home insurance in 1987:

*Figure 4.2* Examples of Direct Line's promotional literature

We decided that 1990 was to see a major thrust from the company to acquire more household business. We launched a forceful press and TV campaign in early June aimed at challenging the dominant position held by building societies in the home insurance market. At the same time we made a formal submission to the Office of Fair Trading asking them to consider whether the customer really has a free choice in the selection of his household insurer. Our initiative gained widespread, quality coverage on TV and in the press and has prompted a growing number of consumers to direct their own complaints to the Office of Fair Trading.

In its advertising Direct Line guaranteed to cut household insurance costs to new policy holders by 20 per cent provided houses were purchased during the previous five years via mortgages from seventeen of the twenty leading building societies and had been continuously insured through them. The campaign and the related press coverage prompted a defensive response from many of the leading building societies which had previously actively promoted household insurance through themselves to mortgagors, on which they received commissions of some 30 per cent from the insurance companies. As a result the number of quotations and acceptances of household insurance via Direct Line increased dramatically. Commenting, Peter Wood added:

> While the objective of all this activity was to increase our sales we, nevertheless, believe in a fair deal for the consumer and in the consumer's right to choose the product which best meets his or her requirements at the right price.

## The provision of personal service

Peter Wood believed that much of Direct Line's success could be attributed to the company's emphasis on high quality customer service. Unlike traditional insurers who had little or no direct contact with policy holders, Direct Line encouraged customers to talk to them by telephone. During the financial year to 30 September 1990, Direct Line received 1.7 million telephone calls. By 1992 this number had grown to 4.4 million. Not only had the company attracted many new policy holders but the customer retention rate was substantially higher than that of most other leading insurers.

Customers seeking a quotation were greeted by a telephone system which could prioritize incoming calls, direct them to a free operator and identify to the telesales operator the type of call he or she was receiving. The operators were based in each of Direct Line's four operating centres and received extensive and continuous training in telesales techniques to ensure customers and potential customers received friendly, courteous and efficient service.

On receipt of a call, operators would effectively complete a proposal form via a computer screen which would prompt the operator through the data required. Within the software, automatic back-up systems would identify for the operator specific models of automobiles and the like, which had been preprogrammed to cover underwriting risk. This database was being continuously updated as new underwriting experience developed. After completing data entry the computer would generate automatic quotations dependent upon driver background, area and model of car, with alternatives covering different degrees of risk. When a quotation was made, if accepted by the customer, immediate cover could be granted if required, or deferred to a time convenient to the customer. Quotations remained in effect for a given period. The whole process took usually no more than three minutes for motor insurance. In the event of acceptance the computer file was transmitted to a laser printer which operated day and night to ensure all policies issued during the previous day were sent out to customers within 24 hours. Details of all quotes made but not accepted were also stored on the central data base. This data was used to compare success and failure so as to structure marketing efforts. Failed quote prospects were also sent an unsolicited direct mail quotation on the first anniversary of their original telephone enquiry. Only 10 per cent of the Direct Line Portfolio was for non-comprehensive insurance compared with an industry average of 29 per cent. In addition, Direct Line had a strict policy of not accepting fast or exotic cars and young drivers.

Claims were also dealt with as rapidly as possible as Peter Wood believed strongly that customer service did not end at issuing policies but rather began there, and that the real quality of an insurance company lay in its speed in settling claims. In the case of smaller motor claims, the Direct Line telephone claims department could issue immediate approval to motorists. In other, more substantial cases, Direct Line's own engineers aimed to settle as quickly as possible and the company rather than the repairers guaranteed the quality of repairs if customers chose one of a carefully selected list of automobile repairers around the country.

For both motor and household policy holders Direct Line provided 24-hour helpline numbers. In the motor section these were manned by friendly experts in accident and claims procedures, and a free accident recovery helpline was provided to ensure that help was quickly available following an accident. Vehicle recovery costs and emergency breakdown care were also provided as options on Direct Line policies.

Home policy holders were provided with a free household emergency helpline offering 24-hour access to qualified tradesmen identified by Direct Line in the event of an emergency such as burst pipes, storm damage, broken windows or damaged locks.

In the consumer magazine *Which?* an independent survey of some 100 motor insurance companies in 1990 placed Direct Line as one of only three companies achieving a top rating for its speed and efficiency in claims handling. The company is proud that this position has been maintained in subsequent years. After the Lockerbie air disaster in Scotland, Direct Line paid out emergency aid to policy holders in less than 24 hours.

The telesales quotations and claims service is also visible to management via the Direct Line integrated MIS system. This reports in real time the number of quotations made by area, by operator and the conversion rate by operator, thus providing a clear view of performance in real time. Moreover, operators with lower conversion success rates can be individually counselled to improve performance. Successful operators or units can also be rewarded via bonuses or special rewards.

## The pursuit of efficiency

Direct Line was an innovative user of technology to help keep down the cost of premiums. For example, the company only accepted payment by credit card or direct debit. In this way payments could also be received electronically, with the minimum of paper, which kept staff levels and, therefore, costs to a minimum. A combined effect of the level of personal service and low cost delivery systems meant that Direct Line, despite product/services imitators from the traditional service industries continued to show substantial growth throughout the 1980s and early 1990s. Moreover, via its integrated MIS system, the company constantly monitored its customer base to identify claim abuse, extra policy marketing opportunities and the like and adjusted premiums charged based on the level of overall actuarial risk.

## The leading products of Direct Line

By 1992 Direct Line insured some 4.5 per cent of all cars in the UK and was amongst the top five of motor insurers (out of some 600). Moreover, the company's swift and efficient claims service enhanced the Direct Line image. Direct Line, apart from offering standard motor insurance, had extended its product offer by allowing customers to add Motor Legal Protection cover for a fixed rate fee. This meant that if a policy holder should ever need assistance in recovering uninsured losses following an accident that was not their fault, the matter could be pursued through the Courts on their behalf.

Further, Direct Line made breakdown cover available to motor policy holders at prices much lower than traditional organizations like the RAC and AA. The company had also expanded its policy holder base by purchasing the motor book of Refuge Assurance made up of some 7,000 policy holders. Peter Wood considered this purchase as merely a dry run to test the risk and return of other insurers' motor books, because he felt that other leading composites would be getting rid of their usually unprofitable motor books.

'It was only four days' new business, in current terms, so I couldn't get excited about it,' he commented, 'It occurred to me that we would never take this route again because it's easier and better to grow your own business. There are probably 15 million motorists in the UK who pay for private motor insurance. Of them, ten million will have over three years' worth of no-claims businesses. I want 30 per cent of that total.'

In household insurance Direct Line was better able to quantify the effect of low prices. As a result Direct Line had been able to guarantee purchase at lower prices for home insurance compared to those purchasing through building societies. Direct Line was also able to guarantee that the company's premium rate would not increase in the following year. By 1990 Direct Line had achieved cover on £7 billion of property and contents. By 1992 premium income had grown to £35.7 million and the number of policies in force had grown from 166,000 in 1991 to 206,000.

Direct Line also provided insurance for The Royal Bank of Scotland loan clients and credit card consumers. The service was in this case provided via the Royal Bank and covered over 350,000 accounts in 1990, though it was not as successful as the motor or household businesses.

Early in 1993, Direct Line was developing further financial service products to offer on a direct sales basis. Peter Wood commented,

We're doing a prototype now on home loans and deposits to our customers. It should be operational in four or five months' time. Longer term, we are looking at mortgages. However, I'll only give people home loans if they come through our core products. That really streams out some bad costs. It'll be simple – if you want one of our products, you have to have our home insurance.

### Company organization

By 1992 the number employed by Direct Line had grown to 1,086 people in its four regional centres, up from 787 in 1991. These centres were based in Croydon, Glasgow, Manchester and most recently Birmingham. Very roughly there were around 520 in telesales and 330 involved in teleclaims. The company employed 47 in-house engineers and these evaluated 90 per cent of claims on motor business rather than using loss adjustors as was normal in the industry. Household claims were evaluated by loss adjustors but Direct Line used its own engineers to conduct security surveys on high-value properties. There were some 130 employees engaged in information processing with around 40 of these being involved in systems development. In addition, some systems work was subcontracted out. Of the remainder, 40 employees were engaged in accounts, 7 analysed underwriting and 3 were involved in marketing. While premium income had soared in recent years the number of employees had grown at approximately half this rate. The company was still led by Peter Wood who had originally conceived the idea of Direct Line. He was ably assisted by a small executive team, many of whom had

Head
Office

| Peter Wood* |
| Chief Executive |

| Roy Haviland* | Lyndon Thomas* | Mike Flaherty* | Jane Dickson* | Vic Farrow* |
| Executive Director | Executive Director | Information Technology | Company Secretary | Director & General Manager, Operations |

Executive
Management

| Stephen Ashman | Stephen Davis | Andrew Dodsworth* |
| Marketing | Banking Services | Finance |
| Chris Harland | David Jenkins* | Keith Johnson |
| Technical Services | Strategic Planning | Engineers |
| Derick Leath† | Loraine Manzaroli | Chris McKee* |
| Claims | Personnel | Underwriting and Claims |

* Executive Committee Members
† Under temporary secondment to Manchester for one year to head up the new office

*Figure 4.3* Who's who in Direct Line Insurance

been with the company since its conception. The executive team is shown in Figure 4.3. In 1992, Peter Wood became the highest paid executive in the UK when he received a bonus of some £6 million for Direct Line's performance in the past financial year. This sum was based on a formula developed when The Royal Bank of Scotland bought out his original 25 per cent of Direct Line's equity.

## FUTURE PROSPECTS

Peter Wood commenting in 1993 upon the future prospects of Direct Line stated,

Despite its short history Direct Line has already claimed a position among the UK's leading personal lines insurers. During the 1990s many of our competitors suffered losses, in some cases substantial; some of them have responded with increases in premium rates on both their private motor and household buildings' accounts.

We are aware of the problems facing the general insurer ... However, our underwriting success of the past year and the continued development of our infrastructure have put us in a strong position for the future and we consider that such an environment presents Direct Line with the opportunity to grow both its motor and its household accounts.

This we plan to do, at the same time continuing to give our policy holders maximum value through the tried and tested combination of low costs and high quality service. If all things stay the same, Direct Line will be making £100 million in a couple of years. The only things you can't control are the competition and the weather. It could be worth more than the Royal Bank before too long.

## NOTES

1 © D. F. Channon 1993

This case study has been written as a basis for class discussion rather than to illustrate effective or ineffective managerial or administrative behaviour.

2 *Financial Times*

# Chapter 5

# Amtssparekassen: the survival of a regional savings bank

*Børge Obel, Bo Eriksen, Jens Krag and Mikael Søndergaard*

## EDITORS' OVERVIEW

The Amtssparekassen case describes the rejuvenation of a regional Danish bank in the wake of industry deregulation in the 1980s and the run up to the Single European Market scheduled for 1993.

Although Danish banks were technologically advanced, making good use of computerized information systems, they had been accustomed to a growing economy, a relatively high level of inflation, and a generous spread between wholesale and retail interest rates on which there had historically been little competition. When this changed and recession set in, many banks struggled. Amtssparekassen found itself in a bad situation earlier than many of its peers and in adversity changed its leadership, strategy, organization structure and style in a timely and effective way.

The case study reviews the Danish banking industry. It then describes how Amtssparekassen came into being and the organizational problems that arose. These contributed to its severe financial losses in 1987 and 1988, as did Amtssparekassen's dependence on smaller and less creditworthy corporate clients. In crisis, the supervisory Board conferred operating responsibility on two joint managing directors, the current CEO and a former director of the Danish association for savings banks (previously a university professor in business administration).

During the next few years, this 'team' implemented an impressive turnaround strategy. This involved redefining the target markets of the bank, consistent with its regional status and size. They also made fundamental changes to organization structure, making it much flatter, and changed lending policies and accountabilities. As a priority the bank sought to reduce costs and bad debts below the industry average. In 1991 it became a public company.

The case study provides details of a comprehensive and costly change in management process implemented between 1991 and 1994. Throughout, the top team adopted a style of decision making that was neither extremely democratic nor authoritarian: employees were involved in important decisions and had the opportunity to express opinions. It is perhaps this management style that constitutes a new core competence for Amtssparekassen. In any event, when other banks were still hard hit by recession in the early 1990s and many disappeared, Amtssparekassen was 'fighting fit'.

## Discussion questions

- How would you describe Amtssparekassen's strategy? Has it now achieved a defensible strategic position?
- What are its core capabilities and how easy are these to emulate?
- What contribution did the organization development (OD) programme make? What is your view of the decision-making style described in the case as neither democratic nor autocratic?
- Where should Amtssparekassen go from here?

## List of named characters

Poul Balle, joint managing director
Dr Niels Christian Knudsen, joint managing director

## Keywords

Turnaround/rejuvenation; niche; cost reduction; culture change; management by objectives; competence upgrading

## INTRODUCTION

For decades, the Danish banking industry was regarded as well managed and banks were considered very trustworthy by external observers.[2]

> Danish banks and savings banks are among the financially most sound in the world, since the law makes them maintain a ratio of equity capital and reserves to deposits and guarantees of 8 per cent – and nearly all the savings banks maintain a ratio two or three points higher than this.[3]

Danish banks had been at the forefront of technological innovation with extensive use of computers and the introduction of a nationwide system for electronic money transfers between stores and banks. The banks were accustomed to operating within a growing economy experiencing a relatively high level of inflation, and with a generous spread between wholesale and retail interest rates. Losses related to the financing of houses and other kinds of bad debts were minimal. In this setting, growth was the key to profit. The large Danish banks competed on the volume and value of loans they could issue and to this end many small, regional banks made strategic moves to gain national coverage.

A severe blow to Danish banking integrity and pride occurred in the mid-1980s when inflation and economic development decreased dramatically. With the deregulation of financial markets and new banking regulations in the European Community, many banks found themselves in a very difficult position with few options for improvement. An unprecedented number of banks experienced severe losses and several collapsed. Few observers saw much chance for the survival in Denmark of small regional banks. A prosperous industry had turned into a troubled industry.

This case study is about a savings bank that very quickly found itself in a bad situation. But contrary to many of its competitors, Amtssparekassen managed to change its strategy, organization, and management in a timely way. It created a strategy that was different from conventional wisdom in the industry. Thus it has managed not only to come to terms with the problems of the industry, but to become a very sound regional bank.[4]

We first review the general situation of the Danish banking industry. Then we discuss the sector of the industry containing the Amtssparekassen savings, bank followed by its new strategy and management approach.

## THE DANISH BANKING ENVIRONMENT

The structure of the Danish banking system is straightforward. There are two types of banks: savings banks and commercial banks. Their historical roots and forms of legal organization constitute the chief difference between them. The difference is highlighted in the way equity capital was raised and in the way loans and credits were granted, not in the way deposits were received from the public.

The first savings bank was established in 1810 and the first commercial bank in 1846. The early savings banks were more or less charitable institutions. Their main task was to accept savings from, and grant loans to, the man in the street and to promote saving habits in general.[5] The task of commercial banks was to make funds available for the industrial sector based on the strength of their share capital.

Savings banks were non-profit, self-governing institutions, while commercial banks were limited liability companies. The requirements for equity capital differed. For savings banks at least 4 per cent of total liabilities was required, whereas at least 10 per cent of total liabilities was required for commercial banks. The differences in their activities were controlled by formal regulations.

Equality in the legal status of the two types of banks was introduced by the Commercial Banks and Savings Banks Act 1975. Thereafter, both kinds of banks could do the same types of business, the only difference being that savings banks still had to be non-profit, self-governing institutions. This severely restrained them in raising equity capital as they could not issue stocks, which was the prime strategy of commercial banks in this respect. Thus savings banks were severely restrained in their growth.

From the early 1960s until the mid-1970s two trends characterized the Danish banking industry, namely reduction in the number of independent institutions and expansion of retail branch networks. In 1960 there were 159 commercial banks and 477 savings banks. By 1977 there were 74 commercial banks and 170 savings banks. Meanwhile, the number of branches of commercial banks almost doubled from 1,135 in 1960 to 2,078 in 1977, while branches of savings banks rose from 516 to 1,256 over the same period. The two leading savings banks, SDS and Bikuben, had more than half of the branches of the savings banks' network while the three leading commercial banks had almost 40 per cent of the commercial banks' branches. Thus the savings bank sector experienced greater concentration than the commercial bank sector, allied to greater proportionate expansion of its branch network.

The interest rate spread was fixed by regulation. In 1960 it was 4.25 per cent, in 1970 5.79 per cent, and in 1977 it was 6.13 per cent. By 1990 the spread was back to the level of the early 1960s at 4.27 per cent. Since the value of credits advanced was constrained by the prevailing fixed credit/deposit ratio, the competitive advantage of a Danish bank lay in the amount of deposits it could attract. To control an increasing amount of deposits in order to be able to satisfy a booming demand for advances, ambitious commercial and savings banks had either to increase the number of their branches or merge with other, smaller banks. Consequently, the total branch network increased and the number of independent banks decreased significantly.

The banking industry was very prosperous during the 1960s, owing mainly to the expansion of the Danish economy during that period. The gross income of commercial banks increased from DKr.238 million in 1960 to DKr.836 million in 1970.[6] In 1975 their gross income reached DKr.1,888 million.

In the 1970s the activities of the Danish banking industry were subject to rigid monetary policy. In 1970 the Danish Central Bank had imposed a 'credit ceiling' on bank lending commitments that applied both to savings and commercial banks. Given the significant deficit in the national balance of payments, the Central Bank pursued a high interest-rate policy to induce the corporate sector to raise foreign loans. Commercial banks negotiated these foreign loans on behalf of their customers and covered them with guarantees. Because savings banks were not allowed to issue guarantees, they were prevented from easing the pressure on the credit ceiling. Thus commercial banks obtained a competitive advantage in their dealings with corporate customers that extended also to farmers and wage-earners, the savings banks' traditional customers.

In the early 1980s the Danish government anticipated a surge in international growth likely to aid economic expansion in Denmark. Danish banks earned unprecedented profits in the mid-1980s from granting loans to the booming property sector and for private consumption. Capital gains were also extremely important for the banks' profits. In the era of high regulation the Danish banks had been restricted essentially to only traditional banking activities. During the 1980s the banking industry was gradually deregulated under EC rules so that all European banks could now compete on basically equal terms. This meant that Danish banks could now form holding companies, engage in stockbroking, issue real-estate bonds, compete for mortgage financing, enter the insurance industry, and so on. In many cases the banking business became just one of several subsidiaries of the holding company. Similar changes were allowed for the insurance companies, many of which entered the banking industry. These changes increased the competitive environment and the banking industry had to reconsider its situation:

It is a common view that some of the big regional banks and savings

*Table 5.1* Number of branches in the largest banks and savings banks, Denmark, 1988

| | |
|---|---|
| Den Danske Bank | 278 |
| Handelsbanken | 277 |
| Privatbanken | 196 |
| SDS | 334 |
| Bikuben | 277 |
| Provinsbanken | 216 |
| Jyske Bank | 131 |
| Andelsbanken | 240 |

*Table 5.2* Number of employees in the largest banks and savings banks, Denmark, 1988

| | |
|---|---|
| Den Danske Bank | 5,921 |
| Handelsbanken | 5,988 |
| Privatbanken | 5,079 |
| SDS | 4,473 |
| Bikuben | 3,780 |
| Provinsbanken | 3,683 |
| Jyske Bank | 2,430 |
| Andelsbanken | 3,850 |

banks will need to merge with others in order to gain size which can bear the cost of diversification into new types of activity, such as foreign business.[7]

The Danish banking sector was increasingly dominated by a limited number of leading banking institutions and a larger group of regional and local banks. Since deregulation the leading banks were price leaders. They would set rates to cover their operating costs including bad debts and to yield a satisfactory profit margin, given their assessment of prevailing market conditions. Earnings remained relatively high.

But from 1986 the international economy began to contract after several years of high growth. Denmark's economic conditions were then characterized by recession and rising unemployment. The fiscal policy of Denmark was driven principally by concern for improving the balance of payments, an important consequence being that the unemployment rate increased. Long-term financing had typically been made on the assumption of a high inflation rate. As inflation decreased, prices of real estate levelled off and in some areas even fell. Banks and mortgage finance institutions suddenly had to make hefty provisions for losses, mainly on loans to property and property development. During the late

1980s they realized a large number of bad debts. The more aggressive banks also started to compete strongly on price.

The eight largest banks in 1988 were represented in almost every region in Denmark, and controlled an extensive network of branches and employees (see Tables 5.1 and 5.2). Historically, all Danish banks had been full service institutions, offering a wide range of banking services to private individuals, firms and institutional clients. Even after deregulation commercial and savings banks tended to remain close to their core customer groups. The three largest commercial banks in 1988, Den Danske Bank, Handelsbanken, and Privatbanken, had close ties to large corporate customers. Andelsbanken, founded by the co-operative farmers movement, held a large presence in financing farmers and the agricultural industry,[8] which is dominated by farmers' co-operatives. SDS, the largest savings bank, had a strong presence in the private or retail market, and Bikuben, the second largest savings bank, was strong in financing residential (co-op) property.

Foreign banks still accounted for only an insignificant part of the Danish market in terms of branch distribution, even though Denmark was the first Scandinavian country to allow the entry of foreign banks at the beginning of the 1970s. High taxation, high labour costs and high net capital requirements appear to have kept most international banks away, although all exchange controls were lifted by the end of 1988.

The prospect of further liberalization of the international capital markets by 1992 triggered a new wave of mergers in the Danish banking industry after 1988, leading to even greater concentration. In the popular press, Danish banking was often referred to as 'overbanked', due to the large number of branches and employees in commercial and savings banks.[9] This over-abundance of bank resources was widely seen to create significant diseconomies, thus rationalization of branch networks was a principal goal of these mergers: 'We have too many branches in this country [about 2,000]. The branches must be profitable and have a minimum earnings of say DKr.5,000,000 [$US450,000].'[10] The increasing importance of electronic banking also meant that in the near future customers would probably be able to conduct a significant share of their banking business from the office, from home or via automated teller machines (ATMs). Thus electronic banking could reduce dramatically the need for manpower and for wide geographical coverage.

In 1989 the arch-rivals Den Danske Bank, Handelsbanken, and Provins-banken merged to form Den Danske Bank. Additionally, Privatbanken, Andelsbanken, and SDS merged to form Unibank. In so doing Den Danske became the largest Scandinavian bank, albeit still medium-sized in comparison with the largest banks elsewhere in Europe. Thus by the beginning of 1990 the Danish banking sector had changed dramatically,

*Table 5.3* The twenty largest banks and savings banks in Denmark, 1988 and 1992

| Bank | Assets 1988 (*billion* DKr.) | Bank | Assets 1992 (*billion* DKr.) |
|---|---|---|---|
| 1 Den Danske Bank[1] | 166.0 | 1 Den Danske Bank[1] | 320.1 |
| 2 Handelsbanken[1] | 121.1 | 2 Unibank[2] | 213.3 |
| 3 SDS[2] | 98.6 | 3 Bikuben[3] | 93.9 |
| 4 Privatbanken[1] | 97.2 | 4 Jyske Bank | 52.4 |
| 5 Provinsbanken[1] | 63.0 | 5 Girobank | 44.7 |
| 6 Jyske Bank | 60.0 | 6 Sydbank Sønderjylland[4] | 26.8 |
| 7 Bikuben[3] | 60.0 | | |
| 8 Andelsbanken[2] | 56.7 | 7 Sparekassen Nordjylland | 19.4 |
| 9 Sydbank[4] | 23.0 | | |
| 10 Sparekassen Nordjylland | 22.4 | 8 Aktivbanken | 15.6 |
| | | 9 Varde Bank[5] | 12.5 |
| 11 Sparekassen Sydjylland[3] | 19.1 | 10 Arbejdernes Landsbank | 11.9 |
| 12 Varde Bank | 15.6 | 11 Baltica Bank[5] | 10.1 |
| 13 Arbejdernes Landsbank | 13.6 | 12 *Amtssparekassen Fyn* | 9.3 |
| | | 13 Amagerbanken | 8.2 |
| 14 Aktivbanken | 11.9 | 14 Midtbank | 7.3 |
| 15 Amagerbanken | 10.6 | 15 Lån og Spar Bank | 3.6 |
| 16 DK Sparekassen[3] | 8.0 | 16 Forstædernes Bank | 3.3 |
| 17 *Amtssparekassen Fyn* | 6.9 | 17 Hafnia Bank[5] | 3.3 |
| 18 Sparekassen Sønderjylland[4] | 6.8 | 18 Sammenslutningen | 3.2 |
| | | 19 Kronjyllands Sparekasse | 3.0 |
| 19 Hafnia Erhvervsbank | 6.4 | | |
| 20 Midtbank | 5.8 | 20 Roskilde Bank | 2.9 |

*Notes*: 1 Den Danske Bank, Handelsbanken and Provinsbanken merged into Den Danske Bank.
2 SDS, Privatbanken and Andelsbanken merged into UNIBANK.
3 Sparekassen Sydjylland and DK Sparekassen merged with Bikuben.
4 Sydbank and Sparekassen Sønderjylland merged into Sydbank Sønderjylland.
5 Wound up or liquidated during 1993.

though it was still dominated by non-specialized domestic commercial and savings banks. Table 5.3 shows the industry structure before and after the second wave of mergers.

The mergers of the principal banks paved the way for future cost-cutting in the industry. These so-called megabanks began to integrate and rationalize the local branch networks of the newly merged structures. Management systems and especially computer systems also had to be integrated and the chief efforts of the new megabanks were focused on this until the beginning of 1992.

By 1992 and the advent of the Single European Market, the Danish banking industry was still in bad shape, despite or because of recent merger activity. For many banks the future prospects looked grim. Even for the leading banks such as Unibank the problems were severe. One of the few banks in Denmark to avoid losses at this time was Amtssparekassen Fyn A/S, the subject of this case study.

## AMTSSPAREKASSEN: HISTORY AND FOUNDATION

Amtssparekassen Fyn A/S[11] came into being between 1974 and 1976 in the first wave of mergers, through the fusion of twelve independent savings banks in small towns on the island of Funen.[12] In 1975 they established a common central office and a high street branch in Odense, the largest town on Funen. At the outset, the merged company had 220 employees, a number that rose to 525 by 1992. In 1986 a branch was established in Svendborg, the second largest town on Funen, and in 1988 a wholesale bank was established in Copenhagen.

From the beginning, the organization structure of Amtssparekassen Fyn was problematic. Even though the twelve savings banks were technically merged, they continued *de facto* as independently run businesses. The Board of Directors had thirteen members – one from each of the local areas and one from the central office. The dominance of local units was enforced at the centre by tacit agreement among board members not to interfere in local credit decisions, even the larger ones that the law required to be taken at main board level. The attitude was 'if you mind your own business, I will stick to mine, that attitude was a strong element in the tradition of the bank'.[13]

Thus the newly established central office had little authority over local branch managers who still decided credit and marketing policies in their own branches. This situation created a large degree of balkanization in the organization, highlighting the lack of central co-ordination. Because the central office held little power and status, few central staff functions were set up to help management co-ordinate the various tasks in the bank including marketing, credit and personnel policies. Amtssparekassen operated in effect as a collection of savings banks that had simply pooled their accounting data to meet regulatory and other pressures.

The lack of appropriate credit policies and clear lines of responsibility contributed to severe financial losses in 1987 and 1988, years when the rest of the Danish banking industry experienced healthy profits and return on equity (Table 5.4 and Figure 5.1). Furthermore, as Table 5.5 confirms, Amtssparekassen Fyn A/S incurred significantly higher provisions and bad debts than the industry average at this time.

This outcome was not an accident. Only after 1975 had savings banks

*Table 5.4* Main financial figures for Amtssparekassen 1987–92 (thousand DKr.)

|                          | 1987      | 1988      | 1989      | 1990      | 1991      | 1992      |
|--------------------------|-----------|-----------|-----------|-----------|-----------|-----------|
| Assets                   | 6,579,203 | 7,459,290 | 7,523,276 | 7,781,748 | 7,442,026 | 9,273,262 |
| Equity                   | 447,781   | 467,978   | 518,741   | 623,475   | 656,569   | 659,662   |
| Profit after tax         | − 16,563  | − 28,666  | 5,198     | 39,395    | 29,632    | 19,762    |
| Return on equity (%)     | − 3.70    | − 6.13    | 1.00      | 6.32      | 4.51      | 3.00      |
| Return on assets (%)     | − 0.25    | − 0.38    | 0.07      | 0.51      | 0.40      | 0.21      |

*Table 5.5* Losses and provisions for future losses 1987–92: percentage of loans and guarantees

|                  | 1987 | 1988 | 1989 | 1990 | 1991 | 1992 |
|------------------|------|------|------|------|------|------|
| Industry average | 1.1  | 1.5  | 1.2  | 1.8  | 2.0  | 2.9  |
| Amtssparekassen  | 1.3  | 3.3  | 1.9  | 1.3  | 1.3  | 2.3  |

been allowed to extend credit to corporate customers. The smaller banks including Amtssparekassen were therefore confined largely to servicing corporate clients not welcomed by the commercial banks, as well as smaller firms established after 1975. These two groups of potentially unsound customers were soon hit by the recession. Consequently, Amtssparekassen felt the adverse impact of recession much earlier than most commercial banks.

Amtssparekassen was still struggling to find an appropriate organizational structure. But its decision making continued to be grounded in local politics and no general strategy had been agreed upon. The unsatisfactory results between 1986 and 1988 signalled the pressing need for a strategic shift from past practices. The thirteen-member Board agreed to support a new top management team of two directors, with the remainder of them adopting the status of an advisory board.

The top team comprised Poul Balle, who was already CEO, and Dr Niels Christian Knudsen. The two men had very different backgrounds. Poul Balle had a traditional banking education supplemented with an MBA in finance and accounting. He had worked for Danfoss A/S and Sydbank before joining Amtssparekassen in 1979 as chief economist. Niels Chr. Knudsen had spent fifteen years as a university professor in business administration before becoming director of the Danish association for savings banks. However, when he joined Amtssparekassen he had no operations management experience in banking.

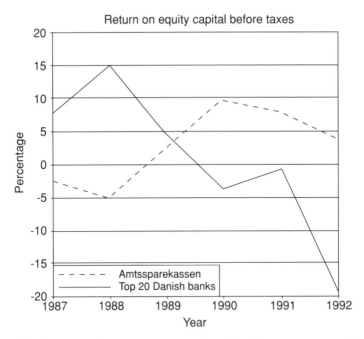

*Figure 5.1* Amtssparekassen compared with the top twenty Danish banks

Despite the fact that they divided their activities into functional areas, the two men held equal power and have run the bank as a genuine dual leadership – a very uncommon practice. During the next few years, this 'team' was to complete an impressive turnaround of Amtssparekassen, initiating a new strategic direction, restoring profits and starting new expansion (Tables 5.4 and 5.6).

Their first step was to establish a central focus for the operations of the savings bank and to design a new organization structure. After only two meetings of the thirteen-member board of directors, 'We simply stopped calling the meetings,' explained Niels Chr. Knudsen, 'They were of no use.' The old local politicking was divorced from the banking operations. The management of the central staff was changed so that all functional chiefs reported directly to the top management team. A new head of the credit department was appointed and two of the local directors whose areas had very significant losses were fired, giving a clear signal to the remaining ten local directors.

*Table 5.6* Amtssparekassen consolidated profit and loss account 1988–92 (thousand DKr.)

|  | 1988 | 1989 | 1990 | 1991 | 1992 |
|---|---|---|---|---|---|
| Interest earned etc. | 550,316 | 630,496 | 699,687 | 749,074 | 891,631 |
| Interest paid | 327,887 | 372,993 | 435,155 | 454,764 | 584,330 |
| Net earned interest and commissions | 222,439 | 257,503 | 264,532 | 294,310 | 307,301 |
| Other ordinary income | 72,807 | 78,159 | 85,756 | 44,724 | 75,930 |
| Profit and loss before expenditure | 295,246 | 335,662 | 350,288 | 339,034 | 383,231 |
| Expenditure | 201,908 | 218,634 | 237,692 | 238,216 | 241,929 |
| Profit or loss before depreciation and provisions | 93,338 | 117,028 | 112,596 | 100,818 | 141,392 |
| Depreciation and provisions | 166,811 | 92,689 | 73,808 | 79,024 | 144,557 |
| Profit or loss before extraordinary income and expenditure etc. | − 73,473 | 24,339 | 38,788 | 21,794 | − 3,165 |
| Profit and loss before tax | − 28,984 | 5,276 | 39,269 | 33,835 | 20,796 |
| Net result (after tax) | − 28,666 | 5,198 | 39,395 | 29,930 | 19,762 |

## AMTSSPAREKASSEN'S NEW STRATEGY: DEVELOPING A CONSISTENT AND DIFFERENT BUSINESS IDEA

The Danish banking sector was now dominated by comparatively few large banking institutions and a bigger group of smaller regional and local banks. The management of Amtssparekassen concluded that in order to survive and compete successfully in these circumstances, two conditions had to be met. First, bad debts and provisions for losses had to be lower than the average of the banking industry. Second, costs could not be allowed to deviate substantially from the industry average. Though crucial, these conditions were not considered sufficient to obtain lasting competitive advantage. More would have to be done later – but it was a start.

Based on their analysis of the changed conditions, the two men decided to look carefully at control of risk and cost efficiency. If the bank could do better or at least as well as the leading banks – the price and cost leaders – on these two measures, the way would be open for the development of a distinct competitive advantage. They decided first to concentrate on control of loan risks. This was a logical priority because, to a large extent, the negative results of the preceding years were caused by substantial losses and bad debts.

As noted, the head office of Amtssparekassen had lacked central control of loan operations. So the firm was unable to manage risks from the perspective of the whole organization, now seen as an imperative in order to balance risk exposure. The team created a strong head office credit management department with the responsibility to manage, control and adjust the loan policy of the bank. A new senior manager for this department was appointed. Together, they quickly established a clear, common loan policy to be implemented in all branches. Over the next few years this strong head office function formed and maintained policies and administration practices that enabled Amtssparekassen to realize lower losses than other Danish banks on average.

However, a clear loan policy could not be established without defining desired market and customer profiles since the risk involved is generally determined by these. Amtssparekassen considered that good risk management required an appropriate trade-off between the risks involved in each market, the risks associated with different customer profiles, and the expertise available in the firm to evaluate and control such risks correctly and efficiently.

To determine the risks involved in particular cases, management needed to answer three basic questions:

1 Which services should the bank offer?
2 Which market and customer needs should be satisfied?
3 What resources would be necessary to achieve these aims?

Moreover, the answers to all three questions had to be consistent. Top management soon realized that answering these questions implied a redefinition of the basic mission of the bank. In other words, the principles and the fundamental goals of the bank had to be clarified.

There were several strands to the approach they adopted. To sustain lower losses than other banks, the team decided it made sense to reduce the number of areas of business operation. In particular, it decided that Amtssparekassen would stay a regional player and try to be the best bank in its chosen region. It would focus on its existing core regional customers on the island of Funen, for whom it would aim to be the preferred bank. As part of this approach, Amtssparekassen closed its office in Copenhagen.

However, Amtssparekassen also decided to decline the status of number one bank for some of the very large corporations on Funen. The team realized that it could not compete effectively for such a clientele, because it lacked specific and sometimes very specialist competences. Rather, for these actual or potential large clients, as well as in the sense of the more general strategy, Amtssparekassen would seek the status of their number two bank. When a number of leading banks merged, this policy proved very rewarding. Many Danish companies found that their number one and number two banks had merged into a single bank and they needed a new number two. Amtssparekassen was now the perfect choice for them. For Amtssparekassen this implied more volume business at comparatively low risk, albeit with lower profit margins.

As straightforward as Amtssparekassen's new strategy may sound in retrospect, it was distinctively different from that of other regional banks at the time. Many local and regional banks of a similar size and structure to Amtssparekassen had broken out of their geographical confines. In expanding geographically these banks had diminished the traditional competitive advantage they enjoyed over the national banks, namely their capacity to evaluate risk effectively by using local inside information about customers through their networks of personal contacts in each local community, which the leading banks evidently lacked.

Furthermore, some had entered new areas of business such as foreign currency and real-estate investment in the more liberalized banking environment. They had diversified into business areas for which they were inexperienced; in particular many were ill-equipped to evaluate and manage the nature and scope of risks. Still, the general assumption in the industry, derived from the old days, was that growth remained the key to success and now they struggled to make their chosen growth strategies work in practice.

Amtssparekassen's regional focus may seem to be a pure niche strategy but it was seen by the team as part of a more general strategy. The team carefully analysed the banking sector and concluded that for national operation there were diseconomies of scale associated with maintaining a presence in every area of the country. There were also diseconomies related to flexibility in portfolio management, for example if a large bank reorganized its portfolio of bonds and stocks it affected market prices significantly whilst a small bank could react quickly with minimal impact on the market. Additionally, they saw several arbitrage possibilities that were difficult for larger banks to exploit owing to their highly specialized staff and structures. Therefore Amtssparekassen developed new products and services for its business customers based on exploiting these perceived diseconomies of scale.

However, the team recognized that there are important economies of scale in banking. The most significant one is the implementation of modern information technology, which was recognized many years ago: 'With increasing use of computer accountancy and other facilities involving high capital costs, many smaller banks will have to merge to stay competitive.'[14]

The small banks did not have the resources to be competitive in that area so they countered the problem by running joint computer centres. Amtssparekassen participated in one such joint venture. Indeed, its strategy has been to create joint operations wherever economies of scale can be realized through co-operation with other commercial and savings banks, large or small. Amtssparekassen has, however, been very careful not to become dependent on any one group or partner. The wisdom of this was seen during the early 1990s when some of its relationships had to be restructured or terminated because banks either merged or were liquidated.

To summarize, Amtssparekassen established a fit between its customers, the nature of the risks they constituted, the products offered, and the specific, even unique expertise Amtssparekassen was able to extend to its clientele. Furthermore, top management dictated that criteria such as the rate of return on equity capital and the capacity to earn in relation to cost of operations were the only meaningful ways to measure the results of the bank. They rejected the measures used by other bank managers who thought of volume – expansion of the deposit base – as a prime indicator of success and guaranteed increases in profit. The rules of the game had changed, but not everybody perceived these changes in time.

## MANAGING THE CHANGE PROCESS

Amtssparekassen's strategic developments can be broken down into phases. The first phase consisted of uniting operations into one firm. A key step was to create a strong head office to establish a common marketing policy, a common product design programme and, as staff are the core resource of a bank, a common set of personnel policies. In parallel the top team set about redetermining the basic goals and principles of Amtssparekassen. The first phase was concluded when the head office organization was introduced and fully in operation.

Phase two focused on creating cost-efficient operations by cost reduction and selective growth. The top team realized that human resource management would be a very important key to efficiency. Whilst budgetary control instruments were necessary, the variation among tasks was thought to be too great in a complex service organization to rely on rules, procedures, and structures as the main instruments of control, especially since the relationship between revenues and costs was somewhat variable and difficult to predict.

Accordingly, the top management team regarded norms, attitudes, and values as well as working relations between people in and outside the organization as key instruments for improving efficiency. Despite the change to a much more centralized structure, the top team involved all personnel in the development of the changes in the bank. For example they were all invited to a general meeting in 1989 where many problems were discussed. Their recommendations and comments were taken very seriously by the team. New plans for corporate image and marketing were initiated at that meeting. Significant changes have subsequently been discussed using teams comprising both staff and line

managers and the management takes great pride in informing all personnel about activities in the bank.

Banks operate in the same legal, political, and economic environment.
Bank managers and employees have the same professional training and
experience. Thus top management believed that 'The difference between
banks is whether the *management* is qualified or not. It is the quality of
management in general that determines whether a bank ceases to exist,
merges or prospers.'[15] So management realized that the exploitation of
the various opportunities identified should proceed in conjunction with
the development of requisite staff skills. They decided to implement a
comprehensive organization development (OD) project rather than rely
exclusively on rationalization and marketing initiatives in the quest for
cost reduction and selective growth. This was remarkable because Danish
firms have been reluctant to undertake OD projects ever since the 1970s
when some firms had traumatic experiences with the programmes then
in fashion.

Amtssparekassen launched an OD programme that, compared to the
size of the organization, was very comprehensive – and very costly (the
total budget estimate is DKr.6 million). The name given to the
programme was 'Quantum leap'. It began towards the end of 1991 with
the top management team and then moved to the next management
level. When completed by the end of 1994, 100 persons had been
involved in it. Quantum leap focuses on leadership profile, addressing
some fifty dimensions related to being a good leader – not specifically
related to banking issues.

These dimensions covered behavioural aspects of ideal and actual
leadership styles, individual scores being assessed by both the manager
and the subordinate. The specific dimensions included skills of communication, delegation, decision making, risk taking, conflict handling,
controlling, awareness of personal capabilities, tolerance of different
opinions, openness and dialogue, goal setting, interpersonal skills and
sensitivity, willingness to change, initiating and accepting changes, and
coping with stress.

In 1991 another phase of change saw Amtssparekassen floated on the
Copenhagen Stock Exchange. Before 1975 savings banks had been able
to acquire the necessary equity capital for expansion of balances only by
accumulating surpluses. From 1975 to 1991 they were also allowed to
issue guarantee certificates but they did not have the same access to the
financial markets as the commercial banks. In 1991 savings banks were
allowed to change their legal status and go public and Amtssparekassen
was one of the first to do so. Amtssparekassen Fyn made its first public
offering of 800,000 shares of DKr.100 each. An additional 417,000
shares, representing the value of the 'old' savings bank's equity capital
were transferred to a related foundation. The stocks were issued at a

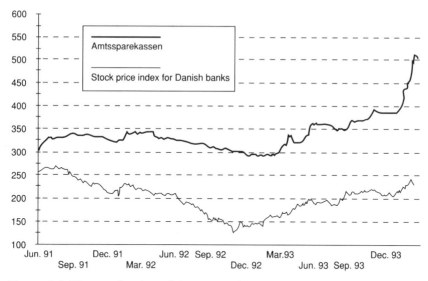

*Figure 5.2* The stock price of Amtssparekassen compared to an index of Danish banks

price of DKr.295 which in February 1994 reached DKr.524. This result was far better than other banks, as shown in Figure 5.2.

## MANAGEMENT COMPETENCE AS SOURCE OF COMPETITIVE ADVANTAGE

With the advent of the pair of top managers at the bank there came a new management style. Arguably, it was made possible through the unique professional skills and personalities of the two individuals. The main features of the new style were as follows:

1 A flat organization structure.
2 Decision making that was neither democratic nor authoritarian.
3 Openness and dialogue.

The number of vertical levels in the organization were reduced. It has been the view of the top team that there should at most be two levels from any client or customer to the decision maker: 'For 80 per cent of the volume of loans/credit only two hierarchical levels exist between the customer and the top management of the bank.'[16] But this change did not mean hasty decision making. Contrary to their competitors' approach, Amtssparekassen marketed itself on its competent and fair decision making. The customer would always be told when a decision would be made. Straightforward cases would be decided quickly, but more complicated ones would take longer. Some competitors advertised a maximum of 72 hours before a decision would be made, which in many situations probably increased their risk.

Management initiated and became involved in daily operations as well as long-term planning. An example of this is found in the early days of the new top team. One of its first activities was to analyse the accounts of the bank. Mr Balle and Mr Knudsen initiated and personally supervised a detailed analysis of all loan accounts of more than DKr.25,000 to acquire a first-hand assessment of the risk exposure of the firm. The direct involvement of the top management in this project was seen as very unusual and made them highly visible in the line organization.

Also as a result of this detailed analysis, the management team began with a conservative approach to provisions, cleaning up the loan book during the first year and making it easier to show early positive financial results and returning to profit during the second year.

In contrast to the previous decision-making process when local managers had to a great extent operated autonomously, the new decision-making process was less democratic without being authoritarian. In practice this meant that:

> Decision-making that is neither democratic nor authoritative implies for instance that there will be no voting at large meetings with the top 18-20 managers of the bank, but (equally) that no decisions will be forced upon managers against their will![17]

The two top managers have a weekly meeting with one of the branches or head office departments. At that meeting all staff members participate. This makes the leadership style and strategy very visible. A recent survey found that 95 per cent of the employees were aware of the main goals and strategies of Amtssparekassen.

The new management style is based on authority and competence. The skills of the top pair are complementary and encompass the economist and the educationalist, allied to appropriate hierarchical authority. Senior managers have demonstrated the professional capacity not only to comprehend fully the risks involved in the business, but also to explain the tasks and priorities in a comprehensive way to other managers and staff.

It is in this management style that Amtssparekassen has perhaps realized a core competence yielding a lasting competitive advantage. The top management team has initiated and continues to take a direct part in an organizational learning process that is turning Amtssparekassen's personnel into a unique resource that will be very difficult to copy or to install in a different bank environment.

## CONCLUDING REMARKS

Because of its difficult circumstances in the mid-1980s, Amtssparekassen was already fighting costs effectively when the leading actors were merging and had scarcely started the rationalization and cost reduction process. Further, Amtssparekassen had already clarified its business idea and was adjusting its organization and management accordingly. Figure 5.1 presents graphically how well its five-year return on equity performance up to 1992 compared with the top twenty Danish banks. None the less, its experiences suggest that having a good strategy is not sufficient, since the timing and approach to implementing the strategy are also vital components for success.

The Amtssparekassen case shows that whilst necessary core banking competences changed over time, most Danish banks very reluctantly changed their perception of what these were. One explanation is that in the 1960s and 1970s when most chief executives received their professional training and experience, core competences were the ability to collect deposits and to manage the technology of an ever-growing information processing task. This was because the success of a bank was measured by its volume, given that interest spread was generous, yet not a focus for competition in the regulated environment. Expansion of banking services and spatial differentiation were the main forms of competition. Moreover, the effects of mistakes were softened by the high rate of inflation.

For a time after liberalization of Danish banking, most banks seem to have acted on unchanged perceptions of the necessary core competences. One bank broke the rules of the game – Amtssparekassen. It adopted rate of return on equity as an appropriate measure of success, not growth *per se*. Hence it refrained from expanding into different regions of the country, preferring instead to focus on core customers in its chosen region where it could evaluate lending risk sensitively by means of its local network of contacts. Additionally it reduced the number of services it offered and then developed new products and services appropriate to its strategy of exploiting modest scale. Though control of risks and costs had been a prerequisite for survival, Amtssparekassen embarked on a substantial management development programme to enhance its risk management capability, whilst other banks were still reducing costs through branch closures and redundancies. It did this because top management attributed the core competence of the firm to its personnel. Finally, it can be said that a special management style has been a distinctive feature of Amtssparekassen's approach to obtaining lasting competitive advantage.

History suggests that Amtssparekassen was right. Many comparable regional competitors which followed mainstream thinking are names not to be found anywhere today, having being forced to close or merge with others due to financial difficulties.

## NOTES

1 © Børge Obel, Bo Eriksen, Jens O. Krag and Mikael Søndergaard 1995. This case study has been written as a basis for class discussion rather than to illustrate effective or ineffective managerial or administrative behaviour. It draws on personal observations and published materials including Niels Åge Nielsen, 'Trends in the competitive structure of banking in Denmark', in Donald E. Fair and François Léonard de Juvigny (eds) *Bank Management in a Changing Domestic and International Environment: The Challenges of the Eighties* (The Hague, Boston, Mass., London: Martinus Nijhoff, 1982); and Amtssparekassen Fyn Holding A/S Annual Accounts.
2 e.g. *Wall Street Journal*, 26 April 1985.
3 Hilary Barnes, 'All change in Danish banking', *The Banker*, December 1985: 56.
4 *Wall Street Journal*, 7 January 1994.
5 Nielsen op. cit., p. 81.
6 Includes taxes, value adjustment of securities.
7 Hilary Barnes, op. cit. p 41.
8 e.g. slaughterhouses, dairies, heavy goods.
9 e.g. Bjerager, *Wall Street Journal*, 18 December 1985.
10 Erik Seligman, The Danish Supervisory Body of Commercial Bank
11 Originally, the name of the newly established entity was Amtssparekassen for Fyns Amt.
12 Assens, Ejby, Faaborg, Glamsbjerg, Haarby, Kerteminde, Marstal, Nyborg, Nørre, Aaby, Rudkøbing, Søby, and Ærøskøbing.
13 Niels Chr. Knudsen, 15 June 1994.
14 Robert Hillbourne, 'The Danish banking system', *The Banker's Magazine*, March 1979: 17.
15 Niels Chr. Knudsen, 15 June 1994.
16 Ibid.
17 Ibid.

# Chapter 6

# Cartier: a legend of luxury[1]

## Sumantra Ghoshal, François-Xavier Huard and Charlotte Butler

### EDITORS' OVERVIEW

The long and interesting history of the Cartier company was inextricably linked to successive generations of the Cartier family until the 1960s. Starting in 1817 with a Paris shop selling sculpted powder horns, successive generations of Cartier moved the firm into jewellery, *objets d'art* and watches. Meanwhile the customer base changed from the frequenters of the first artisanal shop to royalty and the aristocracy and then to the *nouveaux riches*. Moreover, Cartier went international long before Singer or Ford.

However, the case study really starts in 1968 when the firm is drifting, as the close-knit Cartier family loses its cohesion and squabbles over policy. Enter Robert Hocq, a successful artisan entrepreneur with a stylish butane cigarette lighter but no brand name. The complementarity was perfect: Cartier had the well-known name and the prestige image, Hocq had the right product. When he had reached an understanding with the family, Hocq hired Alain Perrin, whose enthusiasm and drive ensured the success of the lighter. Hocq bought out the jewellery interests of the Cartier family in 1971 and in 1972 the trademark 'les Must de Cartier' was registered.

Over the next few years Perrin became increasingly influential, first as general manager of the lighter division, then as the cornerstone of the business following Hocq's accidental death in 1979, ultimately as president of Cartier International from 1981. From 1983 Cartier has been owned by the Richemont Group and in the decade to 1990, the time of the case study, it averaged 27 per cent annual sales growth to reach $US950 million.

The case study explores how Cartier has developed and exploited to the maximum a distinctive, yet paradoxical array of competitive advantages. A number of themes are highlighted in the case study including creativity in product development, combining an exclusive jewellery business with volume sales of the Must line and systematic product diversification into luxury goods of many kinds. Product strategies were complemented by promoting the prestige image of the company and global sales expansion into 123 countries by 1991, albeit with a top level commitment to retain at least half of its sales in Europe.

## Discussion questions

- What are the key strategic decisions taken in the Perrin era? Why are they significant and what have been the consequences? In what terms would you characterize Cartier's corporate strategy and the success arising from it?
- At the heart of current success may lie the seeds of future failure. How might Cartier become vulnerable to competitive initiatives and other environmental threats? From where are these threats most likely to emerge?
- What contribution did Robert Hocq bring to Cartier? What has been Alain Perrin's principal contribution? How does Perrin encourage creativity? How can we reconcile this with the portrayal of him as a benevolent dictator?
- The case study writers attribute Cartier's creativity and innovation to a series of deliberate tensions resulting from paradoxical (apparently contradictory) *dualities* in the strategies it implements: for example, combining secrecy and publicity. Is this explanation quite fundamental to Cartier's success?

## List of named characters

Louis Cartier, the inspiration behind the catalogue of spectacular designs
Robert Hocq, originator of the Silver Match lighter and later CEO
Alain Perrin, lighter salesman and later president and driving force behind Cartier
Jeanne Toussaint, creator of the famous animal collection
Other members of the Cartier family

## Keywords

Entrepreneurship; creativity; exclusivity; related product diversification, centralization, globalization; acquisition strategy

## PAST: THE BIRTH AND GROWTH OF A LEGEND

In 1817 a man named Pierre Cartier returned from the Napoleonic Wars and opened a shop in the Marais, Paris's artisan quarter, where he sculpted powder horns and decorative motifs for firearms. His son, Louis-François (1819–1904) adapted to the more peaceful and prosperous times of the Restoration by becoming first the apprentice and later, in 1847, the successor of Monsieur Picard, a 'maker of fine jewellery, novelty fashion and costume jewellery'. In 1859, Louis–François opened a shop on the Boulevard des Italiens, flanked by the favourite cafés of the smart set. He soon attracted the attention and patronage of the Princess Eugénie, cousin of Napoléon III and soon to become Empress of France.

Alfred Cartier took over from his father, Louis–François, in 1874. In the turbulent decade following the collapse of the Second Empire and the revolt of the Communards, the company survived by selling the jewels of La Barucci, a famous courtesan of the time, in London. Like his ancestors, Alfred adapted to changing times and the whims of a new set of customers, the wealthy bourgeois, adding *objets d'art*, clocks, snuff boxes and fob watches to his range of wares. His son, Louis, became his associate in 1898.

### Louis Cartier

Cartier . . . the subtle magician who breaks the moon into pieces and captures it in threads of gold.

*Jean Cocteau*

Louis brought to the firm his 'creativity, his commercial genius and an extraordinary dynamism'. Full of curiosity, passionately interested in artistic and technical innovation, Louis introduced platinum into jewellery settings, making them lighter and easier to wear, and showed a distinctive flair for design. His was the inspiration for new items such as the watch with a geometric hull, designed for his friend, the Brazilian pilot, Santos Dumont. Jewellery designer Jeanne Toussaint (1887–1978) added her creativity to that of Louis. The result was the famous animal collection, including the beast that was to become Cartier's best-known international trade mark, the fabulous jewelled panther.

Cartier moved to the Place Vendôme, home of the greatest names in jewellery, but Louis had no intention of allowing Cartier to become just another jewellery firm. The clockmaker Jaeger, and Lalique, the goldsmith and luxury glass manufacturer, both worked for him. At the 1925 World Fair it was clear that rather than cling to the company of traditional jewellers, Louis preferred to mix with people from other creative fields, such as the couturiers Lanvin and Louis' father-in-law, Worth.

With his brothers, Louis opened shops in London (1902) and New York (1908), while at the Court of St Petersburg he established Cartier as a rival to Fabergé. Cartier ruled over the crowned heads of Europe, 'the jeweller of kings and the King of jewellers'. Royal warrants came from Edward VII of England (Louis created 27 diadems for his coronation), Alphonse XII of Spain and Charles of Portugal.

In the early decades of the twentieth century Cartier reached its apogee. There was not a monarch, business tycoon or film star who was not a client. Louis even conquered the literary world, designing the swords carried by authors such as Mauriac, Duhamel, Maurois and Jules Romains for their enrolment as members of the Académie Française. And it was Jean Cocteau who, in 1922, inspired Louis to create his famous ring composed of three interlocking circles, a magical symbol in Indian legend.

But Louis' descendants were to live through less glorious times. The Second World War engulfed many of the clients who had been the mainstay of the great jewellery houses and, after four generations of entrepreneurial, successful Cartiers, the firm seemed to lose its sense of direction. The New York store was sold, amid some dispute and discord within the family.

In 1964, a man came knocking at the door of the legendary jewellers. He was a manufacturer of mass-produced cigarette lighters, an inventive spirit who had applied all the latest technical refinements to the development of a new product. To mark the event, he wanted to decorate this new product with silver and christen it with one of the great names of the jewellery establishment. Rejected by other jewellers, he made his way to Cartier.

## Robert Hocq

Robert Hocq was the head of Silver Match. A self-educated man, his dreams were forged among the machines in his workshop. Trailing behind the great names of Dupont and Dunhill, Silver Match had adopted the 'copied from America' style of the new consumer society, furnishing disposable lighters to the mass market. Positioned in the middle range, the Silver Match lighters were sold through tobacco shops.

Robert Hocq had defined the market he was aiming for – the gap between his current products and the 'super luxury' of Dunhill and Dupont. All that his lighters needed was 'a little something' that would elevate them to the realm of 'authentic' luxury goods. And in a world of plastic and cheap imitations, he needed the guarantee that only a name associated with true luxury could provide. Whether prompted by the need for money or the memory of past innovations, in 1968 Cartier agreed to grant Hocq a temporary licence.

The lighter's original design, a simple column in the Greek architectural style encircled by a ring, was slowly elaborated. Two radical innovations were incorporated. First, its oval shape was a direct descendant of Louis Cartier's favourite form, then quite unknown in the world of lighters. Second, Robert Hocq introduced the use of butane gas. The sale of gas cartridges would be a lucrative sideline even though, for the moment, clients were more accustomed to using liquid fuel.

To commercialize the new products, Le Briquet Cartier SA was established. The lighters were to be sold through the same outlets as Silver Match, a network of retailers. By 1968, the deal had been finalized and Robert Hocq turned to the task of finding the right person to sell his Cartier lighter.

## Alain Perrin

The candidate who entered Robert Hocq's office did so in response to an advertisement he had seen in the paper. The meeting began at six o'clock in the evening, and ended at midnight over an empty bottle of whisky. Alain Perrin often exhausted those around him whether at home, at the twelve schools he attended or during the long nights of his student days. He had arm-wrestled with Johnny Halliday, dined with the Beatles and, in short, led the Parisian life of insouciance of the 1960s generation. Born into a family of scientists, he dreamt only of a business career. While at the Ecole des Cadres he imported Shetland sweaters for his friends. Cutting school to trade sweaters for farmers' old furniture, he earned the nickname 'King Pullover'.

After the death of his father in 1965, Alain Perrin directed his ebullient energy towards more serious objectives. He returned to school to finish his studies and then began work in a paper recycling company. Bored by this, he started his own company dealing in antiques. One shop led to another, and finally to three.

In May 1969, he was still only 26.

On the road, a suitcase of the new Cartier lighters in his hand, Perrin visited those existing Silver Match clients who seemed best suited to the new product's image: wholesalers and fine tobacco stores or civettes. The lighter was an immediate success. The civettes gave it star billing; to be able to handle a Cartier product was tantamount to selling real jewellery. In competing with traditional jewellers, this gave them a long-sought legitimacy.

All profits were reinvested by Hocq in order to acquire the permanent and exclusive right to the Cartier name. His relations with Cartier grew ever closer.

Hocq's activities were not confined to lighters. Two days after Cartier acquired a 70-carat diamond in a New York sale, Richard Burton bought it for 14.5 million francs as a gift for Liz Taylor. Cartier's profit on the deal was minimal but the publicity surrounding the sale was invaluable. Orchestrated by Hocq, the event was a media coup for Cartier.

In 1971, backed by a group of financiers, Robert Hocq bought the jewellery business and the Paris and London shops from the Cartier family. In 1976, he bought back the New York store. Alain Dominique Perrin became General Manager of the lighter division.

*Must lighters*

In 1972, the trade mark 'les Must de Cartier' was born.

When the lighters were first launched in December 1969, Robert Hocq was discussing the project with a colleague. Tapping a magazine advertisement, Hocq asked him 'Cartier . . . what exactly does Cartier mean to you?' In English, the man answered: 'Cartier is a must, Sir.' At the time, the reply baffled Hocq, but several years later, he remembered the incident.

> Modern man has a need to let the world know that he has succeeded. To do this, he needs to be able to buy symbols of social prestige. True luxury objects produced by the great jewellers cannot give him the recognition he yearns for, since they are exclusively one-of-a-kind.
> Must lighters are the materialization of social status.

In 1974, following the example of Dupont. Cartier pens joined the lighters in shop windows. Whereas the lighter was, by its very nature, connected with tobacco shops, pens opened up new distribution channels. In 1975, the addition of leather goods opened up yet another.

With the Cartier pen-lighter duo, stores were no longer selling an object but a prestige concept. At the same time, Cartier was anxious to expand distribution of its jewellery. However, although lighters and pens could hold their own amidst displays of necklaces and rings in neighbourhood jewellery stores, Cartier jewels were simply not meant to be surrounded by the ordinary and anonymous.

Exclusive Cartier boutiques were created. In them, under the slogan 'Les Must de Cartier' and set against the rich Bordeaux red chosen for the line, Cartier jewels were displayed to advantage. Later, leathers, lighters and pens too were shown against this same distinctive setting. Strict guidelines defined the product mix, decoration and service which each distributor had to provide. Cartier then began sending inspectors round to monitor discreetly that these conditions were being respected.

The Must line was not to everyone's taste. The very select Comité Colbert excluded Cartier from its membership and shortly afterwards Cartier withdrew from the Syndicat de Haute Joaillerie, the organization of fine jewellers which represented the most prestigious houses of the Place Vendôme. For a time, relations between 'that cowboy Perrin' and the other jewellers were strained.

In 1973, Cartier founded a new company under the emblem 'Les Must de Cartier', to be kept entirely separate from its jewellery interests. Alain Perrin became its President. Concerned that too much of the jewellery business was concentrated in the Paris area (65 per cent of sales), he convinced Robert Hocq that the concept and products should be exported.

> I needed to move from the state of an elegantly sleepy retailer to that of a young, contemporary, international concern, capable of creating products for a worldwide market, and not just Paris, London or New York.

Once a year, Alain Perrin travelled round the world. In ten to twelve stops from the Middle East to Australia, from Hong Kong to the USA, he picked up orders and sold the universality of the Must concept.

*Must watches*

Buying back the New York store in 1976 led to a new activity. As a jeweller, Cartier made a solid gold watch: the Tank. Its reputation (which went back to Louis Cartier) had inspired innumerable imitations. The American market in particular was infested by a plague of watches in plated brass, copies of the Tank. For 500 or 1,000 francs, an imitation of the real thing (costing 10,000 to 15,000 francs) could be bought. Even the New York store, long out of the control of the Cartier family, was selling this type of imitation.

To end these shoddy practices, Alain Perrin fought fire with fire. He brought out a vermeil watch, based on an original model. This meant that for only 2,000 francs more than the price of a cheap imitation, people could buy themselves a real Cartier watch, a true descendant of the masterpieces created by Louis Cartier in solid gold and brilliants.

The extension of the luxury Must line into watches allowed Cartier to surpass Dupont. From then on, Cartier's line of lighters, pens, leathers and watches were always displayed quite separately. Retailers had to reserve 'a space within a space' for them in their stores and the style of presenting the goods had to be in keeping with (and directly inspired by) the Must boutiques.

*Perfume*

The idea of launching a perfume, planned for 1981, presented a dilemma. On the one hand, the very nature of the product contradicted Cartier's expressed wish to limit itself to 'lasting products which clients covet and to which they become attached'. Cartier had originally resolved only to produce objects that were 'never thrown out'. On the other hand, perfume was inevitable. Historically, it had been the first diversification channel for every luxury brand, and constituted the most obvious path in the public mind. A further problem was how to launch the perfume – and hence follow in the footsteps of most other luxury brands – without breaking another of Cartier's golden rules: 'Avoid what is already being done.'

Cartier's product managers came up with the idea of a 'case/refill'. The case was conceived as an object in the Cartier tradition, lasting for ever and never going out of fashion – an expensive product priced well above the competition – while the refill, in utilitarian plastic, would be priced well below the competition for the same quantity of perfume. The bevelled shape of the refill would ensure that it could not stand upright or be used without the case. Sale of the perfume to a client without a case would be forbidden.

The idea seemed simple yet seductive. Opposition came from market specialists, who did not believe that it would work. Previous similar attempts, albeit limited, had failed. But Cartier's marketing team felt that the 'Cartier' cachet would overcome any reservations in the perfume market, and that the very novelty of the case, 'a totally new gift idea', would open up a new area of marketing. Perrin decided to go ahead with the launch. It was an immediate success.

At a later date, having legitimized its entry into the perfume market, Cartier brought out its perfume in a classic bottle – with a leather pouch. It was presented as a 'travel' version.

> In the luxury market, it's the survival of the fittest. You have to have the largest market share and be the most creative. Then you can do as you like with the market.

*Transition*

In 1979 Robert Hocq was run over and killed by a car while crossing the Place Vendôme. His daughter Nathalie became head of the group until 1981, when she moved to the USA. At that time, the Must collection represented a turnover of 250 million francs. The same year, Must and Cartier Joaillier merged, regrouping under the name Cartier International. Alain Dominique Perrin became President of the Board of Directors.

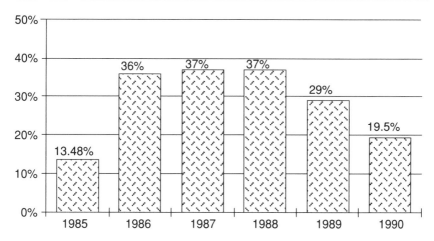

*Figure 6.1* Cartier: rate of growth 1985–90

In 1983, Cartier was acquired by the Richemont Group, a 3.3 billion Swiss francs tobacco and luxury goods conglomerate of South African origin.

## PRESENT: THE FORCES OF CREATIVITY

On becoming president of the company following the Richemont take-over in 1983, Alain Perrin announced to *Business Week*, 'By 1990, we'll show a turnover of 300 million dollars.' The actual turnover in 1990 reached $US950 million, representing an average annual growth rate of 27 per cent per year over 10 years (Figure 6.1). Consolidated sales, including other brands acquired or under licence, amounted to $US1.350 billion. A 1990 McKinsey study evaluated the world luxury market at $US50 billion in retail sales, thus giving the Cartier brand 4 per cent of sales – the largest for any single brand – in a highly fragmented market.

In jewellery, representing 25 per cent of its turnover, Cartier is one of the world leaders after the US firm Winston. It is number one in the sale of luxury watches (40 per cent of the market and 550,000 annual sales), and deluxe leather goods (10 per cent of turnover) with 1.6 million articles sold in 1989 (Figure 6.2).

According to Alain Perrin, creativity is the engine that has powered Cartier to this spectacular success. For him, it is the soul, the very essence of the group. Under Perrin, the lifeblood of the company is derived from the friction between a series of dualities. Thus, creation at Cartier is yesterday's memory, juxtaposed with today's insights into the environment. Perrin loves to cultivate such disequilibrium because 'It forces us to move forwards.'

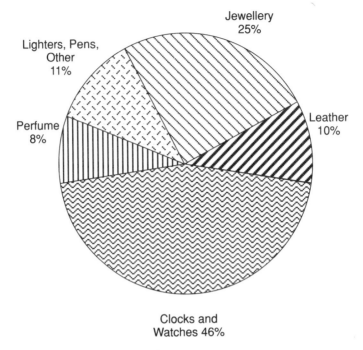

*Figure 6.2* Cartier: sales by product

One of the best sources of profit is creativity. Creativity is what? It is doing something your competitors do not do. Or doing it first. Or doing it stronger or better. Everything that is creative contains a plus on something . . . and creativity is the backbone of Cartier.

### Product development

The design for every new Cartier product is discussed and prepared according to a very precise process involving all the 200 people working at Cartier International. The launch of a product takes two to three years. A 'product plan' three years ahead of the launch describes the evolution of the line: one launch per year and spin-offs from each leading project. Nothing is launched until Perrin is convinced Cartier can 'do it right'. 'I'd rather lose one year than introduce a half-baked concept.'

Once the designs have been selected, the drafting department elabo-rates models and prototypes 'while stressing quality and keeping in constant contact with the creator'. In order to reproduce the audacity of the designs, technical creativity is added to artistic imagination.

The oval pen was a real brain teaser, one which the best specialists in the business refused to touch when we consulted them. It took us two years to bring out the product, since we had to design and produce our own cartridge. We patent designs every year.

Such creativity rests on this paradox: 'Each product is an exceptional creation, but we invent nothing.'

### The old . . .

Cartier's past is where the search for present creativity begins. Each new product launched has its ancestor among the collections of chalk and pastel drawings made by Louis Cartier and represents 'the spirit of creation and the style of Cartier, adapted to our time and to the trends we are setting for the future'.

At the turn of the century, a piece of Cartier jewellery destined for the mistress of a client was accidently delivered to his wife. To avoid a repetition of this error, Cartier began to keep exhaustive records on clients, the models they chose and the gems used. These records became Cartier's archives.

> The first lesson a product manager has to learn is how to navigate his or her way through our archives. In this treasure trove, we search for ideas which will fall onto fertile ground, germinate, ripen and one day, when the time is right, be launched onto a market which is not quite ready for it.

While looking at an archive photograph of the governor of Marrakesh and at the massive watch that Louis Cartier had made for him, Alain Perrin predicted that 'One day we'll have to launch a watch like that.' Today, 'the Pasha watch is one of our star products, and has brought large watches back into fashion'.

Perrin had already delved into the archive's rich seam of ideas for the Must line. When he became president, its use became systematic. Consequently, the company began to develop lines whose names – Santos, Panthère, Pasha, Cougar – owed nothing to the US culture of the 1960s and 1970s that dominated elsewhere.

### . . . And the new

Cartier's business is to be a trend-setter not a follower: 'to influence people in their behaviour, in their choice, in their taste . . . Other companies follow customers; but customers follow Cartier.' To do this, 'We spend a lot of time and money on surveying the market and the competition . . . on getting the information that will lead us to understand and make decent forecasts on trends.'

Perrin has files on each of his leading competitors going back twenty years. 'I know more about them than they do about themselves.' He even has 'people making window checks on competitors' products all over the world, all the year round'.

Starting from concrete information on competition, on distribution, on consumption, on people's choices, on political trends, on fashion, all these ingredients at the end give us the quality of information that we need to be able to create a product which we know will be fashionable, and have an influence on the culture of the year 2000.

**Image**

For Perrin, brand image is the basis of an effective marketing strategy. 'Luxury, for the client and the manufacturer alike, means communicating around a brand in the same way that jewellery communicates around a gem.' But promotion should be based on the name and image of the company rather than the product:

Our brand name was built very slowly, and it's set in concrete. We survive economic, political and regional conflicts without disturbance. Crises seem to stimulate the market for high value added products. In recent years we have even witnessed a growing demand for relatively old Cartier jewels. This is unhoped-for support for our image.

Perrin is proud of Cartier's pioneering marketing methods.

We were the first to use heavy marketing, the first to communicate in the way we do, the first to use heavy public relations to create events around culture, promote artists, and probably the first to succeed in controlling our distribution as we did.

He enjoys manipulating the opposite marketing poles of secrecy and publicity.

*Secrecy . . .*

Through secrecy about past events affecting the company, Cartier is able to protect its legend.

One of our strengths is our ability to maintain a certain mystery about the economic entity which is the company. We bring magic and dreams to consumers who don't want to see their favourite brands discussed in the media, and lacking any sense of the romantic.

According to Perrin, breaching this secrecy could bring the luxury industry crashing down. Thus, he regards going public as a sure way to perdition. 'Waging public battles on the floor of the stock exchange is a serious error for the luxury goods sector. It kills the magic. My craft is to make money with magic.' Luxury businesses who go public 'risk losing their soul. A luxury business has nothing to gain from seeing its name indiscriminately positioned in alphabetical order in the daily quotations listing.'

### . . . And publicity

But then again. 'Cartier is a name which lives in the news.' The luxury goods sector is an important consumer of publicity. Cartier's public relations department has a team of twenty people, and each new product launch is accompanied by astounding creative pageantry, courtesy of a company called Delirium.

Undoubtedly, Perrin himself is Cartier's best communication tool. A high profile figure, he is photographed everywhere: beside Elton John on his French tour, at the launch of the 'restos du cœur' (soup kitchens set up by the French comedian, the late Coluche), on the slopes of a fashionable ski resort, at a Red Cross benefit or attending a conference at HEC (a leading French business school).

Another powerful weapon is Cartier's universal implantation. 'I remember,' notes a competitor, 'finding myself in a tiny airport deep in the heart of Venezuela. The very first thing I saw as I got off the plane and entered the makeshift building was a Cartier watch.' Cartier files all the magazine photos or articles which mention its name, or that of one of its products. Its picture gallery includes the tennis player Jimmy Connors, Dynasty star Linda Evans, French film star Jean-Paul Belmondo, Pakistan's ex-Prime Minister Benazir Bhutto, and also 'rogues' such as Libya's President Gaddafi and the ex-gangster Mesrine giving his companion a Cartier necklace just hours before being shot down by the police. The sale of the Duchess of Windsor's jewels 'among which ours were prominent' also served Cartier well.

Another famous picture shows Perrin perched on the top of a steamroller, on the day in 1981 when he destroyed 4,000 counterfeit Cartier watches. The defence of the Cartier name against counterfeiters costs the company nearly $US3.5 million a year.

Cartier has created its own highly effective communication and marketing weapon: the use of sponsorship and culture.

> By marrying Cartier with contemporary art we seduced the anti-luxury and anti-uniform population. We also seduced the media which, since 1981, has been cool towards the luxury goods industry. By positioning the firm in the future rather than in the past, we at last managed to reach a younger clientèle.

Most famous is the Cartier Foundation for Contemporary Art, a cultural centre established just outside Paris in response to a 1983 market survey which found that young people were interested in contemporary art, and that 70 per cent of those attending exhibitions were less than 25 years old. A meeting place, as well as an exhibition and seminar centre, the Foundation hosts young artists from across the world and offers them financial support. Exhibitions have included a retrospective dedicated to the Solex, the little moped which symbolizes a whole generation of young French men and women, and another on the cars of Enzo Ferrari.

> Sponsorship is an impressive form of communication. It unites Cartier's employees around an adventure which attracts both the media and the public across the world. Patronage costs Cartier 30 to 40 million francs a year. But it earns us media coverage worth 200 to 250 million francs.

## Marketing

Perhaps Perrin's trickiest balancing act has been to maintain Cartier's image as an élite purveyor of expensive luxuries, while thriving in the mass markets of watches, wallets and pens.

*Exclusivity . . .*

At the fusion of Cartier Joaillers and Les Must in 1981, demarcation lines were established to keep the Must line clearly separate. In the company's London office in Bond Street, 'Must people worked upstairs. Cartier people downstairs'. To compensate for the Must 'wide distribution' image and to keep the Cartier name close to its roots, the 'high jewellery' business was relaunched. By developing a line of 'signed' jewels with extremely limited editions, Cartier strengthened its presence in the $US50,000–$100,000 market segment (the top of the jewellery market goes above $US100,000).

One of Cartier's principles is never to test any of its products commercially.

> Our products, whether we are talking about a piece of fine jewellery or a Must pen, must be exclusive. There has to be a 'certain something' that makes them stand out, something that goes against the norms. We do 'anti-marketing'.

*. . . And volume sales*

> With the Must line I was perfectly conscious that by producing thousands of watches or pens instead of one-of-a-kind objects, I was running the risk of affecting the image of our company. If it is true

that men and women wish to call attention to themselves by having a Cartier lighter or pen or sunglasses, it is also true that they wish to be recognized as part of an exclusive milieu and not as just anyone.

Quality must never be sacrificed.

The same care must be exercised over each of the 300 operations necessary to the making of a lighter as in the 1,400 hours it took to make the Odin necklace [\$US600,000]. Industrial quality has to stand comparison with the traditional, painstaking care of the individual craftsman. Cartier's workshop has sixty-seven craftsmen, setters, polishers and jewellers, three times more than most leading jewellers.

Cartier's success in watchmaking illustrates the manipulation of these contradictions. Cartier's adversary was Rolex, whose massive sporty wrist-watches in steel and gold had set the trend. Alain Perrin felt that a watch of equal quality, but with more creative lines and more style could become an effective rival to the Swiss brand. Through his efforts, a large clientèle was now familiar with luxury products. Their appetites whetted, they were demanding more . . . However, he also believed that the Must line would not be strong enough to compete against Rolex. The Must concept, used and reused since 1972, risked becoming stale through repetition.

Perrin decided that henceforth Cartier would develop its exclusive collections under a generic name taken from Cartier's history. 'I was going to put products inspired by the exclusive designs of Louis Cartier within the reach of thousands of people.' On 20 October 1978 twenty Mystère jets brought Cartier's guests to Paris's Le Bourget airport from the four corners of the world. Among them were Jacky Ickx, Ursula Andress and Santos Dumont's grandson. They were to be present at the launch of the 'Santos Dumont', a wrist-watch with a shape inspired by the famous aviator's watch. The first watch to have screws on its body, it was 'immediately copied by the competition'. In 1981, it was followed by another success, the first moonphase Pasha watch.

In 1990, Cartier overtook Rolex as the world leader in luxury timepieces.

## Distribution

We had to get Cartier out of the temple . . . We had to shake Cartier out of its retailer's lethargy in order to make it a profitable luxury goods company, distributing internationally.

*'Leaving the temple'*

Cartier's journey into the light had begun when Perrin set off round the tobacconists with his suitcase full of lighters. The move signalled Cartier's move away from the discreet salons of the jewellers and its entry into the wider world of the gift shop. By December 1989, 33 per cent of Cartier's revenues (15 per cent of volume) came from its network of 135 stores. The rest came from concessions. Cartier used its profits gradually to purchase all the distributors controlling its 7,500 brand-name points of sale. This take-over was complete by 1990.

In Japan, Cartier entered the market early in 1971 by renting the usual corner spaces in hotels and department stores. By 1989 Cartier had bought an entire building, cancelled the contract with its importer and in its place established a joint venture (Cartier controlling 51 per cent of the shares) to manage the sixteen Japanese points of sale.

> It's the only way to consolidate our margins and control our brand name. The retail margin accumulated with the gross margin is what makes us profitable. But more importantly, it's the assurance that the name will be represented as it ought to be, whether it's in Melbourne, Madrid or Paris.

## Logistics

In the mid-1980s Cartier was confronted by an almost total blockade of its logistics system. 'We were no longer able to guarantee supplies, but at the same time we were troubled by an increase in intermediary inventory. Our network took some hard knocks.' Cartier responded by reinforcing the co-ordination between sales and production and introducing a sophisticated computer system. This system was designed around thirteen months' sales projections and was piloted from Freiburg in Switzerland by Cartier's General Agent (Switzerland is a duty-free zone where products can be circulated quickly with the minimum of customs formalities). Freiburg, Cartier's central supplier, manages all plant deliveries and covers subcontractors supplying all twenty-two sales affiliates. It then centralizes the statistics needed to update sales and manufacturing plans.

Freiburg also controls the customer service file. 'We have to be able to repair all our models, including those we no longer produce. After-sales service is assured indefinitely. It's a valuable contact with clients and it makes them return to our stores.' Product maintenance costs Cartier 7 million dollars each year, and represents 240,000 repairs.

## Strategy

*Focus . . .*

Cartier is one of the rare luxury houses that will not allow any licensing of its name (with the exception of the development of a brand of cigarettes, a decision imposed by the holding company which also owns Rothmans). Perrin will never develop a new line simply because there is a market for it. Except for scarves, he has not ventured into the fashion business.

> There is no Cartier make-up, clothes, shoes or ties, and as long as I am here there never will be . . . Cartier could do what the other luxury houses do: a little bit of everything. We haven't wanted that, since every name has strict limits. Our business is gems, jewellery, watch making, lighters, pens.

*. . . And diversification*

On the other hand, 'We have developed all of our traditional products. Now, Cartier is condemned to external growth.' Acquisitions will prevent the Cartier name becoming over-exposed and besides, 'If there is something that can add to the group, it is better to buy it than to leave it to your competitors.'

Every acquisition is designed 'to consolidate our leadership in the luxury industry'. Thus, in 1988, Cartier bought the two Swiss watchmakers, Baume & Mercier (70,000 watches per year in a market segment close to that of the Must line) and Piaget (17,000 watches in an exclusive market 'more than Rolls Royce, maybe Lagonda'). They were, says Perrin, 'sleeping beauties'. He has separated the two 'for their own good. I don't want them to talk to each other any more'. Cartier also acquired the distinguished jewellers Aldebert (FFr.80 million in annual sales), which has seven stores in Paris, Cannes and Monte Carlo.

Since 1989 Cartier has held a 6 per cent share in Yves Saint Laurent, the high fashion firm for which it had produced a line of jewellery (Figure 6.3). A contract with Ferrari allows Cartier to go beyond the defined limits of luxury goods, as it did years ago with cigarette lighters.

> We wanted to introduce our expertise, our distribution, our know-how into the male and female accessory businesses. The deals also set a kind of barrier at the bottom of the pyramid . . . With Ferrari and Yves St Laurent we have got the market share we could not have got with the Cartier name . . .
>
> We will go no further in diversification, which has remained relatively restrained.

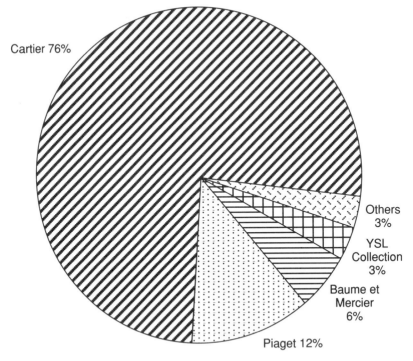

*Figure 6.3* Cartier: sales by brands

## Management

> If you decentralize creativity too much, it is no longer creativity, it's a
> mess ... the information must come from the satellites, from the
> subsidiary or from the markets, but the final decision must come from
> one man.

*Absolutism ...*

Under Perrin, absolutism lives on in France. 'In a company with a strong
name, a strong personality, the President must be in charge.' Perrin is the
ultimate arbiter of what is produced by the firm. It is he who decides which
products will be launched, he who examines, refuses or approves each of the
1,200 designs submitted to him by the marketing department, he who pulls
apart each product before its launch. 'I am,' he says, 'that kind of man. I want
to participate in the daily life of this company and I do it . . . I participate very
much in the creativity, in the production, in the quality. I am an active
executive.' But all these choices are, he maintains, 'the choices of any good
manager . . . anybody could be Alain Perrin at the head of Cartier'.

At Cartier, we are a management team. I can disappear tomorrow morning . . . My management people are very able to go on . . . The team is built around Cartier, not around me . . . It took twenty years, but there is no recipe . . . It is by finding the people to match . . . It is the quality of these people which guarantees our growth.

Observers note a sense of shared excitement among a workforce embarked on 'the adventure at Cartier'. 'Everyone sees him, and he enters anyone's office at any time. Ask anyone here and you'll get the impression that they know him personally. They'll tell you, "his greatest assets are his attentiveness to others and his great generosity".'

Such a direct relationship can cause difficulties. It is an area where Perrin's balancing act has occasionally failed. When Perrin took over the management of Cartier, he was assisted by an executive committee composed of the fifteen managers responsible for different areas of the company. However, Cartier's expansion rendered this system increasingly difficult, whereupon Perrin appointed a general manager. Unsurprisingly, Perrin's direct, impulsive and omnipresent management style had trouble accommodating this new structure and so he modified it, transforming the general manager into a vice-president. Three general managers were then appointed to run the operational functions of marketing, finance and operations (co-ordinating the sales affiliates from Freiburg).

Perrin also has a group of close advisers, 'people who have been with me for a long while, between about six and twelve years'. They help him with his top management tasks of creation, communication and production and have been selected because 'I found in them all the qualities that I don't think I could find in myself. So let's say I am always looking for complementary colleagues.' He also uses them as 'a task force to check and control what is being completed and achieved on the operational side'.

Any occasional conflicts between the normal line organization and his advisory group Perrin sees as another source of creative energy. 'A company without conflict is a company without life . . . If you take it the positive way, a conflict must end up with something creative. So I believe in conflicts.' His role is to 'be the referee' of this 'calculated chaos', so that it does not result in paralysis. 'If you know how to manage conflict, it ends up being very constructive.'

*. . . And autonomy*

At the same time, Perrin insists that 'a company is not only a money machine' but 'a mosaic of men and women . . . a place where people live together . . . And the relationships that you have to create inside a company are human relationships, they give everyone the opportunity to express themselves.' One of Cartier's great successes has been 'in motivating people . . . And you cannot motivate the 4,600 people working for Cartier if you don't give them the absolute conviction that a soul exists.'

At Cartier, this soul is composed of 'the partners plus the management, and before taking any final decision, the top man 'must take the time and go round the world if necessary, and listen to the partners'. At Cartier, it is

> natural for many, many people around me in this company to come up with a new concept . . . They can always try, they know they can try . . . The art of management is to put the ideas of others together. Creativity is something you manage exactly like an industry.

Perrin believes that 'everybody has within himself a fantastic power of creation and of interpretation'. The modern executive is 'one who knows how to use what is inside the brain of the people, not only what he knows, not only his techniques, but his power of creation'.

'The secret of Cartier,' says Perrin, 'is that we try to extract something from everybody, and give everybody the chance to participate in the creation.' And by this, he means not just the product, but 'the way you decorate a new office, the way you organise a new factory, a new distribution network . . . I like to have creative meetings, and this is the way we work.'

> You must allow people the freedom to express themselves. I very often say in meetings, and we all do the same, express yourself. If you say something stupid, don't worry, we will let you know. But I prefer people to say ten stupid things, because the eleventh one will be the idea.

## FUTURE: A NEW TEMPLE

In 1990 Cartier International was installed in its new offices on the rue François 1er in Paris. Housed in one of the city's grandest former private residences, Cartier is within striking distance of the large foreign luxury shops on the avenue Montaigne, and demonstrably a long way from the old-style jewellers of the Place Vendôme. All its stores will eventually be transformed along the same lines as this new corporate headquarters.

A considerable investment programme will see the renovation of the boutiques. There will be room for leisurely browsing, as well as intimate alcoves in which to personalize private sales. Luminous window displays in green, ivory and mushroom tones will be reduced in size and show only a few items. The centrepiece will be a column decorated in gold leaf, against which some of Cartier's most exclusive jewels will be thrown into sharp relief.

The next generation of acolytes in the Cartier temple is also being assured. Recruitment is based on student placements. Every year, 100 students work in the company, vying to fill 20 positions. In 1990 Cartier created a sales school, Sup de Luxe, which will train salespeople from the stores as well as distributors of Cartier products.

Perrin prefers managers who have 'experienced the terrain'.

> The manager who is only a technocrat and who has never gone out into the field, talked to a client or gone to a factory and talked to the workers, worked with them, understood how to transform a piece of steel into a watch ... understood what the process of production is really like, as well as distribution ... is somebody who is less complete ...
>
> When you hire four guys D-day, and after two years look at them, one has been everywhere and knows everybody, and this is the one you are going to promote right away ... One day, the fact that he has learnt so much from all kinds of horizons will help him have a broader view and have this famous intuition, the power to make a decision ... The others are already stuck in one direction, doing what they do best.

## Global strategy

The expansion of Cartier outside France began in the 1970s, with the export of the Must concept. By 1991 Cartier was present in 123 countries with 145 boutiques and a network of 10,000 concessions. Cartier spread early to Hong Kong (1969) and Japan (1971). At the time, few believed there could be a market for Cartier's products in the Far East. To fight off the competition in Hong Kong, Cartier played its cultural card and launched the Cartier Master Series in 1988. The first year was 'an unbelievable success'. By 1990, Hong Kong had five boutiques and 114 retailers and was one of Cartier's three regular international launching pads, along with Paris and New York.

And yet, Perrin is clear that Cartier will never stray too far from its heartland. 'We must be strong at home. America represents 20 per cent, of which the greater part is the United States, and Asia 25 per cent.' Since 1983, Cartier has gradually pulled back from the Middle East market (only 3 per cent in 1990, which left the company less exposed to the effects of the Gulf War) (Figure 6.4).

> Our European penetration is a voluntary strategy. Europe is the origin of luxury. It is a product of our culture. I believe that the market most loyal to the artistic professions is the one that has

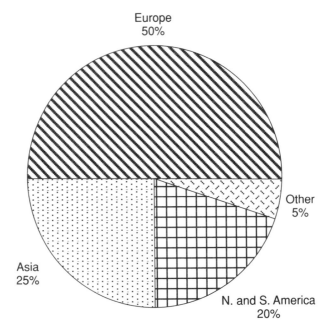

*Figure 6.4* Cartier: sales by region

conceived them. I will always ensure that Europe never represents less than 50 per cent. Most of the major names have chosen the opposite strategy and Asia claims between 60 per cent and 80 per cent of their revenues. But who can guarantee that there won't be a reversal in the Asian market?

In the early 1990s Cartier looks to expand into East Europe. Openings are planned in Budapest, Warsaw, Prague and Moscow. The Cartier name is already known in Hungary. At the turn of the century, Louis Cartier directed the company from a palace in Budapest, where he lived for six months of the year while pursuing an affair with the beautiful Hungarian woman who became his second wife. Meanwhile, Cartier is strengthening its position in the American market. A consumer research firm was commissioned for a study to identify areas with the most highly paid populations. Shops will be opening in San Diego, San Jose, Phoenix. 'We're going to places where money flows like ice in the sun.'

## Integrated manufacturing

Perrin sees the integration of its industrial facilities as Cartier's next strategic challenge. The process will be led from Saint Imier in Switzerland, the headquarters of Cartier's industrial arm, CTL (Luxury Technology Company). With the exception of a few smaller outfits and its jewellery workshop, Cartier has hitherto lacked the means to manufacture its other products. Some of them, such as glasses frames (introduced in 1983 and manufactured by Essilor) and perfumes, are subcontracted to leading industrial companies. For the rest, Cartier depends on networks of small local craftsmen who have traditionally supplied the fashion and luxury goods industry. Paris is rich in such craftsmen, who are closely tied to the greatest names in jewels. Cartier's leather goods are produced in France, Italy and Spain. Nothing comes from the Far East.

In 1988 Cartier completely integrated its cigarette lighter and pen production by opening a plant in Freiburg (100 employees) and another in Franconville (200 employees). 'We decided that the artisan watch manufacturing in Switzerland should be integrated, as this activity accounts for more than 40 per cent of sales'. Relations with the watchmakers, to whom Cartier subcontracted 80 per cent of its watch-making business, had been strained. 'Respect for deadlines among some of our subcontractors had deteriorated drastically. The big companies are fighting to dominate a network of manufacturers who are themselves struggling to keep up with the expansion of the business.' In 1989 Cartier invested in a 50 per cent shareholding in Cristallor, the watch-case manufacturing affiliate of Ebel (a very exclusive Swiss manufacturer and a long-time Cartier subcontractor). With Piaget and Baume & Mercier, Cartier also acquired two manufacturing companies, Prodor and Complications. Further additions have resulted in an industrial armoury which Perrin hopes will make Cartier invincible first in watches, and then in jewellery. Since October 1991 the majority of watches made by the company have been assembled at the plant in Saint Imier. As a result, Cartier has reversed the proportion of watches it subcontracts.

In the future, Cartier will be able to manufacture 75 per cent of its production, the remaining 25 per cent will give the company flexibility. 'This push towards integration allows us to consolidate our margins and our quality, and affirms our leadership.'

By a twist of fate, Piaget and Rolex face each other on opposite sides of the street in Geneva. Alain Perrin likes to feel the vibrations from his closest rival so nearby. 'In 1991,' he predicted, 'the battle will really start.' The future of the luxury industry, considers Perrin, will be 'in the hands of two or three or four groups, no more'. The names that will dominate? 'Cartier, of course, as number one. Chanel. Vuitton. Dior. Yves St Laurent. Dunhill. Hermes.'

Cartier is planning a three-pronged strategy: to reinforce its presence where it is already strong; to expand in East Europe; and, in anticipation of 1993 and the end of duty-free shopping, to open shops in every European airport. These will become 'centres of luxury products, at the expense of alcohol, tobacco and perfume'. But even as he describes the changes to prepare for the future, Perrin is equally emphatic about the inherent continuity and timelessness of the company:

> There is no significant change in the spirit of Cartier between 1847 and 1990, and there will be none by 2000 or 3000 . . . Cartier has been the companion of all the success stories of the world for 150 years. As long as the world is the world, that success story will never cease.

## NOTE

1  © INSEAD-CEDEP 1990, Fontainebleau, France. Revised 1992.
This case was written by François-Xavier Huard and Charlotte Butler, Research Associates, under the supervision of Sumantra Ghoshal, Associate Professor at INSEAD. It was written as a basis for class discussion rather than to illustrate effective or ineffective managerial or administrative behaviour.
Financial support from the INSEAD Alumni Fund European Case Programme is gratefully acknowledged.

# Section 2

# Creation and upgrading of competences

# Chapter 7

# The Richardson Sheffield story: revolution in the cutlery industry[1]

## *Robert Grant and Charles Baden-Fuller*

## EDITORS' OVERVIEW

Richardson Sheffield was founded in 1839. The primary focus of this case study is on events after 1966, particularly the 1980s. From 1974 to 1986 the company experienced considerable growth in sales (averaging 29 per cent p.a.) and profits (21 per cent average return on capital). Its performance was substantially above the UK cutlery industry as a whole (average return on capital for 1974–82 of 12.2 per cent). Behind this impressive result is a story involving considerable technical innovation, changes in market orientation, and team work.

This case study raises many interesting issues. The case outlines the declining performance of the UK cutlery industry in the face of low cost overseas competition. Thus one may ponder how this context constrained the strategic options open to Richardson after Bryan Upton became Managing Director in 1966 and how the competitive situation affected the managerial style and culture of the organization.

Over time Richardson's approach evidently diverged from that of most firms in the Sheffield cutlery industry which adhered to a well-established, but, as it turned out, losing 'recipe'. It is worth thinking carefully about the assumptions which Richardson's managers rejected or reframed. It is also worth reflecting on the link between the various strategies of the company, its financial policies, and the expectations of its owner, Jerome Hahn of the USA, during the 1956–86 period in which the company was run with considerable parsimony.

After something of a crisis arising from economic recession in 1979, the firm's strategy centred on three important issues according to the management, namely, efficiency enhancement, new product development, and marketing and customer service. The case study examines these in some detail.

Efficiency drives involved continuous improvement in technology and manufacturing processes and emphasized the duty of all employees proactively to seek cost savings for the company. Product innovation was accelerated with the realization of the concept of the ever-sharp Laser knife and subsequent innovations.

Richardson's marketing approach was also unusual. It captured a 35 per cent share of the UK retail kitchen knife market with very little advertising or promotion expenditure. Instead, it determined to respond flexibly to the needs of trade customers in terms of delivery and matching their requirements quickly to production schedules. In addition it sought to emphasize the Laser brand, and to make kitchen knives much more than a utilitarian product. Over time its business became increasingly global in scope.

The Richardson case outlines the development of a small, but well-integrated and flexible management team which now includes particular expertise in general management, marketing, production and advanced mechanization techniques. The role of the managing director Bryan Upton in creating a team well matched to the desired competitive advantages is also emphasized. The entrepreneurial attitudes within the firm towards learning, risk taking and capitalizing on perceived opportunities are also treated during the case discussion.

### Discussion questions

- What are Richardson's principal resources and competences? How have these been upgraded over time?
- To what extent has Richardson's success been planned as opposed to being experimental, a kind of continuous adaptive learning process? Can the latter concept be applied systematically to secure operational enhancements, hence superior performance relative to the industry?
- Discuss the role of innovating in Richardson's success. Which innovations have made the greatest contribution since 1980? What are their implications for managing the linkages between marketing, production, distribution, etc.? Which innovations are hardest for competitors to emulate and why?
- How did the industry context in which Richardson was operating affect its response to problems and opportunities during the Upton era? What factors could inhibit the continuing high performance of Richardson in the cutlery industry? What contingent responses should Richardson prepare?
- How important has continuity of management – style and personalities – been to Richardson's success? Why?

### List of named characters

Jerome Hahn, chairman and owner from 1956 to 1986
Bryan Upton, managing director since 1966

Gordon Bridge, deputy managing director
Dick Ellis, managing director prior to Upton
Bob Russell, chief engineer
Kathy Sanchez, sales director
David Williams, chief of electronic engineering and robotics
Denise Ogden, production supervisor
Harold Bearston, managing director of Kitchen Devils

**Keywords**

Innovating; technology; entrepreneurship; leadership; cost reduction; differentiation; learning; teamwork; industry recipes; upgrading; culture

## INTRODUCTION

Richardson Sheffield Ltd have been unusually successful in international markets, and this study provides a simplified story of how that success has been achieved. Many writers, such as Michael Porter, have suggested that there are only two export strategies available to UK-based companies: the low-price, large-scale, mass-market approach; and the high-price, small-scale, niche-market strategy. Richardson appears to have adopted the niche strategy – but with a difference. Whilst some of its output, such as the Laser knife, is in the higher priced segment, the company still makes good profits in the lower price segments. Richardson recognizes that international markets are segmented, even for a mature product such as the kitchen knife. It exploits those segments that it can serve well – such as the customer who wants a cheap knife produced quickly – with flexible production systems.

Creating international success does not rely on a single source of competitive advantage, but on many such sources. Above all, a successful company demonstrates a capacity for change. The Richardson story exemplifies this.

Little about Richardson Sheffield is typical of the Sheffield cutlery industry. In an industry which has seen output and employment more than halved over the past fifteen years, Richardson has expanded its annual sales from under £500,000 to £9 million and has increased employment fivefold. Against a flood of low-cost imports that has sunk several of the leading companies in the industry and resulted in import penetration rising to over 90 per cent in some segments of the market, Richardson has taken 35 per cent of the UK market for kitchen knives, has established itself as the largest supplier of kitchen knives in West Europe, and has rapidly growing export sales to Japan and North America. In contrast to other Sheffield cutlery companies where production methods have been little changed for half a century and where machinery is typically between 10 and 20 years old, Richardson has pioneered the use of automated grinding and polishing techniques and is currently applying robotics and computer-control to knife manufacture.

Our study traces the development of Richardson Sheffield Ltd and explores the reasons for Richardson's success in an industry characterized by decline and failure.

## THE UK CUTLERY INDUSTRY

The cutlery industry is one of the longest established and most tradition-bound of Britain's manufacturing industries. Its founding in Sheffield pre-dates the Industrial Revolution and its emergence accompanied the development of the iron smelting industry in that area. Many features of the UK cutlery industry have remained unchanged for over a century. It remains a fragmented industry dominated by small, family-owned companies, many of which have been in existence for over a hundred years and few of which have ever employed more than a hundred persons. The industry remains concentrated within the City of Sheffield.

The post-war histor of the industry has been one of near-continuous decline. The general demand for table cutlery has shrunk as a result of the greater informality of family meals and the 'fast-food' revolution in the catering industry. The output of UK producers has declined even faster as their share of the domestic market has been eroded by an influx of low cost imports from South Korea, Taiwan and Japan and increasing imports of quality cutlery products from other West European countries. The result has been depressed profitability and a decline in output and employment which gathered pace during the late 1970s and continued into the 1980s before bottoming-out in 1982–3. Decline has been marked by the failures of a number of the leading companies in the industry. In 1982–3 two of the largest companies in the industry went into receivership: Viners Ltd – by far the largest company in the industry, with 530 employees and over £12 million sales – crashed in 1982, and Richards of Sheffield which had dominated the pocket knife market finally went into liquidation in 1983.

The industry's decline has not been uniform across all segments. The most heavily hit segment has been stainless steel table cutlery, where low cost imports from the Far East have largely displaced domestic production. Scissors manufacturers have faced a similarly catastrophic decline in sales as a result of competition both from low cost imports from the developing world and high quality imports from West Europe. In other sectors the pressures of international competition have been less severe. In silver-plated cutlery and tableware, a number of small companies and a few medium-sized producers have survived by supplying quality products to a traditional market. The kitchen knife sector has also escaped annihilation by imports. Although competition from producers in France, Germany and Japan has been strong, the kitchen knife sector has not suffered the flood of imports from South Korea and Taiwan that has driven most Sheffield producers from the mass market for table cutlery. At the same time, the demand for kitchen knives has been comparatively buoyant.

A study of the cutlery industry by the Centre for Business Strategy found that by 1985 the ranks of the British cutlery companies had thinned considerably.[2] The two leading companies in the table cutlery and silverware segments were Oneida Silversmiths, a division of the large US cutlery company, Oneida, and Terence Mason Investments, a relative newcomer to the industry that had acquired a leading Sheffield cutlery manufacturer, George Butler, together with the remnants of

Hawker Marris's Cavalier tableware business. Terence Mason Investments was itself acquired by Crown PLC in 1986. The other companies surviving in the industry were primarily family businesses producing quality silverware, such as Arthur Price and Company, Parkin Silversmiths, Frank Cobb and K. Bright. The primary characteristics of the surviving companies were that they had limited involvement in the sectors most open to low-cost import competition (stainless steel flatware and scissors) and they were focused on the high-price/high-quality market segments. Most of the survivors had pursued comparatively conservative strategies: on average they had invested little in capital equipment, in developing new products or in marketing; they had survived intense market competition, recession and high interest rates through a defensive approach, minimizing outgoings and concentrating on the efficient operation of traditional production methods.

## THE HISTORY OF RICHARDSON SHEFFIELD

The Richardson cutlery business was established in 1839. In 1929 the business was incorporated as Westall Richardson Ltd, but it continued as a family business owned and managed by Westall and his wife, Minnie Richardson. In 1956 Jerome Hahn of New York State visited Sheffield seeking a source of knife blades for his New York-based knife company, Regent. Richardson was unable to supply the 20,000 blades a week that Hahn needed. Hence, in order to obtain a secure source of supply, Hahn shipped machinery from the USA, provided finance for buying a new factory building, and took a 51 per cent share in Richardson. By 1960 Jerome Hahn had acquired 100 per cent ownership of Richardson through buying out the shares owned by the then managing director Dick Ellis. Mr Hahn remains chairman of Richardson.

Until the mid-1960s Richardson produced only knife blades, a substantial proportion of them for its US associate. Others were supplied to knife manufacturers in Britain and Germany. In 1966 an urgent request from a London distributor of kitchen knives resulted in Richardson beginning the manufacture of complete kitchen knives. Since then, its sales of finished knives have grown relative to its sales of blades to other manufacturers. In mid-1987, Richardson was producing around 750,000 knife blades a week, of which about 400,000 were sold to other knife manufacturers, and 350,000 were used in Richardson's own knife production. Finished knives make up by far the larger proportion of Richardson's sales revenue.

Bryan Upton, the present managing director, began work at Richardson in 1959. He was taken on as a 'progress chaser' which involved monitoring production and solving technical problems. He had left school at 13 and trained as a tool maker. He was later appointed works manager and in 1966 was made managing director, a position he has held to date. Under his leadership Richardson commenced upon a programme of continuous improvement of its manufacturing processes, aimed at increasing both the quality and the efficiency of blade manufacturing. During the latter half of the 1970s Richardson's sales revenue increased by an average of 16 per cent per annum in real terms – mostly coming from increased exports.

During 1979 and 1980, Richardson's sales stagnated in nominal terms and fell in real terms. This was primarily a result of a return to normal levels of business after a very large, one-off order from Germany had boosted sales in 1978 by some £500,000. At the same time, home demand was hit by recession and export demand suffered from an overvalued sterling exchange rate. During this pause, Richardson looked for new directions of growth. The breakthrough in Richardson's development occurred in 1980 when the 'Laser' kitchen knife was introduced. This product launched Richardson as a leading knife maker, rather than a manufacturer of blades, and established the company in the UK retail market. Promoted as the knife that never needs sharpening and backed by a 25-year guarantee, the Laser knife attracted considerable publicity and quickly gained reputation both with retailers and consumers. In 1980 Richardson's turnover was £2.4 million with 160 employees. By 1986 it had overtaken the UK market leader in kitchen knives, Kitchen Devils, and was exporting finished knives to over seventy countries of the world (see Figure 7.1) Sales revenue in fiscal year 1986–7 was just short of £12 million; far in excess of that of any other cutlery manufacturer and a substantial proportion of the total industry's output and exports.

To consolidate its position as a manufacturer of complete kitchen knives, Richardson acquired its principal supplier of plastic knife handles in April 1984. Elford Plastics Ltd is a manufacturer of plastic, injection-moulded components. At the time of acquisition its sales were about £700,000 per annum, 40 per cent of which were to Richardson. Under Richardson's management it has expanded sales, not just to Richardson, but also to third-party customers. In 1987 turnover is expected to increase to £2.5 million, of which Richardson's purchases will account for one-third. Profits of Elford have risen from £30,000 to £200,000.

Jerome Hahn's offspring showed little inclination towards careers in the cutlery business and, in view of his own advancing age, Hahn sought a suitable buyer for his companies. A chance meeting at a trade fair in Chicago resulted in his agreeing to sell both Regent Sheffield and Richardson Sheffield to McPherson's Ltd of Melbourne, Australia. McPherson's is a diversified company with interests in publishing and engineering and is the largest Australian manufacturer of kitchen knives and cutlery. Its leading product is the 'Wiltshire Staysharp' knife. Its aim

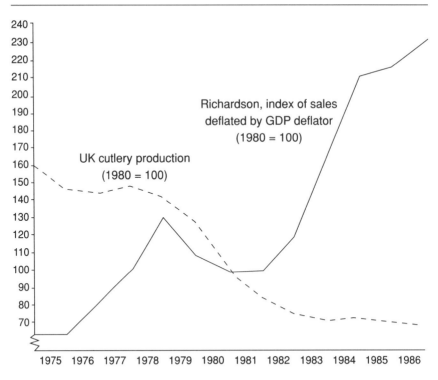

*Figure 7.1* Trends in production 1975–86: Richardson Sheffield Ltd and the UK cutlery industry

in acquiring Regent and Richardson was to extend its interests in the cutlery business outside Australia and to expand the marketing of its Staysharp knife into North America and Europe. On 6 February 1986 Regent and Richardson were together sold to McPherson's for $US18 million and Richardson continues as a wholly-owned subsidiary.

Since acquisition, Richardson has continued along its path of expansion. Sales growth has been assisted by the continuing success of Richardson's Laser knives in overseas markets and a broadening of Richardson's product range. To offer a professional range of knives, Bryan Upton visited Thiers in France and purchased, after a long period of negotiation with the French government and Sabatier Knife Association, one of the nine French Sabatier knife manufacturers. Richardson now distributes a range of French-manufactured Sabatier professional knives. Early in 1987 Richardson introduced its 'Kitchen King' range of kitchen knives similar in design to the kitchen knives supplied by Kitchen Devils, the previous market leader in Britain. In autumn 1988 Richardson will begin to manufacture a range of Wiltshire Staysharp knives, the marketing of which will take Richardson into television advertising for the first time.

In December 1986 Richardson purchased a 140,000 square foot factory close to its existing factory site on Upper Allen Street. The factory was formerly a steel rolling mill and is being rebuilt to house Richardson's production, warehousing and administration. During 1988 Richardson will vacate its present overcrowded, fragmented facilities and move to the new factory.

## Financial performance

Table 7.1 gives details of Richardson's financial performance. In contrast to other companies in the cutlery industry (and in contrast to most other companies in the metal goods industry), Richardson's sales have increased at an annual average rate of 29 per cent in the 12 years between 1974 and 1986.

Sales expansion has necessitated considerable expansion of production capacity, although on the basis of accounts figures, it appears that, between 1974 and 1982, Richardson's expenditure on plant and equipment was a smaller proportion of sales revenue than that for several other of the larger cutlery companies (e.g. Viners). However, because of Richardson's parsimonious approach to capital investment and its preference for developing and building its machinery in-house, accounts data may understate the value of Richardson's investment in fixed assets.

Despite rapid expansion of sales and capital employed, Richardson has taken on no long-term debt. The only borrowing has been on overdraft and this has only exceeded £100,000 in two years (1979 and 1980). The absence of debt is a reflection of Richardson's consistent profitability and its policy of reinvesting all profits in the company. Between 1974 and 1985 pre-tax return on capital employed averaged 21 per cent. In the period 1980–85, that is since the introduction of the Laser knife, the return on capital has risen to an average of 26 per cent. This return is far in excess of the average earned by the cutlery industry as a whole. Between 1974 and 1982 the average pre-tax return on capital employed by thirty-four larger UK cutlery companies was 12.2 per cent.[3] Until 1986 when the company first paid a dividend to its Australian parent, all profits had been reinvested in the company. Interestingly enough, Jerome Hahn received no return from Richardson during the period 1974 to 1985 either as chairman of the company or as its principal shareholder. This is not typical of the cutlery industry. In general, cutlery companies in Sheffield have had to support through dividends and directors' emoluments several family members. In a competitive industry with very low profit margins, this placed a severe constraint on investment and development in these family companies.

Table 7.1 Richardson Sheffield Ltd: financial performance 1974–86

| | 1974 | 1975 | 1976 | 1977 | 1978 | 1979 | 1980 | 1981 | 1982 | 1983 | 1984 | 1985 | Jan.–June 1986 | Year to June 1987 |
|---|---|---|---|---|---|---|---|---|---|---|---|---|---|---|
| Turnover (£000) | 632 | 752 | 1113 | 1595 | 2422 | 222 | 2446 | 2698 | 3458 | 5059 | 7000 | 7776[1] | 4700[1,2] | 12391 |
| Operating profit before interest and tax (£000) | 50 | 44 | 42 | 107 | 254 | 199 | 210 | 227 | 263 | 410 | 554 | 856 | 942[3] | 2096 |
| Cash flow from operations (£000) | 40 | 45 | 56 | 122 | 278 | 213 | 243 | 265 | 334 | 510 | 778 | 1018 | 1019[2] | 2433 |
| Stocks (£000) | 122 | 91 | 196 | 327 | 503 | 703 | 703 | 787 | 823 | 1130 | 1417 | 1926 | 2450 | 3320 |
| Capital employed (£000) | 250 | 280 | 324 | 408 | 662 | 843 | 1074 | 1292 | 1542 | 1991 | 2302 | 2522 | 4593 | 5993 |
| Overdraft and short-term loans (£000) | 38 | 28 | 48 | 27 | 28 | 148 | 108 | 15 | 0 | 22 | 5 | 7 | 511 | 670 |
| Expenditure on plant (£000) | 13 | 9 | — | 19 | 31 | 77 | 47 | 148 | 265 | 552 | 213 | n/a | 139 | 574 |
| Profit before interest and tax/capital employed (%) | 12 | 11 | 12 | 26 | 37 | 20 | 18 | 21 | 18 | 21 | 24 | 34 | 41 | 35 |
| Turnover/stocks | 5.2 | 8.3 | 5.7 | 4.9 | 4.8 | 3.2 | 3.5 | 3.4 | 4.2 | 4.5 | 4.9 | 4.0 | 3.8 | 3.7 |
| Employees (at year end) | — | — | — | 120 | — | 155 | 160 | 159 | 176 | 221 | 339 | — | 367 | 405 |

Notes: 1 Does not exclude intercompany trading
2 Six months
Source: Annual Accounts

## Strategy

Under the leadership of Bryan Upton, Richardson has pursued a consistent strategy of growth and development within the kitchen knife market. This strategy has not been formalized into any planning document. Indeed, Upton noted that it was not until Richardson's acquisition by McPherson's that he was ever asked to produce a formal business plan. Nor is there indication that the evolution of the company has followed any particular long-term development which has existed in the minds of either the chairman or the managing director. The critical turning points in the development of the company, the entry into manufacturing complete knives in 1966 and the development of the Laser knife in 1979–80 were both the result of external initiatives. Hence the strategy of the company that has emerged over the past two decades has been entrepreneurial and driven by identifying and exploiting opportunities, rather than the product of clearly formulated intentions.

At the same time, it is apparent both from Bryan Upton's accounts of the company's development and from the pattern of actions over time, that Richardson has benefited from a clear sense of direction and from some basic guidelines as to how the company would compete in the knife market. Upton attributed the success of his company to a strategy that comprised three factors: efficiency, product development, and customer service and marketing. We start by considering the pursuit of efficiency.

## The quest for efficiency

Between 1966 and 1980 the principal thrust of Richardson's strategy was increased efficiency of its manufacturing operations through process innovation and cost saving.

> When I took over in 1966, we were manufacturing blades in such antiquated methods, you wouldn't have believed it. In 1966, the Chairman and I put our heads together and realized that we would be out of business in ten years if we carried on like that. There were plenty of guys in the Far East developing automated methods of production that would kill us. So we decided to spend our time working out how we were going to produce blades on an automated basis so that we could be competitive. We threw every penny we had into the plant and we designed and built our own equipment. It took us a long time.
>
> (Bryan Upton)

Most of this improvement was the application of electrics and pneumatics to semi-automated existing processes. Virtually all the technical improvement took place in-house and nearly all Richardson's machinery has been developed and built within the plant, much of it under the guidance of Chief Engineer Bob Russell. The biggest area of technical development was in blade grinding. Under traditional methods, an operator would grind one blade about every 35 seconds. With the automated grinding machines developed in-house, one operator can supervise five machines and seven blades are produced from each machine every 35 seconds. Similar productivity increases have been achieved in blade polishing. Polishing is traditionally a highly labour-intensive operation. Richardson has developed its own automated polishing machine. In addition a Siepman automated polishing machine was purchased from Viners when it went into liquidation. When at Viners the machine was operated less than one day a week; at Richardson it operates continuously. In most instances Richardson has gained considerable cost saving from in-house building of its machines. Richardson's own polishing machine cost around £35,000 to build – far less than the cost of anything similar from an equipment supplier.

Technical improvement is a continuous process. There have been very few significant innovations. Technical development is primarily applying and developing ideas and techniques used in other industries and other companies and building on Richardson's own experience. The in-house design and development of machines have been a key feature of the continuous increase of productivity at Richardson. As Bob Russell explained:

> Doing it ourselves meant that we could design machines that were precisely what we wanted, and it was at about half the price of what it would have cost to have bought anything similar from outside suppliers. They were simple, basic machines. But we continue improving them and there is always money available for the technical development of our machines. Downstairs we have over one hundred grinding machines, each time we have built one we have improved it marginally. Without our in-house engineering capability it would not have been possible to successfully introduce new product designs. Take the Laser knife. These require the manufacture of crush rollers that form the grinding wheels that make the edge on the Laser blade. To make these rollers you simply cannot buy a machine from an outside supplier. You have to sit down, draw it and build it. From start to finish, starting from scratch, this took twelve weeks. It's a good machine that does its job, but it's a simple machine. We could have contacted a specialized machinery builder and bought something costing half a million pounds, but it would have been their machine and done their job, not our machine doing the job that we want done. And, best of all, our machine cost about £5,000.

Improving productivity has also involved reorganizing the production process. The flow of product through the factory, from the initial pressing of steel strip to final packaging and warehousing, is constantly being improved. For example, the press shop will be reorganized in July and August 1987 which will allow the automated transfer of blades from the press to the next process. This will cost around £55,000 and will save the equivalent of about six jobs. Upton believes that the main increases in productivity over the next two years will come from reorganizing manufacturing to speed the flow of production and to permit the application of automation and computer control. An important advantage of mechanical transfer is that it enables the work rate of operators and assembly and packaging workers to be controlled. The payment structure reflects the fact that Richardson has an integrated production system. A chief difference between Richardson and other Sheffield cutlery companies is that Richardson's production workers are on hourly wages rather than piecework.

> Piecework was a nightmare. It meant more supervision, more quality control problems, more wages clerks and more disputes. Abandoning piecework in favour of hourly wages was an essential factor in management gaining control of the manufacturing process and developing a system of production.
>
> (Gordon Bridge, deputy managing director)

Some manufacturing operations are avoided altogether. While many of the smaller Sheffield knife manufacturers temper knife blades after grinding, Richardson purchases ready heat-treated stainless steel strip. Although this means heavier wear on tools and machines it results in substantial cost saving.

Current developments are aimed at further automation of production processes. David Williams, previously at Cranfield, joined Richardson in 1985 as manufacturing systems manager. He is mainly involved in the application of electronics to the manufacturing process to increase machine speed, reduce down time, and lower labour input. His work on Richardson's edge grinding machines has resulted in a machine that is totally automated. The edge grinding time has been reduced from 20 to 5 seconds and dramatically reduces machine down time by automatic redressing of grinding wheels. Electronic sensors measure wear on the grinding wheels and automatically change the grinding wheels as necessary. This reduces downtime from about half an hour to 10 minutes and dispenses with the need for a skilled fitter to reset the machine.

In addition to electronic control of existing machines, computer control will be extended to the production process as a whole. In the near future the grinding machines will be linked to a computer which will monitor production and quality. Eventually all machines will be linked to a single computer and the company is currently working on the software needed for such a system.

Steps are also being taken to automate those parts of the production process that have so far been heavily labour intensive. A knife assembly machine has been developed that joins knife blades to handles. Under the traditional method one worker assembles 3,000 knives a day. The new machine with one operator assembles 20,000 knives a day.

Cost reduction is only one objective of the present developments in manufacturing systems. Electronic technology also permits higher quality and greater product consistency. In some cases, improved quality control is possible with very small investments in off-the-shelf equipment. An optical projector costing only £2,500 allows the quality of knife blade edges to be constantly monitored. Substantial productivity improvements have also been achieved through improved organization of the production process. Upton envisages that one of the principal benefits of the application of robotics to knife manufacture will be the ability to produce knives of consistent, high quality.

This development of manufacturing efficiency through continuous improvement of machines, organization and work methods is a classic case of a company gaining cost advantage through steady progression down an experience curve. Consistent with conventional experience curve analysis, Richardson has expanded output more rapidly than its rivals and consequently has moved down the experience curve faster than other companies, opening up a widening cost gap. However, this is not quite the whole story. Observation of other Sheffield knife manufacturers suggests that, rather than a slower movement down the experience curve, they are failing to achieve any benefits from 'learning by doing'. This clearly illustrates the point that economies of experience are not automatic; they must be exploited by management. At Richardson Sheffield, cost economies have been actively sought, opportunities for improving existing processes and machines have been perceived, and the engineering expertise to exploit the opportunities has been available or has been acquired. Other Sheffield manufacturers do not exhibit the same quest for cost reduction, in general they do not believe that there are opportunities for reducing costs, and few have the expertise necessary for adapting and developing machinery.

The quest for cost reduction extends beyond manufacturing to all aspects of Richardson's operation. Bryan Upton's desire to find new sources of cost reduction is evident everywhere. Upton closely monitors the development of Richardson's new factory:

> The guy I've got here as civil engineer is the father of our sales director. The money he has saved me on this project is unbelievable. He argues the toss, he screws all the contractors down, he won't

accept anything until he knows he's got the right price – a brilliant bloke.

Upton is particularly proud of his ability to successfully market the Laser knife and build Richardson's share of the UK kitchen knife market from a half per cent to over 35 per cent without spending a penny on advertising.

To avoid the high costs of employing in-house specialists, Upton has looked outside the company for the skills and talent his company requires and has employed people on a consultancy basis. This has been the case in public relations, some technical areas and design:

> I've got one of the best designers in the world and he costs me next to nothing. He's a Sheffield silversmith who does all our design from blades to handles to packaging. Whatever we want, he is the guy who sits down and makes the model. He's brilliant, he has an aptitude for design . . . It's the same in other areas. For some jobs I've had to go to the big agencies. For the Staysharp launch, for example, we have had to employ a major advertising agency. But most jobs we do on a piecemeal basis and we pick out the best person for the job, wherever he may be.

This no-frills approach is also evident in public relations, which has been extremely important to the development of the company, particularly in gaining publicity for the Laser knife. Upton initially employed a London agency but found their services expensive and ineffective. Public and press relations are now handled in-house utilizing the expertise of Frazer Wright, formerly industrial editor of the now-defunct *Sheffield Morning Telegraph*, as an outside consultant.

Throughout the company employees are expected and encouraged to find ways of reducing costs. On our arrival at Richardson's factory, the shipping manager informed Mr Upton that he had just negotiated a saving in postage charges of 25 pence per set on an order of 100,000 sets of knives being supplied as part of a promotional campaign by a leading British oil company.

## Product development

### *The Laser knife*

The introduction of the Laser knife in 1980 was the breakthrough which was to transform Richardson from a medium-sized blade manufacturer into one of the world's largest suppliers of kitchen knives.

The idea for the Laser knife did not originate with Upton. The starting point was a request to Jerome Hahn at Regent Sheffield from

Sears Roebuck for a kitchen knife that would not need sharpening. Sears were faced with an array of kitchen knives from different manufacturers, all similar in price and performance. If a knife which didn't need sharpening could be devised, they reasoned, a large market was assured. Hahn came and talked to Upton in 1979. Upton recalled the meeting:

> 'Bryan,' said Jerry, 'we've got a project to work on. I've got the name, I haven't got the product. We'll call it Laser. All we have to do is to develop a knife that doesn't need sharpening.'
>
> 'Big deal,' I said. 'Who is going to do that?'
>
> 'We are,' said Jerry.
>
> So that was that. First of all we worked out what was the sharpest edge we could get on a piece of 1.2 mm stainless steel. We produced blades in a range of angles from 10 degrees to 30 degrees. By edge testing, we found that 18–20 degrees was optimal. Then we said, 'Now that we've got the sharpest edge, how the hell do we keep it that way?' So we began playing around with edge configuration. And what we came up with, after a lot of blood, sweat and tears, was a knife blade with a series of minute serrations. By testing our blade against those of every other manufacturer we proved to ourselves that the Laser edge starts sharper, stays sharper and lasts longer than any other knife. The reason is that the edge of the knife is made up of hills and valleys, the hilltops protect the valleys, and the valleys maintain a sharp edge at the optimal cutting angle.

Despite the technical superiority of the knife, it was not an instant success in the British market. Upton recalled:

> So, we brought out Laser. But the retailers still wouldn't buy it. So what's the best way of getting attention? Start an argument. I contacted the press and the radio and said 'Look, here's a Sheffield-made knife. It's the finest knife in the world with a 25-year guarantee. Still the buyers won't talk to us.' Well, that was that. Next day the buyers were on the phone and within three months we were into every department store in the land.

*Product development since 1980*

Following the successful introduction of Laser, most of the product development was in extending the range of knives and increasing its customer appeal through a broader range of handles and colours.

> It's a fashion business. We were the first knife manufacturer to bring out coloured handles. We'll give the customer knives with any colour of handle he wants. We regularly revamp the packaging. The packaging must be professional and attractive. It's got to appeal to the

customer and capture his attention. We change our retail displays every year – no one else in the business does that. It's new items and new images all the time.

(Bryan Upton)

The original Laser was followed by the Laser 5 in 1982 and the Laser 7 in 1986. The new knives featured improvements both to handles and blades. Richardson continues to seek opportunities for improving and maintaining customer interest in this remarkably successful knife. One problem with the Laser knife, noted Upton, is its tendency to stick when cutting swede, turnip and certain other vegetables. Richardson is currently experimenting with different types of blade coating to solve this problem.

Despite the strong engineering orientation of the company, Richardson gives meticulous attention to the design of its knives. This is evident in the plans for introducing to the British market the Wiltshire Staysharp knives currently manufactured by the parent company, McPherson's. Richardson has redesigned the handle of the knife to make it more comfortable to hold and to increase its appeal to the British customer. The handle design and general appearance of the McPherson product were not appropriate to the British market, believed Upton, and would not justify a price tag of £16 or more.

The company's commitment to product development is apparent in a variety of projects aimed at improving the performance of Richardson's knife blades.

We are working here on the knife of tomorrow. We also have engineers at Manchester University working on a project. We have several ideas up our sleeve: some will be coming out next year, some in ten years. We don't know what the knife of the year 2000 will look like. But you can bet your bottom dollar that the Japanese are working on some ideas. We are staying one jump ahead.

Over the next five years, Richardson will be broadening its range of products even further. Both to spread risks and to maintain the company's growth momentum, Bryan Upton foresees expansion into other kitchen tools and also into fashion tabletop cutlery. His key criterion is that whatever products they bring out, there must be an element of novelty and innovation.

If we go into table cutlery, it will not be silverplate. Silverplate is very nice, but it's old hat. That's not what I'm interested in and it's not the style of this company. If we were to go into table cutlery it would be into fashion products – something new, something exciting. . . . We would only go into a different product if our product is better than anything else on the market. That has got to be one of the first essentials. If it's not better, if it's a me-too, I don't want to know.

## Developing a marketing orientation

The Laser knife marked the change of the company's business from supplying producer goods (knife blades) to supplying consumer goods (knives). This transformation in the business of the company was accompanied by a shift in the focus of the company's activities. Until quite recently, manufacturing operations dominated the company and its thinking. So long as Richardson was primarily a supplier of blades to other knife manufacturers, the dominant theme of its strategy was the efficient production of good quality blades. One of most interesting features of Richardson's development has been its ability to change from being a component supplier dealing with knife manufacturers to being a consumer product company dealing with retailers and distributors. The foundation of the company's success in the knife business was the innovatory Laser knife edge, however, and the continued growth of the company's business owes much to its competence in developing its marketing capability.

Richardson's approach to marketing has much in common with its approach to manufacturing and product development: a common-sense, parsimonious attitude which utilizes talented individuals and small budgets. Even after the introduction of the Laser knife, Richardson operated with few marketing resources. A remarkable feature of Richardson's development is that it entered the retail market for kitchen knives and built a 35 per cent market share without any expenditure on advertising and promotion. This has been possible through having a good product with an unprecedented 25-year guarantee and an evocative brand name. It has also been facilitated by Upton's public relations aptitudes that have enabled Richardson to obtain considerable free publicity since 1980.

Evidence of a more market-driven approach to its business comes from observing the increased emphasis given to product styling and packaging and in the expansion of the sales and marketing staff. The sales director, Kathy Sanchez, is now supported by a new marketing manager and a new export sales manager, in addition to an expanded sales office staff. Upton admits that the addition of a marketing function in a sales-driven company and integrating the two has been one of the most difficult transitions that he has had to manage.

One aspect of the increased marketing focus is Richardson's policy of providing a full range of kitchen knives and even extending into other kitchen tools. The Sabatier professional range and the Kitchen King range mean that Richardson has a product in virtually every segment of the kitchen knife market. As a result Richardson is now able to offer retailers a standard display stand which features a range of kitchen knives that no other supplier in Europe can match. Richardson now controls the display of its products in all leading retail outlets, with the exception of John Lewis which prefers to organize its own display.

Richardson's marketing does not simply involve taking market share from others, it has also sought to develop the market for kitchen knives in new areas. Richardson is making particular efforts to develop a gift market for kitchen knives. To this end it is marketing sets of knives which are sold in a wooden block or in an attractively designed package. It is also developing the market for knives as promotional gifts for petrol companies and other promotional purposes.

A substantial area of growth has been supplying special ranges of knives for particular retailers. In many cases these are not specially manufactured knives, but simply standard knives embossed with the retailer's name and in special packaging. Richardson supplies knives packed under the distributor's own brand to Debenhams, British Home Stores, Boots and House of Fraser. 'We will make anything for anyone,' stated Bryan Upton. One of Richardson's largest customers is Argos. Currently a line is being developed for Marks & Spencer.

The marketing of the Staysharp range of knives breaks new ground for Richardson. Prior to launching the product a market research study was commissioned from Booz Allen and Hamilton. The results were encouraging: even at the high price of £17 there was strong consumer interest in a smooth-bladed knife that kept a razor-sharp cutting edge, and a sizeable market demand was forecast. Still Bryan Upton was sceptical. To test the market Richardson displayed the new Staysharp knives at Debenhams, Oxford Street, for one week. Everyone who bought one of the knives was contacted afterwards. The reports were glowing, convincing Upton that people would pay £17 for a carving knife and that the product was a winner. A new marketing manager was hired late in 1986 specifically to manage the launch of the new range, a leading feature of which will be national TV advertising. An advertising budget of £1 million has been set.

Growth in the home market has been matched by the expansion of export sales. Initially, Bryan Upton developed export sales, but subsequently sales director Kathy Sanchez took over responsibility and since mid-1986 she has been assisted by an export sales manager. Trade fairs have been extremely important for Richardson in providing contact with potential customers. These contacts are then followed up either by Richardson's sales staff or by Richardson's sales agent in the country. The export sales manager explained the vital importance of personal contact in building export sales:

It is essential that we go there and are seen to be interested. For every single country that we sell to it is vital that distributors and retailers see us taking the trouble to go and meet them and talk to them.

One of the principal successes has been the development of sales to Japan, itself a leading manufacturer of kitchen knives and the world's largest exporter of cutlery products. Gordon Bridges reported:

> We will do between three-quarters and one million pounds of business with the Japanese this year. Most of the orders are flown out there. We are more efficient than the Japanese. The Laser 5 and 7 have caught the imagination of the Japanese and even with the additional costs of transport and sales, we can sell and earn a satisfactory margin.

The starting point for developing sales to Japan was a visit by the sales director to Japan which resulted in the appointment of a sales agent who has methodically expanded sales of Richardson's products. In May 1987 Richardson will participate in a BOTB-sponsored exhibition in Japan, which will assist the company in contacting new customers. The export sales manager viewed the expansion potential of exports as tremendous:

> We've won the Queen's Award for Exports twice, and we are going for a hat trick. We've got the product, the manufacturing capability, the presentation, the flexibility, the right prices, most of all, we've got the right attitude. The opportunities are fantastic.

**Customer service**

Although the nature of Richardson's business has changed radically since 1980, a consistent theme of the company's development has been serving the customer. Explaining the edge that Richardson has on its competitors, both at home and abroad, Gordon Bridge, deputy managing director, identified two factors:

> No one can match our prices or our delivery times. Take the order we got from Italy. There are some big knife manufacturers there, but we got the order because they couldn't offer as low a price or as quick a delivery. We had six weeks to manufacture a million-and-a-half knife sets, to print the cards, to get the packaging approved and to deliver them. There is no way a Far Eastern supplier could compete on an order like that.

The company's philosophy of serving the customer essentially involves speed of response and flexibility of response. Commitment to speed of response is summed up in Bryan Upton's 'Three Golden Rules':

We operate three rules here. Letters are answered the same day, samples are supplied within 48 hours, telexes are answered in minutes.

Gordon Bridge explained how the sales department is organized for responsiveness to customers:

At the sales office, we have coverage from quarter to eight every morning. If you go into the sales office at ten past six there will be four girls there. They stagger their lunch breaks so that from quarter to eight until quarter past six there is always someone to respond to a customer whether he telephones in or telexes in.

Within the range of knives that Richardson's manufactures, it offers the maximum variety possible in order to meet the requirements of individual customers. These preferences include the colour of the handle, the name that is embossed on the blade, the type and design of the packaging, and the range of knives offered in a set. At the time of our visit Richardson was developing a set of knives for Marks & Spencer that required a specially designed plastic package printed in Marks & Spencer's 'harvest' design.

To offer speed of delivery together with the ability to accommodate customers' individual requirements for product variations or particular types of packaging requires considerable flexibility of production operations. Although Richardson traditionally operates a single shift, weekend and evening working are frequently needed to complete orders on time. Because sales expansion has outstripped increases in production capacity, overtime working has become routine and a twilight shift is being introduced. The chief problem Richardson has experienced in increasing the hours of factory operation is the burden it places on the managerial and supervisory workers.

Upton did not consider that competing through speed of delivery and offering products which were differentiated to meet the requirements of specific requirements significantly increased production costs. Richardson produces a standard range of knife blades, so product differentiation is primarily in terms of handles, brand names and packaging, and most of the special orders are for fairly large numbers of knives. At the time of our visit Richardson was completing an order for 1.5 million knife sets for Italy and was currently producing 100,000 sets of knives as part of a promotion for BP petrol. These orders meant considerable overtime working, but by increasing the total volume of production they helped spread overheads. The principal cost of speedy delivery arose in transport. A substantial proportion of exports, including those to Japan, are air freighted.

## EXPLAINING SUCCESS

Why has Richardson Sheffield been so outstandingly successful in comparison with other companies in the British cutlery industry? Part of the explanation may be that the kitchen knife segment has been relatively more buoyant than other segments of the cutlery industry and less subject to low cost overseas competition. Certainly the demand for kitchen knives both in Britain and elsewhere has shown modest growth in comparison with the demand for table cutlery. Also it is a market where customers are willing to pay a premium for a product with superior performance. Most important, the market has not been invaded by ultra-cheap imports from South Korea and Taiwan. However, choice of market segment is only a minor factor in Richardson's success. Other British kitchen knife manufacturers, notably Prestige and Harrison Fisher, have performed poorly both in terms of sales growth and profitability. Moreover, competition in Europe has been very strong. Several German, Swiss and French manufacturers were large and well established. During the 1970s imports into the UK increased substantially. These included high quality fully-forged knives (professional knives) from Europe and cheaper kitchen knives from Japan.

Its appears, therefore, that Richardson's success is almost entirely attributable to its own efforts. In the earlier sections we have outlined the strategy pursued by the company since 1966. The strategy textbooks tell us that a sound business strategy is one that is consistent with both the market environment of the company and its resources. In terms of both criteria Richardson Sheffield has pursued a sound strategy. The knife industry is strongly competitive in the high price, high quality segment from West European producers, with competition in the low- and medium-priced segment primarily from domestic and Japanese companies. Richardson has used manufacturing efficiency together with the relatively low British wages to gain a clear cost advantage in blade manufacture. This was followed by product innovation to gain a product advantage in the mass market.

However, these advantages of low production cost and product innovation are not easily sustainable. In an internationally competitive market, such as that for knives, cost advantage is vulnerable to exchange rate fluctuations, international differences in steel prices and the emergence of competition from low wage countries. The Laser knife with its technical superiority in cutting and its durability is subject to imitation. Although Richardson has protected its innovation by patents, these do not apply in every country of the world and Richardson is subject to increasing competition both from similar products and direct counterfeits. Hence Richardson's emphasis on continual product development to stay 'one jump ahead of the competition'.

In terms of sustainable competitive advantage, a key factor is Richardson's commitment to speed and flexibility of response to customer requirements. Here the company makes use of locational advantages in terms of identifying the needs of domestic and European customers and its organizational flexibility in terms of speed of response to customers. Richardson claims that the delivery times which it is able to offer, even on large contracts for specially differentiated knives are unmatched in the industry.

To observe Richardson's strategy and analyse its wisdom is easy. To explain why Richardson has been able to adopt and successfully implement a winning strategy while most other Sheffield companies have stagnated or declined is more difficult. Underlying all three strands of Richardson's strategy – efficiency, product design and customer service – is a constant quest for improvement. Probably the starkest contrast between Richardson and other companies in the cutlery industry is the desire for change. From earlier interviews with the senior managers of cutlery companies, it was apparent that few perceived any opportunities for significant changes either in products, production processes or management methods. While some of these companies did introduce new styles of cutlery, few have attempted to design any product ranges that are innovatory in appearance, materials or performance. Similarly, few companies have introduced any significant changes in production technology. For many Sheffield companies the trend has been the reverse. Because of declining production volume many companies have abandoned semi-automated processes and reverted to more traditional labour-intensive methods of production. For example, in pressing flatware and knife blades, most cutlery producers use steel sheet rather than the cheaper and more easily automated continuous steel strip.

The inability to perceive the potential for profitability through change has led most companies in the industry to seek profitability through protection. Most managers in the industry see the problems of the industry as primarily the result of low cost competition from the Far East, a situation which they believe should be resolved by the imposition of import quotas.

Upton compares the approach of his company with that of Kitchen Devils, the previous brand leader in the British market. 'They had a damn good product and they marketed it well,' he admits. 'The trouble was they did nothing with it and it soon became tired.' By contrast, Richardson's success with the Laser knife did not stop the company from seeking further development. Richardson has made continued technical improvement to the blade, it has sought to increase the consistency of product quality as well as the efficiency of its manufacture, and, most of all, it has emphasized the continued regeneration of market interest through coloured handles, design variations and new approaches to packaging and display.

This quest for improvement and continuous development has its basis in Upton's attitude towards his job as managing director. His energy and relentless drive to make the company better are sustained by his enthusiasm for what he is doing:

> I enjoy what I'm doing – its like a hobby to me. If McPherson's were to come over tomorrow and were to say, 'Look, Bryan, we've got someone else to do your job,' I'd say, 'Fine, I've had 27 fantastic years', and I'd go and do something else. Every day here is something different. There's never a dull moment – always new things.

This attitude is characteristic of others in Richardson's management team. David Williams, in charge of electronic engineering and robotics, commented:

> It's a challenge. I feel that I'm pushing back the frontiers because no one else is doing this particular job. I'm finding out new solutions to problems all the time. It's very exciting and it's a great place to work.

Continual improvement is most easily observed in manufacturing operations. The machinery, the organization of the factory and working methods are the product of continual, incremental improvement made over twenty-one years. Our visit to the Richardson factory was just before a substantial reorganization that would economize on the manual handling of knives between each production process. 'Our goal is to manufacture knives so that at no stage in the production process do they ever touch the floor,' noted Upton.

Upton believes that continuity in the company's management (Hahn has been chairman since 1956, Upton has been MD since 1966) has been an important factor in maintaining development of products and manufacturing efficiency. A significant cause of the failure of other companies has been changes in ownership that have disrupted management and have involved managers in fighting internal power battles rather than managing and developing the business. He cited Kitchen Devils as one example of this. Kitchen Devils was the most successful company in the UK kitchen knife market. Under the leadership of Harold Bearston it developed an excellent product and marketed it effectively. However, the business was acquired by Wilkinson Sword; Wilkinson Sword was acquired by British Match, which was itself acquired by Swedish Match. One consequence of this was that Bearston's expertise and commitment were lost and the business stagnated.

## The people

The ability of Richardson to identify the potential for development and to implement improvements successfully in product, processes and marketing owes a great deal to the abilities and the personalities of the company's managers. Most important have been the managerial and entrepreneurial capabilities of Managing Director Bryan Upton. Though lacking any formal management training – he left school at 13 and his managerial experience has been entirely with Richardson – Upton shows a remarkable breadth and versatility of business competence. Although his background is in engineering, the main feature of his twenty-one years as managing director has been the outstanding leadership and skill he has demonstrated over a wide range of managerial functions from production and product development to design, public relations, marketing, and recruitment. The only area where Upton acknowledges lack of expertise is in finance. Here he admits his dependence on the deputy MD.

> He has a remarkable business sense. He has an ability to go straight to the heart of any problem and pull out the nuts and the bolts. He may not know the solution in precise terms, but he will know what to ask and who to ask.

The most obvious characteristics of Upton's management style are his opportunism, his attention to detail, and his insistence on getting things done. His opportunism is evident from his ability to turn chance meetings whether they are on business trips or holidays into business for the company, and his reluctance ever to turn away an order. 'I'm a hands-on merchant. I do things and I worry about them afterwards.'

His bias for action extends into all aspects of the company's operations. Even with the growth of the company and the expansion of the management team, Upton saw many of the details of company operation as too difficult to leave to others. For example, he has taken personal charge of the development of Richardson's new factory.

> I was down there yesterday, and I noticed that up near the roof there were pigeons. Now, you know the kind of mess that pigeons are going to make in a new factory. So, I've arranged for them to be got rid of. There are not many managing directors that you will find checking on the little details of the development of a new factory, but it's important to me and it's important to the company, and I'm going to make sure that we do a good job. That's what being a managing director is about. If I'm sure that someone is doing a good job, I let them get on with it. But I've got to be satisfied that they are doing it right, and I can only be sure by going and seeing exactly what is

happening. The trouble with a lot of MDs is that they wear dark suits and red ties and sit behind a desk. We once had an MD like that. He had three cars and nearly ran the company into liquidation.

But Richardson is no longer a one-man band. Rapid growth has necessitated considerable expansion in the managerial staff and one of the essential ingredients of Richardson's success has been Upton's ability to build a management team of highly capable individuals who share Upton's enthusiasm for their work. Upton explained the broadening of Richardson's management as follows:

> As we grew I found it increasingly a strain to be an expert on every aspect of business life without anyone to lean on other than a Chairman who was three thousand miles away. My first step was to get some part-time guys in who had the skills that I needed. And that's what I did. I sought advice from the bank and I eventually found what I needed: a finance man, a marketing man, and a good all-rounder – someone who knows everyone from the Queen down. After a while this was not enough, so our financial adviser, Gordon Bridge, came in as full-time Deputy Managing Director. We also appointed Kathy Sanchez as Sales Director, and we are now needing a Production Director.

To this core of executive directors, Richardson has added managers for marketing, exports, manufacturing systems, sales, and data processing. Recruitment has been from several sources: agencies, direct advertising, head hunting and personal contact. Upton admits that management recruitment has been one of the most important and most difficult of his jobs in recent years. It was difficult to know who would fit into the company and work out well. What he looked for in particular were people who were self-starters – who would see what needed to be done and would get on and do it.

> One of the most difficult things in recruiting is hitting the right level. One of our problems in the past was that we aimed too low. The way the company is going – into robotics, into more sophisticated quality control, into marketing – means that we need people with brains. On the other hand, there's no point in having people who think they're too good. Some blokes want a nice office with assistants and secretaries running around after them. They may be all right for some companies – they are no good to us.

One of the most difficult jobs to fill had been that of production manager:

> The person who we need for running production here may not even

exist, but we keep looking and I think that the guy we have starting this month may be just right. He knows nothing about making knives, he works for a confectionery company. But what he does know about is how to get product through a factory fast. And that's what we need.

While it was usually possible to identify when people had the right skills for the job, it was more difficult to assess whether they would fit in with Richardson's way of doing business. Gordon Bridge explained:

Managers come here and they either love it or hate it. If they love the place they tend to stay a long time. If they hate it or if they don't fit in, they go quickly. We must have people who work our way and work to the required standards. If they don't, then they may prejudice the business.

Upton had precise expectations of what he expected from managers in particular jobs; if they did not match up to expectations, they were asked to find another job. In the four weeks between our first and second interviews at Richardson, two managers were identified by Upton as 'not fitting into the company' and 'not making progress with their jobs' and replacements for them were being sought.

As well as bringing in experienced people from outside, Richardson has grown its own managers. As Gordon Bridge explained:

We have got some terrific people here who have grown with the company. Our production supervisor Denise Ogden was one of the first people we hired to pack kitchen knives about fifteen years ago. She is unbelievable. She has a natural business sense and a determination to produce goods on time. Linked with that is an ability to manage people – and managing up to 140 girls aged between 16 and 21 is no easy task. What helps, of course, is that she knows every single job on this factory floor. With Kathy Sanchez it's a similar story. She came here as a Sales Secretary and was promoted to Sales Director. She now speaks five languages. That's a fantastic asset for a company like ours. We arranged to go to a trade show in Milan a few years back. A few weeks beforehand she bought some tapes and by the time she went there, she was speaking Italian.

## Maintaining flexibility and responsiveness

As a one-man band, it was relatively easy for Upton to impose his entrepreneurial, hands-on style of management. However, as the organization has grown, maintaining the commitment to change and the opportunism that has characterized the company's strategy, is more difficult. A key feature has been maintaining flexibility by maintaining a closely knit team that avoids nearly all bureaucratic procedures. The offices are along a single corridor and staff are continually in and out of each other's offices. Responsiveness to customers and the drive to improve manufacturing methods are also assisted by rapid decision making. The export sales manager told us that in accepting an order from a customer, if he could not individually negotiate the price, then he would telephone or telex the sales director or deputy MD and obtain a firm price either immediately or within half an hour. Bob Russell, chief engineer, reported no significant delays in gaining authorization for buying items of new equipment.

Reconciling a high level of autonomy by individual managers with Upton's passion for detail and involvement in all aspects of the company's business is no easy task. Upton explained that his approach was essentially one of management by exception: if someone was doing their job properly and achieving the right level of performance, then Upton let the person get on with it.

Speed of response also necessitates taking risks. Bryan Upton recalled a recent order from Germany:

> The contract was a huge, thick thing, all in German and stuffed full of penalty clauses. If I had waited to get the thing translated and okayed by the legal people, we would have lost the order. My philosophy is that, if we can deliver products of the required quality by the date specified, then you can burn the contract – it's irrelevant.

Responsiveness also means a willingness to make mistakes and change direction. Gordon Bridge believes that a willingness to learn from mistakes and revise plans accordingly is an important feature of the company's operation:

> If anyone makes a mistake, whoever it is, they are quite open and admit it, and we try to avoid the same mistake again. When it comes to major decisions, if it proves to be wrong we quickly change it. We don't say, 'We made a decision, we must stick with it.' We change it and get on with the job.

### Richardson's independence from the Sheffield cutlery industry

If we explore the reasons why the company has been able to adopt so progressive and innovatory an approach to its business in comparison to other cutlery companies, a key factor must be Richardson's distancing itself from the rest of the Sheffield cutlery trade. Several empirical studies have identified the tendency for 'group think' to emerge within an industry. This is most likely to manifest itself in an 'industry recipe' –

a consistent view between companies as to the nature of the industry environment and the appropriate kinds of strategies which companies should pursue. In a traditional, craft-based industry, such collective thinking may impose a substantial barrier to change. In an industry which is suffering catastrophic decline, it is likely to induce fatalism and pessimism.

A distinguishing feature of Richardson Sheffield has been its limited involvement with other companies in the Sheffield cutlery industry since the accession of Bryan Upton. A key factor here was its US ownership and the influence of Chairman Jerome Hahn.

> I learned a great deal from Jerry Hahn. I had the basics, but he taught me most of what I know about management. More than that, I learned from him how to think like an American. A lot of British managers look very pretty in their ties and suits, but they can't actually get things done.
>
> (Bryan Upton)

Deputy managing director Gordon Bridge confirms the important influence of the US Chairman:

> The input of Jerry Hahn was a key factor behind the success of this company. He stopped the company from thinking like a traditional Sheffield company and broadened everyone's horizons. This attitude of challenging everything and never accepting No for an answer has been a key feature of the company's development. It's good to have an outside influence, and we still benefit from having non-executive directors. In addition we have the benefit of the experience and views of our main board directors from McPherson's. There's always a danger of becoming too parochial and thinking that Sheffield is where the world begins and ends.

The distancing of the company from the traditions of its own local industry is apparent in many aspects of Richardson's operation. Richardson has only recently become a member of the Sheffield-based Cutlery and Silverware Association of the United Kingdom – mainly to participate in wage negotiations and government-sponsored trade missions. None of the present management team have worked in the cutlery industry before. Several were previously employed in the motor industry, two from a confectionery company and one from a household products supplier. As Bryan Upton emphasized several times: 'We are an engineering company, *not* a cutlery company.'

## Motivation and commitment

Richardson's strategy of continuous development and constant improvement works only because of the commitment of the company's employees.

Gordon Bridge, deputy managing director, explained the attitude of people as follows:

> The example starts at the top. We don't flag. We are always here. You won't catch the MD or myself having a day off other than for our regular holidays. We don't slope off to the golf course on a Friday afternoon. We are never late in. I don't think that either of us have had a day's illness in years. That is how it is here – the managers just are not away ill. And it's the same throughout the company. When an order needs to be completed we work evenings, we work weekends, and the people just come in. And the main thing is that they come in willingly – they don't have to be bullied into it. That is the sort of people we want. They enjoy doing a good job, they enjoy working for a successful company, they enjoy the rewards they get. If people come here and do a good job they get rewarded for it.

This commitment to the company which is indicated by the conscientiousness and flexibility of employees throughout the company reflects the influence of Bryan Upton. Not only do his own attitude and work habits provide an example, but he actively provides encouragement to others and, because of his attention to detail, he is well aware of activities and the performance of his colleagues. Many of his ideas of how business should be conducted are now deeply ingrained in the operating practices of the company. One of these is the 'as well as' principle which Upton outlined:

> We are constantly taking on urgent orders and starting special projects. People used to ask me, 'If I'm taking on this job, what shall I drop?' My answer was, 'You drop nothing. You do the special project or the special order as well as your normal work.' Now I don't have to say anything, it's understood that we do the additional things *as well as* whatever else we are doing.

## THE FUTURE

Under its new owners, Richardson is embarking upon the most rapid period of expansion in its history. Development is taking place on several fronts. Later this year the entire factory will be moving to the large new site. The single-building, single-storey layout will enable much better linkage of production processes and product will flow continuously from the steel store to the warehouse for final goods. In addition, the manufacturing process will be revolutionized over the next five years through the application of computers and robotics. A substantial sales expansion in the home market is expected from the introduction of Staysharp knives in October 1987. In addition the prospects for increased exports of Richardson's kitchen knives are considered excellent.

Looking ahead, Bryan Upton is exploring the possibilities of new kitchen and table-top products: a range of fashion table cutlery has been designed with a view to launching it in 1988. Richardson's business plan projects sales for 1990 at about £23 million with Elford Plastics contributing another £4 million. While the move to the new factory will ease the space constraint on expansion, a further constraint will be the increased burden of work on the management team. Richardson is now giving greater attention to management development and will be hiring two graduates this year.

Bryan Upton has two ambitions for the future. The first is to see Richardson's sales exceed £50 million a year, the second to export to Russia and China. Upton confidently expects to meet both objectives:

> I went to a seminar on exporting to China. The speaker told me that I had a problem. The Chinese, apparently, don't use kitchen knives – they have a cleaver that is used for all kitchen jobs. That may be so, but there are hotels and restaurants as well. Our job is to find the potential buyers and show them what we have to sell . . . . As for Russia, I'm going to the Black Sea for a holiday this year. I intend to find time to talk to a few people and see if I can generate some business.

## NOTES ˙

1 © London Business School 1987
  This case study has been written as a basis for class discussion rather than to illustrate effective or ineffective managerial or administrative behaviour. It could not have been written without the help of those working in Richardson Sheffield, but the views expressed here are those of the authors, and are not necessarily those of the Richardson Sheffield management. We also thank the ESRC for their financial support.
2 R. M. Grant and S. Downing, *Industry Adjustment, Business Strategy and Firm Performance in the UK Cutlery Industry, 1973–83* (Centre for Business Strategy, London Business School, 1985).
3 Grant and Downing op. cit., Table 14.

# Chapter 8

# Woolworths: the refocusing of a leading retailer[1]

## Joshua Bamfield and David Williams

### EDITORS' OVERVIEW

This case study covers Woolworths' history from 1909 to 1994. Its principal emphasis is, however, on the period from 1982 when F. W. Woolworth PLC was taken over by Paternoster Corporation. The strategies subsequently followed by management resulted in the transformation of the group from a profit of £26 million in 1982/83 to a profit of £232 million in 1993/94. Underpinning this financial turnaround is a story of considerable change in market focus, organization structures and systems, corporate identity, and staff motivation, training and rewards.

Although Woolworths remains the core retail format, by 1994 the Group additionally comprised the DIY chain B&Q, Comet Electrical Stores, Superdrug PLC, Charlie Brown's Autocentres, and Darty SA, the largest French retailer of electrical goods. Moreover, a number of other competing retail chains had been acquired and integrated with the above. In 1989 the Group changed its name to Kingfisher PLC. Despite out-performing many competing retail groups with which it had been unfavourably compared in earlier years, Kingfisher was the subject of adverse commentary in the financial press in the wake of disappointing results in 1994.

Woolworths' history evidences early corporate success that was sustained until the late 1950s. Thereafter there was a long period of slow decline as changes in the market-place and new approaches to retailing were not reflected in new strategies at Woolworths itself. Management remained stubbornly attached to old ways, notably, persisting with an unfocused 'variety chain' approach to merchandising that involved some 70,000 product lines. To counter lack of progress in the core business, 1981 saw diversification into DIY retailing with the acquisition of B&Q and Dodge City.

The time was right for overhaul. A consortium called Paternoster Corporation was formed to try to take over the chain, and the US parent was persuaded to sell out late in 1982. The Paternoster team faced many difficulties and opportunities. The new team may perhaps have had greater freedom to consider radical change, as contrasted with the inertia of previous incumbents, but they moved cautiously to begin with. Still, by 1984 improvements were evident and in 1985 Operation Focus was launched. Between 1985 and 1989 the firm was concentrated on six core activities, the retail outlets were reorganized and refurbished and there were many changes in supplier arrangements, information systems, staff policies, and a new corporate approach to managing the massive high street property portfolio. The performance of other elements of the group was also improved. In 1986 a take-over bid by rival retail group Dixons was successfully repulsed.

The case study provides the opportunity to consider the many aspects of managing a large, geographically dispersed retail organization. Woolworths is a prime example of the truth of the often quoted phrase 'retail is detail', but what were the key operational details that Woolworths management had to control and improve as part of the longer-term strategy? The case details many incremental investments in the form of experiments with market focus involving, for example, new store formats, policies and operating systems, some of which eventually emerged corporate-wide. These experiments provide an insight into how new strategies emerge over time as incremental steps are preferred to radical overhaul in the change process.

The case outlines key innovations in staff training, motivation and reward which were initiated during the 1982–89 period. It is worth considering what effect these schemes had on the success of the Woolworths' strategy as a whole and how well the cost-benefit assessment was analysed. The issue of cultural change also relates to many of these 'rejuvenation' initiatives.

The case also examines issues of a broader strategic dimension such as corporate governance, the interests of the various external and managerial stakeholders in the firm – the latter including the chairman and group managing director, other board members, regional managers, and the various merchandise teams. It points to the changing roles and power bases of these various actors during a lengthy and sometimes traumatic change process. One such issue is the appropriate balance between decentralization and centralization of decision-making.

The case provides financial data on the organization enabling the reader to analyse the events in terms of their potential financial implications. The reader may also wish to reflect on whether the property portfolio extended the breadth of options open to Woolworths relative to competitors or whether it was essentially a distraction.

## Discussion questions

- What was Woolworths' principal problem when Paternoster took over?
- Evaluate the effectiveness or otherwise of Paternoster's strategic turn-around of Woolworths after 1982. To what extent have its core competences been upgraded?
- Discuss the role of experimentation and incremental development in the turnaround process. If past success creates inertia and managerial unwillingness to change, how can this tendency be resisted? Are crises inevitable, even desirable?
- Detail the principal changes in organizational structures, systems and procedures. How important were these in comparison with repositioning in terms of market image and focus and associated product policy?
- Assess the Group as a portfolio of business activities. Where does the Group go from here? Who are its benchmark competitors?
- Are Woolworths' post-1994 problems mainly about strategic position, mainly about inferior competences to benchmark competitors, or mainly about continuing difficulties of strategy implementation? What is your reasoning?

## List of named characters

See Appendices 5 and 6 for detailed lists

## Keywords

Retailing; turnaround; rejuvenation; experimentation, incrementalism; managerial roles and styles; (de)centralization of decision-making; culture change and motivation; corporate governance; acquisition strategies

## INTRODUCTION

At the beginning of the 1990s, the Board of what had originally been F. W. Woolworth PLC was able to feel that it had met all the promises to shareholders made at the time of the take-over or management 'buy in' by the Paternoster Corporation in 1982. The take-over had been the culmination of three decades of continuous decline by F. W. Woolworth, once one of the dominant UK high street retailers. Since 1982, the Woolworth high street chain had been transformed, whilst the Group (renamed Kingfisher PLC in 1989) had meanwhile become a substantial holding company. Its portfolio of retail and retail-linked businesses included Comet (electrical goods), Superdrug (drugstore/chemist), B&Q (hardware/do-it-yourself), and Chartwell Land (property) turning Woolworths into what the Times called 'one of the fittest retail businesses around':

> Geoffrey Mulcahy, the chief executive of Kingfisher, has confounded critics of his strategy for Woolworth, once one of the worst performing retailers on the high street. The chain now has the biggest share of the home entertainment, confectionery, and toys market and claims to be the best performing mixed merchandise store in Britain . . . Earnings per share rose for the eighth year in succession.[2]

During the recession of the early 1990s, whilst many retail competitors were struggling to maintain profitability (or even to survive), Kingfisher was able to increase turnover and maintain profits. The turnover of the Group rose from £1.2 billion in 1982/3 to £4.8 billion by 1994/5, whilst pre-tax profits had grown from £12.4 million to £309 million over the same period. Kingfisher had become an international retailer with the acquisition of the largest French electrical retailer, Darty, in 1993. The company's results for 1995 did, however, raise a number of questions about the future.

This case deals with the 1982 take-over of F. W. Woolworth PLC by the Paternoster Corporation and the strategies which the new management used to turn around and reposition the group. It deals primarily with the *Woolworth* high street core business, although sister companies in Kingfisher are discussed where appropriate. A chronology of Woolworths is given in Appendix 1.

The store chain has always been known by generations of shoppers as 'Woolworths' or more affectionately, 'Woolies'. Until 1989, the company and financial commentators always used the term 'Woolworth' to describe the chain, although in 1989, the Kingfisher Group, reflecting common usage, registered the Woolworth chain as 'Woolworths PLC'. Throughout this case the company is known as 'Woolworth' until 1989 and 'Woolworths' thereafter.

## 1909–82: FROM THE ORIGINS OF WOOLWORTH TO THE PATERNOSTER TAKE-OVER

The first British outlet of the American retail chain store F. W. Woolworth & Co. Ltd was opened in Church Street, Liverpool in 1909. The US parent company had been founded by Frank Winfield Woolworth in 1897 on the simple idea of selling as many goods as possible for five or ten cents. The British operation offered a great variety of goods for a penny, threepence or sixpence.

After the First World War, the chain expanded rapidly; by 1931 it had 434 branches. The *variety chain*[3] format became the role model for a number of imitators including Marks & Spencer, Littlewoods, and British Home Stores. Unlike Woolworth, however, other variety stores concentrated on textiles.

The Woolworth slogan in its early years was 'Nothing Over Sixpence'. It was a cut-price store, the company insisting on special deals based on buying direct from manufacturers rather than wholesalers. The Woolworth stores were large, well-lit and open, and encouraged shoppers to stroll around without any pressure to buy. Apart from department stores, most retail outlets were fairly small and specialized, and used salespeople who tried to make a sale to everyone who entered the shop. In contrast Woolworth was an emporium; it concentrated on staple goods including food, clothing, haberdashery, toys and gifts, soft furnishings, lighting/electrical, paint and hardware. F. W. Woolworth became a cornerstone of the high street, and an established part of the main shopping expeditions of a substantial proportion of UK households.

Until 1931, when 48 per cent of the British company's shares were floated on the British Stock Exchange, F. W. Woolworth operated as a wholly-owned subsidiary of the US parent. In the following years the UK operation became increasingly autonomous from the parent company and by the 1950s was operating as an independent company – though the US parent retained its majority stake in the business.

The retailing revolution of the late 1950s–1960s presented a problem for well-established formats such as Woolworth. Its failure to take full advantage of the growth in retail sales and to utilize new merchandising and promotional techniques led to dissident shareholders forming the so-called Ginger Group in 1969 to change the company's trading strategy (the profit record of F. W. Woolworth is given in Appendix 7). The share price had more than halved between 1960 and March 1970. However, changes in product range, judicious pruning and cost control improved Woolworth performance so that by 1972, the *Observer* was announcing, 'the odds were heavily in favour of Woolworth making a High Street comeback sooner rather than later. It has happened a lot sooner than many expected.'[4] However, by 1975 Woolworth's problems had become more acute. Specialist multiples seemed to understand customer requirements more comprehensively and were more selective in the goods they stocked. Successful regional multiples had become national businesses based on superior merchandising and promotional skills combined with high sales per square foot; their significant buying power was used to obtain concessions from suppliers which were passed on to customers, thus eroding Woolworth's price advantages. Customers were also more demanding; the range of goods in Woolworth was seen to be unadventurous and its stores were much less inviting than their newer competitors, the specialist multiples. In addition, during the 1970s there was a shift by many retailers away from the high street in favour of new developments (both in-town and edge of town) that were operationally more cost-effective for retailers as well as being more attractive to shoppers.

Woolworth tried to take account of the changes in the retail marketplace. It opened the first Woolco, an out-of-town hypermarket, in 1970, making it one of the pioneers of superstores. Other new formats designed to attract middle-class customers included Shoppers' World in 1975, a chain selling goods from a catalogue. To get its message across, Woolworth became one of the largest retail advertisers; its 1975 theme, 'The Wonder of Woolworth' is still remembered, even though it was replaced in 1981 by 'You'll Love the Change'. The well-known 'Winfield' own-brand name was dropped in favour of simply 'Woolworth'.

Another attempt to appeal to affluent consumers in the late 1970s involved widening the product range to include high-ticket lines such as furniture and electrical goods, including TV and hi-fi, and removing haberdashery and food from many of their stores. Thus the chain which had initially advertised 'Nothing Over Sixpence' was now selling a range of expensive electronic and electrical goods in its larger outlets.

During the 1970s, recognizing that its stores needed improvement, 65 new outlets were opened, and 602 extended or modernized out of a 1970 total of 1,140 stores. Seventy-one stores were closed. Cash-flow problems led to the modernization programme being cut back – many stores only received a temporary facelift. By the early 1980s continuous low profitability had created a vicious circle of neglect for the organization. It could not be decided whether large city centre stores such as Birmingham, Nottingham or Bristol should be closed or modernized; their profitability was, at best, marginal, and experience elsewhere had shown that full modernization could not be justified by increased returns. Yet without modernization, Woolworth stores looked increasingly dowdy and failed to reflect the quality image which the firm hoped to achieve.

Woolworth undertook considerable market research into its problems. Based on the results, the company attempted to centralize control of in-store retail operations by the use of detailed store manuals laying down standard operating procedures for stores. Detailed space allocation formulae were adopted to determine shelf space and department location. Self-selection was introduced into Woolworth stores, with the customer paying at centrally situated cash points; this enabled staff numbers to be reduced.

However, the notion of selling anything and everything – the classic variety chain format – in 66 individual departments was still the basis of the business, with the difference that the removal of many of the staple lines had alienated many traditional shoppers without bringing in sufficient new customers. Company figures showed that the percentage of households shopping at Woolworth every week fell from 38 per cent in 1978 to 33 per cent in 1980. New concepts, whether successful or unsuccessful, were doing nothing to improve the performance of the core Woolworth business.

By the early 1980s Woolworth's results were getting worse not better. Geoffrey Rodgers, Woolworth's chairman, writing in the 1981 Company Report, blamed poor performance mainly upon high cost inflation combined with the sharp downturn produced by the economic recession.[5] The new policies being followed by the Board also affected profitability. These policies included several new concepts introduced in 1981 and the acquisition of B&Q.

New Woolworth retail formats launched in 1981 in an attempt to provide a significant repositioning of the company included Footlocker (shoes), Furnishing World (out-of-town discount furniture), and 21st Century Shopping. The 21st Century Shopping format was launched as a proposed new approach for the Woolworth core business. The earlier new formats remained – Woolco, which by now had 11 stores and Shoppers' World with 40 units.

The B&Q (Retail) business was purchased in 1981 to give Woolworth 39 stores in the rapidly growing do-it-yourself (DIY) and hardware business. Woolworth did not attempt to change the B&Q format or trading methods and left the existing management in place. This was followed in 1982 by the acquisition of the Dodge City chain, the early pioneer in the UK of out-of-town DIY trading, which with B&Q made F. W. Woolworth the owner of the largest DIY store group in the UK. The Board announced that the B&Q sales area was to be increased by 50 per cent over the following twelve months.

The announcements of new launches and acquisitions could not obscure the decline of the company between 1960 and 1980. In 1960, a little over twenty years previously, Woolworth had dominated the high street, being larger and more profitable than other variety chain stores such as Marks & Spencer. Then, Woolworth's turnover of £194 million (1960) had been 35 per cent higher than Marks & Spencer, and its net profitability as a percentage of sales was also greater. However, by 1980

Woolworth's turnover was 42 per cent smaller than that of Marks & Spencer, which itself had become a benchmark of retail effectiveness. Woolworth net profits (measured as a percentage of sales) had fallen to 5.9 per cent compared to Marks & Spencer's 10.2 per cent.

## 1982–84: THE PATERNOSTER TAKE-OVER

### The Paternoster Corporation

Paternoster Stores was formed in September 1982 as a consortium of several leading investment funds for the sole purpose of taking over F. W. Woolworth PLC. It was called together by Victor Blank, Head of Corporate Finance at Charterhouse, the merchant bank, whose address was Paternoster Square, London.

By November 1982 Woolworth's US parent company had agreed to sell its 52.68 per cent stake in the British operation. Paternoster installed a new management team, led by John Beckett, former head of British Sugar. Beckett brought with him from his previous company Geoff Mulcahy and Nigel Whittaker.

The purchase price was £310 million, only £100 million of which was equity capital. Up to that time this represented the most highly geared acquisition of a leading firm in the UK. Soon after the take-over, Paternoster changed its name to Woolworth Holdings PLC.

### The company in 1982

On assuming control, the new management team put in hand a thorough review of Woolworth operations. They found that the company they had taken over consisted of the following assets:

- One of the best-known names on the high street, visited by 14 million shoppers every week.
- 990 Woolworth stores with a selling space of 10 million square feet; only 90 stores were larger than 20,000 square feet sales area.
- Eleven Woolco out-of-town superstores, and other ventures including Shoppers' World and 21st Century Shopping.
- The DIY chain B&Q.
- The company's valuable freehold and leasehold property portfolio.

Geoffrey Mulcahy, the main architect of the company's recovery described the company as follows (1988):

> F. W. Woolworth had lost its way in the retailing scene of the 1970s, and became a misery stock for its ever hopeful shareholders. Yet it had one great strength: its huge property portfolio. It could never sink with the buoyancy provided by such assets, whose value was

twice the company's capitalization. But it was doing the next thing to sinking – it was floundering badly.[6]

The new management team did not have a detailed strategy when it took over Woolworth. The team gave itself seven years to get the new Woolworth into shape. Research in the early weeks and months after the take-over identified several key problems.

In 1982 Woolworth was still a classic 'variety chain' with a range of merchandise that was inconsistent and confused; pricing policies were often uncompetitive. John Beckett, who had replaced Geoffrey Rodgers as chairman, stated in the 1983 Annual Report that 'the company was confused about the market it was trying to meet and this resulted in a less than clear message to its customers'.[7] Stocks were £525 million at the time of the take-over compared with annual sales of £1,120 million; this was clearly excessive. There was little real management information at shop level apart from records of daily sales takings. Woolworth did not know which of its 70,000 product lines were selling well or badly. Control of stock was ineffective; breakdowns of stock-holding details at branches were only known at the half-yearly stocktakes. Hence buyers were unclear about what to order.

The view of the new team was that the previous business had attempted to develop new forms of retailing, but had failed to identify what it should sell in its Woolworth outlets. Two of the new trading ventures, Shoppers' World and 21st Century Shopping were unprofitable and seemed unlikely to ever become profitable.

The new management team was also concerned that the programme of property disposals, inherited from the previous board of directors, was not related to a clear business strategy or the needs of a well-managed property portfolio. It might well prove to be inconsistent with new trading policies developed for the company. As a result the programme was suspended.

The organization structure was thought to be top heavy and slow; communications were poor. The head office employed around 1,000 people to deal with co-ordinating the work of the regions, central policy, running central services (including personnel and mainframe computing) and corporate affairs.

In the past, control had been wrested away from central management and devolved to the regions. The eight regional managers were an alternative centre of power within Woolworth and were known as the 'Barons'. Regional managers were consummate politicians; their offices were larger and better equipped than the chairman or managing director of Woolworth. The next managing director or chairman would be chosen from the regional managers. Each regional office had about 350 staff, and these provided administration, merchandising, buying and other support services for over 120 stores in each region. The regional manager's control over operations within his region was much more complete than that of head office. Communications with head office were via the regions, and there were many examples of central initiatives being abandoned as a result of opposition from the Barons. The regions replicated national functional structures: at regional level there were also regional merchandise controllers, departmental managers and personnel managers.

The regions were subdivided into several districts. There were 72 districts in all, each with a district manager, supervising the store managers in his region. The company was dominated by buyers and the route for advancement for most store managers would come from progressing through the various positions at district and regional level, and gaining buying experience before joining head office. One executive commenting on this era suggested: 'Senior managers were all home grown and many of them started off sweeping the floors. They had to. No one recruited from outside could have understood the business.' There were poor links between buyers and store (sales) management, a feature of the many organizational tiers and compartments of the business. The main channel of communication between purchasing and stores was via regional department managers; the powerful buyers rarely met store managers directly.

Woolworth was lacking, too, in its management of the supply chain from manufacturer to retailer. Aggressive buying based on price (for which the company was renowned) had neglected to address the operational inefficiencies caused by an outdated distribution system. Three-quarters of its requirements were still being delivered direct to each store by the manufacturer with the heavy administrative, delivery costs and back-door reception costs that this implied. Control over suppliers' delivery dates was poor. Poor supply chain management meant that Woolworth was not routinely aware of overstocked items or merchandise shortages either on a company or an individual store basis.

The 1983 Chairman's Report, the first report from the new team headed by Beckett, listed the problems that analysis had shown to be most critical. Comment in the financial press was, however, unenthusiastic.

> City analysts and other retailers have seen little sign that the 'wonder of Woolworth' . . . is likely to re-emerge in the near future . . . In fact all that has really happened is that the new management has openly admitted the problems that exist.[8]

Although the FT reported[9] that the institutions which bought the group seemed happy to accept the seven-year target, others believed that the City's involvement in Woolworth was an each-way bet. If Beckett and his new team turned Woolworth around, then large capital gains would be made by the original members of Paternoster; if they failed, then the break-up value of the company would be well in excess of the original price paid, mainly because of Woolworth's substantial portfolio of freehold high street assets.

## 1983: the good housekeeping year

'It will take time; no one should expect a decline of a decade and more to be arrested and turned into success in the short term.'[10]

In the first full year after the take-over, the management team made many changes (which they described simply as 'good housekeeping') aimed at reducing waste, improving business control, and simplifying retail activity to place Woolworth on a surer footing. In the six months to July 1983 losses were cut from £18.4 million to £1.8 million. This was achieved mainly by lowering prices, by cutting stock levels (down £30 million) and eliminating slow-moving product lines.

A senior executive of the period commented:

When the new management came in, it was clear that they rejected the 1970s-style variety chain, but what the new Woolworth store would finally look like was a matter of great dispute. The previous management had done a lot with the operation. After Beckett and Co had, rightly, cut costs to the bone the question still had to be answered of what was wrong with Woolworth and what changes should be made to put it right.

The company was already the market leader in many different product areas and needed convincing before giving up any of this leadership in pursuit of a more specialist merchandise range. In order to discover what could be done with Woolworth several experiments in new store layout and merchandise mix were carried out. This was an attempt to provide the company with basic marketing information to be used in developing longer-term strategies for the Woolworth core business.

The use of better market research and more professional buying was intended to improve the standard of the Woolworth offer. It was felt that the previous management's prestige advertising campaigns using entertainment stars promised more than Woolworth could actually deliver and confused the store's image in the mind of the customer. The advertising account was moved to a new agency.

Although the company was dominated by buyers, the buying function was considered by Beckett and his team to be one of the weakest parts of the business. Half of the buyers were made redundant. Buying was centralized. A marketing department was set up for the first time in Woolworth which, with the buying teams, attempted to study more closely what Woolworth should be selling.

Three regional offices were closed down, a complete tier of management eliminated, and responsibility for merchandising, store development, and lay-out was centralized. The company was reorganized. Woolworth, along with B&Q, became a subsidiary of the holding company, Woolworth Holdings PLC. Overseas interests were grouped separately with the Republic of Ireland.

Woolworth Properties was established to hold all the properties owned or leased by the company. Operating companies, including the Woolworth chain, were charged the full market rent lease for the property they occupied. Although this approach had long been recommended, it was still fairly rare in retailing. The introduction of market rents showed that the real profits made from retailing were even lower than had been feared. Woolworth store managers, who had generally felt that their business was quite profitable, began to recognize that the performance of many of the shops had been dependent upon historically-based occupancy charges. Many other retailers have now adopted the Woolworth approach.

The new management team raised pay scales for staff, who were thought to be demotivated, and tried to cut down the proportion of staff time spent engaged in tasks other than serving customers. Communications with staff were improved to keep them informed about the new objectives for the organization.

There was concern that any changes carried out should preferably be inexpensive, cost-effective and provide a return in the shortest possible time. Thus when, in the following year, 1984, an attempt was made to brighten up the whole chain by repainting all stores, lowering counters and widening aisles, the programme was carried out by shop staff in six weeks and cost only £3 million. Operation Facelift, as it was called, had a significant effect on the Woolworth trading environment at a very low cost.

One of the first tasks of the new management team was to recruit a well-known retailer to the group. Beckett and his team were strong in the financial area, but lacked a retail specialist who could provide additional operational expertise and, perhaps, vision. The team was, of course, supported by senior executives with considerable retail experience. Attempts to recruit a well-known retailer failed. Changing Woolworth was seen as 'Mission Impossible'.

The Board decided to give up the search for a Woolworth 'super retailer' and get on themselves with the task of revitalizing the company. However, there was considerable concern about the company in the City. David Churchill reported in 1984 the unease felt in the City that

Geoffrey Mulcahy, the finance director, had been appointed chairman and chief executive of the Woolworth chain as well as taking responsibility for overseeing the whole group as group managing director.[11] Mulcahy had no previous retail background. Mulcahy saw his role, however, as co-ordinating the abilities of others and ensuring that the marketing plan was implemented – thus reducing the need for a retailer to be in charge.

By 1984 retail profit of Woolworth Holdings had risen to £28.4 million, and the *Guardian* was able to report the 'best dividend for years'.[12] Of this, however, B&Q's contribution rose to £19.3 million. Unease in the City about the slow pace of change at Woolworth enabled Dixons, the high street electrical chain, to mount a take-over bid for Woolworth in 1985. This was unsuccessful, largely because a majority of City institutions came to believe the case that Mulcahy and colleagues were making about the future of Woolworth.

## 1984–89: THE DEVELOPMENT OF NEW STRATEGIES FOR THE WOOLWORTH CORE BUSINESS

### Remodelling the core business

The 1984 Annual Report announced that the process of discussion and experimentation had enabled the company to decide its strategic options. 'There are core strengths which have been confused by all the clutter; we are focusing on these strengths and developing others.'[13]

Recognition of the fact that Woolworth stores generally looked out of date and were often dowdy can be seen in Operation Facelift. This exercise was only a short-term palliative and was recognized as such by the Board. However, in 1984, stores in Halifax and Goole were subject to extensive modernization and refitting. But although the modernized stores gained large rises in turnover, the profits produced from the new turnover could not justify the expenditure. The estimated costs of similar work (approximately £15–£20 per square foot) carried out on all stores in the Woolworth chain would have been around £150 million, which was 2.5 times greater than the annual profit from Woolworth. As a result the policy finally adopted was one with a lower cost and less risk. However, many multiples at this time such as BhS (British Home Stores), Next, Sears Group, Marks & Spencer, Burtons and Boots were paying up to £60 per square foot to obtain radical changes in the appearance and layout of their stores.

It was accepted that Woolworth could not continue as a traditional variety chain. Beckett and his colleagues had assessed the case for redirecting Woolworth in a radical new way by specializing in one product area such as clothing or do-it-yourself, and building up activities in related areas. This was the basic strategy of many of its successful high street competitors such as Boots and Marks & Spencer. Companies like Next were showing how substantial sales growth could be generated by focusing on comparatively small specialist markets. The relevance of this to Woolworth was that Next had been used to turn round the moribund Hepworth menswear clothing business. The Woolworth board rejected the radical strategy, however, in favour of developing a multi-purpose generalist store with a wide appeal.

In 1984 the company planned to remodel the chain, moving away from the generalist approach of sixty-six selling departments to concentrate on only six main market areas: do-it-yourself, clothing, leisure, convenience, daily provisions and housewares. These market areas would have been covered by twelve departments. However, linked with these main market areas, there were to be other departments which were included to generate extra customer traffic or to sell associated products, with the result that most stores would now have twenty-nine departments. This was far less than the sixty-six departments of the old Woolworth, but obviously an inadequate response to the need for a more concentrated approach to the business.

Although this approach was abandoned, its importance lay in a special project developed from it called 'Weekend and General'. Shops were designated as either weekend stores or general stores and concentrated on the needs of weekend or general shoppers. Extensive ranges of existing products which did not fit into the new concepts were eliminated from each chain and considerable work was done using market research and buyers to improve the ranges that remained. Careful experiments and store refurbishment were carried out in twenty stores to assess the effects of making changes in merchandise, ranges, layout and design and staff training. Fitch and Co., the largest UK retail design group, was used to work out the final retail concept. Mulcahy took personal control of implementation, which was directed by a team of specialists drawn from outside the day-to-day operational management of the business. This was to avoid resistance from inside the company.

The disparity of Woolworth store sizes led to the emergence of the two store formats with merchandise ranges related to store size. 'Weekend and General' (later rechristened 'Comparison and Convenience') was experimental, but Woolworth's experience of the concepts led to a further refinement of its strategy for the stores. The new programme was launched as Operation Focus.

Operation Focus was introduced in 1985 and involved the elimination of a further part of the existing range along with the radical improvement of the new areas of concentration. The market segment to target was identified as the young family shopper. The strategy of Operation Focus was for Woolworth to continue as a multi-purpose non-specialist store,

*Table 8.1* Woolworth product categories after Operation Focus (1987)

| | |
|---|---|
| Gifts and sweets | 29% |
| Kids | 19% |
| Home and Garden | 18% |
| Entertainment | 17% |
| Looks | 10% |
| Kitchenshop | 5% |
| Other | 2% |
| | 100% |

*Source*: *Verdict*

but to concentrate on key areas where Woolworth was already strong. Credibility was to be enhanced by ensuring that within every focus area, there would be broader ranges of better quality merchandise displayed in radically improved stores. The business was to concentrate (1985) on six specialist key areas:

1 *Kids*: mainly children's clothing, toys and books.
2 *Confectionery and gifts*: including Christmas confectionery and gifts.
3 *Entertainment*: records, tapes, CDs and videos.
4 *Kitchenshop*: crockery, glassware, ovenware, cutlery, kitchenware, etc.
5 *Home and garden*: including seeds, bulbs, peat and other garden requisites.
6 *Looks*: toiletries, cosmetics and fashion accessories aimed at the young.

The share of each focus area by 1987 (after Operation Focus had achieved its immediate goals) in Woolworth's total turnover is given in Table 8.1.

Every focus area represented a market sector where Woolworth was already strong. Toys, entertainment and confectionery were seen as representing 'family' leisure and entertainment requirements. Research showed the company that consumers perceived Woolworth to have a natural advantage in those areas. The company concentrated in areas not only where it had a large share of national trade (e.g. toys, chart records and entertainment and the confectionery market) but where it also believed it was able to be authoritative. However, although Kitchenshop was a traditional area of strength for Woolworth, only part of the previous product range was continued into the new section.

An emphasis upon higher quality products led Woolworth to introduce brands in a carefully controlled way. A policy of selling co-ordinated ranges of merchandise was adopted. Own brand ('Woolworth') was to compete against other 'surrogate' lines in the same product category. In kitchens and bathrooms, Monarch, Country Style and Design Plus were each developed to appeal to different customer interests. This also reflected the company's policy to stock several quality levels of product, ranging from the basic commodity to more upmarket ranges. The Ladybird clothing brand was purchased to help give the Woolworth infant clothing range a stronger identity (eventually being used for all young children's clothing) and in 1988 the Chad Valley trade mark was purchased to brand its toys.

The cost of implementing Operation Focus was £93 million. All stores were converted to the new format by July 1987, whilst the refurbishment of the chain was completed by 1988. Refurbishment, a necessary part of remodelling Woolworth, entailed shifting from the traditional Woolworth grid layout using standard counters to a more flexible layout using varying types of display fixtures. Most stores were given new exterior fascia; inside, the use of softer colours, carpeting in certain areas, different heights of fixtures, and the redesigned store layout which included browsing areas (e.g. for records) were intended to make the stores less hard, more welcoming, and to split them into different areas.

Operation Focus was a key strategic step. It involved moving Woolworth from a variety chain to a more focused multi-purpose store. Although this might have been seen to be a compromise between the existing variety chain concept with 15 million customers per week and the more radical 'specialist' option, it was still a risky strategy.

Departments were eliminated dealing in grocery, adult outerwear, electrical appliances, etc., giving up £250 million in sales, equivalent to 25 per cent of turnover. However, six marketing-directed departments replaced the previous 55 and the range of merchandise lines was reduced from over 50,000 to 20,000. This in turn could lead to greater clarity in other areas of the business including supply chain management (the number of suppliers was cut from 8,000 to 1,000) and company structure. The focus approach also involved new management structures, better communication, and improved staff motivation and training.

The approach meant that many Woolworth stores were now too large for the product range they were allowed to sell. A fully-merchandised store with all six focus areas needed to be only 25,000 square feet. Many Woolworth stores were much larger than this. The company found that stores of 15,000 square feet and above were less profitable and had lower sales per square feet than smaller stores. In addition, many Woolworth stores dating from the 1930s or 1950s were too large for the local trading area or were badly located. Woolworth closed twenty-seven stores in the first three years of Paternoster management, which, with the sale of the Woolco operation, cut Woolworth selling space by 1 million square feet. The selling space in many other of the larger Woolworth stores was partitioned off, let to other retailers, or transferred to other parts of the Group. In Milton Keynes for example, the Woolworth sales area fell from 30,000 square feet to 14,000, with the

*Table 8.2* Woolworth sales area (million square feet)

| | |
|---|---|
| 1982 | 10.0 |
| 1985/6 | 8.2 |
| 1986/7 | 7.4 |
| 1987/8 | 6.8 |
| 1988/9 | 6.4 |
| 1989/90 | 6.2 |
| 1990/1 | 6.2 |
| 1991/2 | 6.1 |
| 1992/3 | 6.1 |
| 1993/4 | 6.1 |
| 1994/5 | 5.9 |

*Source*: Company Report

surplus space being used to create seven new shops. The reduction of Woolworth selling space within its remaining stores accounted for a fall of 1.7 million square feet between 1983 and 1986.

As a result, the Woolworth trading area which had been 10 million square feet in 1982 had fallen to 7.1 million square feet by the completion of the Operation Focus programme in 1987, and the proportion of the chain's total floorspace accounted for by stores of under 15,000 square feet rose from 54 per cent (1985) to 65 per cent (1988). By 1988 Woolworth had no presence in the central areas of a number of principal towns such as Norwich, Bristol, Cheltenham and Birmingham. By 1991/2 the Woolworth high street sales area had fallen to 6.18 million square feet (Table 8.2).

Whilst very little detailed information exists to substantiate Woolworth's claims about the success of Operation Focus, analysis of the performance of the Woolworth chain store reveals profit per square foot (before deducting rental charges) rising from £3.8 in 1982/3 to £12.1 in 1987/8 after the chain had been fully converted to the new format.

## Staff policies and the Excellence Programme[14]

An attitude survey carried out in 1985 by Woolworth showed that management style in the stores was authoritarian. According to Don Rose, Woolworth personnel director,

> People were there to be directed, manipulated and disciplined . . . The existence of staff managers in shops, assistant store managers, and staff supervisors meant that the organization seemed to be geared around keeping the store manager separate from the sales staff and on a 'good' day a store manager might only meet one or two sales staff.

Managers regarded themselves as managers of systems, procedures, stock and property rather than people . . . Staff at the time lacked pride in themselves, their job and the company.

The penalties for non-performance could involve pay cuts, demotion to a smaller store, or the sack. The survey showed that shop floor staff lacked skills and were often afraid of customers. Their jobs were typically defined in terms of manual procedures with no reference to customer service.

The new company adopted more effective training methods. Operation Focus itself involved the retraining of staff so that they could deal with customers and understand the new company procedures. A more thorough grounding for new staff, a two-day induction course and the use of mentoring, following a lengthy recruitment interview gave new staff more self-confidence. New recruits were kept away from customers until they had built up the basic skills and self-confidence to face them.

By 1987 Woolworth had introduced a systematic approach to the induction, training and motivation of staff called the Excellence Programme. It was developed by Don Rose and was based on a series of training modules, designed to equip every member of staff with necessary sales skills and knowledge of one or more product areas. Whilst there was nothing unique about the various components of the training and motivation package, what was striking was the effective way in which these components had been blended together. A parallel scheme called Partners was introduced for warehouse staff.

Progress in training enabled staff who completed four core modules dealing with generic store skills and behaviour (and entitled 'Induction', 'Feelings', 'Till Skills', 'Secondary Selling') plus one module concerned with a merchandise product area, to obtain a personal staff badge with **EXCEL** printed on it. Work on the other focus areas earned the other letters in Excellence for the badge and up to five stars. Possession of the full badge showing completion of the course became a source of pride to staff and a matter of comment for many customers. The scheme involved all existing and new staff, both full time and part time. In 1987 the training was estimated to cost about £300 per person. Completion of the programme, which took about a year, brought a certificate and a lump sum equivalent to about 4 per cent of salary (more for part-time employees) plus a salary increment of 1.5–2.0 per cent for the next five years, subject to evidence of satisfactory involvement in the training programme. The company also introduced team briefing techniques and quality circles to improve communication and to encourage staff to identify and deal with issues that they faced. Staff elected delegates to represent them at the quarterly regional meetings which discuss company and staff issues and take forward ideas from the quality circles.

Research undertaken before and after the Excellence Programme showed a rise in consumer satisfaction. Weekly customer complaints had fallen by 21 per cent at the end of 1988 compared with 1987. Annual staff turnover for all staff had fallen from 60 per cent in 1985 to 30 per cent (1987). Saturday staff remain with the company three times as long as previously.

### Changes in organizational structure

The management career structure of the old F. W. Woolworth had many rungs to the ladder and was regarded as inflexible. Company policy was to promote from within, thus reinforcing the internal culture and denying the organization diversity of experience.

Within the stores, the posts of assistant store manager and that of staff manager were phased out, forcing store managers to become more directly responsible and simplifying communications with staff. Structural change was intended to reinforce the change in store managers' responsibility to include staff and customers. Operation Focus reduced the complexity of the business, enabling several tiers of hierarchy to be eliminated. The basic unit of management was seen as the merchandise team – one per focus area. Each focus team was headed by a section manager, who was regarded as first line management; the six section heads were all directly responsible to the store manager. Cutting out middle management at shop level resulted in a simplified structure with clearer responsibilities. This created many more promotional opportunities for shop floor staff who had little chance of significant promotion under the old system.

During 1984–88, regional and head office staff was further streamlined. Head office staff was cut to 400. The regional offices were closed, and much of their work was moved to head office assisted by new computerized central systems. Woolworth kept a handful of staff in six regions, mainly to deal with sales and personnel issues. Under the new organization, regional managers were responsible for around 120 stores each, and district managers (who reported to regional managers) controlled around fifteen stores.

### KINGFISHER PLC: 1989–95

Starting with the purchase of B&Q before the Paternoster take-over, the Woolworth Group had pursued a strategy of related diversification. By 1989 the Group had been restructured into a broad-based portfolio of retail brands, including B&Q, Superdrug, and Comet as well as Woolworth, mainly positioned at the volume end of the market, along with the property company Chartwell Land. The group was clearly more than Woolworth, hence in 1989 the Group changed its name to Kingfisher PLC and adopted a new corporate identity. Kingfisher was a distinctive

*Table 8.3* Main operating companies of Kingfisher PLC in 1994

| Company | Date acquired | Profit 1993/4 (£ million) | Turnover 1993/4 (£ million) |
|---|---|---|---|
| B&Q PLC | 1981 | 82.0 | 1,151 |
| Comet Group PLC | 1984 | 16.4 | 526 |
| Superdrug Stores PLC | 1987 | 31.5 | 617 |
| Woolworths PLC | | 74.5 | 1,314 |
| Darty SA, France | 1993 | 79.2 (8 months) | 694 (8 months) |
| Chartwell Land PLC | 1988 | 42.9 (investment income) | |

*Source*: Company Annual Report, 1994

name, the Group hoping that it 'gives all of our companies clearer identities, especially Woolworth which was so often confused with Woolworth Holdings'.[15] The main Group companies were all restructured as PLCs, Woolworth now becoming Woolworths PLC. The 1989 Annual Report emphasized, 'we will also be objective in analysing the success of our operations and be prepared, where appropriate, to withdraw from those areas not showing adequate rewards'.

The growing self-confidence of the Group led to its making a £461 million hostile take-over bid in December 1989 for the Dixons Group. This time Kingfisher was bidding for a leading retailer – one which had itself attempted to take over Woolworth Holdings three years previously. The proposed merger was turned down by the Monopolies and Mergers Commission (23 May 1990) on the grounds of potential adverse effects on competition in retailing electrical goods.

In 1993 the Group took its first steps towards becoming an international retailer with the acquisition of Darty, the largest consumer electrical goods retailer in France. This was followed in 1994 with a DM 20 million (£7.8 million) stake in the German office superstore company Maxi-Papier-Markt GmbH, in conjunction with Staples Inc., its US partner in the new chain of office superstores in the UK. By 1995 the Group's turnover had grown from £1.2 billion in 1982/3 to £4.5 billion. There were 2,300 shops and 75,000 employees.

Table 8.3 shows the main Kingfisher subsidiaries and activities. As well as the operations of the six main Kingfisher subsidiaries shown here, other Kingfisher retail operations in 1994 had 200 stores in total and included Charlie Brown's Autocentres, Entertainment UK, Staples and Titles. Further information about Kingfisher's operating companies can be found in Appendix 4.

**Corporate governance**

In common with an increasing number of British companies, the Board of Directors contained a majority of non-executive directors. A list of Board members is given in Appendix 5. The Group's Executive Committe, made up of executive directors and supported by a small team at the corporate centre, had responsibility for recommending and implementing Board policy. The Executive Committee worked with each of the operating companies to develop and implement Group policy. The Group's management style was explained by Geoff Mulcahy as follows:

> The small team at the centre works closely with the operating company managements to ensure that we are heading in the right direction, keeping our minds open all the time to make sure that we don't miss any opportunities to get a better return on our shareholders' money. A key part of our job is to see that the strategy is turned into successful results by building teams of top quality management in each of the companies. Only in that way can we expect to realize our ambition: to bring restless and vigilant professionalism to an industry that has in the past too often made do with gut instinct.

Or as a senior executive commented:

> Kingfisher is results-oriented and is obsessive about performance rather than interfering or preoccupied with the detailed implementation of policy. But if performance is less than that promised, then Kingfisher takes no hostages.

Below the level of Board members, the Management Committee comprised members of the Executive Committee plus the managing directors of the main operating companies (see Appendix 6). Its main functions included the following:

- Sharing information experience and best practice.
- Exploiting opportunities for collaboration between operating companies.
- The development, implementation and communication of Group strategy.

Each of the operating companies had a company board which was responsible for recommending strategy and for the effective day-to-day management of the business.

Two of the five executive directors, Mulcahy and Whittaker, had been members of the management team at the time of the Paternoster take-over, emphasizing the degree of continuity at the top of the company. The departure of Archie Norman to Asda (former finance director, one of only three executive directors and also one of the Paternoster managers) had left a gap at the top of the Group which took some time to be filled. In addition to the new finance director, the team was strengthened when Alan Smith joined as chief executive from Marks & Spencer in 1993. Geoff Mulcahy, formerly both chief executive and chairman, became executive chairman. Tim Breene joined the Board from United Distillers in 1994 as director of strategy and international development. The 1992 Board, which had only seven members (including three executives) had become twelve by 1994 (with five executives). The same trend was apparent in the Management Committee; the five executives of the old 1992 management group had become eleven by 1994.

**Further developments after 1989**

The period 1989–94 saw continued improvements in Woolworths' performance. Staff productivity and sales per square foot increased much faster than the rate of inflation, at the same time as market leadership was maintained in confectionery, entertainment and toys. By 1994 sales per square foot of selling space had risen by 7.1 per cent compound since 1989, whilst sales per employee rose by 11.7 per cent in 1994 alone. Woolworths was the largest advertiser of any mixed retail business (The Media Register figures) and was the largest mixed business in terms of sales or store numbers.

Woolworths stores returned to cities like Birmingham, Norwich and Bristol as part of a store development programme in the early 1990s. Further improvements in the Woolworths supply chain produced additional benefits; Woolworths became one of the leaders in quick response (or just-in-time distribution) with the introduction of a scheme to cut delivery lead times from five to ten weeks to five to ten days in its 'Kids' clothing operation. Ninety per cent of all Woolworths supplies came through central warehousing and the company was a pioneer of electronic data interchange (EDI) with its suppliers. However centrally-driven stock replenishment was only introduced to the company in 1993 (in Kidswear) and was to be extended to other product areas in 1994/5. Woolworths had also been slow to introduce electronic point of sale devices (EPoS) in stores, because it argued that it could get most of the benefits of EPoS using less sophisticated devices. It had made considerable progress with EPoS since 1993, but in April 1994 EPoS had been installed in only 200 stores. The whole chain was converted to EPoS by Christmas 1994, enabling Woolworths to obtain detailed and accurate information about the daily and weekly sales of each product line by store.

By 1994 the Excellence staff programme had been replaced by the Woolworths Customer First training scheme. This was supported by a new in-store customer service initiative called VIP, the aim being to train staff to deliver consistently high customer service standards, providing VIP treatment to every customer. Awards were given to staff who met customer service criteria.

In spite of its success in developing Woolworths and other group companies, Kingfisher had been less fortunate in developing new retail concepts. Although Titles (96 music and video stores) and Staples had both been successfully developed, and the new Music and Video Club (MVC) seemed to have considerable promise, many Woolworths-based formats proved disappointing. These included a two-year pilot of stand-alone Kidstores, Volume One book stores, a tight focus strategy for certain smaller Woolworths stores based on only three focus areas, a Thornton-style confectionery chain and Kids At Woolworths. However, within Woolworths careful experimentation with new product ranges had led to new pet care products, adult casualwear and denim clothing, and snacks and drinks being introduced to the main stores.

Although Operation Focus had been very successful in rescuing the business and providing a development strategy for Woolworths, by 1994 several investment analysts were suggesting that Woolworths stores and the retail offer looked boring. It was argued that Woolworths needed the infusion of new skills and flair, such as good housekeeping, attractive merchandising, and a better sense of in-store style associated with a group such as Marks & Spencer to boost the number of customers. The chain was known to be trialing several new formats and refurbished fifty-three stores in 1993 and modernized a further one hundred in 1994. Mair Baines, the Woolworths chief executive who had done so much to streamline the business, left early in 1994 and was replaced by Jonathan Weeks, Kingfisher's strategy and business development director. Weeks had originally been distribution and operations director of Woolworths before becoming managing director of Entertainment UK. New Woolworths appointments in 1994 included Saaed Hattea, merchandise director (ex-Marks & Spencer), and Bharat Patel, finance director (ex-Tesco) (see Appendix 8). Along with Alan Smith, Kingfisher chief executive, who was expected to be closely involved with Woolworths, these new appointments were thought likely to provide a greater sense of purpose for the chain.

## The retail environment

Over the period 1989–95 the retail environment in the UK changed markedly. During most of the 1980s retail growth had been linked to rising consumer spending and buoyant expectations. The beginning of the period saw the end of the so-called 'Thatcher' boom. Government action to correct an over-expansion of the UK economy and the high level of personal indebtedness gave rise to more difficult trading conditions for retail companies. Mulcahy had been one of the first retailers to recognize this change and in 1989 reaffirmed his belief that 'retailing in the Nineties will be about achieving the highest points of competitive advantage against the lowest cost base'.[16]

As a result the Group was much better prepared to manage during the recession of the late 1980s-early 1990s than many groups who had overextended themselves or realized too late how their trading environment was changing. Some of the best-known retailers of the 1980s such as Next, Burtons, Dixons, Storehouse and Sock Shop had to engage in substantial cost-reduction or turnaround strategies to survive. Whilst Kingfisher was not immune to the difficulties of trading through the recession with pre-tax profits falling from a peak of £294.7 million in 1989/90 to a low of £195.7 million in 1991/2 the Group remained financially sound.

Mulcahy's belief that there had been a permanent change in the retailing environment led the Group to adopt a new strategy. 'Everyday low pricing' (EDLP) emphasized the need to cut prices, recognizing the industry background of low sales growth and price inflation. The basis of the strategy was that where retail chains were able to control costs tightly, lower prices should increase sales volume and market share, generating improved profits and buying power. Once this outcome was achieved, prices could be cut further thereby leading to a virtuous circle.

Whilst the theory behind the strategy of EDLP was appealing, publication of Kingfisher's 1993/4 financial results raised questions about whether the strategy was working. Whilst pre-tax profits rose from £204.8 million to £309.3 million, this was largely due to the inclusion for the first time of a contribution from Darty (£79.2 million) and a smaller than expected interest charge. UK retailing profits had actually fallen, with Comet, Superdrug and Woolworths all recording reductions.

City analysts were divided about the future prospects of Kingfisher whilst it continued to pursue a strategy of EDLP. It was a strategy that was difficult to execute effectively without a dominant market position and the ability to increase productivity and reduce costs. '(EDLP) . . . is designed to attack the lower growth and more competitive environment of the 1990s . . . I am convinced the strategy is right and it is working.'[17]

Some analysts supported Mulcahy's position, arguing that it takes time for customers, especially where infrequent purchases are concerned, to appreciate the change in strategy and for sales to respond. The alternative view was that in the case of the high street chains, Woolworths and Superdrug, the benefits of the new strategy should already have been apparent.

*Table 8.4* Woolworths' sales performance by focus area*

| Product area | Percentage change first half 1993/4 | Percentage change second half 1993/4 | Percentage change 1993/4 |
|---|---|---|---|
| Home | + 11.6 | + 6.7 | + 8.6 |
| Entertainment | + 12.0 | − 1.6 | + 3.0 |
| Confectionery | + 9.4 | + 6.4 | + 7.7 |
| Kidswear | + 16.6 | + 14.0 | + 15.1 |
| Toys | + 12.8 | − 2.5 | + 2.1 |
| Overall | + 12.0 | + 3.8 | + 6.9 |

*Source*: Kingfisher Preliminary Results, 23 March 1994
*Note*: * All percentage changes are comparable year on year

## Performance of the Woolworths business

The questions being asked about Kingfisher Group strategy were highlighted by the performance of the Woolworths chain. Sales had risen by 6.9 per cent, but operating profit had declined by 4 per cent. The Street Values campaign (part of the EDLP strategy) had been a failure, but only 500 lines had been included. Across the five main product areas, sales performance had shown a marked variation (Table 8.4).

In 1993/4 Woolworths had experienced especial difficulties in the second half of the year in two of its product areas: Entertainment and Toys. Entertainment had been adversely affected by sales of video games. The Sega MegaDrive price war with Dixons (Christmas 1993) and overstocking of hardware and software items for this market, anticipating a rise in sales, had subsequently required price reductions across the range. Similarly for Toys, a strong first half performance led to over-optimistic buying for the second half. Again correction of the position resulted in significant mark-downs to clear stock. As a result of these difficulties, Mair Barnes, Woolworths' managing director, was replaced.

The performance of Entertainment and Toys also served to emphasize the continued dependence on highly seasonable merchandise with the majority of profits being earned in the second half of the year. Management were working to correct this imbalance (Table 8.5).

Woolworths' disappointing performance in 1993/4 broke a period of continuous increases in profit going back to 1985/6 (see Appendix 3). In addition to the specific problems encountered in Toys and Entertainment, analysts continued to question the applicability of EDLP to Woolworths. In 1995 Woolworths' profits fell by one-third, and a poor performance from the rest of the Kingfisher Group led to Geoff

*Table 8.5* Woolworths' operating profit 1994

|  | *Operating profit (£ million)* |
| --- | --- |
| Half year to 31 July 1993 | 2.1 |
| Half year to 29 January 1994 | 72.4 |
| Full year to 29 January 1994 | 74.5 |

Mulcahy taking over once more as the chief executive and the departure from the Group of Alan Smith, James Kerr-Muir, Nigel Whittaker and Tim Breene as part of corporate restructuring. For the first time, the heads of the Group's operating divisions were made members of the main board. Sir Geoffrey commented, 'What we are doing is focusing management more clearly and making those responsible for running the businesses more accountable.'[18]

Woolworths itself was a unique retail format: there was no other store with a comparable range of products. Whilst this was certainly a strength, it also meant that Woolworths needed a strong relevant trading identity to compete with a range of other specialist and non-specialist formats, including discount companies such as Argos and Poundstretcher, as well as Boots, W. H. Smith, Our Price, Toys 'R' Us, BhS and Littlewoods. Appendix 2 lists the main competitors to Woolworths in different product areas.

Kingfisher's objective for the second part of the 1990s was as follows:

We aim to be world-class retailers with market-leading businesses that meet customers' needs by offering reliable and consistent value . . . [Kingfisher's] aim is to provide outstanding financial performance for its shareholders, above-average rewards for its employees, opportunities for its suppliers and to make a positive impact in the community.[19]

The question facing Woolworths' management was how they could achieve this objective for the chain in the next few years. Many of the Kingfisher Group's assets had been used to diversify away from the core business. Should the Group have spent more on developing Woolworths itself?

## NOTES

1 © J. Bamfield and D. Williams 1995.
  This case study has been written as a basis for class discussion rather than to illustrate effective or ineffective managerial or administrative behaviour.
  The assistance of senior executives from Woolworths PLC and Kingfisher PLC is gratefully acknowledged. The case was developed from material

produced in conjunction with the Consortium of Retail Teaching companies (CORTCO), by Professor Joshua Bamfield (Nene College, Northampton), Liz Barnes (Staffordshire University), Bob Halsall (London Institute), Joanna Gaukroger (Further Education Funding Council), Charles Moss (University of Sunderland), Stuart West (Oxford Brookes University), John Willans (Northumbria University), and David Williams (Bournemouth University).

2 *The Times*, 28 March 1991.
3 A *variety chain store* carries an extensive assortment of relatively inexpensive items, primarily non-food, in large functional stores with one or two floors.
4 John Davies, 'How Woolies managed to stop the rot', *Observer*, 10 April 1972.
5 Chairman's Statement, Company Report and Accounts, 1981.
6 Geoffrey Mulcahy, 'Woolworth Holdings', in Rebecca Nelson with David Clutterbuck (eds) *Turnaround: How Twenty Well-known Companies Came Back From the Brink* (London: McGraw Hill, 1988).
7 Chairman's Statement, Company Annual Report, 1983.
8 *Financial Times*, 26 April 1983.
9 David Churchill, *Financial Times*, 5 October 1983.
10 John Beckett, 1983 Company Report.
11 David Churchill, *Financial Times*, 30 August 1984.
12 Mary Brasier, *Guardian*, 23 March 1984.
13 Chairman's Statement, Company Report, 1984.
14 This section draws on the comprehensive article by Don Rose 'Woolworth's drive for excellence', *Long Range Planning*, 22(1), 1989: 28–31.
15 *A New Name, A New Identity*, Kingfisher PLC, 1989.
16 *Sunday Correspondent*, 10 December 1989 and *The Independent*, 8 December 1989.
17 Peggy Hollinger, 'Darty helps Kingfisher to £309m', *Financial Times*, 24 March 1994.
18 Patrick Donovan, 'Kingfisher chief sacrifices his oldest ally', *Guardian*, 14 February 1995.
19 *Kingfisher PLC Annual Report and Accounts 1994* and *Profile of the Group*, Kingfisher PLC, 14 June 1994.

## APPENDIX 1: CHRONOLOGY OF WOOLWORTH OPERATIONS

1909  First British F. W. Woolworth store opened
1931  UK company floated on the Stock Market, 52 per cent being retained by the American parent
1969  A succession of poor results leads to the formation of shareholder Ginger Group
1970  First Woolco hypermarket opened
1975  Shoppers' World chain established
1981  B&Q DIY chain acquired
1982  Dodge City chain purchased. Paternoster Consortium formed, led by John Beckett, and buys US parent's controlling shareholding. John Beckett becomes new chairman and Geoff Mulcahy group managing director. Company name changed to Woolworth Holdings.
1983  'Good housekeeping' reforms implemented at Woolworth; rapid expansion of B&Q. Woolworth Properties formed to hold Woolworth Group Property.
1984  Acquisition of the Comet chain
1985  Launch of Operation Focus to reposition the Woolworth core business
1986  Dixons' take-over bid for Woolworth Holdings unsuccessful. Sir Kenneth Durham takes over as new group chairman, Geoff Mulcahy becoming chief executive
1987  Acquisition of Superdrug Stores PLC. Purchase of Charlie Brown's Autocentres – merged with B&Q autocentres. Ultimate chain acquired and merged with Comet. Record Merchandisers purchased from EMI and renamed Entertainment UK.
1988  Creation of Chartwell Land; purchase of Tip Top and Share Drug, integrated into Superdrug
1989  Name of holding company changed to Kingfisher; subsidiaries become PLCs. Medicare chain acquired and integrated with Superdrug. Take-over bid launched for Dixons. Lasky Electrical chain acquired.
1990  Monopolies and Mergers Commission oppose Kingfisher's bid for Dixons. Mulcahy becomes Kingfisher chairman and chief executive.
1991  Kingfisher reports best ever retail results with strong performance from revitalized Woolworths. Titles video chain established.
1992  'Value' campaigns start in Comet, Superdrug, Woolworths and B&Q. Agreement to develop Staples superstores in the UK reached with Staples Inc. (USA).
1993  'Every Day Low Prices' campaigns start. First UK Staples store. Largest French electrical goods retailer, Darty SA, acquired. Joint venture with Staples Inc. to run office superstores in Germany through acquisition of Maxi-Papier-Markt GmbH (Germany).
1994  Woolworths' MD resigns. Kingfisher UK retail profits fall, leading to criticism by the City of company strategy.
1995  Profits warning in January, leads to resignations of main board executive directors. Geoffrey Mulcahy reverts to being Group chief executive.

## APPENDIX 2: MAIN COMPETITION TO WOOLWORTHS CHAIN

| Product | Main competition | Comment |
|---|---|---|
| Toys | Toys 'R' Us<br>Argos<br>Children's World | A highly fragmented market: key area for Woolworth to expand. Note increased importance of computer games. |
| Entertainment | Boots<br>Our Price<br>W. H. Smith/Virgin, HMV<br>Ritz, video shops | High sales growth is being maintained by Woolworths |
| Kitchen | Boots Cookshop<br>Multiple retailers<br>M. & S. BhS, Littlewoods<br>Department stores<br>Argos, Habitat | Woolworths' gross margins in this area have shown great improvement, but there is strong competition |
| Confectionery and gifts | Supercigs<br>Martins; NSS/Forbuoys<br>Supermarket groups<br>J. W. Thornton, Clintons<br>Convenience stores/CTNs<br>Petrol Stations | Woolworths has a leading presence in this market |
| Looks | Boots<br>Miss Selfridge<br>Department stores<br>Signet | A weaker area for Woolworths |
| Home and Garden | Wyvale, Nottcuts<br>Fads<br>Independent garden centres<br>DIY superstores, e.g. B&Q<br>Department stores<br>Wilkinsons | A weaker area for Woolworths |
| Kids (children's clothing) | Adams, Peacocks and discount chains<br>Children's World<br>M. & S., BhS, Littlewoods<br>Department stores<br>Mothercare<br>C & A | Woolworths is doing better with the under 7 market than with the 8–12 market where strong competition is being encountered |

# APPENDIX 3: SUMMARY FINANCIAL STATEMENTS OF WOOLWORTH HOLDING PLC AND SUBSIDIARY COMPANIES (NOW KINGFISHER PLC.)

Table 8.6 Consolidated profit and loss account (£ million)

| Year | 82/83 | 83/84 | 84/85 | 85/86 | 86/87 | 87/88 | 88/89 | 89/90 | 90/91 | 91/92 | 92/93 | 93/94 |
|---|---|---|---|---|---|---|---|---|---|---|---|---|
| Turnover | 1124.0 | 1268.6 | 1661.1 | 1757.0 | 1828.6 | 2172.0 | 2660.4 | 2910.0 | 3117.1 | 3388.8 | 3547.9 | 4479.0 |
| Retail profit | | | | | | | | | | | | |
| B&Q | 9.1 | 19.3 | 28.6 | 34.2 | 45.5 | 60.2 | 76.4 | 87.1 | 95.7 | 90.3 | 81.1 | 82.0 |
| Comet | — | — | 14.9 | 13.7 | 17.4 | 20.1 | 25.5 | 17.9 | 7.6 | 9.1 | 17.7 | 16.4 |
| Darty | — | — | — | — | — | — | — | — | — | — | — | 79.2 |
| Superdrug | — | — | — | — | — | 13.0 | 22.2 | 29.7 | 34.5 | 34.6 | 34.8 | 31.5 |
| Woolworths | 1.3 | 7.6 | (5.1) | 17.6 | 38.7 | 45.1 | 50.2 | 55.6 | 63.0 | 71.4 | 77.8 | 74.5 |
| Other | 2.0 | 1.5 | (0.6) | (0.6) | (4.6) | (7.4) | (8.5) | (9.3) | (9.8) | 0.0 | 3.0 | 6.8 |
| Total retail profits | 12.4 | 28.4 | 37.8 | 64.9 | 97.0 | 131.0 | 165.8 | 181.0 | 191.0 | 190.7[2] | 214.4 | 290.4 |
| Property Income | 34.3 | 33.3 | 48.5 | 45.1 | 49.4 | 52.4 | 59.8 | 62.4 | 54.4 | 39.1 | 8.1 | 43.0 |
| Profit before interest[3] | 46.7 | 61.7 | 86.3 | 110.0 | 146.4 | 183.4 | 225.6 | 243.4 | 245.4 | 207.5 | 205.5 | 316.9 |
| Net interest payable | 40.6 | 32.3 | 29.5 | 28.7 | 31.1 | 36.2 | 38.7 | 36.0 | 30.1 | (11.8) | (0.7) | (7.6) |
| Profits before tax | 6.1 | 56.5 | 105.8 | 81.3 | 115.3 | 177.0 | 224.1 | 294.7 | 252.5 | 195.7 | 204.8 | 309.8 |
| Taxation | 19.9 | 1.5 | 2.1 | 16.2 | 30.5 | 37.6 | 51.8 | 63.3 | 63.7 | 61.5 | 56.9 | 77.4 |
| Extraordinary items | — | 1.6 | — | 29.1 | 16.0 | — | 3.4 | 5.8 | 4.4 | — | — | — |
| Profits for the financial year | 26.0 | 53.4 | 85.8 | 36.0 | 68.8 | 139.4 | 168.9 | 225.6 | 184.4 | 134.2 | 147.9 | 231.9 |

Source: Company Accounts

Notes: 1 Exceptional items have not been separately shown due to changes in the reporting standards in the UK affecting their position on the face of the profit and loss account.

2 Includes restructuring provision of £14.7 million.

3 Other non-retail profits/losses are not separately shown, but included in this summary figure.

# APPENDIX 3 (continued)

## Table 8.7 Consolidated statement of source and application of funds (£ million)

| Year | 83/84 | 84/85 | 85/86 | 86/87 | 87/88 | 88/89 | 89/90 | 90/91 |
|---|---|---|---|---|---|---|---|---|
| **Source of funds arising from trading** | | | | | | | | |
| Profit on ordinary activities before taxation | 29.4 | 56.8[1] | 81.3 | 115.3 | 177.0 | 224.1 | 294.7 | 252.5 |
| Property realization profits | — | — | (2.7) | (6.2) | (6.4) | (4.1) | (87.3) | (37.2) |
| Profits on sale and leaseback of properties | — | — | — | — | (35.2) | (44.7) | — | — |
| Exceptional cash items | (15.8) | (1.4) | — | — | — | — | — | (0.4)[2] |
| Depreciation | 15.9 | 19.3 | 21.2 | 28.3 | 41.3 | 54.4 | 54.3 | 62.0 |
| Total | 29.5 | 74.7 | 99.8 | 137.4 | 176.7 | 229.7 | 261.7 | 276.9 |
| **Funds from other sources** | | | | | | | | |
| Disposal of fixed assets | 59.2 | 95.8 | 12.8 | 44.2 | 102.0 | 141.9 | 208.6 | 285.9 |
| Shares issued | — | 6.6 | 12.1 | 3.7 | 253.4 | 5.7 | 9.0 | 31.6 |
| Other | (21.0) | 35.2 | 14.6 | 1.1 | — | — | — | — |
| **Total sources of funds** | **67.7** | **212.3** | **139.3** | **186.4** | **532.1** | **377.3** | **479.3** | **594.4** |
| **Application of funds** | | | | | | | | |
| Increase/(decrease) in working capital | | | | | | | | |
| Stock | (47.0) | 38.9 | 16.9 | 48.8 | 37.9 | (7.7) | 20.2 | 45.1 |
| Debtors | 5.5 | 10.1 | (4.3) | 13.1 | 23.2 | (12.2) | 33.1 | (7.8) |
| Creditors | (23.1) | (0.9) | (29.8) | (41.8) | (12.9) | (33.4) | (7.7) | 9.1 |
| | (64.6) | 48.1 | (17.2) | 20.1 | 48.2 | (53.3) | 45.6 | 46.4 |
| Other applications | | | | | | | | |
| Purchase of subsidiaries | — | 128.9 | 0.7 | 6.2 | 282.7 | 46.7 | 11.8 | 35.3 |
| Investment in associates | — | — | — | — | — | — | — | 40.5 |
| Purchase of tangible assets | 33.4 | 77.0 | 123.5 | 175.9 | 196.2 | 241.5 | 225.1 | 325.4 |
| Extraordinary items | 3.2 | — | 4.9 | 18.0 | — | 4.8 | 5.8 | 4.9 |
| Tax paid | 0.6 | 8.4 | 13.0 | 20.3 | 18.9 | 35.7 | 47.8 | 70.3 |
| Dividends paid | 1.3 | 7.0 | 15.0 | 21.6 | 32.9 | 40.1 | 47.3 | 52.0 |
| Other | — | — | 3.1 | — | — | — | — | — |
| **Total application of funds** | **(26.1)** | **269.4** | **143.0** | **262.1** | **578.9** | **315.5** | **383.4** | **574.8** |
| **Decrease/increase in borrowings** | **(93.8)** | **57.1** | **3.7** | **75.7** | **46.8** | **(61.8)** | **(95.9)** | **(19.6)** |

*Source:* Company Accounts
*Notes:* 1 Exclusive of exceptional items.
2 Retained by associated undertakings.

Changes in Financial Reporting Standards in the UK
In the early 1990s significant changes took place to the financial reporting standards in the UK. In particular both the source and application of funds statement and the profit and loss account were remodelled. As a result of these changes the source and application of funds statement was replaced by a cash flow statement. Consequently, for the period covered by the case study discontinuities in the presentation of financial data have occurred.

**APPENDIX 3** (*continued*)

*Table 8.8* Consolidated cash flow statement (£ million)

| Year | 91/92 | 92/93 | 93/94 |
|---|---|---|---|
| **Net cash flow from operating activities** | 239.8 | 237.1 | 371.1 |
| **Returns on investment and servicing of finance** | | | |
| Interest received | 26.5 | 32.8 | 43.6 |
| Interest paid | (46.2) | (36.0) | (62.5) |
| Dividends received from associated company | — | — | 1.0 |
| Dividends | (57.8) | (64.6) | (83.5) |
| **Net cash flow from returns on investment and servicing of finance** | (77.5) | (67.8) | (101.4) |
| **Taxation** | | | |
| Corporation tax paid | (64.9) | (47.3) | (46.5) |
| **Investing activities** | | | |
| Purchase of subsidiary undertaking (net of cash and cash equivalents acquired) | — | — | (124.8) |
| Payments to acquire tangible assets | (80.3) | (165.1) | (179.6) |
| Payments for additions to investment | (6.0) | (4.0) | (7.7) |
| Net purchase of short-term investments | (3.1) | (36.9) | (10.7) |
| Receipts from the sale of tangible fixed assets | 34.7 | 25.5 | 52.5 |
| **Net cash outflow from investing activities** | (54.7) | (180.5) | (270.3) |
| **Net cash (outflow)/inflow before financing** | 42.7 | (58.5) | (47.1) |
| **Financing** · | | | |
| Issue of ordinary shares | 17.7 | 9.8 | 320.6 |
| Net sale (purchase) of short-term investments | (36.8) | 14.1 | 16.8 |
| Net repayment of loans | (6.3) | (48.2) | (356.1) |
| **Net cash outflow from financing** | (25.4) | (24.3) | (18.7) |
| **(Decrease)/increase in cash and cash equivalents** | 17.3 | (82.8) | (65.8) |

*Source:* Company Accounts

# APPENDIX 3 (*continued*)

## Table 8.9 Consolidated balance sheet (£ million)

| Year | 82/83 | 83/84 | 84/85 | 85/86 | 86/87 | 87/88 | 88/89 | 89/90 | 90/91 | 91/92 | 92/93 | 93/94 |
|---|---|---|---|---|---|---|---|---|---|---|---|---|
| **Fixed Assets** | | | | | | | | | | | | |
| Tangible Assets | 549.1 | 663.3 | 685.2 | 806.0 | 971.5 | 1096.3 | 1225.0 | 1213.8 | 1120.4 | 913.2 | 992.4 | 1249.2 |
| Investments | 5.9 | 5.8 | 4.3 | 3.3 | 1.2 | — | — | — | 40.9 | 43.2 | 37.2 | 44.9 |
|  | 555.0 | 669.1 | 689.5 | 809.3 | 972.7 | 1096.3 | 1225.0 | 1213.8 | 1161.3 | 956.4 | 1029.6 | 1294.1 |
| **Current Assets** | | | | | | | | | | | | |
| Development work in progress | — | — | — | — | — | — | — | — | — | 134.3 | 59.3 | 37.3 |
| Stocks | 208.7 | 161.7 | 262.7 | 279.6 | 335.1 | 422.9 | 431.0 | 463.9 | 509.0 | 505. | 571.7 | 734.0 |
| Debtors | 70.7 | 97.0 | 84.2 | 65.1 | 84.6 | 126.2 | 128.8 | 172.0 | 165.0 | 231.9 | 254.7 | 390.9 |
| Investments | — | — | — | — | — | — | — | — | — | 128.7 | 153.9 | 149.9 |
| Cash at bank and in hand | 28.1 | 32.8 | 47.3 | 70.9 | 42.7 | 61.5 | 76.0 | 102.2 | 159.2 | 210.0 | 161.7 | 236.6 |
|  | 307.5 | 291.5 | 394.2 | 415.6 | 462.4 | 610.6 | 635.8 | 738.1 | 833.2 | 1209.9 | 1201.3 | 1548.7 |
| **Creditors: amounts falling due within one year** | (278.8) | (290.7) | (373.4) | (417.6) | (518.4) | (658.3) | (669.4) | (691.6) | (651.2) | (851.0) | (940.2) | (1283.9) |
| Net current assets | 28.7 | 0.8 | 20.8 | (2.0) | (56.0) | (47.7) | (33.6) | 46.5 | 182.0 | 358.9 | 261.1 | 264.8 |
| Total assets less current liabilities | 583.7 | 669.9 | 710.3 | 807.3 | 916.7 | 1048.6 | 1191.4 | 1260.3 | 1343.3 | 1315.3 | 1290.7 | 1558.9 |
| **Creditors** | | | | | | | | | | | | |
| Amounts falling due after more than one year | (207.8) | (132.7) | (193.9) | (243.5) | (249.6) | (295.8) | (328.9) | (298.5) | (368.7) | (233.0) | (132.3) | (465.8) |
| **Provision for liabilities and charges** | (3.2) | (3.8) | 4.7 | (13.2) | 0.7 | — | 2.4 | — | — | — | (0.6) | (0.9) |
|  | 372.7 | 533.4 | 521.1 | 577.0 | 666.4 | 752.8 | 860.1 | 961.8 | 974.6 | 1082.3 | 1157.8 | 1092.2 |
| **Capital and reserves** | | | | | | | | | | | | |
| Called up share capital | 34.2 | 34.2 | 40.5 | 89.1 | 90.9 | 106.9 | 108.9 | 110.0 | 113.5 | 120.8 | 124.7 | 166.4 |
| Share premium account | 55.0 | 55.0 | 54.2 | 14.6 | 16.5 | 17.9 | 19.7 | 27.6 | 55.7 | 117.2 | 150.3 | 189.9 |
| Revaluation reserve | 249.3 | 363.2 | 310.9 | 341.9 | 394.8 | 375.0 | 400.9 | 350.6 | 207.6 | 126.3 | 85.3 | 113.9 |
| Other reserve | — | — | — | — | — | — | — | — | — | 19.8 | 19.8 | — |
| Profit and loss account | 34.2 | 81.0 | 115.5 | 131.9 | 164.2 | 253.0 | 330.6 | 473.6 | 597.8 | 698.2 | 777.7 | 620.9 |
| Equity shareholders' funds | 372.7 | 533.4 | 521.1 | 577.0 | 666.4 | 752.8 | 860.1 | 961.8 | 974.6 | 1082.3 | 1157.8 | 1091.1 |
| Equity minority interests | — | — | — | — | — | — | — | — | — | — | — | 1.1 |
|  | 372.7 | 533.4 | 521.1 | 577.0 | 666.4 | 752.8 | 860.1 | 961.8 | 974.6 | 1082.3 | 1157.8 | 1092.2 |

*Source:* Company Accounts

**APPENDIX 3** *(continued)*
*Table 8.10* Retail price index

| Year | All items other than seasonal foods | Inflation index |
|------|--------------------------------------|-----------------|
| 1982 | 100.0 | 1.000 |
| 1983 | 104.7 | 0.955 |
| 1984 | 109.7 | 0.911 |
| 1985 | 116.5 | 0.858 |
| 1986 | 120.4 | 0.830 |
| 1987 | 125.4 | 0.797 |
| 1988 | 131.6 | 0.760 |
| 1989 | 142.1 | 0.704 |
| 1990 | 155.5 | 0.643 |
| 1991 | 164.6 | 0.608 |
| 1992 | 171.1 | 0.585 |
| 1993 | 173.9 | 0.575 |

*Source:* CSO

## APPENDIX 4: KINGFISHER SUBSIDIARIES IN THE MID-1990s

| | |
|---|---|
| B&Q | *DIY goods for homes, businesses, cars and gardens.*<br>279 out-of-town do-it-yourself superstores. Acquired in 1982. Dodge City group integrated with B&Q in 1983. Total share of national DIY market 15.1 per cent. |
| COMET | *Electrical goods for home use.*<br>231 electrical stores, more than one-half of which are now out-of-town. The chain was acquired in 1984. |
| DARTY SA | *The leading specialist electrical retailer in France.*<br>137 outlets with 1.73 million square feet sales area. Acquired in 1993 |
| SUPERDRUG | *Toiletries, beauty aids, vitamins, over-the-counter medicines, snacks and household products.*<br>Acquired in 1987, Superdrug has 696 stores, making it the largest high street drugstore chain. A number of smaller chains have also been acquired and integrated into the group. |
| WOOLWORTHS | *Children's clothes and toys, entertainment, confectionery and items for the garden and home, including gifts and stationery.*<br>With 788 stores in the UK, this is Kingfisher's core business. |
| CHARTWELL LAND | Kingfisher property interests are vested in Chartwell Land, launched in 1988. It is now one of the largest UK property companies. |
| CHARLIE BROWNS AUTOCENTRES | *Car parts and accessories, combined with fast fit service.*<br>Acquired in 1987, with 50 outlets. |
| ENTERTAINMENT UK Ltd | *Buyer and distributor of compact discs, cassettes, videos and computer games.* |
| STAPLES | *Superstores selling a range of office equipment, furniture and supplies.*<br>Five stores in 1994. Partnership with Staples Inc. (USA). |
| TIME | *Retail credit card service to Kingfisher retailers.* |
| TITLES | *Videos for rental or sale.* |

Group sales have grown from £1.1 million (1982/3) to £4.5 billion in 1995

*Source*: Company information

## APPENDIX 5: KINGFISHER BOARD OF DIRECTORS 1994

| | |
|---|---|
| Sir Geoffrey Mulcahy | **Executive chairman** since March 1993. Formerly chairman and chief executive. Aged 52. A member of the original Paternoster team. Former finance director of British Sugar PLC and Norton Abrasives. Graduate of Manchester University and a Harvard MBA. |
| Alan Smith | **Chief executive** since April 1993. Previously a director of Marks & Spencer. Graduate of Edinburgh University. Aged 53. |
| James Kerr-Muir | **Group finance director** since April 1992. Aged 53. Former managing director of Tate and Lyle (UK division) and vice-president of Redpath Industries, Toronto. Graduate of Oxford University and a Harvard MBA. |
| Nigel Whittaker | **Corporate affairs director.** Aged 45. A member of the original Paternoster team. Former general counsel for British Sugar PLC. Graduate of Cambridge University and Yale Law School. |
| Tim Breene | **Strategy and international development director** from April 1994. Former marketing director for Global Operations of United Distillers, with experience in Unilever, Mars, McKinsey and WCRS Group. Aged 44. |
| | **Non-Executive Directors** |
| Sir Nigel Mobbs | Deputy chairman, chairman of Audit Committee. Aged 56. Non-executive director since 1982. |
| Lady Howe | Aged 62. Non-executive since 1986. |
| Michael Hollingbery | Aged 60. Former chairman of Comet prior to its acquisition by Kingfisher. |
| Ronald Goldstein | Aged 57. Former joint chairman and co-founder of Superdrug. |
| Peter Hardy | Aged 55. Former MD Merchant Banking of S. G. Warburg PLC. |
| John Bullock | Aged 60. Chairman of Coopers and Lybrand until 1992. |
| Bernard Thiolin | Aged 65. President of Banque Colbert and president of Credit Lyonnais in Belgium and Portugal. Board member of Financiere Darty SA and Eurotunnel. Joined Kingfisher board after merger with Darty SA. |

## APPENDIX 6: KINGFISHER MANAGEMENT GROUP 1994

| | |
|---|---|
| Richard Cowan | Aged 47. Managing director, Entertainment UK. Appointed February 1994, formerly operations manager. Degree in Economics. |
| Philippe Frances | Aged 53. Chief executive of KERL (Kingfisher Electrical Retailing Ltd), Chief executive of Darty. Appointed in 1986, formerly general manager and development director. Joined Darty in 1973. |
| David Jobson | Director of international development, Kingfisher Group. Appointed in 1994, formerly B&Q buying director. |
| Alan Jones | Aged 53. Managing director, Chartwell Land PLC. Appointed in 1987, previously property manager of B&Q and property executive at Woolworth. FICS. |
| Roger Jones | Aged 56. Managing director of Superdrug Stores PLC. Appointed in June 1992, previously property and service director of Woolworths PLC. Joined Woolworths in 1954. |
| Jean-Noel Labroue | Aged 46. General manager, Darty Ile-de-France since 1990. Joined Darty in 1979, previously with Société Intertechnique and CNRS-CEA, the atomic energy authority. MSc from NorthWest University, Chicago. |
| Roger Paffard | Aged 42. Managing director, Staples UK. Previously managing director of Sharps Bedrooms Ltd. Graduate of Oxford University. |
| Alan Smith | Aged 47. Managing director of B&Q PLC. Joined company as managing director of Superdrug Stores PLC. A former MD of Victoria Wine. BA from Leeds University. |
| Tony Ward | Aged 44. Director of human resources, Kingfisher PLC. Previous HR posts at Grand Metropolitan. University of Leeds. |
| Jonathan Weeks | Aged 55. Managing director of Woolworths PLC since February 1994, previously managing director of Entertainment UK and strategy and business development director at Kingfisher. Joined Group in 1984 as director of distribution at Woolworth. |
| Brent Wilkinson | Aged 43. Managing director, Comet Group PLC. Joined Comet in 1985, previously with Dixons. Before 1986, he was an executive at Dixons; became marketing and buying director of Comet in 1986. BSc from Sheffield University. |

## APPENDIX 7: F. W. WOOLWORTH PROFITS 1962–81
*Table 8.11* Profits before tax (1962–81)

| Year | Profit before tax (£ million) |
|------|-------------------------------|
| 1962 | 37.68 |
| 1963 | 39.92 |
| 1964 | 40.47 |
| 1965 | 42.30 |
| 1966 | 41.85 |
| 1967 | 39.95 |
| 1968 | 42.88 |
| 1969 | 40.72 |
| * change in series | |
| 1970 | 34.56 |
| 1971 | 37.27 |
| 1972 | 40.63 |
| 1973 | 43.31 |
| 1974 | 30.65 |
| 1975 | 36.25 |
| 1976 | 38.19 |
| 1977 | 40.61 |
| 1978 | 46.78 |
| 1979 | 53.10 |
| 1980 | 57.27 |
| 1981 | 39.26 |

*Source:* Company reports

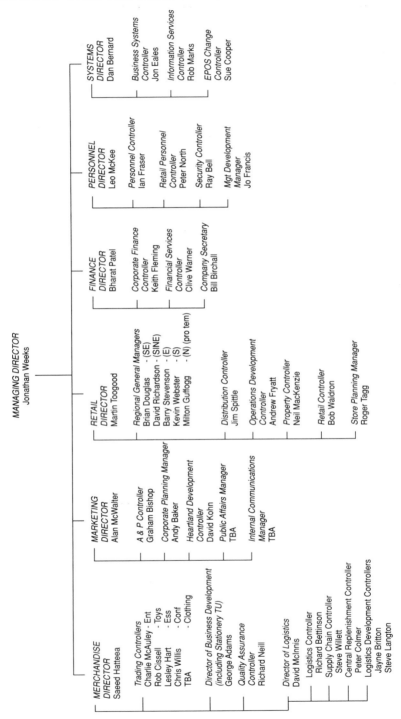

*Figure 8.1* Organizational structure

# Chapter 9

# Rejuvenation of Edwards High Vacuum[1]

## *John Stopford*

## EDITORS' OVERVIEW

Edwards operates in the technologically advanced market for high vacuum pumps. This case study starts with Edwards as a minor division among the 110 divisions in the British Oxygen (BOC) Group. Edwards was not doing well and commanded little attention from corporate management. By the end of the case study Edwards was one of BOC's fastest-growing divisions. It was challenging for leadership in the USA, where it went from nothing in 1972 to a 22 per cent market share in 1987, and attempting to take over a competitor in 1988 to gain a 20 per cent share of the global market.

The central focus of the case is the events between 1970 and 1988. They raise a number of issues concerned with organizational strategy, structure, leadership styles, organizational skills, communication, managing overseas organizations, as well as detailed issues of the global vacuum market. There is considerable detail of the issues faced by Edwards and its strategic options. The reader is given details on the characteristics of the vacuum market and the key competitors within the industry. These help frame the circumstances in which Edwards formulated its strategy.

The early part of the case outlines cutting and re-focusing of the business by then managing director, Robbie Robinson. This raises questions about the logic of cutting out specific sections of a business and the opportunity costs of such exercises. In the case of Edwards it is suggested that this initial cost cutting set the ground for implementing the strategies which led to its rapid growth in the 1980s. The reader may wish to consider whether successful turnaround was dependent on this period of retrenchment.

The decision by the new managing director, Andy Ray, to expand Edwards' business beyond the core business of primary pumps is discussed in considerable detail. Management tackled issues relating to the use of computer technology to enhance efficiency. The emergence of a new management team and the building of bridges between the functional areas are given some prominence. There is also the linkage between emerging corporate entrepreneurship and the role of information in the successful leveraging of resources and capabilities to consider.

The management of rapid growth is a chief issue here. The relationship between growth and the preparatory steps is explored. The case outlines how Edwards' management went about creating a credible proposal for a new capital investment programme. As a small division with a rather poor past track record the steps taken to convince the parent organization that it could implement the programme quickly and effectively were important. The case outlines the three legs of Edwards' product strategy and some of the steps taken towards achieving it. Pricing strategy is also considered.

The case devotes considerable space to the changes in Edwards' organizational structure and culture, and attempts to upgrade its skills base. Communication links between the division and corporate management, between functions within Edwards, and between Edwards UK and its overseas offices are all dealt with in some depth. Thus, one can assess the importance of communicating and managing information in order to co-ordinate strategy across an organization, vertically and horizontally.

The case study closes with a bid for Varian Associate's Vacuum Products Division. The bid raises further interesting questions at a time when Edwards faced other new competitive challenges.

### Discussion questions

- What impact did Robinson's cost cutting and re-focusing have on the development of a rejuvenation strategy at Edwards?
- What were the key elements of the emerging rejuvenation strategy? On what core competences was it based? What mistakes were made?
- How has Edwards upgraded its competences over time? Can it continue to do so?
- Are Edwards' current organizational strategies, structures, culture, etc. congruent, i.e. mutually supportive? What changes, if any, would you wish to encourage?
- Is further investment in Edwards now justified? If the take-over of Varian Associate's Vacuum Products Division is successful, what strategic direction should the enlarged organization take and what problems do you anticipate? What should Edwards do if the bid fails?
- Can strategy formulation and implementation at Edwards be separated in practice? What are the implications for strategic planning?

**List of named characters**

(See Figure 9.8, p. 219, for a complete list of *current characters*.)
Robbie Robinson, Edwards managing director 1974–80
Andy Ray, Edwards managing director 1980–82
Danny Rosenkranz, Edwards managing director 1982–
Jim Thorpe, Edwards chairman 1982–
Barry Kirkpatrick, operations director, 1982–3
Dick Giordano, chairman of BOC
David Pitts, managing director of BOC

**Keywords**

Restructuring and turnaround; organic growth; incremental and radical change; competence upgrading; technology strategy; market dominance; international strategy; organizational structures and leadership styles, internal communications

## INTRODUCTION

In 1978 Edwards High Vacuum was a poorly focused company struggling to stay in the first division of international competitors in the vacuum pump business. At that time, it was a relatively small unit and only one among 110 divisions in the BOC Group. Because it was barely breaking even, it did not command much corporate attention and was on the list of businesses identified for sale. Since then, the company's fortunes have been transformed. It has emerged as one of the fastest-growing units in BOC's much slimmed-down portfolio, and is one of the most successful of the leaders in the world industry.

How this remarkable rejuvenation has been accomplished is the subject of this case study. Written on the basis of interviews held during 1988, it documents the key events from the mid-1970s up to September 1988. The story is necessarily complex, for rejuvenation was not accomplished overnight and was the sum of a myriad of individual actions. The study is written to reflect the stages through which the company built its new capability. Starting from decisions to cut out loss-making activities and to invest in new product design, attention shifted progressively to strengthening the human resources and the information base, to investing in greater efficiency and later to expanding capacity in a hurry. Successive waves of reorganization adjusted the management focus to the new tasks shaped by the arrival of new managing directors. Throughout, the theme is of evolution from an original base of strong but largely unrecognized potential; not a complete abandonment of the past.

To preserve confidentiality, the study excludes a detailed review of the financial performance. An indication of the success is that Edwards' sales grew from £17 million in 1978 to about £100 million in 1988, primarily from organic growth. Figure 9.1 gives a series of indices about the financial performance. For example, profits have grown from near zero to a level greater than leading competitors' and profitability is today well above the average for British manufacturing industry. Figure 9.2 provides further indices about the improving efficiency of the company since 1978.

## LAYING THE FOUNDATIONS (1976–80)

Robbie Robinson was appointed managing director in 1974, some six years after BOC had acquired the company at the prompting of the government's Industrial Reorganization Committee. He inherited a company with a strong reputation in primary pumps and a wide portfolio of other products, including large-scale systems that used vacuum environments for a variety of manufacturing operations. These systems included

*Figure 9.1* Edwards High Vacuum: indices of growth

freeze-drying processes, metal deposition and applications of mass spectrometry; they represented the results of many years of sustained research and development effort. Production was on four sites. Three were in the UK – Crawley, which included the headquarters, Shoreham and Eastbourne – and one in Italy which was dedicated to making freeze-drying equipment.

### Searching for a focus

Robinson started by cutting various marginal activities, but it was not until 1976 or so that he began a more radical approach to focusing the company. He took the view that Edwards could survive profitably only if it were to be reduced to a single core business: the primary pump. (Appendix 1 provides details of the products and Appendix 2 describes the market and the main competitors.) Robinson dropped most of the systems and much of the development work on a range of vacuum-related technologies. The only activities to escape the axe were the Italian operations and some of the instrumentation work at Eastbourne.

By defining the business narrowly in terms of mechanical pumps, Robinson removed Edwards from some of the emerging technologies,

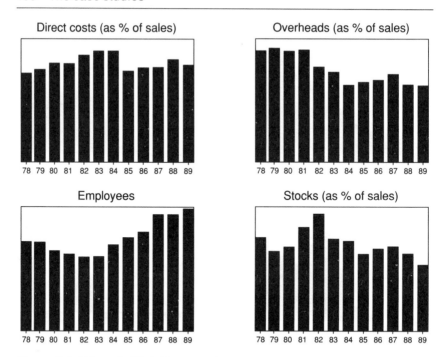

*Figure 9.2* Edwards High Vacuum: indices of efficiency

such as turbomolecular and cryo pumps, and created problems with BOC's central technical department, which wanted to retain a broad technological capability. Not all technologies were dropped, as is described later, but the price of specialization was high. The price, however, seemed necessary; the company could not command the resources needed to become or remain a leader in all possible segments. Moreover, the exit from systems temporarily helped competitors like Leybold in Germany and Balzers in Switzerland, who could benefit from a less contested market-place.

At that time, Edwards was barely breaking even and had a negative cash flow. Managers felt that their lack of credibility would discourage headquarters from accepting any substantial capital request. Headquarters, however, took a different view. Later, David Pitts, who was appointed managing director of BOC Limited and a director of the BOC Group in 1979, was known to have complained that 'Edwards people sit by themselves saying "we are different from BOC". The only time they want to come to HQ is with their hands out for cash.' Despite the elaborate corporate requirements for planning, communications had broken down, reflecting perhaps the contrasting personalities of Pitts and Robinson.

Part of the distrust may have been caused by inconsistent internal investment behaviour. Whereas Robinson prevented the R&D department from spending small sums of £20,000 on equipment, he felt able to spend money on acquisitions. In 1978 he bought a German company, Kniese, which made freeze-drying equipment and had been successful in northern Europe, but had run into trouble as it tried to extend into Japan. Besides adding new opportunities, this was an attack into the backyard of Leybold, the largest company in the industry. Edwards had a sales office in Frankfurt and a small workshop that was wholly inadequate for the needs of the business. Though the reasons for the purchase are now unclear, one manager remembers the logic as:

> Robinson thought the industrial leak detection business was going through the roof and didn't want to miss the opportunity. He bought what was available, basing his case on Kniese's assumed capability in the new business and the fact that he would greatly extend his freeze-drying market by eliminating a competitor. Kniese proved to be an albatross for years, because it had unwisely taken on large contracts it could not supply.

Despite these inconsistencies, Robinson had made a start on the difficult process of weaning the company away from its old philosophy of making anything to do with a vacuum. 'You the customer call the tune, Edwards will do it' was a common expression of the then sales-led view. Robinson promoted the alternative view of, 'let's do well what we *can* do well'.

### Investing in product design

Robinson's decision to invest in a fundamental redesign of the *entire* range of primary pumps was a courageous break from past behaviour and served to dramatize his determination to focus the effort. Hitherto, the company had altered designs only in marginal steps. This time, as one described it, 'we got hold of the entire range and just charged in.'

The spur to concentrate on the primary pumps and to re-design the range was provided by several developments. First, demand from industrial users, notably in the chemical processing industries, was beginning to grow. Second, competitors had been developing direct-drive rather than the traditional belt-driven pumps. Though the engineers still argue about the merits of the two drive systems, it was clear that customers preferred direct-drive, perhaps for no more profound reason than 'an element of fashion', as one manager put it. In short, the existing range was ten years out of date and risked losing Edwards' strong reputation for technical excellence.

During the period 1977–80, the pumps were designed to be rugged as well as vibration-free. The low-vibration characteristics were derived from the early years of the company's experience of selling to R&D laboratories. Though Edwards had long moved away from selling solely to laboratories and into the commercial markets, the low-vibration characteristics were retained as ruggedness was added. The combination proved an important advance over competitors' models. No specific industrial application provided the basic design specification; the designers had a broad concept of the pumps' usage in hostile environments. They believed that the chemical industry was likely to be the main market, and did not anticipate the semiconductor business that was then only just beginning to emerge. A further characteristic of the design process that proved important was the collaboration between the designers and the production engineers: the designs were set within the then-available manufacturing and machining capabilities. As some of these were not yet embodied in Edwards' factories, subcontractors were used initially to provide part of the first production runs.

The development work had to be done in stages and divided across the main parts of the range, for management believed that everything could not be achieved simultaneously. The small pumps, where Edwards was traditionally strong, were first and were in production by 1979. The medium-sized pumps were next, being introduced to the market in late 1979, followed by the large pumps (mainly for the industrial applications and the fastest-growing segment of demand) in 1980. By 1981 all production was in-house. The effort was restricted to the primary pump only and excluded the secondary pumps and the other equipment needed to sell a primary pump 'package'.

Concentration on primary pumps had its costs; other products and support activities were cut savagely and had to be rebuilt later as profits grew. R&D spending was reduced at the end of the decade. Even so, work continued. By 1979 the first prototype of a 'dry' pump had been developed to give Edwards a further technological edge when it was eventually launched in 1984. The instruments business at Eastbourne was considered a candidate for closure, but was kept on without much development effort. When the policy was changed in the 1980s to widen the range of products, instruments proved to be a critical part of the plan.

While the new pumps were being designed and tested, other developments were occurring that later proved to be important. For example, Robinson ended the bonus schemes and introduced a company-wide system of pay parity and pay negotiations to all three UK factories. This required considerable negotiation with unions long accustomed to adversarial bargaining. The new schemes provided the base for a much more flexible approach to control and change in the production function.

## Developing exports

During the late 1950s and early 1960s Edwards had established a few overseas sales offices to add to the efforts of its numerous distributors. Offices in Japan and Brazil were opened in the early 1970s. Though these offices remained remote from the mainstream of the company, they provided a 'toe-hold' in export markets.

In the USA, an offshoot of the Canadian subsidiary had been established at Grand Island, near Buffalo in New York State. The combination of proximity to the Toronto office and loans at favourable rates made the choice of location reasonably obvious, even though it turned out to be remote from the main East and West Coast markets that later developed. Alan Giles was sent out as managing director of this office in May 1976, when he was 27. He had the objective of 'getting closer to the customer' and was soon to be helped by Peter Connock, a recent graduate recruit, who took over the prospecting of new customers when Giles returned in September 1978 as general sales manager for the UK. Their combined interest in actively following up possibilities for the then uncertain future in the industry later proved crucial to the speed at which the company could respond once the demand from the semi-conductor industry took off.

During this period the central selling function was primarily that of allocating supply to customers, some of whom had to wait for over eighteen months for delivery. Overseas selling seems to have been limited to ensuring that the local unit made a profit based on the transfer price set for their imports. Despite supply shortages in the industry prices were not adjusted and Edwards remained largely ignorant about what was happening in the market. One manager remarked later,

> We did not succeed in integrating the international side of the business into the activities in the UK. Each foreign territory was on its own, free to make money however it thought best. Thus there was extensive discounting from the artificial transfer price and great disparity in the prices quoted in different markets. It is remarkable that with such a strong order book we could still have lost money.

Despite the fact that Edwards had a full order book, the company was struggling and losses started mounting. Production planning was based on the sales manager's forecasts that were routinely no more than extrapolations of the previous year's sales within + or − 10 per cent. No attempt was made to link production with actual orders during the budget period. The consequence was that orders and production movements were continuously out of phase, as Figure 9.3 shows. Looking back from the perspective of 1988, the process used at that time was described as 'I used to do it top-down in terms of "I think this is the

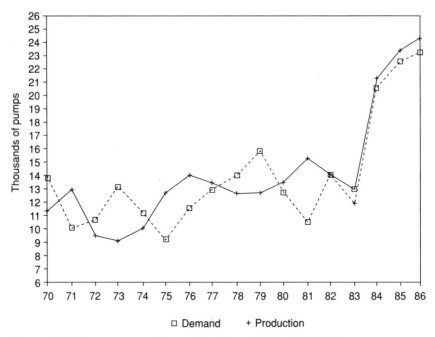

*Figure 9.3* Primary pump demand and production 1970–86

number; now tell me what is going to disturb it"'. By contrast, the same manager described the contemporary process as market-driven with the sales budget directly linked to production planning. A start on the job of sorting out the confusion was made in early 1980 when Robinson promoted Alan Giles to be sales director for the whole company, with the remit to integrate the selling effort more adequately across countries.

## Developing production management

Though Robinson's main preoccupations were with product design, he did not wholly ignore the other functions. Recognizing that production inefficiencies were a drag on profitability, he recruited a new production director, Barry Kirkpatrick, also in early 1980.

The balance of power and the effectiveness of the company were critically affected by the manufacturing developments that ensued. By mid-1980, Kirkpatrick had recruited two new members of the production team, both of whom were to become directors: John Rimer took over as production manager at Shoreham, and Alex Mudge at Eastbourne. They were assisted by the arrival towards the end of 1980 of 'Raj' Rajogopal, an expert on production systems. John Rimer recalled later his sense of shock that he was faced with an order backlog of 3,000 units and his immediate determination to sort out the problem. Among the first changes made were moves towards cell production, better production control (replacing the existing complicated MRP system with a simpler process), simplified sourcing (from three foundries rather than twenty), some pay cuts and some redundancies.

The new team created a sense of urgency for ensuring increasing efficiencies. As Alex Mudge recalls,

> At the time, John and I knew we couldn't do a job for Edwards. We were being asked to be functional. The brief was 'sort out production: it's in a mess'. But that wasn't totally the case, and we could have wasted a lot of time if we'd just kept the blinkers on. We were very concerned about building the infrastructure of the commercial enterprise and started building bridges back from sales to manufacturing right away in 1980.

The team, however, could not make much further progress until other changes had been made, most notably with the help of Keith Pointon, whose work is described later.

Despite these moves to strengthen the team, in 1980 Edwards must have resembled, on cursory examination, more a beached whale than an effective competitor. With hindsight, one can see that the rigidity of the organization caused most of the problems. The functions did not co-ordinate their efforts and little systematic attention was paid to developing relationships with the emerging set of new, internationally-minded customers.

From the vantage point of 1988, managers now consider this to have been a period when Edwards had no shortage of good ideas, but lacked the skills and determination to translate them into coherent business propositions. Moreover, the declared attempt to concentrate down into a smaller company was often modified by actions that served to keep some options open. The consequent dissipation of effort led Danny Rosenkranz, who took over later, to conclude that Robinson had failed fully to exploit the benefits of the new primary pumps by limiting his vision of the company to simple parameters that he 'could get his arms around'.

Yet an 'emergent' strategy was visible if one looked carefully. All the decisions were pointing in the same direction, even if they lacked coherence and clear articulation. One person who looked was David Pitts. He saw that the vacuum pump business had considerable potential for growth. At a time when BOC was drastically pruning its portfolio of diverse businesses, Pitts and his chairman Dick Giordano were looking for other businesses that might become equally large and capable of protecting BOC from the long-run cyclicality of its core gas business.

Though it was not clear that Edwards could achieve that stature, and despite Giordano's scepticism, Pitts took the view that the potential was sufficiently strong to make investment attractive. He set in train a sequence of events that led to the transformation of the company.

## HIATUS AND PROGRESS (1980–83)

Robbie Robinson left rather abruptly in May 1980. Reading between the lines, it seems that he did not get on well with David Pitts, his new boss, and that his departure was directly related to Pitts' determination to make Edwards profitable. It also seems evident that Pitts did not regard Robinson as the man for that task. Whether this was an unduly harsh judgement is a question that cannot be answered. Though his leadership may well have seemed to be modest, Robinson had made the crucial investments that later helped to rescue the company.

Robinson's departure left a hole at the top of the company for almost a year. Despite repeated reassurances from BOC that a new man was coming, it was not until late in the year that Ross arrived, and when he did he stayed for only seventeen days. He, in turn, was succeeded by Andy Ray, who arrived in January 1981. The hiatus of having no internal leader for most of 1980 meant that Pitts was in effect a distant managing director but one who lacked any clear lines of reporting. Opinions differ as to what really happened during this period, but it seems that the functional lines of demarcation were, if anything, reinforced with a consequential worsening of interdepartmental communications.

A climate of new optimism was initiated at a meeting when David Pitts came to Edwards to introduce Andy Ray to the team. He announced, 'after 12 years of neglect, we will now back you'. It took another year for the impact of the changed climate to be shown in the form of the first of a series of spending requests.

### Investing for efficiency

Andy Ray's arrival helped to crystallize manufacturing's growing sense that investment was urgently needed. Just to stay in business, efficiencies across the company had to be improved. Andy Ray had been BOC's technical director and had earlier been Robinson's boss in the Advanced Engineering Division. Thus, he already knew the Edwards business and could quickly start to work closely with the team to produce a £2 million investment proposal by the end of 1981.

This proposal called for £1.5 million on new CNC machinery and the balance on improved layout to improve manufacturing efficiency. Approval was rapid and the new machinery was installed within six months, far faster than originally proposed. There was little of the typical UK shop-floor resistance to the changes in work practice, because of the care taken earlier to ensure good labour relations and the extensive briefings given about the purpose and competitive need for the changes.

The re-equipment was accompanied by the adoption of IBM's computer-based system (MAAPICS) that allowed greater factory-wide control of all costs. This was installed on the recommendation of Coopers and Lybrand, consultants appointed by BOC after Edwards had failed its annual audit and the problems of persistently failing to control the business had become visible at headquarters.

MAAPICS was a success at Eastbourne, but less so elsewhere. Earlier experience at Eastbourne with IBM systems such as PRINCE provided a good platform for improvement, especially given Alex Mudge's initial work to build 'an embryonic matrix across the functions'. More importantly, Keith Pointon led the installation team. Keith had joined the company in 1975 as a graduate trainee in the marketing area after earning a PhD in metallurgy. He spent some years taking a part-time course to become a cost accountant but accepted the job of commercial manager at Eastbourne before he formally qualified. Though by the time MAAPICS arrived he had been promoted to administration and planning manager at Crawley, he could nevertheless lead the work at Eastbourne. Such was the effectiveness of the whole programme then and later that Eastbourne remains a reference site for IBM's continuing promotion of the system.

Difficulties arose at other sites. John Rimer recalls that the system required substantial modification at Shoreham. This was slow in coming as managers had little experience of what was required. At Crawley, the introduction was rated 'a complete disaster', except for its impact in the accountancy area. The basic problem was that 'even with MAAPICS, we still did not know the factory costs properly and could not link them to changes in the market-place'. A start was made to improve the financial understanding of the business when Andy Ray appointed Keith Folkes finance director in February 1981 in the aftermath of a significant problem created by the failure to control stock losses. The full impact of the financial system was not, however, to be felt until other developments described in the next section had taken place.

Despite the impetus from the manufacturing function to create integration of the systems across the entire business, the company remained unfocused and Edwards' managers were confused about priorities. Alex Mudge recalls that some parts of the business remained sales-led while others were driven by technology, regardless of cost. Despite the cuts in the R&D budget, new products kept appearing. Not only was the 'dry' pump technology developed, but also other products such as Spectron, for leak detection, were started in 1979.

The sales function was still chasing volume with little awareness of costs and contribution. Failures resulted because 'sales people deal with problems as they arise; they are "of-the-moment" people. They used to regard service as overhead.' Another said 'sales people did not understand the processes to the extent they do now' and went on to point out that the moves towards integration were continuing in 1988 even though great progress had been made in reducing the friction among the functions.

If the events of 1981/2 had established some greater credibility for the future of the company, they had by no means ensured its success. The new equipment had lowered costs, the backlog of orders had begun to shrink and the new range of primary pumps was well received and now capable of being produced in-house rather than by subcontractors. But the company was only just beginning to become profitable, and the cash drain had increased. Above all, the company lacked a direction for the future: 'We were all concerned to build bridges: the only thing that wasn't coming together was the company. There was no clear definition of what the company was trying to do or where we were going.'

### Emerging leadership

The fog of indecision began to be rolled back in 1982 when two new men arrived from BOC: Jim Thorpe and Danny Rosenkranz. Jim Thorpe arrived as chairman in October 1982, before Andy Ray's departure in December. He had run BOC's welding business, was widely regarded as a tough man capable of sorting out difficult problems, and was known to be trusted by David Pitts. An Australian with wide international experience, Thorpe clearly had the responsibility of sorting out the company.

His first moves were to hit hard at the continuing need to cut costs even further. In addition to the job losses previously identified as part of the package for the investment in new equipment, Thorpe wanted tighter controls on pay structures. At Shoreham, for example, there were negotiations with the unions about shift premia, which were reduced to 25 per cent, below the 35 per cent then in existence. Thorpe also concentrated on efforts to increase volumes, to improve the control of total costs and to revise the pricing structure.

For commercial issues he relied on Danny Rosenkranz who acted as chairman of a newly created pricing committee. In early 1982 Rosenkranz had been seconded to Edwards from other senior responsibilities within BOC to take over responsibility for the 'non-standard' business. It is unclear exactly what BOC had in mind for him in the new appointment.

Given the earlier failure in the appointment of Ross, headquarters may have thought of him as the managing director-designate – certainly managers at Edwards regarded him as such – but Rosenkranz himself is clear that he was not offered the job until Jim Thorpe did so in late 1982. Whatever the real motivations of those involved, Rosenkranz was a powerful figure in the fortunes of the company from the day he arrived and when Thorpe arrived later in the year the pair worked closely together.

The pricing committee depended on a new information system OSACS (Order Sales and Contribution System) for much of the needed data. This system had been introduced in early 1983 by Keith Pointon, whom Thorpe had promoted to commercial manager, to complement the MAAPICS system and provide a fuller understanding of the contributions. The system linked demand planning to production and allowed the company selectively to produce for stock. It also provided much needed cost data to enable a review of the pricing policy. Previously, all products were priced at a mark-up on notional costs, with little regard paid to the price sensitivity of demand, to the effects of competition, or to the effect on costs of the changing volumes being achieved. The costs used were essentially guesses, for there was no system of allocating costs properly or even for understanding the direct costs. The sales effort was primarily that of allocating product to customers and setting customer 'priorities' in the long queue that was only just beginning to come under control. The lack of adequate customer contact and understanding is well expressed by one US customer who is reputed to have said at about this time, 'I thought Edwards was out of the business: I have not seen any product for over a year.'

The effect of the investment in new information systems was dramatic. As Rosenkranz remembers it, 'Just by looking at the pricing policy, we managed to add £2 million to profits in six months.' In practice the results were not so easily achieved, for the systems provided only a base position and it was attitudes in the sales force that had to be changed before improvements could be seen. Sales people were geared not to lose an order, and risking that loss by introducing higher prices at a time when the company was seen to be 'down' took courage.

Work to solve the whole costing problem took time. Keith Folkes took the lead in developing the systems that eventually linked both MAAPICS and OSACS to the financial controls. The problems were especially acute abroad. David Palmer, the current finance director, joined the company in 1983 as overseas controller, where he was immediately plunged into the problem of dealing with profit assessments based on artificial transfer prices to the foreign markets. He says that it did not take him long to understand why each foreign territory was making money while the whole company was in loss: all the overhead charges were being borne by the UK operation.

While all these functional developments were taking place, Jim Thorpe was also working to change the organization to provide a better focus on the constituent businesses. Using his knowledge of BOC's practice in the special gases business, he extended the embryonic developments within the factories into a form of matrix structure. Fitting people into the new slots proved troublesome. First, in November 1982, Barry Kirkpatrick was appointed head of the components business. This did not work and he departed in 1983, being replaced by Alan Giles. John Rimer was promoted to manufacturing director, with the brief to push through the manufacturing changes more effectively. Keith Pointon had a short spell as product group manager for pumps and accessories, before becoming commercial manager and later commercial director in 1987.

## NEW STRATEGY AND NEW STRUCTURE (1983–4)

'When Thorpe asked me to take on the job, I was not at all sure I wanted it. Could I resolve the issues? Besides, the job had damaged previous managing directors. I went away and wrote a memorandum over the weekend.' From that rather unpromising beginning, Danny Rosenkranz took hold of the company and lifted its sights to aggressively seeking leadership in the world industry.

> I had two choices. I could shrink the business down to about one-quarter of the size, where it could be managed as a profitable niche player. Alternatively I could grow it quickly. To do the latter, I had to add more components, for the primary pump was too small a base. What I could *not* do was continue to fiddle around in the middle. Given the growth then clearly visible in the US market, the excellence of the new pumps, plus the good work started to improve efficiency, I chose the growth option. I knew I did not have much time, for the competitive structure was being sorted out by the boom and late entrants would not have much left for them.

Rosenkranz had to work on many fronts simultaneously if he was to catch the boom. He had to increase capacity, redefine the organization to make it work and build a product strategy around the available skills. Today's directors all remember the clarity with which the new direction and the revised structure were articulated in 1983. Though there have subsequently been numerous changes, these have been relatively minor. In other words, the vision that emerged early in the new leadership proved to be remarkably robust.

## Expanding capacity

The earlier US reconnaissance started to pay dividends by the beginning of 1983, when orders from the US semiconductor industry began to appear. Edwards' new pumps had particular features that appealed to this industry at a time of rapid expansion: the pumps lasted longer than competitors' in the highly corrosive manufacturing conditions. Moreover, by having the lowest available level of vibration, the pumps could be installed near to the delicate operations of etching the silicon wafer, thus saving expensive engineering.

The trickle of initial orders soon turned into a flood. The order backlog re-appeared and it soon became obvious that extra capacity was needed. The plan to double capacity at Shoreham was completed by October 1983. Some £2.8 million was needed for 17 extra CNC machines and ancillary equipment. Edwards asked for £3.3 million to allow for a 10 per cent contingency, but in the event spent only the £2.8 million. The plan was presented in five 'tranches' to allow HQ the option of moving more slowly than an immediate doubling of capacity.

This was clearly a high-risk project, for Edwards had no track record of being able to meet the projected cost levels, let alone of managing the project at the speed indicated. It had to be sold on the basis of 'credibility'. This required the analysis to be completed to a degree of detail never before attempted. Rosenkranz had to work hard to persuade his team to prepare a *written* account of all the details needed to support the case for the gamble. In particular, he required a model of the market demand, derived from forecasts of semiconductor production, to be developed. To be credible, the plan required market *evidence*, not hope. This meant that many holes in their understanding of the new demand in the USA had to be filled by purchasing market surveys. Everyone in the company remembers their surprise about the source of the new demand: they had regarded chemical processing and not semiconductors as the more likely source of new business. The work on the market thinking helped to push further the integration of the thinking among all the functions, especially as very detailed sensitivity analyses had to be created to deal with various possible combinations of demand variation, competitor reaction and Shoreham's equipment needs. Rosenkranz remembers,

> We had to be very quick to get the approvals, because this market has a habit of coming up fast and, if you miss the wave, you don't win by coming in after the wave has receded. What happened is that we did all the detail and then just picked a number.

Selling the project to the parent company was not easy. Initial reactions were that only half of the plan should be accepted. Rosenkranz considered that doing one-half was 'obvious' given the state of the market, but that doing the whole lot at once would yield a far greater prize. A half-way house would be sub-optimal and lack courage. Besides, he argued,

> In the context of Edwards at the time, the risk of over-investing was less than the risk of under-investing. The worst thing in my mind was compromising and not having courage. The question was confidence in the market study, not the detailed investment numbers. As I said at the meeting, 'You have a lot of machine tools there. If the worst comes to the worst, we'll make other things on them.'

He stuck to his arguments and won the day.

For Edwards, this decision was putting the company on the line: should the plan fail the whole company was at risk. Viewed from the perspective of BOC, however, the risk seemed less acute, for it was small relative to the scale of the worldwide group. None the less, the review was just as rigorous as those for much larger investments.

Once approved, the plan was put into effect with astonishing speed. Production was *doubled* within less than four months. The speed of implementation was made possible by a combination of factors. First was the decision to use the experience of the earlier investment by ordering precisely the same machines as before. Given the urgency they were not even put out to new tender. Second, the machines had been ordered *before* approval had been granted, but could have been cancelled without serious penalty. Third, because of the exact duplication of the machines, the control systems could readily be expanded. The cohesiveness of the management team at Shoreham, led by 'Raj', combined with strong support from the shop floor were also important in ensuring the minimum of disruption.

## A dash for growth

Management had considered the option of putting the extra capacity into the USA, but rejected the idea because of the extra difficulties of working in an unfamiliar environment and the associated problems of ensuring adequate quality control from day one. By contrast, Leybold in Germany decided to invest in the USA and suffered from serious delays, thus opening even wider the door for Edwards to take market share.

The point of availability of supply at a time of excess demand was crucial, because of the high 'switching costs' for buyers. OEM buyers had to design their systems around the particular characteristics of the vacuum pump. Switching, therefore, required expensive reconfiguration of the production system. Buyers were naturally reluctant to switch

*Table 9.1* Changing leadership in the US market: market shares for rotary vane pumps (% based on value of sales)

| Firm | 1972 | 1979 | 1982 | 1984 | 1987 |
|---|---|---|---|---|---|
| Sargent-Welch (USA) | 61 | 29 | 16 | 7 | 9 |
| Leybold (Germany) | 4 | 22 | 25 | 29 | 22 |
| Edwards (UK) | 0 | 2 | 8 | 13 | 22 |
| Alcatel (France) | 0 | 12 | 16 | 16 | 14 |
| Others | 35 | 35 | 35 | 35 | 33 |

*Note*: 'Others' includes Balzers, Busch, Dresser, Ebara, Gast, Kinney, Normatex, Stokes and Varian.

unless either greatly superior performance was on offer or their existing suppliers had failed to keep up with the growth in demand.

These switching costs had meant that the previous structure of the world industry was predominantly 'multi-domestic'. National champions, for reasons of history, tended to dominate their home markets and few had captured significant shares in export territories. For example, in the early 1980s, Edwards held about 70 per cent of the UK market but less than 10 per cent of any other leading market. The same had been true in the USA, where Sargent-Welch had been dominant. Though Leybold and Alcatel had captured new US customers during the 1970s, it was not until the boom of the early 1980s that the structure of the world market changed significantly in favour of the exporters, as Table 9.1 shows.

Fortune favoured Edwards for it had both superior technology and available supply. It could thus take market share from everyone, especially the US suppliers who had not upgraded their products. Thanks to earlier choices of material inside the pump, the new Edwards' pumps had particularly good anti-corrosion properties and lasted longer than others in the highly corrosive gas streams used in semiconductor fabrication.

The impact of both the increased demand and the new equipment on the costs at Shoreham was dramatic. Figure 9.4 shows that unit costs fell by 20 per cent almost immediately and have been held steady in real terms thereafter, despite considerable complication of the subsequent product range developments.

Not content with success in the USA, Rosenkranz soon turned his attention to Japan where the semiconductor boom lagged behind that in the USA. Thanks to a long-standing joint arrangement with Nippon Sanso, a leading supplier of industrial gases, Edwards was the only foreign company with any significant presence in the Japanese market. Nippon Sanso supplied the leading semiconductor producers with gas and could help introduce Edwards to its customers. That may have

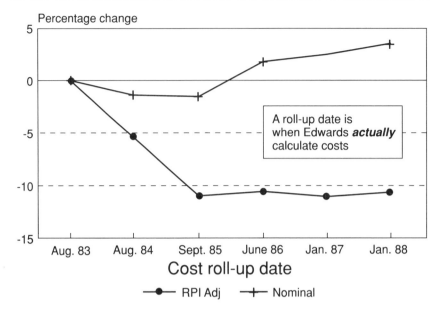

*Figure 9.4* Primary pump cost changes (prime or variable cost only)

opened the door to a new market but developing sales required more than an introduction. Managers with US experience were sent to Japan to transfer their knowledge of the new operating conditions. With a strong push from experienced salespeople and a superior product, Edwards rapidly captured the leading share of the primary pump business in the fastest growing market in the world.

Leybold and Alcatel took until 1985 to organize themselves for the new market and bring out their new corrosion-resistant pumps. By then, the boom was over and Edwards well entrenched. The dash for growth had been repaid many times over.

### Further reorganization

Thorpe had started the difficult process of instilling new values of efficiency and profit consciousness at many levels of the hierarchy. He had also begun to break down the old functional barriers by his trials with a form of matrix structure. Before he left in June 1983 he had effectively laid the foundations on which Rosenkranz could build. As Rosenkranz put it, 'Jim acted as "blood man" for me.' Rosenkranz described the task he faced as basically very simple:

We had to flatten the organization, introduce control systems, build

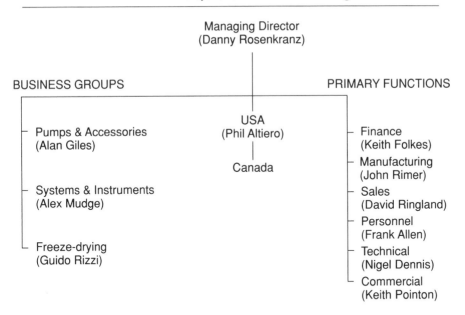

BUSINESS GROUPS

Managing Director
(Danny Rosenkranz)

PRIMARY FUNCTIONS

Pumps & Accessories
(Alan Giles)

Systems & Instruments
(Alex Mudge)

Freeze-drying
(Guido Rizzi)

USA
(Phil Altiero)

Canada

Finance
(Keith Folkes)

Manufacturing
(John Rimer)

Sales
(David Ringland)

Personnel
(Frank Allen)

Technical
(Nigel Dennis)

Commercial
(Keith Pointon)

*Note:* Guido Rizzi and G. Wilk report direct to the managing directors in their capacities as general manager in Italy and Germany respectively.

*Figure 9.5* Edwards High Vacuum organizational structure in 1984 (simplified)

on the momentum which had started in the product and production areas and then make marketing and commercial sense of the whole thing. This is a very complex business, but no one appeared to understand it. I forced them to clear the decks. By flattening the organization, I created much more accountability. I let people run their own patch, but I also changed lots of people and allowed much more visibility for juniors and brought in people from the outside.

The organizational form chosen was a modified form of the earlier matrix structure. Three business directors were appointed: Alan Giles to run the pumps and accessories; Alex Mudge to run instruments; and Guido Rizzi to continue with freeze-drying. Each was given primary profit responsibility for his product line and each was supported by the series of functional activities shown in Figure 9.5. There were some adjustments to the basic logic of this structure to accommodate special needs and save unnecessary duplication of effort. Thus North America was run as a sales territory for all products under the direct supervision of Rosenkranz. Similarly, Italy was combined with the freeze-drying business as it had in effect been run for some years previously.

Rosenkranz also set out to change the climate of operations at lower levels. Immediately upon becoming MD, he went round all the sites to brief everyone about the business, its prospects and problems. His basic message was that 'the strategy of the firm is built on the details that everyone must know and control'. He started a regular programme of six-monthly briefings as part of setting and maintaining a climate of much greater 'openness' from top to bottom of the company.

To reinforce that climate he abolished the directors' dining room at the Crawley headquarters so that everyone there now eats in the same canteen (though there is still a managers' dining room at the Shoreham site). He also re-named the Board the Management Committee and made it clear that he expected all managers to become more flexible in their job expectations. Lateral or even downward moves by managers would not affect their pay, status or perks. Moves between the functions came to be regarded as 'part of the job'. A further measure of the change in climate is provided by the director who stated that 'Today we meet a lot and are trying to get everyone to know each other and what they are doing.'

## Upgrading skills

The developments associated with the new range of primary pumps and their application in the emergent industrial markets made it clear that the company needed more skilled managers, each capable of managing rapid change and increasing technical sophistication. Of the present directors, only three were employed in the company before 1977. All three represent the past strengths that were needed as the foundation of the 'new' company. Nigel Dennis had led the development of the new pumps and was promoted to technical director in 1984. Frank Allen, the personnel director, masterminded recruitment and maintained the traditions of good labour relations. Guido Rizzi, the business director for freeze-drying and the Italian operation, had run the one part of the 'old' systems business to escape Robinson's axe. All the others were recruited specifically to add strength where Edwards was weak.

A measure of the seriousness with which the company took the personnel issue is the fact that from 1980 to 1986 the bill for recruitment and re-location exceeded £5 million, as much as the total expenditure on new plant and equipment. Added to these human investments has been a sizeable, but unquantified, bill for skills training at all levels and for management development.

BOC was involved in the initial work to upgrade the calibre of the team. As Dick Giordano put it, 'Edwards was sitting out as an orphan and had trouble getting good people on its own. We could help.' It did so in two forms: by seconding good people from elsewhere in the group, as has been mentioned earlier; and by recruiting new men specifically for Edwards. The appointment of Keith Folkes in 1981 is a case in point. Such help was not, however, needed for long, for success breeds success. As fortunes and reputation were restored, Edwards became an attractive place for high-flyers. BOC also acted to transfer its culture of systems thinking into a business that had never previously operated in those terms.

Two other parts of the drive to upgrade skills proved to be important. First was the need to weed out those who were not up to standard. As Frank Allen put it, 'One of our first tasks in the period of massive change was to cut, perhaps over-cut, at the top to allow us to rebuild the team completely.' At other levels, many loyal servants of the company disappeared, but this process was managed by attrition and the provision of generous retirement 'packages': no compulsory redundancies were needed after 1982. The second was the willingness to promote younger people on the basis of potential. This was linked to a deliberate policy of moving managers around among the functions. The period from 1981 to 1984 was one of frequent job changes, not all of them successful. None the less, the broad experience gained was a fundamental characteristic of the resource base of the top management cadre. They all knew in considerable detail about others' jobs and could work closely as a team. Without that breadth of experience and perspective the new matrix structure could not have worked as well as it has done: typical points of friction in managing across the sometimes ambiguous boundaries of responsibility could be handled without significant dispute.

The programme of job rotation has diminished in recent years as the top team has bedded down. The same programme is being maintained for the younger managers. Graduate recruits are given a wide functional experience in their early years with the company. By 1988 these younger people were beginning to enter the ranks of junior management to provide the expanded base of capability needed for the continuing additions of complexity to the task.

## Redefining the product strategy

In the early 1980s the effect of the earlier decisions to concentrate on the primary pump had been to make the company overly reliant on only one part of the system that customers bought. Competitors had an advantage from selling a variety of combinations. Rosenkranz was clear that he needed to move the balance of products to emphasize the secondary pumps and all the other possible types of equipment described in Appendix 1. He described the plan in terms of building three legs for the company. First he wanted to strengthen the existing leg of the pumps by growing the company's capability in secondary pumps and accessories. Then he wanted a strong second leg in the area of instrumen-

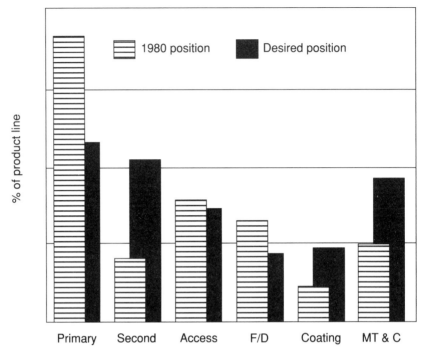

*Figure 9.6* Edwards High Vacuum: product policy for the 1980s

tation. Finally he wanted to plan for a third leg in the systems business. He described this as 'finding a path of increasing robustness that would allow us to attack more geographical segments of the world market and more applications for vacuum technology'. The product strategy was to move in the direction indicated in Figure 9.6, where the 'desired position' was defined in notional terms as building the other product lines to the point where they commanded the same market share as did primary pumps in 1980. In other words, the intent was to add back, in a carefully controlled manner, a large part of the capability lost by Robinson's decision to focus the company.

To ensure that such a plan would not lead to the same loss of competitiveness as it had in the early 1970s, he had to rely heavily on the ability of the organization to upgrade its skills. In the event, the greatest problems lay on the sales side, for the sales engineers had to change many of their approaches to the market and understand more adequately the technical needs of customers. One consequence has been that salesmen in the UK no longer earn commissions. They are salaried so that they can concentrate on selling the appropriate balance of products to customers and move away from what has been described as the 'mechanical pump comfort mentality'.

The plan called for the UK to be the development territory. Successes there were to be repeated abroad. To make this happen required considerable changes in the way the overseas territories were managed so as to integrate them more fully into the needs of the global company.

## MAKING IT WORK (1984 ONWARDS)

The financial record since 1983 has been one of continuing growth in sales. By 1985 the company at last returned to being cash-positive. The principal investments had provided the capacity to ride the demand boom in semiconductors and the whole system was clearly becoming more efficient. The control system was helping among other factors to reduce the amount of stock held and to tie the factories more closely to the market.

Profits reached a peak in 1985, a year of peak demand from the US semiconductor industry and one when the pound was at its weakest against the dollar. As the semiconductor boom later waned, further growth had to be found elsewhere. Rosenkranz considers that the whole strategy was at its most vulnerable in 1986/7, because the company was bearing an upsurge in development costs but not yet gaining commensurate revenues. As he put it,

> It would have been hard to cut back on the growing momentum. We had to believe that we could pull it off. We were encouraged by the fact that the task was getting easier as we built critical mass in the key functions.

A measure of the success is the winning of the Queen's Award for Exports in 1986 in recognition of the regular sales overseas of over 70 per cent of the UK production. Figure 9.7 shows the extent to which the geographical spread of sales has altered from 1983/4 to the forecast position for 1988/9.

### Extending the product line

The range of standard primary pumps has been progressively extended as new pumps have been designed for ever-more specialist applications. For example, niche markets have been developed by adding a range of booster pumps for the high-power laser market and even smaller rotary vane pumps have been made to mirror the trends towards miniaturization in some markets. The most important development in this part of the business, however, has been the launch of the 'dry' pump, described in Appendix 1.

The design work for this new concept in technology was started in 1979, the low point of the R&D cutbacks, and the first prototype was

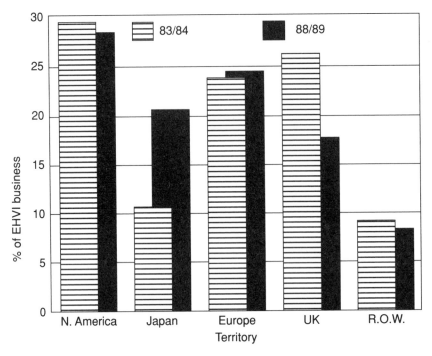

*Figure 9.7* EHVI business spread by territory

running in-house in 1980. Initially the pump was difficult to make
and it was hard to achieve reliability in operation, though these problems were eventually overcome. The launch was delayed until 1984,
despite considerable pressure from Japanese customers. Some argue
that the delay was due to a feeling that success elsewhere needed to
be supported and that internal competition with the 1970s' primary
pumps was unwise. Rosenkranz, however, considers the delay to be
an example of the difficulty of breaking old habits of compromise and
letting things drift: 'It was a breakthrough in thinking and the hardest
part of the whole programme was to convince our own people.' For
instance, the first proposal for pricing the 'dry' pump was based on
the costs of production. Yet the value to customers was considerably
greater, because of the large savings in consumables such as the oil
for the sealing. Eventually the price was set at a premium level and
the pump launched successfully on the Japanese market.

Despite good patent protection, the pump has attracted new competition. There are now numerous Japanese competitors, some using different technologies, and Leybold unveiled an imitative product in early
1988. Even so, Edwards considers its pump the most rugged, and that by

being first into the market it has captured position and customer credibility that will be hard to destroy.

The range of secondary pumps has been expanded. Long reliant on diffusion pumps, Edwards found its position under threat from competing technologies. Both to defend against broad-line competitors and to be able to attack new niches, work was started to create a position in turbomolecular pumps. Initial moves were based on product factored from Elettrovara of Turin. Twice these failed, because of reliability problems. A third attempt had some, limited, success in the market. The factored products have now been replaced by in-house manufacture, with the first of a new range launched in mid-1988. Simultaneously, work went ahead on cryo pumps. Internal development started in 1984, based on a design provided by Osaka Sanso, BOC's associate in Japan, and a new product was launched in 1986. New, more specialist and smaller models are being added to the range. These are, however, meeting severe market resistance, because switching to a new supplier incurs particularly high risks for OEM buyers. In such areas it takes a long time to establish a market position based on new technology. Finally, the range of diffusion pumps continues to be developed with work to reduce costs and increase quality.

The instrumentation side of the business has also received attention. Datametrics was bought in the USA in 1987, primarily to gain access to its technology in total pressure measurement and control. Integrating the new facilities and capabilities has, however, proved difficult. One part of the product range not associated with vacuum was sold and others have been subjected to costly rationalization. Other Datametrics products are being upgraded and yet further instrument technologies are under review as to whether they should be developed in-house or bought in.

More recently the systems business has received revived attention. Part of this was due to the absorption, at BOC's request, of Temescal in March 1987. This Californian thin-film-coating company had been acquired as part of the AIRCO acquisition in 1978. The world leader in thin-film evaporation, Temescal had spawned BOC's extremely successful solar products business, but had got itself into difficulties when it attempted to sell plant based on 'sputtering' technology to the semiconductor industry. After attempts to sell the company had come to nothing, Edwards was assigned the job of sorting it out. Temescal makes thin-film deposition systems and a variety of components for vacuum products. These are reasonably complementary to the line of small, vapour deposition coaters made at Crawley. There are numerous problems still to be solved, not least in upgrading parts of the constituent technology. Competition from Leybold, Balzers and others is increasing and Temescal's problems of reliability and out-of-date designs have caused it to lose some business. Catch-up work is requiring considerable investment and management attention both to cut out the losses and to ensure that Temescal can be fully integrated into the general structure.

Other systems work has involved the leak detection business, where the Spectron range has been launched to give an added technological edge in many countries. The freeze-drying business has been extended with manufacturing added in the USA. Edwards has recently shipped some systems from the USA to Japan and South Korea.

Taken together, these product developments have added complexity to the general task of providing coherent direction and tight operational control of the range. Building the skill with which managers can balance conflicting demands has become an increasingly central part of the drive for world competitiveness.

### Managing the matrix

The organization has evolved from its 1984 form outlined in Figure 9.5. The growing complexity of the product line is mirrored in the current structure, though the basic design remains unaltered. Figure 9.8 shows the top management structure in mid-1988 (names appearing in capital letters denote membership of the EHVI Management Committee). There had been some changes in senior personnel. Alan Giles left in 1985, and David Ringland moved from Sales and Marketing to succeed him. Mike Cole was promoted to sales director from UK sales manager, a position for which he had been recruited in 1984 when he was just 29 years old. Keith Folkes resigned in 1987 to become finance director of Lansing Bagnall and David Palmer was promoted in his place.

The initial efforts to make the new structure work were not always easy. A particular problem was integrating the overseas territories into the total strategy. One director described the effort as follows:

> We had a pile of companies where each guy had his own fiefdom. When I got involved, it was a fundamental that we attempted to run the businesses on group profitability. The main issue was pricing, because overseas people were working against the strategy. We had to know more about their group contribution. It was not easy to do this, for we had to change behaviour. For a year or two, we didn't let them talk about local profits and insisted on measuring them on local overhead management and group contribution. This caused a lot of disquiet. They felt a loss of local accountability and found it hard to work within a wider group. We spent masses of time arguing about numbers that didn't progress the business.
>
> The next step was to raise the level of international thinking and get everyone's consistent with ours. It may seem strange now, but we

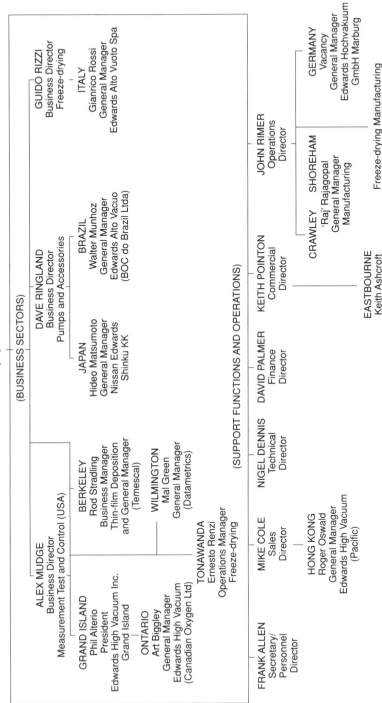

*Figure 9.8* Edwards High Vacuum organizational structure in mid-1988

had to do a lot of fundamental work to understand how each market worked, the pricing pressures and the economic forces. All that thinking basically had to come from here outwards, because of the previous culture of chasing orders.

On pricing, we took a very strong central role and developed central pricing/competitive information. Keith [Pointon] developed list prices around the world and balanced the numbers against the evidence coming in. We stopped all the local decisions. That didn't mean we stopped listening to them: they were involved, but the bottom line was the list prices had to be agreed by those guys.

The strength of our international development today has come about because our form of organization has forced them to build their own market infrastructure. Where needed, they have had to recruit local specialists to fill in gaps. We made them travel a lot to build up relationships. But it would not have worked if we had carried on lobbing instructions from the UK. We changed the budget arrangements to increase the dialogue about what is really going on in the territory and to stop the focus on a single (profit) number. We now tie the budget to the strategy and we use multiple performance measures so that, for example, no one has to go to the wall on a rather arbitrary budget overhead allocation.

By 1988 management was confident that it was mastering the problems of balancing the conflicting demands inherent in the matrix structure. Its view was well expressed by Alex Mudge, who explained that it worked well, because

There is a total management team beyond the business directors with a tremendous level of understanding of the need for business strategy in total. This does not mean we get everything right – we all have misgivings about certain areas where we have not been as successful as we would like – but generally we can focus on the corrective actions.

Another added,

On occasion the balance gets askew, but you can't avoid this. Not everyone in a matrix can be totally aware of *all* the objectives of a business as complicated as this and therefore performing perfectly to balance the short- and long-term objectives. There are too many contrary pulls from geography, technology and the product range.

Improving the ability of the team to manage the necessary balancing act on a global basis is now on the agenda for top management. As one put it,

What has happened is, by definition, *here*, because here is home base.

However much you try overseas, this is where the key guys interact; they walk down the corridor and can be challenged. They can discuss a problem at what I call a better intellectual level. Overseas, they don't have that opportunity. The result is a disparity between the strength of the team here and the quality overseas. Though we have the strategies and all that, the execution needs improvement. We are addressing the issue of building a world organization so that someone in, say, Japan will actually *understand* what the UK is thinking. A lot of work has gone into it, but we haven't succeeded in crossing that bridge.

Various other trouble spots have persisted. A substantial one is Germany, where costs and technical capability have not followed the rest of the company. John Rimer took over line responsibility for this operation in mid-1988, to add to his general manufacturing remit. Such problems, combined with the acquisition of Datametrics and the incorporation of Temescal, served to depress profitability in 1986/7. That good progress has been made to solve the problems is shown by the record profits declared for the year ended in September 1988.

These problems, together with the continuing growth in size and product range, have acted to stretch the capacity of the structure. It was clear to Rosenkranz some time ago that further evolution was needed. Plans to start changing were, however, sidetracked by the proposed acquisition of Varian in the USA.

## Pricing and information management

Within the general structure, a number of key operating decisions have to be taken to ensure that a reasonable balance of effort and focus is maintained. Of these, decisions affecting international pricing and product allocation and the management of information receive much attention.

The basic policy is to price in the local currency in all countries where Edwards maintains its own distribution presence; in countries where agents are used the pricing is in sterling. Agents, thus, carry the exchange risk between the prices in their own local-currency list and those in the transfer. The only exception is France, where the agent is treated as a company distributor. As exchange rates fluctuate during the life of the list price, there are some possibilities for a 'grey' market of agents trading Edwards' products across borders between EC and non-EC countries and among non-EC countries such as the USA and South Korea, though these are seen as minor at present. As Mike Cole put it,

We say to customers 'we offer you warranty and service capability for that product within the territory. If you want to buy elsewhere and later have a problem, then we may have to ask you to return it to the country of purchase where we will honour our obligations.' Where there are price disparities, this approach serves to raise the level of discussion with our important customers about the total life-time cost of the product. We feel this gives us some competitive advantage.

Prices differ across Europe. For example, Germany where Leybold is the leader is considerably more expensive than the UK. Servicing is one factor that acts to keep the prices apart, despite the trade. There are also technical barriers and differences in distribution structures. Mike Cole thinks that these differences will slowly disappear as the Single European Market programme is implemented.

Elsewhere in the world the differences in technical specifications cause some problems for the efficient management of the production flow. Because demand is volatile and the company cannot make to order, estimates have to be made about both demand of particular products and location of that demand. For example, a product made for Germany cannot, at short order, be reassigned to Japan without substantial modifications. The effect of this is to keep working capital levels higher than management would ideally like. As production is increasingly being shared among the various sites in different countries, so the problem is exacerbated.

These developments serve to put increasing pressure on the information system in the company. His colleagues see Keith Pointon as the central figure in managing this part of the organization: 'the hub of a wheel'. There is a two-way flow of data from the centre. Alex Mudge described Keith's function as acting as

> the recipient and manipulator of vital company information into a form that is easy to understand. It helps us to manage our businesses, knowing the data have been brought together and interpreted in the context of running the total business. The key issue is not just data management, but *understanding* the format. If you really do understand the total context, you can go a long way towards making the decision by presenting the information as a couple of facts.

To enable the increasingly complex information to be handled effectively, the systems described above have been augmented. The advent of the personal computer has helped considerably in the effort to make everyone more attuned to the current position. Simultaneously, the finance function has been changing its role. David Palmer is now responsible for ensuring that commercial and product data are interpreted in financial terms as much as possible. There remain difficult issues to be resolved, for it is not yet clear that extra data can be made available without incurring the problems of 'data overload'. A further area of development is improving data and understanding competitors' resources and policies. The difficulties of defining the market, discussed in Appendix 2, are caused by the fact that all leading players are subsidiaries and, like Edwards itself, disclose as little as possible about their performance.

## GOING FOR GLOBAL LEADERSHIP IN 1988

In 1988 Edwards announced a $US60 million bid for the Vacuum Products Division of Varian Associates, Inc., in the USA. This company had been a rival in the world's largest market, though it had been losing market share and had not expanded outside North America. With sales of $US74 million, Varian would catapult Edwards into the leading spot of many of the key sectors of the US vacuum market. Though the bid was accepted by Varian's owners, the US Federal Trade Commission was not equally happy. Because of the dominant position of the two companies in such sectors as diffusion pumps and helium mass-spectrometer leak detectors, anti-trust questions were raised. These had not been resolved at the time of writing, though public speculation was that Edwards or Varian might have to sell part of the range to allow the acquisition to proceed.

If Edwards does capture Varian, it will command roughly 20 per cent of the world market, as defined by the figures shown in Appendix 2. Given that Leybold, with 26 per cent market share in markets similar to Edwards', is currently unprofitable, a high share of the market does not automatically guarantee superior profitability. Leybold, however, is a much larger business than these figures would suggest, for it has carried the vacuum thinking much further and has a strong position in large systems and the losses may not be in the Edwards' range. The lack of detailed financial reporting makes accurate comparisons impossible. Even so, it is clear that the issue facing Edwards today is to ensure it finds and retains sufficient new sources of competitive advantage to stay ahead.

The problems are not simple to resolve. First is the question of the degree to which the industry is becoming more commodity-based. Because competitors can match others' technical advances with increasing speed, price premia for superior technology are, in many instances, at best temporary. The trend is for greater price competition, especially now that there are the possibilities of over-capacity of supply. Advantage will go to those with the lowest costs and the best customer support.

No one knows with any confidence how costs compare among competitors, though it seems that Edwards is currently well placed for much of its range. For the future, the question is whether the UK will remain a favourable site for the bulk of the output. For instance, wage differentials between the UK and the USA have shrunk considerably and the USA has a better purchasing base. The sensitivity to the strength of sterling is considerable. Should the decision be taken to spread more production abroad, the strains on the organization will inevitably increase.

A further issue is the extent to which new specialist producers may emerge to dominate new niches in the market. The trends towards smaller pumps for some applications suggest that the developments in recent years towards advantage for broad-line producers such as Leybold and Edwards could reduce. The extent to which service capability can help to offset both price competition and new competition is an open question. The 'mobility barriers' are still important, though they may be losing some of their strength.

Finally, there is the question of maintaining the momentum for ever-increasing efficiencies. Rosenkranz and his team are acutely conscious that the competitive battle ahead will demand continuous improvements in all departments. Though they have been remarkably successful during the last five years, they know they cannot rest on their laurels.

## NOTE

1  © London Business School 1989
   This case study has been written as a basis for class discussion rather than to illustrate effective or ineffective managerial or administrative behaviour. It was written by John M. Stopford with the help of Charles Baden–Fuller and with the active collaboration of Edwards' management team. Some of the data are drawn from an MBA report written by Ashley Mooney and David Davis.

## APPENDIX 1: VACUUM-RELATED PRODUCTS

Products related to the vacuum industry can be considered in three basic groups: pumps and accessories; measurement, test and control instrumentation; and systems. Each group has its own technological, manufacturing and selling needs. Even so, the boundaries separating them are 'permeable' in the sense that customers often demand, and Edwards supplies, assembled combinations of products, depending on the particular application.

### Pumps and accessories

The pumps and accessories sector is divided into three product segments. Primary mechanical pumps are used to generate rough and medium vacuum levels down to $10^{-4}$ mbar and to provide the first pumping stage for high vacuum. Secondary pumps are used to create high and ultra-high vacuum. All secondary pumps need a primary pump to get them started. There are a variety of methods used to create vacuum levels down to $10^{-8}$ mbar. It is also possible to create an ultra-high vacuum of $10^{-11}$ mbar, though Edwards does not currently make such pumps.

### *Primary pumps*

The most common primary pump adopted for the production of system pressures down to $10^{-3}$ mbar is the rotary vane pump. During its operation the blades of an eccentrically positioned rotor compress gas molecules entering the inlet of the pump and discharge the gas into the surrounding atmosphere. A thin oil film provides the sealing medium between the rotating parts and also continuously lubricates the pump.

To increase the speed of pumping or to handle high gas loads, a mechanical booster is often connected in series with the vane pump. Typically a mechanical booster pump uses two figure-eight shaped impellers, rotating in opposite directions inside a stator. The gas trapped between the impellers and the stator wall is transferred from the high vacuum inlet to the discharge side of the pump, through the vane pump and so to the atmosphere.

Traditional applications for primary pumps are for scientific instruments, general pumping in electrical and industrial applications, atomic energy and metallurgy, and more recently in the manufacture of semiconductors.

In addition, a new concept in vacuum-pumping technology has resulted in the *dry pump*. This pump does not require any lubricant or sealing fluid within the pumping chamber, with obvious advantages for use in applications demanding pure atmospheres. Dry pumps can create a vacuum below $10^{-1}$ mbar, similar to that produced by a conventional, single-stage primary pump.

Primary pumps are made in three ranges of size. Small pumps handle volumes of less than 30 cubic metres/hour and are used primarily in research applications. Medium and large pumps handle greater volumes in industrial processing applications.

*Secondary pumps*

These are used in conjunction with primary pumps to provide higher levels of vacuum. There are three principal technologies employed.

*Diffusion pumps* are based on heat and speed. A supersonic stream of heated vapour is blown into the vacuum chamber at an angle. Gas molecules diffusing into the stream are impelled towards a backing pump, where they are expelled. Small diffusion pumps are used in research and instrumentation applications, whereas large ones have application in industrial processes such as vacuum furnaces. This used to be the dominant technology route, and one where Edwards holds a strong market position. Alternative technologies, however, now offer a cleaner vacuum, higher reliability and simpler operation and have been taking market share.

*Turbomolecular pumps* use high-speed rotors (up to 60,000 rpm) to compress gas molecules to a pressure at which the primary pump can remove them. By contrast, *cryo pumps* employ low temperatures (down to 10 degrees Kelvin) to freeze the gases. They provide the cleanest method of producing a high vacuum.

*Accessories*

Accessories fall into three main categories: those which enhance the performance of the main pumps; consumables such as pump fluids; and components used in the construction of vacuum systems.

There is a wide variety of products in each of these categories, each with relatively low volumes of demand. For Edwards the largest category is the consumables, due primarily to its proprietary range of PFPE (Fomblin) fluids developed by Montedison. Some components, such as valves, are now produced by the Temescal subsidiary, but most of those sold by Edwards are factored.

## Measurement, test and control

All vacuum systems need some form of control instrumentation. At the simplest level, a meter is required to indicate continuously the pressure of the system. In the most complex cases, the system needs complete computer control and performance analysis of pressure, temperature, time and process rate measurement along with the switching of relays to various components in the system according to programmed and feedback-controlled parameters.

For Edwards, the product line comprises electronic measurement and control equipment such as sensors, gauges and controllers (manufactured at Eastbourne); Datametrics pressure and flow control equipment (made in Massachusetts); and medical mass spectrometers from Eastbourne and marketed through Ohmeda. For example, in partial pressure analysis Edwards has developed (under the direction of Ohmeda) a dedicated mass spectrometer for respiratory and anaesthetic agent monitoring.

### Systems

'Systems' is a broad term covering a wide variety of applications of vacuum-related process applications. Most pump manufacturers make some systems and their customers make complete production systems in which the pumps account for 1 to 2 per cent, sometimes 5 per cent, of the total installed cost. Of the systems made by the pump manufacturers, the most important are those for freeze-drying, coating and leak detection. There are also special pumping systems, usually made from non-standard elements and designed for such specific customer applications as evacuating and 'gunning' cathode ray tubes, pumping carts for aluminizing and pumping stations for large heat treatment furnaces.

A *freeze dryer* is a vacuum system arranged so that the material can be dried from the frozen state by sublimation of water vapour. Throughputs vary from a few milligrams in laboratories to more than 25 tons/day in food freezer dryers. A typical system has inbuilt freezing facilities, a vacuum system with microprocessor recording facilities, often with additional hydraulic system, pressure steam sterilization and automated material handling systems.

Freeze-drying systems are used in laboratories, pilot plants and industries such as food and pharmaceuticals. Edwards makes industrial systems in Italy, Germany and assembles European-sourced main structures in the USA. These are typically custom-built. Small and pilot-plant dryers are made in all three of these countries and small standard laboratory freezers are made at Crawley in the UK.

*Coating systems* are used to deposit very thin films of material (usually metallic such as gold or aluminium or semiconducting such as silicon) on a substrate in a vacuum chamber. Electron beam guns or 'sputtering' devices are used to transfer the material.

The range of application for these systems is constantly expanding as research programmes in large customers and universities find new ways of solving old problems. For example, there were trials in 1988 for the deposition of amorphous silicon for the manufacture of solar cells and thin-film transistors.

*Leak detection* equipment plays a role in many processes to ensure that the equipment used is reliable and does not leak. Simple leaks can be detected under water as all bicyclists know. In industrial applications water-based testing can detect leaks equivalent to a car tyre taking three months to lose 10 per cent of its pressure. Other more sensitive applications require leaks of less than one ten-millionth of this rate to be detected. For these purposes, mass spectrometer technology is used. The item on test is evacuated and helium search gas is sprayed over potential leaks. Any helium passing through a leak is detected by the mass spectrometer, the output of which is an electrical signal.

## APPENDIX 2: THE WORLD MARKET AND COMPETITORS

The market for vacuum-related products is extremely difficult to determine with precision, as Appendix 1 indicates. The problem is defining which products should be included in the industry. In addition to the primary and secondary pumps, there are accessories and instrumentation products, and a wide variety of systems that incorporate pumps together with associated equipment. For some purposes of analysis it is useful to consider only the pumps; for others all the related equipment should be included as well. Some competitors are vertically integrated from electronic instrumentation through to large-scale systems, while others are specialized.

It is not clear whether verticality provides for extra competitive advantage, nor is it always possible to gather reliable data on the extent of trade in the various segments of the 'broadly defined' industry. Nevertheless, some crude estimates are possible and are shown below. They should be treated with some caution, as they are no more than estimates drawn from a wide variety of, sometimes conflicting, sources.

### Segments of the world market

By 1988/9 the world market had grown to a sales value of approximately £800 million. This figure includes the systems, instrumentation and accessories produced by leading suppliers of pumps. The total figure for all products embodied in customers' operational systems would be somewhat higher. The industry had grown rapidly during the 1980s, more than tripling in value since 1980. Growth rates had, however, slowed in more recent years. Industry estimates put the growth in sales value for 1988/9 at approximately 4 per cent.

This estimate for the world market can be considered as the sum of various segments. Most people in the industry consider that three segments are of most importance: the equipment, the territory and the type of end-use.

Figure 9.9 shows the value of sales for each of the principal types of equipment. The figures do not match the total estimates for the market; they are limited to those sectors where Edwards competes. The basic pumps account for nearly half of the total value. Measurement, Testing and Control equipment (labelled 'MT&C' in the chart) is the next largest sector and includes leak detection equipment. Accessories ('access') hold about 15 per cent of the total, and freeze-drying systems ('F/D') and coating systems ('coating') account for the rest. The balance of supply by type of equipment has hardly changed during the five-year period, despite considerable growth.

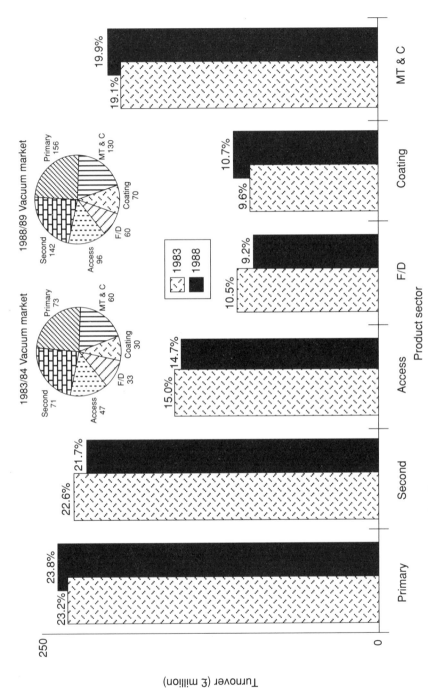

Figure 9.9  Global vacuum market by sector

The second way to examine the composition of the market is by territory. Figure 9.10 shows that North America remains the largest market, though its share has declined in recent years. The main growth has been in Japan, which has raised its share of demand from 16 per cent to nearly 25 per cent in five years. European share, including the UK, has grown only slightly to 29 per cent, still larger than Japan. Within Europe, the largest market is Germany.

The third view of segmentation is provided by the type of end-use. Figure 9.11 shows the principal shifts in demand for Edwards' primary pumps among the various types of buyer and highlights the dramatic growth of demand from the semiconductor industry and the relative decline of demand from other industrial users. Similar shifts have occurred for other parts of the product range.

## Competitors

The data shown in Figure 9.12 need some explanation to identify the leading players listed. L-H stands for Leybold-Heraeus, the largest supplier in the industry. Some details of this company are given in a separate section below. Of the others, EHVI stands for Edwards High Vacuum International. Balzars is Swiss, a subsidiary of Oerlikon, and particularly strong in turbomolecular pumps. Varian is a subsidiary of the US company, Varian Associates, and is subject to a bid from Edwards. Ulvac is the largest of the Japanese competitors. Alcatel is a subsidiary of the French Alcatel Group. S-W indicates the US company, Sargent-Welch. The other competitors are a myriad of smaller, much more specialized firms, many of them limited to operations in a single country.

Several features of the competitor set stand out. First is the dominance of the Europeans. The top four account for nearly 60 per cent of world industry, and have increased their share slightly during the last five years. Second, is the decline of the US producers. If the bid for Varian succeeds, there will almost no locally-owned suppliers left in the world's largest market. Third, is the relative lack of success of the Japanese, despite the growth of their home market.

The reasons for these trends are hard to discern with any confidence. Most observers, however, feel that the winners have all had policies of sustained investment in technology, building market access and improving levels of service, mirroring the history of Edwards.

## Leybold-Heraeus

Leybold is based in Germany and has foreign manufacturing subsidiaries in France and the USA. It has over one hundred sales and service centres around the world. With sales of over DM 1 billion, Leybold is

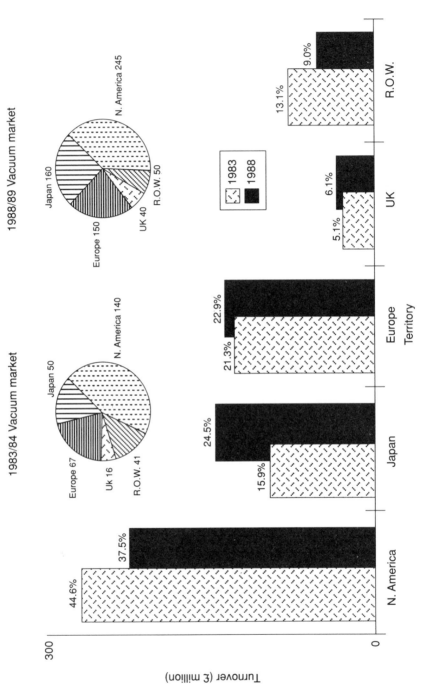

1988/89 Vacuum market

N. America 245

Japan 160

Europe 150

UK 40

R.O.W. 50

1983/84 Vacuum market

N. America 140

Japan 50

Europe 67

Uk 16

R.O.W. 41

1983

1988

300

Turnover (£ million)

0

N. America 44.6% / 37.5%

Japan 15.9% / 24.5%

Europe 21.3% / 22.9%

UK 5.1% / 6.1%

R.O.W. 13.1% / 9.0%

Territory

*Figure 9.10* Global vacuum market by territory

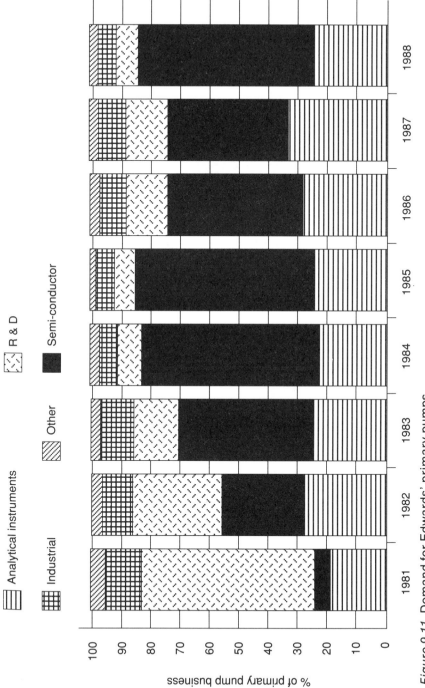

*Figure 9.11* Demand for Edwards' primary pumps

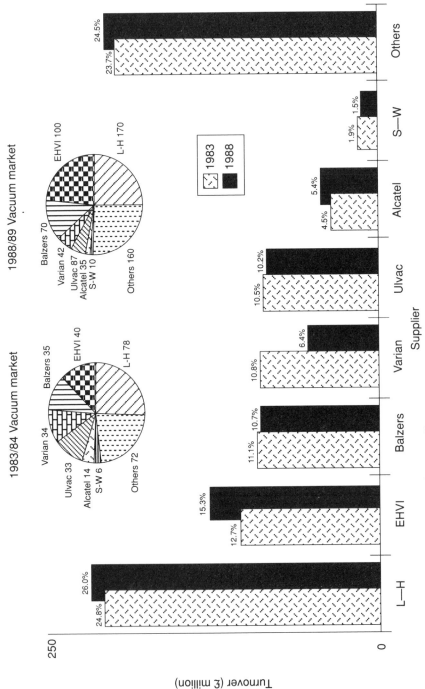

Figure 9.12 Global vacuum market by supplier

*Table 9.2* Performance of Leybold-Heraeus 1983–7 (DM millions)

|                          | 1983  | 1984  | 1985  | 1986  | 1987   |
|--------------------------|-------|-------|-------|-------|--------|
| Sales                    | 663   | 838   | 967   | 1,117 | 586    |
| of which, foreign sales  | 74%   | 79%   | 79%   | 70%   | 68%    |
| Net income               | 15.3  | 19.2  | 22.2  | 13.1  | (46.9) |
| Total assets             | 462   | 599   | 712   | 812   | 719    |
| Fixed assets             | 87    | 106   | 141   | 187   | 198    |
| Capital expenditure      | 20    | 40    | 61    | 80    | 49     |
| Employees                | 3,946 | 4,419 | 5,038 | 5,609 | 5,692  |

by far the largest competitor in the industry. Its performance is illustrated in Table 9.2.

The 1987 results are for only nine months, reflecting a decision to change the reporting procedures to confirm to the policies of Degussa AG, Leybold's sole owner since September 1987. Previously the company had been owned by three companies since the original merger of E. Leybold's Nachfolger and Heraeus Hochvakuum GmbH in 1967. In 1987, however, the other partners, Heraeus and Metallgesellschaft, decided to pull out. Leybold-Heraeus GmbH then changed its legal form to Leybold Aktiengesellschaft, a joint-stock company, with consequent effect on the public reporting requirements.

Management stated in the 1987 annual report that the fourth quarter of the calendar year was historically the strongest quarter for sales, so that the 1987 results shown above were unduly depressed in comparison with previous years. They also announced that the volume of orders for the large systems were reduced, that the sales in the USA were diminished by the weak dollar and that volumes in the domestic market had held up to previous levels. It is impossible to tell from the information made publicly available what caused the substantial loss of DM 47 million, nor in which product group the loss principally arose.

Leybold's product range is far wider than Edwards', notably in vacuum-process technology (mainly the large-scale systems) which accounted for 46 per cent of the 1987 sales. Vacuum-technology products accounted for 33 per cent of sales and measurement and analysis products for 15 per cent. The balance of sales came from diversification into scientific training and related services.

The spread of sales by region in 1987 was as follows:

| | |
|---|---|
| Federal Republic of Germany | 32% |
| European Community | 19% |
| Rest of Europe | 11% |
| North America | 23% |
| Rest of World | 15% |

Like Edwards, Leybold is dominant in its home territory and has North America as its principal market outside Europe. Unlike Edwards, however, Leybold has not expanded so much on a proportional basis into Asia and the rest of the world.

# Chapter 10

# Ariston-Indesit: the story of merger integration[1]

## *Charles Baden-Fuller and Carlo Boschetti*

### EDITORS' OVERVIEW

This case study focuses on the merger of two Italian major domestic appliance makers in the late 1980s. It covers the period 1987 to 1992. Ariston-Merloni and Indesit were of particular significance in the context of the European 'white goods' sector (washing and drying machines for clothes, dishwashers, refrigerators, freezers, etc.) since 40 per cent of European productive capacity was then located in Italy. Brief histories of both companies before the merger are provided. Whilst the Italian industry had expanded fast in post-war Italy and later began a substantial export drive, by the 1980s all the main firms had experienced financial difficulties as excess capacity in Europe (estimated at between 20 and 40 per cent in 1988) depressed prices and profit margins. Ariston's arch-rival Zanussi had been effectively bankrupt in 1983 and was taken over by the Swedish conglomerate Electrolux.

As of 1988 seven producers controlled over half of world sales, conservatively estimated at $US40 billion. In descending rank order these were: Electrolux (US5.1 billion); G.E. (USA: US4.4 billion); Matsushita (Japan: US4.2 billion); Whirlpool (USA: US4 billion); Bosch-Siemens (Germany: US2.2 billion); Philips (Holland: US2 billion); Maytag-Hoover (USA: US1.6 billion). In 1988 Whirlpool acquired 53 per cent of Philips' major appliance business with an option to acquire the rest, which would lift it to the number one position.

Up to this time, European manufacturers had remained competitive in large domestic appliances and had deterred entry by Japanese manufacturers. In small appliances such as vacuum cleaners, Japanese brands such as Hitachi and Panasonic have established a limited presence in Europe, in marked contrast to the 'brown goods' sector where in microwave ovens, televisions and hi-fi equipment they have become dominant.

The acquisition of Indesit by Ariston took place on 1 January 1988. During the first year of the merger, described in the case study as the 'frozen period', there was no attempt at integration, as the new owners reflected on the potential of each organization. Consider how the views of Ariston's management prior to the merger compared with the picture they began to see after the acquisition. Things were evidently not as they expected. Consider also whether management could have anticipated the problems likely to be faced during the early post-acquisition period and hence, been more decisive from the start. Alternatively, perhaps a more protracted process of exploration and learning is beneficial to the ultimate success of a merger.

The case presents a variety of issues that required attention, organizational, structural and cultural. The reader may find it useful to categorize the main problems and opportunities facing management, and the associated responses. What resources and capabilities did each firm bring to the merged company and how could these best be exploited in the post-merger operation? Indeed, the theme of distinctive competences may be a very useful lens though which the reader can analyse the issues of this case study.

The reported clash of organizational cultures also provides the reader with an opportunity to consider the role of cultural change and convergence in such a merger. Reflect first on the processes by means of which a new management team may identify cultural differences and their potential significance. Given the diagnosis, how can cultural change then be initiated, what are the circumstances in which such changes can be effective, and how does one actually know?

The case outlines the drive towards greater integration of the two organizations' activities. The degree of difficulty and success of various initiatives are noted. These involved substantial changes in the composition of management teams and styles of working. Inevitably, some managers were made redundant, some teams were almost completely reformed, and there was some movement of staff between functions and countries. One may ponder the effects of managerial upheavals on strategic change. Inevitably, the integration of activities led to substantial costs, and one may wish to consider whether these were increased by the delay in starting the process. Tables detailing the performance of the merged company can be used to analyse in financial and market share terms how effective have been the subsequent changes implemented by management.

The case study offers the opportunity to analyse the nature of the resources and capabilities in the two firms, and the extent of complementarity. One may wish to consider the role that managers at various levels can perform to rationalize, exploit and develop resources and expertise. More specifically, to what extent can the outcomes of a merger be planned from the top? If they cannot be planned with any certainty, what 'levers' are available for top managers to pull in order to enhance the prospects for success? Are they, for example, primarily structural or cultural? How much should one rely on project teams as opposed to individual change 'champions'? Thus one can discuss the scope for internal entrepreneurship in driving the integration process, including the harnessing of resources and capabilities in new and productive ways.

Throughout the case it is worth remembering the state of flux of the industry at this time. Over-capacity had led to shakeouts and concentration of production via mergers and acquisitions. Ariston-Indesit was not operating in a vacuum. Are the other leading players involved in synergistic organizational integration, or merely consolidation of marketing positions and rationalization of production capacity? Perhaps more fundamental reconfiguration of positions, resources and capabilities are in train to sustain new global competitive advantage. Such changes would almost certainly involve further upgrading of resources and competences. So how important in the future will be economies of scale and scope, and which firms will be best placed to compete on this basis? Finally, this raises the question, can the merged Ariston-Indesit rely on a 'Fortress Europe' arena of operations or is the industry becoming a truly global market? If the latter is the case, will Ariston-Indesit be large enough to compete?

## Discussion questions

- What were the key resources and capabilities Ariston and Indesit separately possessed? How distinctive were these in relation to external competitors?
- What were the main opportunities for complementarity/synergy in the activities of the merged firm? What had to be done to attain such synergies? Discuss the opportunities for leadership and internal entrepreneurship in the post-merger rationalizing activities.
- Explain the nature of the cultural differences between these companies in the early stages. How important were they in creating barriers to integration and the creation of sustainable competitive advantages?
- In retrospect, did Ariston gain more from the merger than if it had kept its distance and allowed Indesit to go bankrupt?
- Looking beyond 1992 what key challenges will face management of Ariston-Indesit? Evaluate these challenges and outline how you would begin to meet these if you were advising the Ariston management team.

## List of named characters

Del Neri, commercial director, Ariston
Garbero, managing director, Ariston/Indesit Spain
Vittorio Merloni, CEO, Ariston

Nicolai, finance and personnel manager, brought to UK operation in
1990
Sallustro, finance/administration director, Ariston
Santini, technical/production director, Ariston

**Keywords**

Domestic appliances; industry concentration; merger; integration/ration-
alization; strategic change; resources and capabilities; distinctive competences; synergy/complementarity; organizational structures and cultures

## INTRODUCTION

In 1992 Vittorio Merloni, president of the Ariston-Merloni group reflected on the past five years. The most significant event had been the acquisition and integration of its closest and larger rival Indesit. At the time of the acquisition, in 1987, the Ariston-Merloni group held about 5 per cent of the Italian appliance market, and about 3 per cent of the wider European market, making it about number ten in the European scene. Indesit was larger, having about 6 per cent of the Italian market and 4 per cent of the wider European scene. The result of the merger was to put the group into about number four position, just after Bosch–Siemens and alongside Thomson.

'Buying a company is far easier than integrating it,' admitted Vittorio Merloni and his top management team.

> We were ill prepared for the task of integration. We had had some experience of smaller mergers, having bought companies such as Colston in the UK, but Indesit was quite different. It was bigger than us, and it was in trouble. We made many mistakes, but we managed to pull through. Five years after the event, we are vindicated, the combined firm is not only bigger but stronger than either part was before.
>
> We have learned from the experience. The most important lesson is that after a merger, initial perceptions may be misleading. We failed to realize that our initial perceptions of Indesit were at odds with the reality. We thought we knew Indesit because we had competed with them for a long time. But we were wrong. After acquisition one needs to be flexible and quick, adjusting rapidly to new circumstances.
>
> I think we in Ariston need to know the full story of what we did. We have much to learn from our past, for it influences the present and the future. For this reason, I want you to hear the views of our managers, hear about our debates and see the documents.

## THE CONTEXT

### The market

Many factors triggered the merger between Ariston-Merloni and Indesit. First were the acquisitive activities of Europe's largest appliance producers. The Scandinavian-based multinational and locally dominant appliance producer, Electrolux, had in 1985 bought Zanussi. Zanussi, which was in receivership, was at the time Italy's largest appliance producer and one of the largest in Europe. Coupled with acquisitions in France

*Table 10.1* (a)  Leading European major appliance firms 1987

| Name | European share % | Italian share % | UK share % | French share % |
|---|---|---|---|---|
| Electrolux | 21.0 | 21.2 | 17.7 | 12.9 |
| Philips-Bauknecht | 12.0 | 11.1 | 4.7 | 14.0 |
| Bosch-Siemens | 10.5 | 2.4 | 1.7 | 5.1 |
| Thomson | 5.5 | — | — | 24.3 |
| Indesit | 4.0 | 4.0 | 3.7 | 1.3 |
| AEG | 5.0 | — | 0.6 | 1.5 |
| Hotpoint | 4.0 | — | 23.8 | — |
| Miele | 5.5 | 0.3 | — | 1.3 |
| Candy | 4.5 | 12.9 | 2.2 | 4.0 |
| Merloni | 4.5 | 14.0 | 2.6 | 1.8 |

*Table 10.1* (b)  Washing machine market share 1987

| Name | European share % | Italian share % | UK share % | French share % | German share % |
|---|---|---|---|---|---|
| Electrolux | 15 | 28 | 8 | 14 | * |
| Philips-Bauknecht | 13 | 5 | 6 | 20 | 7 |
| Bosch-Siemens | 8 | * | * | 4 | 25 |
| Thomson | 6 | — | — | 40 | — |
| Indesit | 4 | 6 | 8 | * | — |
| AEG | 4 | 5 | — | 2 | 14 |
| Hotpoint | 3 | — | 25 | — | — |
| Miele | 3 | * | * | * | 16 |
| Candy | 3 | 15 | 3 | * | — |
| Merloni | 3 | 5 | 2 | * | * |

*Notes:* Country market shares are based on washing machines only
   * Small share, but not measured exactly
   — No active presence
*Source:* Industry estimates, various

and the UK, the purchase of Zanussi made Electrolux Europe's largest firm with 15 per cent of the market. Philips, whose appliance operations were based in Italy, had in 1983 bought Bauknecht, a nearly bankrupt German producer, which put it in second place with 13 per cent of the European market. In 1988 Philips (still struggling to make money) began divesting itself of all its appliance operations to Whirlpool of the USA. Both Electrolux and Philips sought to have a significant presence in all of Europe's leading markets. The next two largest players were

Bosch-Siemens of Germany and Thomson of France. Both these firms were more limited in geographical scope, concentrating their efforts on their so-called home territories. Bosch–Siemens had nearly a quarter of the German-speaking markets: Germany and Austria. Thomson had an even stronger 40 per cent of the French market. Some details of the market shares are shown in Table 10.1.

The merger between Merloni and Indesit was important not only to the two players and others in the industry; there was also a political significance. The often forgotten domestic appliance industry is one of Italy's great success stories. Japanese and Far Eastern competition has made inroads into cars, machine tools, electronics; yet major domestic appliances remain a truly European, if not Italian, industry. Except in microwave ovens, there are no significant Japanese imports into Europe, and such imports as there are, are small and come mainly from the East European countries. The European industry which employs more than 100,000 people,[2] has 40 per cent of its productive capacity and output located in Italy, and about 7 per cent in Germany. A merger between two of the largest Italian firms which were also big exporters was a significant political event.

## The history of Indesit

A second factor that triggered the merger was Indesit's own peculiar history and the trouble in which it found itself in 1987. Until the 1980s Indesit was a very successful organization. It was started in 1957, and it grew rapidly. In the early years it built a factory every eighteen months, a real achievement. By the early 1980s, it was in trouble and by the mid-1980s it was bankrupt.

Indesit was a paradox: both simple and sophisticated. The economics of the business was very simple: obtain attractive credit of 120 days from suppliers, make the product quickly in less than this time and sell the output for cash. To do this required an exceptionally effective production system. The production system, for its time, was sophisticated. Production and engineering were able to work together. The system was focused, and Indesit was among the leaders practising an early version of just-in-time production.

> We shipped the products out as soon as they were made. There were no finished goods inventories. There was no need for expensive warehouses. We put our product directly into the trucks or the trains. We had an uninterrupted flow between production and the market.

The causes of Indesit's difficulties are not the subject of this case study; several are noted, without trying to be precise. The changing nature of the market meant that product variety, quality and new features were becoming more and more important to many consumers, especially in the higher priced segments. Because Indesit's products were not updated, this meant that the consumer became less and less happy to buy them.

Another problem in Indesit was poor productivity. A lack of investment was coupled with overmanning. In 1980 Indesit had 12,000 employees. By 1987 the number was reduced to 8,000 people.

During its period of *amministrazione controllata* (in the hands of the court), it was clear that Indesit had to find new owners. There were three options.

1  Sell to Merloni.
2  Sell to Electrolux.
3  Sell to De Longhi, which was strong in small appliances.

After Electrolux bought Zanussi, the choice became more restricted. De Longhi offered more independence and was preferred by unions and managers who feared the possible effects of outside control. But from a business point of view, all inside Indesit agreed that Merloni was the obvious choice.


### The transformation of Ariston

The third and most important factor influencing the merger was Ariston's transformation during the late 1980s, and the desire of management to capitalize on the past success. When Vittorio Merloni returned from Confindustria in 1984, Ariston was also in trouble. Like Zanussi and Indesit, Ariston had difficulties in making a decent profit. Unlike its rivals steps were instituted to effect change in a rapid manner, resulting in a strong position in 1987.

In 1978 Ariston had been organized into complicated profit centres. There were seven centres in all: four related to production (centred on four factories) and three related to commercial geographic areas (Italy, rest of Europe, rest of the world). These did not always work well. Many of the so-called profit centres operated as loss centres. As a consequence, in 1984, Vittorio Merloni changed the business to a simple functional structure. There were two principal functions: technical (production) and commercial (sales). A third function, (administration), included EDP, human resources and finance. Santini and Del Neri, long-time managers in the organization, were the two principal functional heads. The administrative director was relatively new, with a background in human resource management. Alas, he became seriously ill, and had to leave the organization. Sallustro joined the organization, originally in a finance capacity, and quickly became the third member of the top team, bringing expertise in finance as well as management. Sallustro had a history of involvement in radical situations and joined Ariston because he believed it had an exciting future.

There were other important changes, and this chapter can capture only a few of them. There was a new marking approach. The organization developed the ranges Margherita (for washing products), Supermarket (for refrigeration) and Settecuochi (for cooking products). These were more than names, they were ranges of products pushed in a concentrated manner with advertising and effort. The push took advantage of the hole created in the market by the paralysis of Zanussi and Indesit. Quickly Ariston became number one in the Italian market.

Ariston also captured and exploited the new and rapidly growing built-in appliance market. In 1981 Ariston was selling about 60,000 units; by 1988/90 the number had risen to 450,000 units. Built-in products are very profitable, with a margin of around 8 to 10 per cent, some 5 per cent better than free-standing appliances. Built-in is cheaper to sell, although the channels are different. Ariston's investments were significant.

In production there were also big changes. Between 1985 and 1988 output in the Ariston factories nearly doubled without any new factories being built. There was a drive to improve productivity and efficiency, re-equipping and reorganizing the production systems. For instance, in 1986 Ariston invested 24 billion lire (5 per cent of sales) in the factories.

In the area of systems the company was very simple until 1984. In 1984 systems started to move forward. An IBM mainframe was installed in Fabriano with terminals in the factories. By 1984 Ariston had a system which automatically controlled the supplier's invoices. Since then there have been many important developments: a Copics production system has been installed; the services parts system has been re-organized as has the administrative system; Ariston has introduced CAD systems and factory planning on a weekly basis. The developments have not been exclusive to Italy: France, the UK and Portugal are now integrated.

Logistics was also a backward child. The main role of logistics appeared to be the finding of warehouses for unsold finished products; the role of logistics in solving the integration of production and marketing was ignored. In 1984 the logistics department comprised two people; in 1992 there are eight. Ariston has made large investments in information systems (one billion lire in 1985).

There has been a change in marketing, as the following quotation shows.

The approach to the market also changed radically with Vittorio's return from Confindustria. We used a lot of consultants, such as GEA. We also launched the idea of being more flexible. Before, our planning cycle fixed the next calendar month (which meant that in reality fixing was for an average of six weeks). We then moved towards a weekly cycle. The results have not been wholly satisfactory, but the mentality has changed.

In the area of finance there have been significant changes in the organization. For years finance was a hidden function. However, with the decision to float the shares of the Ariston group on the market, finance became a far more visible function.

People in the organization became much more aware of finance. We had to produce reports for outsiders, and these reports mattered. People saw that finance could help the organization achieve new things. For instance, the fact that we floated on the stock exchange allowed us to buy Indesit. It also helped us raise funds. No longer were we a bad necessity in the organization.

The floatation of the company on the stock market also raised people's interest in the financial performance of the company. However, awareness is not the same as a drive for profits. One executive noted: 'The goal of the Ariston group is not profit for the sake of profit. Our people seem content with a 1 per cent return on sales. Our best competitors are earning 6 per cent.'

## THE MERGER AND THE FIRST YEAR AFTER

### Initial impressions

In 1987 Vittorio Merloni consulted all the managers about the proposed merger with Indesit. This decision to consult reflects Merloni's unusually open style of governance. Three quotations help summarize the differing perceptions which existed inside Ariston of the value of the proposed merger. These quotations were made in 1992 in answer to the question 'What did you think of the merger when you were asked in 1987?'.

The logic of the deal was simple. Indesit was a good brand where Ariston was weak. For example there was strength in the UK and France. As important, buying Indesit gave us the potential to increase our hold on the Italian market. It seemed as though we had reached the limit available to the Ariston Brand.

I was asked what I thought of the acquisition of Indesit, and I said I was against it. From the point of selling 'built-in' equipment, the purchase of Indesit was not a forward step. Indesit did not bring any value to my area. I would have liked us to acquire SMEG. This would have bought more value.

We bought Indesit because it was an *Italian company* and had a good position in Europe. It was also affordable. We felt that it was better to buy a local firm than a foreign one, for instance one located in Germany.

## The frozen period 1988

Ariston bought Indesit on 1 January 1988, and initially Vittorio Merloni decided to wait and watch.

We initially maintained the two companies separately, because we wanted to know Indesit in greater detail. We wanted to give the message to Indesit that we were not the conquerors.

At the very beginning we thought that Indesit was a strongly placed company. We could see that it had low prices and low value, so we thought it was a low cost producer. It seemed to be 'lean on expenses'. It seemed to be a simple business where we, the Merloni Group, could add value.

It was thought that the Merloni management could lift the Indesit brand name out from the bottom of the market. This would create higher value in better margins and better sales.

Others reacted similarly:

In the initial moments, I drew a company map and showed it to Merloni. I said, 'Look how slim Indesit looks, and look at us. In the last ten years Indesit has had a slimming diet, which eliminates the superfluous.'

By early 1989, a year after the acquisition, it was clear that things were going badly. Losses were rising, stocks were rising. Information was scarce. There was a sense of crisis. It is interesting to speculate on the extent to which the subsequent difficulties were the consequence of the original approach of the Ariston management, or other factors. People were clearly divided on this point.

To some the problem lay in radically different cultures:

Between Ariston and Indesit there were radically different cultures. In Ariston every drawer is open, In Indesit every drawer is closed.

Others variously said:

In this company we spend a lot of time and effort on reports and we share this information. In Indesit, information was only shared among the top people. In Indesit there is a question of power. It was a military company and very hierarchically managed.

It is not difficult to integrate. It is a human problem. When you have two different subsidiaries, you have two managing directors. First you have to chose one who will be responsible. Everyone tends to defend his own structure and people. If you do not make the choice, about who is the boss, then you are not able to do anything, that is the point.

Others took the view that the problems were more isolated, and mainly at the top: 'Until Faccio left Indesit, nothing was possible.'

I did not discover until later, but when I went abroad to visit an Indesit location, a telephone call went out from Indesit to the local management warning them that someone was coming from Ariston. Someone told the locals to show only the minimum to the Ariston people.

It took us a long time to realize that we had a problem. We thought that the Indesit people were very open, but the reality was the opposite. Some refused or postponed decisions in favour of integration. They wanted to preserve their autonomy. We could not accept that.

Some suggested that the fault lay in the naïvety of the Ariston group which had little experience of acquisitions.

After the acquisition was announced, we had a meeting with the President. He told us that: 'We have to watch for six months, then we can act. But for the first six months we simply have to understand what Indesit dislikes.' This position seemed very reasonable at the time, but as time passed it became obvious that it was not such a good idea. The possibilities of reducing costs and making synergies were obvious, yet nothing happened. Our hands were tied.

From the very beginning I could not conceive of Ariston and Indesit as two separate companies, even if others did. Our competitors are strong. It is very important for two smaller companies like Ariston and Indesit to exploit product and process synergies. Indesit is only producing 1,300,000 pieces a year, and Ariston 2,000,000 pieces. If you try to go to the market with different projects, for example one washing machine in Teverolo and another one in Comunanza, then you lose when you face Electrolux or even Candy.

Another said:

> One of the most shocking things was that everyone was worried about little things and ignoring the important things. For example, in the top management meetings the Board would worry about whether a DM 1.69 for $1 exchange rate was correct for translating figures. This discussion was out of proportion when the whole business was losing money. After the purchase of Indesit, we had an army of factories, an army of people and the results were poor. Most of the management numbers were a fiction and the true position could only be reconciled at the time of the formal audit.
>
> The real problem was that this acquisition was planned from the heart and not from the head. There was no plan about what to do after the acquisition had been accomplished.

## INTEGRATION 1989–91

### The triggers for action

Vittorio Merloni explained the situation as follows:

> At the beginning of the second year [1989] we realized that we had a serious problem. We then held a seminar in Urbino when we discussed the role of information. To those in Indesit, information was power. This was in sharp contrast to what I believe Ariston stands for. For me, leadership is important.

In the middle of 1989 the signal was given to integrate, and to do this quickly. It is instructive to trace the process of integration from the perspective of different functions. This reveals two key factors. First, not all aspects of integration were able to start at the same time, and some aspects of integration took far less time than others. Second, it was not always the Ariston culture which dominated, sometimes Indesit was on top, and sometimes there was a true fusion.

### Administrative functions

We begin by examining some of the areas where integration was the quickest and easiest to achieve: finance and administration.

To paraphrase one person in the administration,

> The problems were identified, but the staff did not have clear experience. Until 1990 Indesit referred to Merloni if it needed it, they used to send us reports but these were often not accurate or precise and often did not follow our instructions. When we started to integrate with Indesit, it was clear that there were problems not profits.

However, integrating finance was relatively easy. It took three months. We insisted that all the financial controls were ours. We did it all on the Fabriano computer.

Regarding the small central human resources function, the following quotation speaks for itself:

In Human Resources, integration was greatly helped by the fact that the unions wanted to bargain with just one counterpart. They wanted, and we made, one agreement for the two companies.

Logistics took a little longer:

At the beginning of 1990 things began to change. It was clear that physical distribution had to be integrated. For instance Ariston had a warehouse in Rome which cost 3,000 lire per item, Indesit had a different arrangement with another warehouse which cost 5,000 lire a unit. For one year we were paying out 2,000 lire more a piece just because Indesit was not integrated with us.

It only took six months to integrate Indesit's Italian system to ours, that is to put computers in all the locations. We were lucky that it took so little time, for Indesit really had no systems.

At the end of the six months, most but not all of the job was done. The old Indesit central systems had to be torn out and everything replaced. This took sixteen months. Subsidiaries are taking longer, and it is anticipated that the last country will be Netherlands where integration will be complete by 1993.

You can see this in the control of stocks. In Indesit production and marketing did not talk. Production produced, on a seasonal basis, what they thought was appropriate (almost) regardless of the situation. As a result in [spring] 1989, at the peak, there were 700,000 finished goods pieces in inventory of which 338,000 pieces were from Indesit, in all more than a quarter of the whole year's sales. It was 'ridiculous'.

**Integrating the factories**

Production integration took longer. Those in production realized that there were problems. Before the merger, Ariston had six factories whose average production was 300,000 pieces and whose total production was 1,800,000. Indesit had six factories whose average production was 200,000 pieces giving their total of 1,200,000 pieces. Indesit had more than 2,500 people tied up in their factories. Products did not match factories, so the group had fourteen different production locations: 5 for washing machines, 4 for refrigerators, 4 for cooking equipment and 2 for dishwashers.

The target for integration seemed easy to rationalize. In 1988, the group invested 40 billion lire in plant and equipment; in 1989 63 billion lire was invested. As one manager explained:

> We started immediately on the integration of factories and information systems. We worked very hard. The Indesit people in the factories were OK, they wanted to know how we did things, They wanted to know our systems. Within a year, we had some commonality of systems. This does not mean to say that the mentalities were the same.
>
> We worked well together. Their equipment was terrible. They wanted investment. They came to see our factories, and we visited theirs. All employees were involved in exchanges.

Another explained:

> We organized teams to study the potential of factory integration. Some of these meetings occurred in Indesit locations, for instance Torino, and some in Fabriano in Ariston locations. Not everyone liked the idea, but we did it. We focused on synergies and analysis. We started by looking at the information systems, for we recognized the need to speak the same language. For me, information systems are very important in an integration process.

Another explained:

> We had a team approach to the problem. Sallustro, Del Neri and Santini sat down and worked out seven different scenarios. Then they decided to move. They cut one factory in the South. At the time the group was running at around 60 per cent of actual capacity. It is clear that the sense of crisis helped us integrate more fully.
>
> I can identify two phases in the production integration. First we had to reshuffle production and close some factories. We also redefined the products, with some Indesit branded products being made in Ariston factories, and some Ariston branded products being made in Indesit factories. We experimented with the mix to find the best way. Now, in 1992, we are in the second phase where we are replanning the whole system to obtain the best advantages.

One of the chief problems was the lack of flexibility in the Indesit factories. It seems that Indesit was making only a few variants of a basic model whereas Ariston was making much greater variety more flexibly. (For example, in a refrigeration factory Ariston was able to make nineteen different sizes and 220 different models with perhaps twenty different types being produced each day in a daily run of 1,800 units.) Integration of production has yet to extend to full integration of components. The models are different and the number of common components are small.

## The challenge to marketing and commercial sections

In the marketing area things were not so easy:

> Ariston and Indesit were historically two brands which fought each other. The sales people in each company found it difficult to change their attitudes. Before the merger, Ariston sales staff were used to listing the disadvantages of buying Indesit, and likewise the Indesit people were attacking Ariston.

Another manager in built-in appliances said:

> Indesit had no position in the *built-in market*. However, in my few contacts with Indesit, I confirm that there were differences in culture, the way of approaching the market. Problems seemed to emerge on every occasion.

Another senior manager explained that the time allocation for integrating the Ariston and Indesit organizations was an ever-rising crescendo. He explained that for him the integration was only half done.

> As far as I was concerned, it was the first time that I was involved in an integration process. The amount of time required to talk to the people of Indesit and Ariston to get the potential synergies was enormous.
>
> In Indesit, they sold what they produced. There was no marketing approach. It was a successful formula fifteen years ago, but not now. For Indesit it was difficult to understand the idea of marketing and an approach based on the concept that markets are complex in terms of segmentation etc.
>
> We have organized to develop what we call a multi-brand strategy. This means that the two brands, Indesit and Ariston, have to be complementary. We started to develop this idea in the UK; it was an easier country thanks to the distribution concentration. The results [there] are favourable. When the commercial staff visit a [retail] customer, he or she can offer two brands with different images and positions. This is less expensive than having two organizations.
>
> In Italy we have not yet fully integrated. We still have two separate sales organizations and two independent sales managers. Ariston is positioned on the traditional channel and Indesit is geared more

towards wholesalers. In the near future, I anticipate keeping the two sales organizations separate but having a single common marketing group.

In the future we must change. We need a more flexible organization with less fixed costs, and less variable costs. This will allow us more money to invest in advertising and services.

Another senior manager put the view more controversially:

We keep changing our minds. In the beginning Ariston was superb and Indesit rubbish. Now that integration has taken place, people's perceptions have changed, and people are praising Indesit, because it is the better known brand across Europe. These are conflicts in people's heads. We have to face reality. There is a market out there. The problem of labels is irrelevant. We need to generate as many sales as possible to fill the factories. Our job is not to define Ariston and define Indesit and sell this to the market; our job is to work out what the market wants and work back from there. So you see there is debate in the organization.

**After sales and spare parts**

In spare parts and after sales service, the process of integration has been much more difficult.

It took until 1991 to integrate spare parts. Now we have a warehouse in Fabriano for both Indesit and Ariston products. The integration of after sales service is not yet tackled.

In 1988, after the acquisition, Indesit signed a contract with a company that was managing the after sales service of Indesit. This gave this company an exclusive right to service Indesit appliances in Italy until December 1992. The contract had two important provisions. One was a high reward to this company for servicing Indesit appliances, and this remuneration was higher than the costs incurred by Ariston when servicing Ariston products. Second, this company had the right to sell damaged appliances. This latter part of the contract gave this company the right to pay a small sum of money for a damaged appliance and the ability to resell at a much higher price. This was worth about one billion lire a year in profits. This company is costing us a lot of money, moreover, we are losing out on possible benefits from integration.

**Outside of Italy**

It is to be expected that the situation in other European countries would be different from that of Italy. In Spain the integration was relatively speedy:

> In Spain this was the situation. Ariston had a small operation, and all its sales went through one channel, called 'Expert'. Expert is a buying group which operates on behalf of independent retailers in Spain, and it represents about 10 per cent of the Spanish market. In contrast, Indesit had a much bigger presence in Spain, for it had more than twenty years experience of this market. Traditionally Indesit worked with wholesalers, but more recently it had moved to supplying retailers direct, with the result that it had to serve a highly fragmented population of very small dealers. It had become, in actual fact, a wholesaler itself. It was, however, profitable, whereas Ariston was losing money.
>
> I was sent from Fabriano with an explicit brief to investigate the possibilities for integration.
>
> When I arrived, the Ariston and Indesit organizations were completely different, as one would expect, both in size and management style. Moreover, at Indesit the links with the parent company had traditionally been looser and the local management enjoyed a sort of 'entrepreneurial' autonomy. Still, both seemed to match the requirements of the specific channel of distribution each one served. Still, it was clear that there would be cost advantages in merging some of the operations such as service.
>
> But the key problem was strategic: how to move on from there, mainly in terms of distribution development for each brand. To tackle the strategic issue and carry out the integration it was clear that we had to start from the top. The first move was then to put both organizations under one head. Garbero, Indesit's Managing Director, was appointed to the job.
>
> By the time I left Spain the business was in profit, and this was only three months after I arrived. Later, most of the Ariston staff (some 8 or 9 people) were dismissed. The Ariston office in Barcelona was closed and the whole operation was transferred to the Indesit offices in Madrid.

In the UK, the situation was very different. Part of the differences lay in the personalities involved, and part in the far greater size of the respective businesses. The current management of the UK operations explains:

> You need to understand that historically Indesit was a very strong

firm in the UK market. Now when I first came to the UK in 1984, Ariston was presented with an opportunity because of the crisis in Indesit. In 1984 Indesit's share was close to 6 per cent and Ariston less than 2 per cent if not 1 per cent. When I left a few years later, Ariston had increased its share to 3 per cent, selling more than 210,000 units a year up from 100,000 units in 1984. The increased volume was not wholly reflected by increased profits, because at this time it was hard for us to make money in this low priced market with its competitive margins. The strategy at that time, which was agreed with Del Neri, was to pitch Ariston above Indesit, which was located in the lower part of the market.

When I left the UK in 1987 we still faced some critical problems. After sales service was not under the control of sales, but under the direction of someone else. For the operations in the UK to be effective, it is necessary that these two be integrated under one management. The second problem was in the quality of the products sent from Italy. We were the first company to offer a washer/dryer in the UK, but the reliability of our machines was poor and they broke down frequently. The washer/dryer became successful in the UK market only when Hotpoint entered with their machine. It was Hotpoint's credibility and attention to quality which made a real difference to the British consumer; the Hotpoint machine was much more reliable.[3]

Between 1977 and 1989 a discreet veil is drawn. In the spring of 1989 an Indesit manager was appointed managing director for both companies. By the end of the summer most of the Ariston staff had been made redundant (with the exception of most of the service engineers) and all that was left of Ariston Domestic Appliances moved to the Indesit premises. In the new operation, Indesit and Ariston sales and marketing operations were kept rigidly separated. One Italian noted: 'I was in the UK on the second day of the integration [in 1989]. I saw foolish things being done. We [in Ariston] were used to planning the details. What I saw was tragic.'

In June 1990, the managing director left and a new managing director arrived. He had previous connections with the UK. He continues the story:

When I arrived, a number of things had happened. There was some integration, but it was not always satisfactory. The top management had been from Indesit, and their policy had resulted in this situation:

• The business was unprofitable due to low margins rather than high costs. It was clear that the old attitude had been to sell everything based on cutting price.

- The business was very unbalanced. The Indesit brand was selling about 360,000 units a year versus 80,000 units from Ariston. As you can see Ariston had lost ground since 1987.
- There was a low level of motivation internally The Ariston and Indesit cultures were constantly clashing, with 'them' and 'us'.
- Finally, in the UK everyone seemed to believe that Indesit and Ariston were in the same segment, something which was in contrast to the situation of some years previously, but probably true at the time.

What did the UK management do? The actions seemed simple, but this is the benefit of hindsight. At the time they were difficult and powerful moves. Nor were all these moves wholeheartedly supported by the Italian headquarters, where resistance also had to be broken down and top managers persuaded.

Soon after I arrived, the previous managing director left. Most of his old team were to leave the company within weeks as they would not fit into the new set up. There was a key man sent from Italy, Nicolai, the finance director, who since the autumn of 1989 had managed to carry out most of the integration work. Two more Italians, both from the Ariston 'school', were in the management team. Apart from these, I had to build a wholly new team. The new team consists of eight people and we have a very flat structure. There is a free-standing director, a built-in director, a finance and personnel manager (Nicolai), a marketing director and after sales service director, a logistics director and a manager for the newly created customer services. The eighth person is, of course, myself. Five of us were new to the company. Building this new top team took a lot of effort, but only six months of time.

One of the things I had to sort out was the brand strategy. One alternative was to focus on Indesit and try and upgrade the brand. But this seemed risky, for Indesit's strength in the UK lay in the low 'entry price' segment. Therefore we chose the brand differentiation route, which seemed to be the best strategy. This meant that Ariston had to be further 'up-market' than Indesit. Ariston was to be the innovator in the medium-priced segment. However, it was not possible to do anything without funds.

To gain funds we had to improve profitability. We had to alter the mix and the margins. This meant down-playing refrigeration and moving the emphasis to higher margin products. We also had to strike a blow to fixed costs. But we could not continue to make redundancies in order to carry on doing the same things with less people. We had to change the way we were operating and at the same time improve motivation and make people more effective. There was only one way. Two brands but one team.

At the beginning we had two separate organizations, one dealing with Ariston and one dealing with Indesit. But from December 1990, we integrated Ariston and Indesit on the commercial side. This was only six months after I arrived. Two brands and one team. All salesmen are account managers and offer a portfolio of brands. The same concept was applied throughout the company: by the end of 1990 everybody was behind both brands. By this process we were able to save 20 per cent of the staff *and* sell more in total. This meant a dramatic improvement in our profitability. We have created a virtuous circle. From the savings we were not only able to pay a profit (to Fabriano), but also able to invest two million pounds a year (more than four billion lire) in advertising.

The difficulty of the task forced us all to be more creative. The 'customer service' concept was first introduced in the UK and is now in the process of being 'exported' to Italy and other subsidiaries. We also had to create new values and new ways of doing things.

Although the UK had still to undertake a complete restructuring of the after sales service, by the end of 1990 all of the operations were fully integrated.

## MEASURES OF PROGRESS

In 1992 many of the functions had completed their integration. For instance, in finance and systems the progress had been so great that those managing the departments did not see integration as a significant future issue. They said that they faced a stream of general problems rather than ones emanating from the merger. In other functions, as we noted earlier, progress has still to be made. Vittorio Merloni, the president, summarized the situation: 'After three years hard work (i.e from the beginning of 1989) we have done three-quarters of the task of integration. But we still have another quarter to do.'

Measures of progress are not just felt, they are also reflected in the results. Three aspects of progress are detailed here. First is the question of market position.

In Table 10.2, it can be seen that the merger allowed Ariston to 'purchase' market share, increasing its position from 4.7 per cent of the European market to about 10 per cent. Since the merger, the position of the brands in Italy has strengthened, by about one or two percentage points. The top management view is that this reflects better marketing, efficiency and quality. The group's position has also improved in the

*Table 10.2* Market size and share data 1984–90

| Year | 1984 | 1985 | 1986 | 1987 | 1988 | 1989 | 1990 |
|---|---|---|---|---|---|---|---|
| **Market size in millions of units** | | | | | | | |
| Europe total | 30.3 | 32.5 | 35.0 | 37.9 | 39.9 | 40.4 | 41.0 |
| Free-standing | 22.9 | 24.1 | 25.6 | 27.4 | 28.4 | 28.6 | 28.7 |
| Built-in | 7.4 | 8.4 | 9.4 | 10.5 | 11.5 | 11.7 | 12.3 |
| **Indesit and Ariston share (%)** | | | | | | | |
| In Italy | 14.5 | 15.8 | 18.0 | 18.6 | 20.2 | 20.3 | 21.3 |
| In Europe | 4.7 | 5.0 | 7.1 | 8.5 | 10.0 | 10.0 | 9.0 |

*Source:* Annual Reports
*Note:* The market share figures for 1984 are for Ariston alone

*Table 10.3* Ariston-Indesit: principal financial results (billion lire)

| Year | 1984 | 1985 | 1986 | 1987 | 1988 | 1989 | 1990 | 1991 |
|---|---|---|---|---|---|---|---|---|
| Total sales | 340 | 441 | 512 | 597 | 1,059 | 1,076 | 1,152 | 1,192 |
| Italian sales | 160 | 221 | 293 | 319 | 475 | 455 | 448 | 450 |
| Overseas sales | 180 | 220 | 219 | 278 | 584 | 621 | 704 | 742 |
| **Cash flow** | | | 28 | 42.6 | 48.5 | 38.9 | 51.1 | 61.1 |
| Depreciation | | | | 24.5 | 32.3 | 38.8 | 44.5 | 49.4 |
| Operating profit | | | 23.4 | 36.2 | 45.9 | 17.9 | 36.1 | 41.5 |
| Net profit | | | 5.6 | 18.1 | 16.2 | 0.1 | 6.6 | 11.7 |

*Source:* Public financial statements
*Note:* Year ends 31 December

UK. However, taking Europe as a whole, the position has declined, with most of this decline being accounted for by the absence of the group from the German speaking markets where the demand has been growing strongly.

The financial figures tell a more potent story. Here it can be seen that in the initial year of purchase of Indesit, profits rose considerably. Yet these profits were not a fair reflection of the true situation. 1988 was a boom year, and many of the true problems of Indesit, a formerly bankrupt company, were hidden behind the numbers. Debt was high, inventories were not under control and profits were, unknown to management at the time, inflated.

A look at the income statement (Table 10.3) shows how operating profits and profits after financial charges fell in 1989 and were recovered by the end of 1991. It is Vittorio Merloni's view that the statistics look good when one realizes that the market was generally depressed.

Table 10.4 presents some key operating statistics. These highlight the debt and inventory difficulties of 1989, mentioned earlier in the text.

*Table 10.4* Ariston-Indesit: some key operating statistics on debts and stocks

| Year | 1984 | 1985 | 1986 | 1987 | 1988 | 1989 | 1990 | 1991 |
|---|---|---|---|---|---|---|---|---|
| Financial debts | | | 118 | 119 | 135 | 259 | 191 | 194 |
| Net assets | | | 78 | 125 | 139 | 147 | 175 | 212 |
| Net assets/debt | | | 0.66 | 1.1 | 1.0 | 0.55 | 0.92 | 1.1 |
| Total sales | 340 | 441 | 512 | 597 | 1,059 | 1,076 | 1,152 | 1,192 |
| Inventory | 56 | 50 | 53 | 85 | 176 | 216 | 176 | 191 |
| Inventory/sales | 0.16 | 0.11 | 0.10 | 0.14 | 0.17 | 0.20 | 0.15 | 0.16 |
| Units sold (millions) | 1.13 | 1.35 | 1.60 | 1.86 | 3.15 | 3.33 | 3.34 | 3.43 |
| Inventory units | | | | | 0.52 | 0.48 | 0.34 | 0.37 |
| Ratio | | | | | 0.17 | 0.14 | 0.10 | 0.11 |
| Total staff | 3,100 | 3,086 | 3,338 | 3,459 | 5,950 | 6,173 | 5,402 | 5,479 |
| Crude index of output/ employee | 365 | 437 | 479 | 538 | 529 | 539 | 618 | 626 |

*Source:* Public financial reports and internal documents

(The figures in the table are year-end figures, and it should be noted that there is some seasonality with peak inventories being recorded in the spring.) The figures also show the extent of progress; by the end of 1991 debt had been reduced. In addition, inventories were brought under better control, and their valuations better managed.

The last rows of figures of Table 10.4 show the extent to which the group has been able to achieve a better utilization of its human resources. The crude number of machines produced per factory operative has improved over the last few years. Factory operatives form about two-thirds of all employment, and factory costs are a big part of total costs. Thus the closing of several factories with appropriate rationalization has had a big effect on margins. For example, by investment in flexibility and better working practices and transfers, the number of Italian cooking factories has been reduced from two to one, the number of cooling factories (freezers and refrigerators) from three to two, a dishwasher factory has been closed and efficiencies gained in the three washing machine plants.

The production departments claim that the figures understate the progress. There has been a great increase in the complexity of output, with once inflexible plants now required to produce wider and more complex ranges than before, with more sophisticated models and shorter production runs. For instance, in a typical refrigeration plant producing some 1,800 units a day, the capability may be to produce nineteen

*Table 10.5* Ariston-Indesit: numbers employed by department 1989–91

| Year | 1989 | 1990 | 1991 |
|---|---|---|---|
| **Italian position** | | | |
| Central | 221 | 199 | 190 |
| Commercial | 324 | 276 | 280 |
| Technical | 248 | 200 | 226 |
| Factory | 3,716 | 3,187 | 3,205 |
| **Overseas position** | | | |
| UK | 590 | 436 | 413 |
| Spain | 109 | 91 | 96 |

*Source:* Internal documents
*Note:* Italian data excludes numbers employed in after sales service

different sizes of machines and 220 different models. Flexibility would be great with between nineteen and twenty-four model types being produced each day; making daily runs of less than a hundred per model.

The gains in other areas of the business can be gauged by some crude breakdowns in numbers employed. Some simple statistics on the breakdown of employment illustrate the point (Table 10.5).

## NEXT STEPS

When Vittorio Merloni talked of the future of the company, he was very buoyant:

> We were a late entrant into this industry, producing our first appliances in 1970. Now, by 1990, we are a very significant player. My goal is to capture 10 per cent of the wider European market. This means we shall have to consolidate our position in other markets. I am delighted that we are about to announce a link up with a producer in Turkey. This helps to cement our position. We have an important presence in France through our acquisition of Scholtes [a leading producer of cooking appliances]. We also have an important presence in Portugal with our partners there.

## NOTES

1  © C. Baden-Fuller and C. Boschetti 1993
   This case study has been written as a basis for class discussion rather than to illustrate effective or ineffective managerial or administrative behaviour. The authors are grateful for the assistance of Vittorio Merloni and his colleagues at Ariston-Merloni.

2 Authors' estimates based on data given by Merloni for its employment directly and through subcontractors.
3 This can be confirmed by reference to the UK Consumer Association reports of the time which independently evaluated the products.

# Section 3

# Leadership and entrepreneurial styles

# Chapter 11

# Pyrochem Ltd: entrepreneurship in action[1]

## Martyn Pitt

### EDITORS' OVERVIEW

This case study highlights what many would consider the classic entrepreneurial style of management. It describes how a charismatic young innovator, Hamish Dean, founds his first company, then quickly sells it when he discovers what seems to be a better business opportunity. There follow several years of struggle against adversity, as the opportunity proves less attractive than he supposed.

None the less, the entrepreneur persists and ultimately his firm, Pyrochem, prospers. The case describes Dean's willingness to take risks, to confront emerging difficulties and crises, and the imaginative, innovative measures he took to ensure the survival and ultimate success of Pyrochem. It tries to impart a sense of his leadership style and some significant changes in organization structure and ethos after the mid-1980s. The case also describes a number of diversification activities that Dean justified to himself on the basis that they related to and/or supported the firm's core activity.

From the perspective of strategic management, a number of pertinent issues are addressed. A recent text highlighted the linkages between strategy and leadership, arguing that leadership style is a significant, but by no means deterministic influence on strategy formation.[2] Other influences are the operating contexts provided by the firm's external environment, its organization structure and culture, and the effects of past history on future possibilities. From this perspective the leader of a small firm contributes a set of values, stylistic norms and visions of where the firm is going and might go in the future, which have then to be interpreted by the key players in the light of the many, often ambiguous external forces and events. Examples of these can be found in this case study.

Strategic decision making in Pyrochem has been a paradoxical process. Dean draws attention to the ability of Pyrochem's senior executives to grasp detail without losing sight of general direction, seeing the 'big picture'. He himself delegates important decisions to trusted staff, yet wanders about, spotting detailed problems needing attention. Strategies emerge from a combination of analysis and intuition, consistency and idiosyncrasy, boldness and prudence, riding one's luck yet contriving situations where luck is not a principal determinant of outcomes. Dean's perception of a 'five-year unwritten plan in the head', informed by the core threads of fire protection and specialty chemicals, contrasts strikingly with his emphasis on 'adaptive flexibility', the former underpinned by his unwavering faith in his vision for the firm and dogged persistence in adversity, the latter a self-declared obsession to maintain multiple options when implementing any new venture.

According to colleagues, Dean is a master of understanding the customer perspective, having flair for creative and sometimes counter-intuitive solutions to intractable problems and the creation of considerable advantage when applying these solutions. Yet here too there is a paradox. Although he has established a dominant position in a specialist market niche, he says he has constantly sought new challenges and in so doing he may have compromised the development of the core business to some degree.

## Discussion questions

- Describe Pyrochem's strategy in conventional terms. What are its principal sources of advantage and why?
- Can Pyrochem's success up to the 1990s be attributed more to the pursuit of clearly envisioned opportunities than to the systematic development and exploitation of core competences? What part has context played in this?
- How much has Dean's leadership style contributed to Pyrochem's success? Is it possible (probable?) that it would have been more successful under a different managerial style? How would that style have to differ and what might its effects on the firm have been?
- How valid is the use of the word *paradoxical* to characterize strategy formation in Pyrochem and the thinking of its chief executive?
- What lessons, if any, can be drawn from Pyrochem about making the strategic conduct of bigger firms more entrepreneurial?
- What changes to Pyrochem's strategy would you propose if it were taken over and became a business unit in a more diversified corporation?

## List of named characters

Hamish Dean, chairman
Jimmy Jones, facilities manager

Mike Simmonds, managing director
Dick Thomas, product manager
Paul Quinn, technical director

**Keywords**

Small firms; strategy formation; flexibility; leadership style and vision; organization structure and culture; market innovation/pioneering; growth and diversification

## ENTREPRENEURIAL BEGINNINGS

Hamish Dean is the founder and chairman of Pyrochem Ltd. Though trained as a computer programmer, he became a salesman in his wife's family merchanting firm in his early twenties. Two years later he was running his own firm as a fire prevention contractor. He had become aware of new fire regulations imposing stringent constraints on private hotels and recognized that fire officers and contractors were poorly prepared to advise proprietors:

> The national boys were used to putting in huge systems for factories, they couldn't cope with small installations. So you had local electricians charging £2,000 for a £500 job. Legislation demanded something and no single company was geared up to supply it.

Dean began to service this market, using mainly subcontract labour. Clients paid cash on completion. Within eighteen months he employed about twenty full-time and part-time staff:

> Learning literally by the minute . . . flying by the seat of the pants. Every minute a new problem came up and I had to find a way of solving it. It was fabulous fun. The carpenters I hired came on the understanding that if we hadn't any chipping that week they would help the electricians – if there wasn't any electrical work they would help the steel fabricators put up fire escapes or help prepare for redecorating at the end of the contract. They had to be very, very flexible.

Soon Dean was also distributing branded fire alarms, selling to third parties and to his own clients. In 1974 he found a special fire-retardant paint. This so-called thin-film intumescent paint was brushed or sprayed on to exposed surfaces. In the heat of a fire the paint would swell into a two-inch thick charred cladding, protecting the supporting structure until the fire brigade arrived: 'Within six months we were the biggest user [of intumescent paint] in the country. We weren't using very much, but we were using far more than anyone else.'

In 1975 Dean bid opportunistically for a much bigger job than any he had so far done. He quoted what he thought was a ludicrously high price. He still got the order! 'We got halfway through when they doubled the size of the contract. We suddenly realised there were jobs around with a lot of profit potential.'

## THE SWITCH TO DISTRIBUTING INTUMESCENT PAINTS

Thereafter, Dean had no doubt about the potential of intumescent paints. He reacted decisively by selling his contracting business to specialize in distribution. He called the new firm Pyrochem. Although he understood that large UK chemical firms had access to the technology, they declined to trade with him, so he scoured West Europe and found German and French products for protecting wood and steel respectively. Neither was selling well in its own country and Dean managed to negotiate UK distribution rights.

Despite these chemicals being the subject of patent applications as early as 1938, the UK regulatory authorities viewed them with suspicion. Perhaps the situation would have been different if a leading chemicals firm had put its reputation solidly behind the technology, but mindful of contingent product liability in the USA, no one had done so. So Dean had great difficulty persuading the authorities that his products were trustworthy. Their most serious objection was that in a serious fire the promised 30-minute protection time was inadequate. Also, because intumescents were seen as paints it was assumed, erroneously, that structures would need re-treating every few years, which would be costly and impractical.

Dean persisted with applications for wood, especially where regulations were less stringent or did not apply. He persuaded clients to use his products as, in effect, an insurance policy – but without the aesthetic or health drawbacks of competing products like asbestos. He ran the firm from home, storing imported chemicals in outbuildings where they were repackaged into smaller quantities for distributors. The products were marketed under distributors' names and the continuing absence of leading competitors allowed Pyrochem to charge high prices. By keeping overheads low, Dean developed a modest, but cash-rich business. Between 1976 and 1980 the firm grew slowly, because large industrial projects remained elusive.

Dean and his wife had both been raised in an exclusive religious sect. As Pyrochem grew, Dean recruited new staff from the sect, as was expected of him. By 1981 he employed eight full-time staff and distributed via regional agents, some of whom were also subcontractors as well as sect members. Dean's brother, an industrial chemist, joined the firm in 1977 and worked on product testing and improvement. Pyrochem sent its products to the laboratories of the industry association for testing.

By 1980 they had achieved 57-minutes fire resistance with an enhanced version of their main product. Not quite the magic hour, this result still proved a highly symbolic sales message. This advance, allied to the convenience of intumescent paints and growing concerns over the use of asbestos, began to legitimize its use in structural fire protection. As Paul Quinn, who joined in 1981 as a sales representative, explained:

> If any company was associated with intumescents it was Pyrochem. It seemed like manna from heaven, this magical paint which could give fire protection, rather than use clumsy boards and casings. But legislators and contractors found it very difficult to believe in, there was still a great deal of resistance over the longevity of the material.

Dean is in no doubt that his self-belief kept the product alive at that time: 'Without Pyrochem, intumescents would have died a natural death in this country, if not far wider.'

## INNOVATIONS IN MARKET POSITIONING

Dean accelerated Pyrochem's growth from the late 1970s in several ways. To negate continuing scepticism over the technical performance of intumescents for steel he repositioned them as *functional aesthetic*, extending the core benefit of his wood products to the steel paints. Thus Pyrochem could offer aesthetic, cost-effective protection on *any* exposed beam or panel structure.

Dean directed his message at structural *specifiers*, principally architects, as opposed to builders or fire protection agencies. He discovered that when architects wanted exposed steel work they saw intumescents as a liberating design factor and would argue with building control officers to get intumescents approved. He began a concerted propaganda campaign using attractive and informative sales literature and intensive mailing, supported by face-to-face selling. This ploy gained wide awareness of the product at a time when steel-frame structures were becoming increasingly popular because of faster construction and lower cost than traditional methods.

A third innovation was to offer a top (sealing) coat in the full British Standard range of colours, positively encouraging architects to regard exposed steel work as a design feature. Pyrochem had no experience of colour mixing, but that did not bother Dean. As site manager Jimmy Jones explained:

> We were just left to get on with it – we used to mix it in tubs with a big wooden paddle. At times we were at our wit's end to get a colour match, but we did it! I'm not saying we were up to Dulux standard but we weren't far away. The complaints we got were few and far between.

Dean also used the fire protection industry association as a vehicle to lobby the regulators. He aimed to win full acceptance of intumescents and to enhance Pyrochem's legitimacy by excluding 'cowboys'. Thus Pyrochem's thin-film products in effect established and came to dominate the UK 'aesthetic fire protection market', with a peak share by value of around 70 per cent.

## BANISHMENT FROM THE SECT AND ACCELERATED GROWTH

Refocusing on structural steel applications required knowledgeable sales staff. To talk intelligently to engineers, architects, building control officers and other professionals they had to appreciate where and how intumescents could be applied, an advisory technical role. Dean also wanted them to identify new projects, negotiate supply contracts, stay in close contact through the construction phase, and ensure that good quality work was done. His problem was to attract suitably qualified people to his small firm. By 1981 he was looking beyond the sect for the calibre of staff he wanted. This became a source of friction with the elders of the sect.

Pyrochem had by now generated sufficient cash for Dean to acquire commercial building land in a down-at-heel part of Lanchester, where he commissioned several small industrial units. Pyrochem occupied one of these and Dean sub-let the others. This was a catalytic event. The elders were concerned at Dean's commercial ambition and he was disillusioned with their obstructive rules. Matters came to a head when they told him to hand over the ownership of Pyrochem to the sect and and become the firm's manager. He refused. All the staff including his brother and his accountant quit. Only his wife and a recent non-partisan recruit remained. Distributors severed their links and Dean and his wife were banished from the sect.

But if the elders thought their action would make Dean cave in they were wrong. He immediately hired Dick Thomas as sales office administrator and Jimmy Jones as storeman. As Thomas recalled:

When Hamish asked me for interview the offices were empty, there was nobody at all. He offered me the job there and then, kept upping the offer, threw in a company car and petrol, a good salary – it became an offer I couldn't refuse. I was out of work and I joined at once.

The phone never stopped ringing and I was the only one there to answer it. Each week I spent three days answering the phone and two days driving all over the country to sort out technical problems on site. Typically, each day brought a few little orders, then perhaps a year later they'd come back with a big job. After six months or so it was clear that Hamish had a decision to make. He asked, should we stay the size we are or expand? It was clear we should expand. Safety lay in expansion, so he appointed a sales manager and then set up the sales force.

Dean hired three field sales representatives, building to eight over two years. The first was a trained architect, Paul Quinn, later promoted to technical director. According to Quinn, it was uphill work:

> In my first twelve months there was an awful lot of door knocking, starting to build the name Pyrochem in the market-place. Preaching the story of what it could do, the one hour product, cost comparisons with other materials, the decorative aspects – a lot of work. The main object was to get Pyrochem's name on the specification, into the drawing, the bill of quantities.
>
> There was opposition about, competition from Europe, but none seemed to have their act together as well as us. The literature we had then, it's not very good compared to what we have now, but it was streets ahead of anybody else. We did a lot of evening seminars, we'd lay on a bit of food, a few pints of beer. We did live burn experiments – people love to play with fire. We designed quite spectacular little tests, the more you appeal to another sense – touch and smell and the like – the more impact it has compared with meeting in an office and just talking, with nothing to see.
>
> We would get letters of thanks and requests to go back and do it again. So that worked very well for us. It got our name very firmly established. We got a lot of relatively small orders and as confidence built in the material it started to be seen in larger projects. The timber product formed a high percentage of our low price orders but there was a steady rise in the use of steel frame construction. The credibility gap was filled, but having filled it for ourselves, we were also clearing a path for others.

Between 1980 and 1983 these pioneering initiatives enabled Pyrochem to grow substantially. The strategy of targeting architects paid off, as Pyrochem's name became widely known for protecting steel structures. Several former distributors attempted to compete directly. Dean responded by emphasizing customer service. His small team frequently rushed supplies to impatient contractors so that work would not be interrupted. Even today, company myths invoke heroic stories of Pyrochem engineers loading their cars at 4 a.m. and driving hundreds of miles to get product on site for the start of the early shift.

Dean also encouraged reputable non-specialist painting contractors to apply intumescent coatings, effectively demystifying the process:

> We took technology that previously had been regarded as sacrosanct to specialist contractors and we said the specialization is in defining

the requirement, not in the actual application. There is no reason why non-specialists can't use this product without any problem if they follow the rules.

Dean wrote a detailed specifiers' manual to guide architects and contractors. Mindful of the trade's inclination to cut corners, it specified coverage rates, provided thickness gauges to check work, and instituted a process of job certification whereby the subcontractor confirmed in writing to the client that he had complied with specifications. Thus Pyrochem not only avoided the expense of 'flying squads' of specialist contractors but contingent liability arising from faulty workmanship. Sales and profits again accelerated.

By 1984 Pyrochem employed some twenty staff, mostly in sales and promotion, working under a sales director. According to Thomas, growth was:

> absolutely explosive. At that time we could afford to make mistakes and we did . . . but it didn't matter. We'd cock up one order and the next day we'd have the biggest order we'd ever had – and we didn't necessarily even know where it came from. We had a 100 per cent increase in turnover in a year. That went on for two or three years, then down to 70 per cent a year for a couple of years then down to about 50 per cent a year where it is now. It was terribly exciting then, pioneer days.

Direct competition from major UK chemical firms was still muted, though some firms offered less advanced thick-film products. In late 1984 Dean hired an experienced chemist from a competitor to set up a small R&D facility. Pyrochem's expansion continued through 1985 and 1986, when the head count reached sixty. It also began to export to the Far East and North America, winning some substantial contracts such as the treatment of new power stations. To accommodate expansion, Pyrochem reclaimed its sub-let factory units on the Lanchester site as leases expired.

The export initiative came to the attention of, and evidently displeased, the parent company of the French supplier. Pyrochem began to detect variable quality in its bulk supplies, a significant embarrassment since most customers assumed that Pyrochem was the manufacturer. When a leading customer complained, Dean insisted that French technicians visit his clients. Subsequent failure to improve the product caused Dean to step up Pyrochem's own product development efforts in Lanchester. He recruited a French chemist with complementary expertise in sealing mastics who established a parallel R&D unit near Paris. By autumn 1985 relations with the French supplier were beyond repair and Dean launched Pyrochem's own range of steel intumescent paints. The UK laboratory prepared the 'magic' ingredients and a local subcontractor mixed and repackaged the product for sale.

For customers the only obvious change was improved product consistency. As Dean reflected, the transition was

> Extremely easy – in terms of specialist kit and numbers of people, it didn't make much difference. We had already got the lab to carry out the quality control function. It was a remarkably easy transition. I still wonder today what happened.

However, the French supplier took exception to summary termination of contract and alleged patent infringements. Litigation followed, which took several years to resolve. Meanwhile, the gamble on in-house manufacturing enabled Pyrochem to continue growing rapidly and largely pre-empted competition in the UK market. Pyrochem's growing technical expertise in Lanchester duly led to a range of improved intumescent paints, whilst Paris developed intumescent mastics and foam seals for structural voids and cable ductings. As Jimmy Jones, by now facilities manager, saw it:

> Dean ploughed a hell of a lot of money back in, which gave confidence to the people working with him – this guy isn't a flop, he ain't here just to line his pockets. Independent testing is an expensive game, three or four thousand pounds per test – you can see why a lot of competitors didn't go down that road. We could give you documented evidence to substantiate what we were saying. On the marketing side there were lovely brochures all beautifully art-worked.

Still, competition in the UK market-place remained and further innovation in products and technology was needed. Pyrochem extended protection times of the core product to two hours and developed new products for different kinds of steel sections, for cast iron, for brush and for spray application. Soon the range included a wide range of seals, electric cable protection, new wood paints and sealing coats. An improved system of contractor approval was introduced for complex applications. Export sales also grew apace. By 1987 turnover exceeded £4 million and Dean claimed that, 'To our knowledge – we know most countries – there is no one else in the world selling as much thin-film intumescent paint for steel as us.'

## ORGANIZATION AND MANAGEMENT STYLE

Between 1981 and 1986 Dean was fully involved in day-to-day affairs. Yet except for sales, he lacked the management team one might associate with a multi-million pound business. He managed in an informal, rather paternalistic way, aiming for a caring, goal-oriented culture in which personal initiative was encouraged and actions were justifiable on the basis of results and keeping the customer happy.

He was willing to trust people, delegating as much as he felt they could handle. To retain loyal staff he offered a generous range of benefits, including company cars and the use of several company-owned holiday homes in Britain and abroad. That way:

> If someone is asked to work for a couple of hours one evening his family don't mind – they remember the lovely holiday in Lanzarote which they might not have had otherwise. These perks aren't just for directors, eligibility is based on length of service not seniority. Staff know that and they see it's a mark of respect for their efforts. I want them to benefit from the firm. I genuinely appreciate the commitment I get from them. I would like to be the best employer in Lanchester.

In return Dean expected a high degree of commitment from staff. Those who failed this test soon quit! Dean's generosity and personal charisma made dedicated staff willing, metaphorically speaking, to walk through brick walls for him. He retained the knack of keeping his finger on the pulse, as Jones explained:

> Hamish never interferes while a thing is OK but he has this uncanny knack of sensing anything untoward. You never feel he's coming to tell me off, but here with friendly, constructive advice. He'll say, has the wife got over her cold? Staff have affection for him because of that. He doesn't have to shout at people, he just looks crestfallen – you've done that have you . . .? Another guy could be thumping the table and you'd say, *up yours mate*! Even the ones who've come and gone, some out-and-out sharks, have said to me afterwards – OK I'd rob my grandmother but I wouldn't rob Hamish.

Dean's style evidently produced results, but in his opinion it also encouraged poor budgetary controls and inconsistent staff treatment. He saw himself as an ideas-driven person, his good ideas being implemented by subordinates without delay. Unfortunately, staff could not always distinguish the best from the rest and Dean found his role increasingly burdensome. Moreover, 1986 had been financially disappointing:

> I was getting bogged down in the detail, I didn't mind, but I wasn't coping well. I left loose ends. I would define a strategy and a general sense of direction and I expected people beneath me to pick up the threads. I needed a senior management level to take up strategy very professionally, very thoroughly. I didn't want to get to the stage of so many businesses where the founder gets to his late fifties and he hasn't delegated and now he can't. I wanted to delegate completely.

He confronted the possibility that his style was 'creating a managerial bottle-neck'. He sought professional advice, the upshot being that he recruited an experienced managing director (Mike Simmonds, formerly operations director of a US multinational), a new sales and marketing director and various other experienced staff into middle management positions.

Turning Pyrochem into a more professionally managed firm was a change everyone in the firm recognized. Thomas reflected:

> Hamish decided the original sales director's skill had been utilized to his fullest extent and for the company to grow he would have to go. That was a very major step – he really was the company in many customers' eyes. He had a lot of friends, was on a lot of technical committees. Hamish set him up in a personnel recruitment business, bought the company for him, said, off you go. . . . He took a very brave step getting rid of him. Recognized inadequacies and acted on it. Terribly brave, determined, single-minded.

Dean assumed the role of chairman which he saw as liberating. Some staff doubted the extent of change, saying he still meddled in operational details. Indeed, though he claimed to have given up detailed control of operations, he said:

> I do have the ability to go round any department and put my finger on a letter that should never have gone out, or a customer complaint, or I'll find out we didn't get a supplier discount we should have done. I'm always putting my finger on the pulse, it's almost a sixth sense.

In any event, having agreed the broad direction, Dean allowed Simmonds to get on with running Pyrochem's day-to-day affairs. The latter set about improving Pyrochem's operational controls, implementing new budgeting and business planning systems. Simmonds also tackled the issues of personnel appraisal and remuneration. He was in no doubt why he had been hired and had no illusions about the culture change this implied in Pyrochem:

> I'm bound to say that the company was not very well organized then. It had grown through Hamish's supreme enthusiasm and ability to motivate people and perhaps even more important, his superb marketing skill. The company spent money like there was no tomorrow – if somebody thought it was a good idea we spent the money. Hamish tended to do things very much on the spur of the moment. And things that motivated one employee sometimes had a negative impact on others.
>
> When I arrived some senior people became anxious. It's counterproductive because it makes them less likely to achieve. Others just doubted their own abilities, the sales force was incredibly laid back –

*you don't expect us to make more than two calls a day, do you?* But I'm not an autocratic manager, 95 per cent of the time I reach a consensus decision. I thrash things out with the key managers. People know they are now measured with respect to how well they perform against budgets. Setting objectives is a major part of my style and people understand this. We've talked about why it's important that we are all going in the same direction, that we have targets and objectives. I'm very target-oriented.

According to Jones:

At the beginning there were a lot of reservations, everyone was apprehensive. What's going to happen next, are we all for the chopping block, they've brought in a hit man! People were genuinely very worried. I said, if you're giving it your best shot you can't do any more, you shouldn't be worried whether he's an authoritarian or a laid-back type of guy. As it turns out, Simmonds is strict, he doesn't suffer fools gladly, but even though he's alienated a few people he's been what the company needed to keep people on their toes now it's getting bigger. He's brought a whole new approach – very procedural minded – you could say to Hamish, I need an extra pair of hands, he would say, OK Jim, go and get somebody. That wouldn't wash with Mike, you would have to have it justified on paper.

Simmonds was confident that his and Dean's respective styles harmonized:

It is difficult to follow Hamish Dean . . . in all kinds of ways. You know, if the boiler goes wrong he'll go out and repair it. You might walk in one day and find him lying flat on his back putting his desk back together. He likes creating and developing things, he hates nitty-gritty, balls-aching jobs. I involve him almost like a consultant at an early stage of projects to get his marketing concept, especially if it involves a major change or a major investment.

If somebody has a good idea we can do inexpensively, I'm quite happy to take that decision. But if somebody is talking of a quarter of a million pounds of capital plant, I'm not going to do something intuitive without having done the homework. Whereas if Hamish thought the idea was right, he would slap a quarter of a million down without thinking twice about it.

Given the healthy state of the structural fire protection market in the late 1980s, Pyrochem was by 1990 a leading force, supplying product to some fifty countries. After three years the Dean–Simmonds pairing had trebled turnover to over £12 million pounds and the firm employed 125 staff. Pyrochem's sales literature was recognized to be so good that one competitor had actually plagiarized parts of it! Even so, Dean was neither complacent nor dogmatic. He claimed the UK market alone harboured over twenty actual or potential competitors:

> Others are beginning to follow because we have laid the tracks. So far none of them have been successful but there's always the threat. If they posed too big a threat we would probably go into a different market.

## BUSINESS DIVERSIFICATION

Dean's freewheeling approach to business development is exemplified by a decision in 1983 when Pyrochem had begun promoting its name heavily:

> I was very frustrated with the creative designers we were using. They and the others we were looking at all seemed to put their energies into creating award-winning designs for themselves – if they were any good at all – instead of coming up with designs that had empathy with the objective of the exercise, which was to get business for the client.

His solution was to invite the agency's chief designer to establish a new graphic design agency. Its prime objective was eye-catching and informative literature for Pyrochem, and its six designers created excellent promotional material at lower net cost than Dean felt an external agency could have achieved. Whilst not a substantial profit generator, it has subsequently attracted some twenty other blue chip clients as its reputation grew.

Dean's increasing need to travel to Europe prompted him to learn to fly and acquire a twin-engined light aircraft which he then chartered per day to defray running costs, employing professionals to fly it and manage the business. As Thomas interpreted the situation:

> Hamish has enjoyed a sort of cash mountain. That's probably the reason behind the aircraft. He had a small fleet, two Partenavias and a Golden Eagle. He bought the Partenavias second-hand and hired them out. One was used by the National Coal Board for overnight data transport, the other transported jockeys and entertainers up and down the country. Because the planes weren't pressurized they had some bad experiences, vomiting for hours at a time, so he got the Golden Eagle, a turbocharged twin-engined machine which is cabin pressurized and flies above the weather.

In 1987 Dean considered executive jet charter, but held back in the light of airline industry deregulation. Instead, he acquired a retail travel agency. Between 1981 and 1988 he set up or acquired at least eight businesses, though the fast-growing Pyrochem remained the core business. All were managed separately from Pyrochem, and reflected Dean's declared need for new challenges – even if he occasionally lost money. Thomas explained:

> He's got that sort of mind – in 1981 he moved into quite lavish offices which he built. He bought the land for cash, actually supervised the subcontract labour, so he owned a whole row of factory units. He was always dealing, he did quite a lot of property development in the early years, obviously making a profit on it.

Simmonds' presence allowed Dean to direct his attention towards new challenges:

> I'm now able to look at possibilities in terms of acquisitions, new product ranges, new uses for our present products. It will be interesting and challenging. I suddenly realized our product range is terribly narrow. I was thinking in a rut, saying we were in intumescent structural fire protection. When I started to look at our resources I saw they could cope with a lot of products in a far wider context without diluting our effort on anything. There was scope for broadening our product base, markets and geographic territories.

He considered merchanting building products, then he began to explore diversification options more directly related to the core business. He identified a potential target for take-over:

> Their product range would fit superbly with ours: decorative, flame-retardant, specialized, sold largely to architects. It would also give us a lever into a new area, shop fitting and exhibition areas and those could utilize some of our existing products as well. So it seems logical. ... I wouldn't mind taking them over.

However, on Simmond's advice, Pyrochem's first acquisition in 1988 was a small firm manufacturing epoxy intumescents for the defence and aerospace industries. A year later Dean acquired another specialty chemicals company and over the next eighteen months he immersed himself in reorganizing it, reducing staff numbers from 105 to 70, bringing in a new general manager, and making it more market-oriented.

> It appealed to me to buy a company and, with a bit of trepidation, think I can improve the management structure, the marketing, and turn a good chunk of their turnover into profit. I definitely needed a challenge, it's a different size of business and a very different culture, not easy to turn it into something profitable. It's got some unique products. I didn't know they were there when I bought it!

Overall it was definitely a good move, I've learned an awful lot and I'm making money out of it. I've learned so much – I feel I've been cutting my teeth. Still, I've made some bad decisions because of inexperience and if I do any more acquisitions – which I want to do – I've got to make better decisions next time. This one is my time at school in short trousers. Getting the odd rap over the knuckles!

The next firm in Dean's sights was:

A logical fit to our existing product range. We either buy them outright or we attack and weaken them, take their turnover, then buy them and put the prices back up. That kind of strategy excites me just planning it, *playing Monopoly for real.*

Meanwhile Dean had bought much larger premises in another district of Lanchester. In a move reminiscent of his 1981 thinking, shrewd timing of the deal meant that the new premises were acquired for a net outlay of only around £50,000:

Of the three factory units here, one is 25,000 sq. ft., the others are 20,000 each. We had only 7,500 on the old site! We're using the biggest and the others are on short-term leases. I can't imagine how we would fill 65,000 square feet but we'll rent space out until such time as we need it.

## FUTURE DIRECTIONS

As Pyrochem entered the 1990s concerns over future competition in the core business were still largely unfounded. Growth of intumescent products was in line with plans and because of acquisitions, group turnover had expanded faster than anticipated. Gross margins were maintained. In 1990 he promoted Simmonds to group managing director. There seemed little doubt that Dean, still in his early forties, would continue to grow his empire. Simmonds commented:

Hamish and I have talked a lot about whether one should set up separate companies to do different activities. There are quite good defensive reasons for doing it . . . such as litigation. That apart, I believe in keeping things small. If we grow as I hope, we'll split the firm up and run it as autonomous centres. The more people who see the bottom line, the more successful an organization will be. If you get to the point where the chief executive doesn't know everybody, that's the point when you've really got to start thinking about splitting it up.

Looking ahead, Thomas commented:

Hamish obviously has the drive to continue. He gets pleasure from creating things, making them grow and going on to something else. If I'd made a million I'd retire, that would be it. But that's not Hamish's way. He has this desire to go on building because he gets fun, excitement out of it.

He is intuitive, so he sometimes makes mistakes, but because he's been successful it's difficult for his managers who have to justify their ideas with logic, facts and figures. He doesn't have to! An ex-director used to say he had to have all his ducks in a row, do all his preparation, spend an enormous amount of time assembling a logical argument for doing something and then find Hamish would just overturn it, say no, we're not doing that. He's a very complex person, you have to know how he'll feel about a situation before you expose your own views. He doesn't really take kindly to people who think differently to him. On the other hand, he will change his mind immediately if somebody puts a point of view which he sees is correct, better than his.

Simmonds had experienced such a situation:

When I handed my visiting card to people soon after I joined most of them said yuk! I said to Hamish, I'm not very happy about the logo, I think we ought to redesign it. He said *good idea* – which I took to be the case. I've subsequently learned that *good idea* can be said in one of several different inflections from *bloody awful idea* to *really good idea*! I think deep down he was really quite against it, but we did it anyway.

Thomas conceded that:

He is touched with genius. He has terrific courage. Based on the figures you or I would probably not make a decision, but he doesn't do that, he just thinks it and does it. You can make a go of anything fairly sensible, even marginal, if you throw everything, all your assets, all your energy into it. But if you fart about, play with it. . . . He's had good luck, but he's also had the guts to do it and the determination to make a go of it.

Like Dick Thomas, Jimmy Jones defended Dean's style and was in no doubt that Dean would continue to innovate:

Hamish is an entrepreneurial chap. He's very sharp – but that doesn't mean to say he rushes in. He uses people as a sounding board. He goes through the permutations before making his decisions. It's not just, let's try that one and see how that works and if it goes wrong we change. Nobody can be right that many times otherwise. OK, you might get a duff egg sometimes, but he's quick to say, *enough*.

I've got great confidence in him. His track record is exceptional. He likes the challenge of building things up. It's great for him, but you must also have back-up, people to keep the spark alive, get the thing into a big flame and to keep fuelling, so that when you look back there's a big row of blazing beacons. And he can say, well I started all that. That's where he's going to get his kick. Your kick will be standing there at one of the beacons fanning it.

For Mike Simmonds:

He is the most creative person in terms of marketing concepts I've ever come across. He never stops having ideas, some of which are awful but some are absolutely brilliant. He's got an ability to always look at things from the punter's point of view, he does it quite instinctively.

In his own terms, Dean remained hungry to learn and improve:

The things I hate about myself now I hated fifteen years ago. I get to the end of a day and I'm totally dissatisfied with what I've achieved. I'm not worth my salary – I wonder how the company copes. I've learned to delegate a little bit in fifteen years, how to read a balance sheet, and I've learned from experience how to recognize fairly good people and fairly bad people and companies, but the fundamentals of how I deal with people remain the same.

I like any company I'm involved with to be thought of as doing things better than anyone else, being very professional. That to me is much more important than making money, which I don't believe is necessarily an accurate yardstick. I'm more concerned with being around in fifteen years' time, because we have consistently done things better, than I am in making big profits today and only breaking even in five years' time. I'm not inclined to follow the line of maximum profitability, I follow the line of maximum ultimate achievement, which might or might not be the same thing. I will definitely do things I enjoy rather than things that will get me a lot of money.

I like to do different things. I have to do something different every year as part of my learning process. I like challenges. If I hear that lots of firms have tried and failed at something and I still believe it is right and there is a way through, I like to try it for the hell of it. I like doing things better than anyone else. I can't do that in an academic sense, because I'm not bright enough. I can't do it in a physical sense because I'm not strong enough. So I try and do things better commercially, against competitors, that is my arena.

I always prefer strategies with lots of options. I like there to be permutations to exploit. I like everything to be very, very flexible. Flexibility doesn't necessarily incur a liability or sacrifice. It simply requires anticipation of what might happen. I never planned to build a second floor on the 1981 premises. *I planned in case we needed to.* I didn't expect ever to be using three units on that site but I designed it so that we could. I don't like there to be only one success route or escape road.

Looking ahead, Dean rejected the notion of Pyrochem going public:

> The megastars like Richard Branson of Virgin have had to come to grips with the fact that you are answerable to a lot of investors who aren't very keen on mavericks and unconventional management styles. You can end up killing the inspiration and killing the fun. One of which is no good for the business, one is no good for personal satisfaction. I'd sell out first.
>
> I wouldn't mind being a micro Lord Hanson, though – buying companies and injecting enthusiasm into their managers, putting in a good management information system, and letting them run it themselves with a bit of supervision.
>
> Mike Simmonds has said I have the ability to think broad and then focus all my attention on minute detail because it is very important. Mike has that ability. Though I think broader than him sometimes, I can't focus as tightly. Our accountant sees no difference between a pound and a million, as long as it all balances it doesn't matter. He doesn't see scale at all.
>
> I live, eat, sleep and breathe Pyrochem. The five-year plan is in my subconscious, evolving all the time, changing shape slowly, responding to what I hear about the competition, products, costs, etc. If I sat down and worked out a formal, five-year plan I'm sure a few inspirational things would come out of brainstorming with the other directors, but I don't think it would be fundamentally different from what's in my mind now. My guess is that when you have someone heading an organization who has been there for some time and emotionally, not just practically involved, the five-year plan is an unwritten thing in the head.

## NOTES

1 © M. Pitt 1995
  This case study has been written as a basis for class discussion rather than to illustrate effective or ineffective managerial or administrative behaviour. All names are disguised. The author wishes to thank all those in the company who gave very willingly of their time.
2 See B. Leavy and D. Wilson, *Strategy and Leadership* (London: Routledge, 1994).

# Chapter 12

# Salomon: a fast growing sports goods company

*Roland Calori*

## EDITORS' OVERVIEW

This case study relates the history of Salomon from its origins in 1947 to its position as a world leader in winter sports equipment by 1992. The product range grew from components – ski edges – in 1947 to include ski bindings (1952); cableless toe- and heel-pieces (1967); ski boots (1979); cross-country shoes and bindings (1980); and skis (1989). Additionally, a line of hiking shoes was developed and marketed by 1991. Parallel to these product developments in winter sports equipment, Salomon also expanded geographically and acquired a golf club manufacturer in the USA (1984) to counterbalance the seasonality of winter sports.

Financial performance reflected this rapid growth. Sales rose from approximately FFr.500 million in 1981–2 to FFr.3 billion in 1991–2. Georges Salomon's policy of reinvesting profits in capital plant and equipment meant that profit performance was less spectacular.

The case presents some of the typical problems faced by a start-up firm in a specialized market with established competition. One may consider the entrepreneurial reactions of Salomon when facing barriers to entry in various new product lines and the degree to which additional products complement the existing range and affect the stability and cumulative expertise of the firm.

Salomon provides a good example of increasing internationalization and the changes this process brings – notably in organization structure and financial arrangements. The resolution of competing claims on investment resources, for example between R&D, production and marketing, is a theme that runs throughout the story. The strains that emerge when sudden environment-induced shocks arise are also apparent.

Although the word marketing is rarely used in the Salomon case, one can argue that Salomon applies a wide range of marketing skills over time, including targeting of up-market niches and the development of distribution channels both at home and abroad.

Great attention is also paid to promoting the market of tomorrow by supplying equipment to the French national junior ski team and by signing on big name world championship skiers to endorse Salomon products.

Issues of control are latent in the case. Georges Salomon brought in his son Bernard, but the firm is now a public company. The case provides some insights into the influence of the various stakeholders and how their influence may be changing. The interaction of the leading players seems to take place in a setting of informality which fosters personal initiative and creative tensions that historically have served the firm well. Will this continue in the future?

## Discussion questions

- Is there a coherent strategy behind Salomon's growth or did it just happen? What leadership contribution have the various Salomon executives made?
- Discuss the nature and extent of competitive advantage that Salomon has developed to overtake more established rivals. How sustainable are these advantages in the long run?
- As Salomon expanded so the organization structure changed. Do these changes make sense? Were they implemented effectively? Are the present structure and culture an adequate springboard for the 1990s?
- What lessons, if any, can be learnt from Salomon's reaction to adverse business conditions in 1989–91?
- What other products and markets might be logical future expansion areas for Salomon? How would its core competences need to change? How else might it continue to develop? How important will innovative thinking and action be in future?

## List of named characters

François Salomon, co-founder of the firm and father of Georges
Georges Salomon, co-founder and chairman of the Supervisory Board
Jean-François Gautier, president of the Management Board
Bernard Salomon, managing director and son of Georges
Michel Barthod, personnel manager and from 1978 to the late 1980s, joint managing director

## Keywords

Strategic innovating; technology; vision; related diversification; entrepreneurship; environmental shock

## SALOMON IN 1992

A modern office in the Metz-Tessy zone near Annecy (Savoy, France) is the head office of the Salomon company. Georges Salomon is the chairman of the Conseil de Surveillance (supervisory board) of the leading winter sports equipment company in the world. He founded the company with his father in 1947.

Jean-François Gautier (40 years old, engineer from the Ecole Centrale) is Président du Directoire (Management Board); he was taken on in 1990 and was previously chairman of the CIAPEM (belonging to the home appliance division of the Thomson Group). Bernard Salomon (36 years old, son of Georges) graduated from the Lyons Business School. He is Directeur Général and has spent his entire career at Salomon. Jean-François Gautier and Bernard Salomon have managed the firm since the end of 1991, when Georges Salomon took the chairmanship of the Conseil de Surveillance after forty years of leadership.

During the period 1947–92 the company went through several diversifications within the winter sports equipment industry and into the golf equipment business (in 1984); continuous high growth was disturbed by a crisis in 1989–90 and 1990–91[2] before recovering in 1991–2 (see Figures 12.1, 12.2 and Tables 12.1 and 12.2).

The positions of Salomon in its diverse businesses are summarized below (1991–2):

- Salomon was the world leader in Alpine ski bindings, having a 44 per cent market share (the number two being the Austrian Tyrolia).
- Salomon was number two in ski boots, having a 21 per cent market share (increasing to 23 per cent according to estimates for 1992–3), the leader being the Italian Nordica.
- After two years of manufacturing skis, Salomon had a 10 per cent market share of the up-market segment. Estimates for 1992–3 showed that its sales and market share would double in this segment (representing about 4 per cent of the *whole* market for skis).
- The group was the world leader in cross-country ski shoes (42 per cent market share) and cross-country ski bindings (62 per cent).
- A line of complementary equipment called 'Club-line' (bags, gloves, caps, clothes, etc.) amounted to FFr. 128 million.
- Taylor Made, the US-based company of the group involved in golf equipment, was the world leader in 'metal woods', having a 20 per cent market share of the woods segment. It had launched a line of putters in 1990 and irons in 1991.
- More than 92 per cent of the sales turnover of the Group came from foreign countries, mainly the USA (27 per cent of total sales) and Japan (35 per cent).

*Table 12.1* Salomon: summary financial data, 1987–92 (million FFr.)

|  | 1987–8 | 1988–9 | 1989–90 | 1990–91 | 1991–2 |
|---|---|---|---|---|---|
| Sales turnover (before VAT) | 2,542 | 3,152 | 3,263 | 2,653 | 3,005 |
| (% abroad) | 89% | 90% | 92% | 93% | 92.2% |
| Operating profit | 441 | 550 | 158 | 27 | 203 |
| Net profits | 193 | 236 | (91) | (257) | 66 |
| Cash flow | 360 | 413 | 103 | 6 | 241 |
| Investments | 241 | 268 | 250 | 259 | 131 |
| Total assets | 2,426 | 2,765 | 3,056 | 2,650 | 2,637 |
| Equity + net profits | 1,347 | 1,590 | 1,396 | 1,128 | 1,179 |
| Financial debts | 532 | 505 | 1,034 | 847 | 697 |

*Source*: Annual Report 1991/92

Table 12.3 summarizes the positions of the main competitors in the winter sports equipment industry, based on estimates for 1992–3.

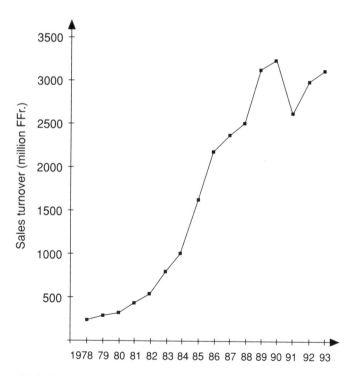

*Figure 12.1* Salomon: sales turnover (1977/8–1991/2 and 1992/3 estimates)

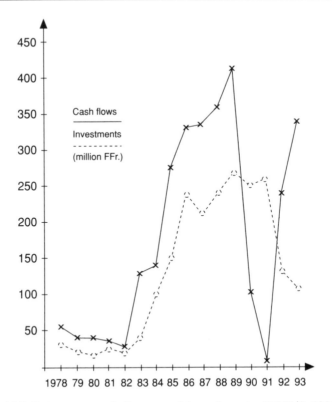

*Figure 12.2* Salomon: cash flows and investments (1977/8–1991/2 and 1992/3 estimates)

The closest competitor to Salomon was Rossignol, a French company also located in the French Alps (Voiron, Isère). Rossignol was the world leader in skis (having a 26 per cent market share, including its subsidiary Dynastar) and number three in ski boots since it had acquired Lange in 1989. At the beginning of the 1990s Rossignol also diversified into the golf equipment business by the acquisition of Cleveland, a small US-based company. Rossignol had also diversified into tennis (rackets) in the late 1970s (having 4 per cent of the world market). The Austrian Head-Tyrolia was number two in ski bindings (Tyrolia) and number three in skis (Head). Benetton Sport System (belonging to the Benetton Group) was the leader in ski boots (Nordica) having a 25 per cent market share, and had diversified into skis (Kästle).

The winter season 1991–2 was dominated by the Albertville Olympic Games. The competitors using Salomon's equipment won 18 medals in Alpine ski competitions and 116 medals in cross-country ski, which was the best performance among the manufacturers. At the end of March

*Table 12.2* Salomon: breakdown of turnover, 1990–91 and 1991–2

|  | 1990–91 | 1991–2 |
|---|---|---|
| **By division** | | |
| Alpine ski | 61.2% | 60.1% |
| Cross-country ski | 5.6% | 7.3% |
| Golf | 27.9% | 26.8% |
| Club-line and miscellaneous | 5.3% | 5.8% |
| **By country** (thousand FFr.) | | |
| Parent company | 1,455,933 | 1,649,396 |
| *Winter sports* | | |
| USA | 269,720 | 263,839 |
| Canada | 114,192 | 101,238 |
| Japan | 708,667 | 789,378 |
| Sweden | 43,988 | 95,324 |
| Norway | 27,478 | 23,926 |
| Finland | 44,212 | 36,777 |
| Great Britain | 27,806 | 28,220 |
| Germany | 95,313 | 135,172 |
| Austria | 60,974 | 79,188 |
| Switzerland | 144,262 | 128,065 |
| Italy | 107,237 | 153,110 |
| Spain | 37,509 | 58,456 |
| Belgium | 18,362 | 16,969 |
| Other | 20,068 | 41,794 |
| | 1,719,788 | 1,951,456 |
| *Golf* | | |
| USA | 459,525 | 553,608 |
| Japan | 269,482 | 284,955 |
| Great Britain | 29,635 | 37,118 |
| Canada | 28,643 | 29,575 |
| Sweden | 3,761 | 4,640 |
| | 791,046 | 909,896 |
| (Sales within the Group) | (1,313,433) | (1,505,156) |
| **Total** | 2,653,334 | 3,005,592 |

*Source*: Annual Report 1991–2

1992 the Salomon group employed 2,526 persons (1,716 in France and 810 abroad). A high percentage of manufacturing was subcontracted to small units in the region and abroad (about 40 per cent of the assembly of ski bindings, even higher percentages of the assembly of ski boots and shoes, and 100 per cent of the manufacturing of Club-line equipment). Salomon always spent more than its competitors on R&D and personnel training, respectively 7 per cent and 5 per cent of sales revenue in 1988–9 before the crisis.

*Table 12.3* The five leading suppliers in the winter sports equipment
          industry

| Company | Sales turnover (billion FFr.) |
|---|---|
| 1 Salomon (France) | 2.4 |
| 2 Rossignol (France) | 1.5 |
| 3 Head-Tyrolia (Austria) | 1.4 |
| 4 Benetton Sport System (Italy) | 1.3 |
| 5 Atomic (Austria) | 0.9 |

*Source*: *Capital* (estimates for 1992–3)

All European manufacturers suffered from a crisis in 1989–90 and
1990–91, after three mild winters. Among them, Salomon had losses two
years in a row, sales decreased and cash flows plummeted for the first
time in the history of the company. 1991–2 was the year of recovery.
The net profits amounted to FFr.66 million, and the net cash flow
increased up to FFr.241 million, for a sales turnover of FFr.3,005
million (increasing by 13 per cent compared to 1990–91). The net
financial debts represented 11 per cent of the equity in March 1992 (as
compared to 33 per cent the year before). Such results were in line with
the high performance of the company during the ten years which
preceded the crisis. Between 1977–8 and 1987–8 Salomon had multiplied
its turnover tenfold (from FFr.264 million to FFr.2,542 million), the
number of employees had doubled (from 1,090 to 2,170), and net profits
had been multiplied by 20 (up to FFr.193 million).

## 1947–52: THE CREATION OF AN ARTISANAL BUSINESS

In 1947 François Salomon, Georges Salomon's father, was 49 years old
and working as a craftsman in a small business of three people which he
had helped to create. This workshop manufactured band saws and ski
edges. François invented a new type of edge and submitted it to his boss
for future developments. After his boss declined, he decided to go out
on his own. His wife was to help him. Georges, his son, had just
finished his schoolteacher training and did not want to leave Annecy for
a country post. He gave up his comfortable career and decided to join
his parents in their risky venture.

Machines had to be bought. The family's savings went towards this
FFr.500,000 investment, including the grandmother's treasury bills which
she had saved to buy a country cottage in her old age. Another difficulty
cropped up: how to choose the machines, how to service them and use

them? These sophisticated machines were very different from those that François Salomon had been using in his former work for twenty years. As for Georges, his technical knowledge was even more elementary. However, it was Georges who became the business technician while his father took charge of sales. To begin his new career, Georges enrolled in evening classes and at the end of each day he learnt to countersink, to solder and to use a lathe. This is how the Salomon company began in a 50 square metre premises.

The product developed by François was an immediate success. The ski edges were sold to regional retailers who assembled them. With increasing orders, money started coming in and the workshop grew. The Salomons dropped the band saw production and a ski-pole manufacturing project. Five years later, in 1952, the company produced a full line of edges (nearly 700 kilometres a year). The workshop was transferred to a facility with a surface area of 250 square metres in Avenue de Loverchy. In 1949 the big boom in winter sports began when the mountain villages were equipped with ski-lifts. Up to 1975 the growth in the winter sports equipment market went hand in hand with Salomon's growth. But thereafter Salomon grew faster than the market.

## 1952–67: A SMALL HIGH GROWTH COMPANY

At the beginning of the 1950s ski edges were assembled by the retailers. However, ski manufacturers began increasingly to assemble the ski edges themselves and because of this evolution Salomon risked becoming a mere contractor for ski manufacturers; this was something Georges Salomon wanted to avoid. He decided to turn to the manufacturing of ski bindings. With this shift in direction, his role in the company became more important. The turnaround had to be achieved quickly.

A Parisian inventor had created a new model for ski bindings that he had presented to Tyrolia (Austria), the leading manufacturer in the world at the time, to Kandahar the number two (Switzerland), to Ramillon the leading French company, and to Franco-Suisse of Saint-Etienne. They had all turned it down. Salomon accepted the product and decided to work on this patent. The gamble paid off. Presented at the Grenoble exhibition, the boot-stretcher 'Lift' achieved great success and was soon selling by the million.

As the Salomon ski bindings had no clear superiority at the time, Georges Salomon decided to avoid direct confrontation in the French market and to develop his business by exporting to the USA. The company focused on exports, acting as if it were ignoring the domestic competition. When the other competitors tried to fight back, it was too late, the room was occupied. Success came quickly: 1,200 sets were sold during the first year (1952), and 10,000 orders came from the USA in

1953 (almost as much as the total French production). Also, from the beginning Salomon opted for an industrial process. The bindings were ordinary perhaps, but they were handier for the retailers who fixed them on the skis, as they were already assembled. The range of products was wide enough and the bindings were mass-produced at relatively low cost (compared to competitors). When Salomon was strong enough, it targeted the French market, and its market share continuously increased during this period.

The company moved in 1962 and built new premises in the industrial zone of Annecy. At the time it employed thirty persons. In 1967 the employees numbered 150 and the sales turnover was FFr.8.2 million. The surface area of the premises had doubled to 4,000 square metres. Georges Salomon travelled widely and had developed a network of relationships with sports equipment importers. The firm participated in most winter sports exhibitions worldwide.

## 1967–78: ESTABLISHING AN INTERNATIONAL NETWORK OF SUBSIDIARIES AND THE SKI BOOT PROJECT

Georges Salomon gave high autonomy to the manufacturing manager and to the sales manager. His own personal taste for invention made him more interested in the R&D department (*le bureau d'études*) where he liked to spend his time and which he regarded as the core of the company. In 1967 the R&D department perfected the first cableless heelpieces for competition and for all types of snow. This was a radical technical innovation. The product range has been continuously improved since then. In 1972 Salomon sold 1,000,000 sets of toe-pieces and heelpieces and became the world leader in the ski-binding business with a sales turnover of FFr.72 million.

It was during this period that the sales manager created several subsidiaries abroad:

• Switzerland in 1969.
• Austria, Germany and Italy between 1969 and 1971.
• USA in 1973.
• Sweden in 1977.

This international distribution network was to be one of Salomon's greatest competitive advantages.

From 1974 onwards the company subcontracted some of its manufacturing (up to 60 per cent). At the time the concept adopted by Salomon was relatively new. Salomon perfected the assembly machines, tested them and installed them in the firms, usually in villages or small towns, and took charge of training and maintenance. Quality control remained with Salomon, in order to supervise all aspects of the process. This strategy allowed the company to adapt more easily to fluctuations in demand, depending on the weather conditions. It also allowed quick growth while keeping the number of employees down and maintaining the entrepreneurial family spirit. It was known as a strategy of 'Vietnamization' of troops.

At the same time, during the 1970s, the Bureau d'Etudes was working on potential new products. There was talk of a combined ski boot and binding. If this idea proved viable, Salomon would be 'in the hands of' the boot manufacturers and risked finding itself a subcontractor. Aware of this threat, Georges Salomon put a team to work on a ski boot in 1974.

At the end of the 1970s Salomon was organized in a functional structure: R&D, manufacturing, and sales, which matched the single global business. The three directors had been in the company from the beginning and had great autonomy. The manufacturing department was by far the largest (employing about 600 persons at the end of the 1970s). The sales manager had full responsibility for the sales subsidiaries which he himself had created. The R&D department had high status in the company and was Georges Salomon's favourite working place as he attached upmost importance to the quality of the products. Quality control and 'secretariat general' were two small departments reporting to Georges Salomon. Management control was not developed and personnel management was under the supervision of each of the three departments (R&D, manufacturing and sales), often described as 'baronies'. The relationships between Georges Salomon and each of the three directors were close and informal, and there was no formal executive committee at the time. Salomon had good products and was highly profitable. It could easily finance its quick growth, especially as Georges Salomon re-invested the profits. Debts were low despite the seasonal fluctuation of the industry. Salaries were relatively high in order to avoid social problems.

Georges Salomon behaved typically as an entrepreneurial leader. He was described as anxious, and never satisfied in his search for market leadership and perfection. This stress was felt throughout the company: 'Work hard and be the best!'

At the end of this period, Salomon was the world leader in ski bindings, having a 32 per cent market share. The breakdown of the turnover of the company by geographical zones corresponded exactly to the breakdown of the total world market as shown in Table 12.4. No other competitor had achieved such a worldwide coverage of the market.

*Table 12.4* Breakdown of turnover, Salomon and the world market (ski bindings, 1977–8)

|  | Breakdown of the world market (%) | Breakdown of Salomon's turnover (%) |
|---|---|---|
| France | 8.8 | 11.0 |
| Other Alpine countries | 41.5 | 35.5 |
| North America | 26.7 | 31.8 |
| Japan | 13.3 | 8.9 |
| Others | 9.7 | 12.8 |

## 1979–1984: THE SKI BOOT DIVERSIFICATION

As the market for winter sports equipment became more mature at the end of the 1970s, Salomon looked for growth in other businesses: ski boots and cross-country ski shoes. The Alpine ski boot market offered several synergies with bindings (same sales network, same customer groups, same brand image). However, the technology was different. The world ski boot market represented a potential for 4.5 million pairs a year. It was dominated by Nordica (having a 26 per cent market share), followed by a group of challengers (Koflach: 11 per cent, Dachstein: 8 per cent, Dynfit: 8 per cent, Lange: 6 per cent), and a number of small competitors. At the time the manufacturing of boots was relatively unindustrialized.

In 1977 Salomon's R&D team developed innovations that could give a strong competitive advantage:

- Back entry and internal regulation.
- Manufacturing by horizontal press injection.
- Inside shoe moulded in a cast of polyurethane foam.

Such characteristics would provide higher comfort for the user, and opportunities to improve the effectiveness of manufacturing.

Bindings required R&D and manufacturing skills in mechanics and metalwork, whereas ski boots required skills in injection of thermoplastic. The R&D team had recruited new staff with the new technological skills. However, when the industrialization phase began, involving manufacturing, some problems arose and the launch was delayed. This was partly the consequence of the very high autonomy given to the ski boot team, which was separated from the rest of the company. George Salomon decided to involve the manufacturing department and the Bureau of Methods and Industrialization, and the ski boot pilot workshops were transferred to the manufacturing department. Such delays created financial problems. Investment in the ski boot project was above

FFr.100 million, an enormous amount of money at the time compared to competitors' R&D budgets.

Two financial institutions which had about 20 per cent of the capital refused to increase their involvement in Salomon, who paid little dividends, re-invested profits and was running the risk of such a diversification. Indeed Salomon was the first firm in the sector of winter sports equipment to venture outside its original business and have two product lines in the industry. Moreover, Salomon was also planning to launch a new business by 1980: a cross-country ski shoe, which the R&D team had started in 1977. Finally the SIPAREX and other investors in the Lyons region gave their support and became shareholders up to 10 per cent of the capital.

In 1978 Michel Barthod was taken on as personnel manager and soon Georges Salomon appointed him managing director of the company, thus sharing top management responsibility. This was certainly a profound change in Salomon. Michel Barthod, a little younger than Georges Salomon, had followed a fairly original career before finally settling down in Annecy. His training was in philosophy; he had worked for ten years as an assembly line worker in the car industry to live fully a philosopher's life! Then he had been a management consultant with CEGOS. His human qualities helped him to instil new practices and new values which corresponded with the new demands of the time: communication, participation, training. His consulting experience in organization helped him to make a success of the necessary structural adaptation.

The functional structure had shown its limits. In 1979–80, in order to solve internal communication and power problems, and to adapt to the diversification strategy, Salomon adopted a new structure with product divisions and geographical areas. More precisely, three divisions were created:

- Bindings.
- Alpine ski boots.
- Cross-country ski shoes and Club-line.

Cross-country ski shoes and Club-line were related, with the same basic technology (assembly of soft material, cloth) and subcontracting strategy (in Italy and South East Asia). The distribution branches were grouped under three geographical zones according to market similarities: North America, Alpine countries (including France), and the rest of the world (see Figure 12.3). The three product divisions and the three geographical sales zones were to report directly to Michel Barthod and Georges Salomon.

Several functional areas were strengthened and six functional departments were created: personnel, finance (including a new team in charge

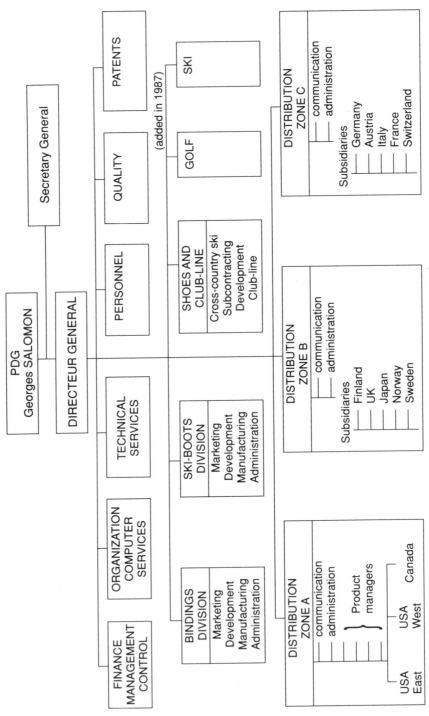

*Figure 12.3* Salomon: organizational chart 1980

of management control), computer, technical services (tools and machines), quality control, and patents. The technical services department was organized by project. The personnel department was charged to develop the participation of personnel in decisions and launching work groups. A pilot group, including equal representation from managers and labour unions was to co-ordinate the whole process.

Several committees were created; the most important were the Management Board (which included the top management, the Secrétaire Général, the directors of divisions and the main department directors), the Marketing Board (which included the directors of divisions, the Secrétaire Général, and the heads of distribution zones), and New Product Committees in each division (which included the general management and marketing of the division, the heads of distribution zones, and the top management).

In 1979–80 the first boots were sold in a fairly rigid French market. Then the distribution was extended worldwide through the strong international distribution network. The product range was extended from the up-market segment to other mid-market segments. The break-even point was passed in 1981–2 when 400,000 pairs were sold. In 1983 620,000 pairs were sold, representing 12 per cent of the world market. During this period nature made things harder; in 1980 and 1981 the winters were mild with little snow in Europe. Thanks to its subcontracting strategy and worldwide sales network, Salomon was able to survive without too many problems.

In 1980 Salomon entered the cross-country ski shoe market with a significant innovation: the Salomon Nordic System, a combined shoe and bindings offering skiers greater reliability, solidness and performance. The market leaders were Adidas, Trak and Karhu but the whole market was fragmented. There was high demand in Scandinavian countries (30 per cent of world demand at the time), thus Salomon established a subsidiary in Norway in 1982. The product range was quickly completed and 100 per cent of the manufacturing was subcontracted. In 1984–5, Salomon became the world leader in cross-country ski shoes, having a 16 per cent market share.

During this period the group also created new foreign subsidiaries in the UK and in Japan. The implantation in Japan was made with measured steps. For seven years Salomon worked with a wholesale distributor (a *sogo-sosha*). The subsidiary was established in 1980. It first selected 350 retailers, hand-picked from the 6,000 working in Japan. A young Japanese who had studied in France and previously worked at Salomon was appointed managing director.

From 1983 onwards Salomon's finances improved greatly. Given the high growth, Georges Salomon decided that the company should go public. It did so in November 1983, when 10 per cent of the capital was offered at a unit price of FFr.650. The institutional image of Salomon was strengthened, and the work on a new head office in Metz-Tessy started.

During this period new skills were developed. Boots and shoes were influenced by fashion and Salomon had to learn a slightly different product marketing: the importance of aesthetics and broad product ranges. New technological skills were also implanted: computer-aided design and manufacturing as well as the use of composite materials. Work relations become more relaxed, more modern. A more collegiate type of management developed, as well as strategic thinking. The original values remained strong: product perfection, innovation, desire to succeed, heedfulness, and hard work. But gradually new norms of behaviour began to emerge: responsibility and teamwork.

## 1984–92: GOLF, SKI AND THE TRANSFORMATION INTO A MULTINATIONAL SPORTS EQUIPMENT COMPANY

### Golf

In August 1984 Salomon took over Taylor Made, a small US company involved in the golf equipment business. The top management believed that the ski equipment market had reached full maturity and they knew that winter sports would always be subject to the risks of climatic hazards. For this reason they looked for growth in a new business. The market for golf equipment appeared to be particularly attractive at that time:

- The total market was higher than that for sports equipment (around FFr.14 billion, of which 45 per cent was clubs, and the rest balls, shoes, and miscellaneous items.
- The products allowed relatively high margins.
- The market was fragmented: in 1985 the four leaders Acushnet, Footjoy, Titleist and Wilson had only a 22 per cent market share, Spalding had 3 per cent and Ben Hogan 3 per cent.
- The sales peak was in spring and summer, inverse to winter sports.
- Demand was growing by 6 per cent a year especially in Europe and in East Asia (10 per cent).

In 1984 the US market represented 59 per cent of the total, Japan 29 per cent, the UK 2 per cent and the rest of the world 10 per cent.

Brand image was important in this business, the main distribution channels (80 per cent in pro-shops and specialized retailers) were different from the ones in winter sports, and the technologies (welding) were also different. Thus Salomon looked for opportunities to acquire an innovative company in the USA.

In 1984 Taylor Made (San Diego, California) was a small firm of eighty people specializing in woods, one of the three types of golf clubs used for long and medium shots (the others being irons and putters). The company had innovated by perfecting a combination of metal and wood, 'metal-wood', which gave superior performance to the traditional wood. It had a good distribution system and a good brand image (given the innovativeness and superiority of its metal-woods). Taylor Made was a young business in search of capital, which had financed its growth by loans. Under-capitalization hindered its development and the firm was on the brink of bankruptcy. In 1984 its sales amounted to $US12 million (and $US0.4 million losses). Its sales represented 2.5 per cent of the total US market for clubs, 6 per cent of the US market for woods, and 50 per cent of the market for 'metal-woods'. Attempts to manufacture irons and putters had failed. Taylor Made focused on product development and assembly, and subcontracted the manufacturing of parts.

Salomon was to keep Taylor Made as a foothold in the American market but R&D was brought back to Annecy, soon to be followed by the marketing department. Teams mixed US (Taylor Made) staff with French (Salomon) staff. Salomon had to learn the techniques of manufacturing golf clubs and the Anglo-Saxon golf culture which was different to the winter sport Alpine culture.

In 1986–7 the sales turnover had increased to $US31 million (of which 90 per cent was in the USA) and the strategy was to increase sales in Japan and Europe, first by creating commercial subsidiaries (UK and Japan) to broaden the product range, including irons and putters (by 1990), and later to include more soft goods, golf shoes and balls. Clubs represented only 45 per cent of the total market for golf, of which woods represented 40 per cent, irons 50 per cent and putters 10 per cent. In 1987–8 the sales of the golf division amounted to FFr.361 million, and in 1988–9 it increased by 103 per cent to FFr.733 million (mainly woods). Salomon certainly was growing faster than the market which was estimated around FFr.8 billion for clubs and FFr.12 billion for the other products.

## Developing a new ski

With high potential marketing synergies and financial resources available, it was tempting for Salomon to consider a diversification into ski manufacturing. Georges Salomon decided to launch a project team in December 1984. He believed that there was no reason to launch a new ski unless it was 'revolutionnaire', and that in order to develop a radically new concept you need time and money. A small, three-member team was formed and involved other managers, technicians, marketers and researchers in creativity groups (all Salomon employees and excellent skiers). Dozens of retailers and skiers were interviewed.

In autumn 1985 the team presented its conclusions, a model and a report on the feasibility of the project. Indeed, the concept was new: an 'integral welded body' ski made of a composite. Compared to the traditional process – thin sheets glued together – the integral welded body process would allow the automatization of manufacturing while preserving high regularity in quality. The new ski concept would also allow higher performance in taking bends and higher comfort for the skier. Salomon hired top R&D engineers from other companies to strengthen the home team in the area of composite materials and in ski development (the head of R&D from Rossignol, and the head of R&D from Dynamic). Semi-prototypes were manufactured in 1986-7 and tested by top skiers. The new ski got its final form in 1988; more than fifty patents were registered. A new plant was being built at Rumilly and a market test was prepared for winter 1989–90 in Switzerland. During this period the investment in the project amounted to FFr.300 million, much more than competitors had ever spent in developing a new ski.

In terms of organization, the two new businesses – golf and ski – were integrated as two new product divisions in 1986. The high growth of the golf division and the perspectives of future growth led to changes in the organization again at the end of 1987. Two 'poles' were created: the *Direction* Golf and the *Direction* Winter Sport including five product divisions and the distribution zones. Market and technological synergies were to be improved within the complete line of ski products. *Direction* Golf was strengthened, having its own distribution network (subsidiaries) and functional departments (see Figure 12.4).

Salomon increased its capital in 1984 and 1985, but the family kept 40 per cent of holdings and the majority of votes. Management control was improved and the finance department took greater care in managing currency exchange rates especially US dollars (as 89 per cent of the sales of the Group were abroad).

During this period great progress was made in personnel management, especially in training, although the system remained relatively informal. According to Georges Salomon, 'Employees should see personal success as being part of the company's success.' At Salomon you had to be a winner and accept working under stress, but employees were also very proud of their company. In 1987, they held 3 per cent of the capital, the 'participation' amounted to 3.2 per cent of the salaries and the 'intéressement' amounted to 17 per cent of the salaries. Collective salary increases were limited to around 3 per cent and priority was given to individual salary increases when promoted.

In 1987 Salomon strengthened its relationships with retailers. It began with the French subsidiary which offered partnership agreements to

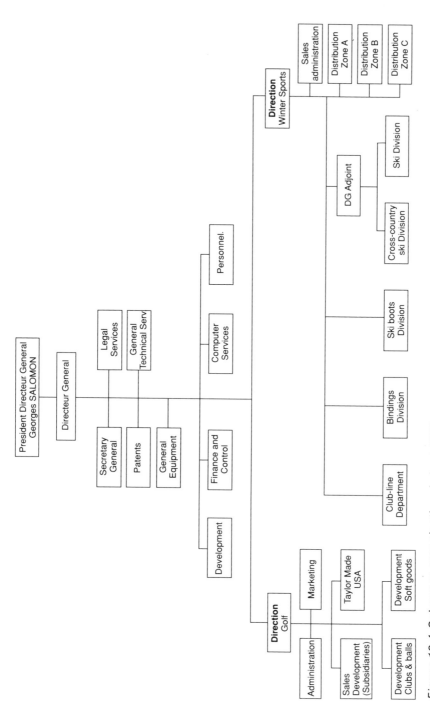

*Figure 12.4* Salomon: organizational chart 1988

selected retailers. The top management preferred strategic thinking to strategic planning (i.e. consolidated revolving plans at the corporate level). On the other hand solid three-year marketing plans were prepared at the level of product divisions. However, none of these management systems could predict the severe crisis of 1989–91 which resulted from the coincidence of several unrelated events.

## The crisis 1989–91

There had been two mild winters in a row, 1987–8 and 1988–9, and usually the year after a winter with little snow the retailers reduced their purchases and got rid of their inventories. Thus one could foresee decreasing sales for manufacturers. Unfortunately 1989–90 was also a mild winter in Europe, resulting in sluggish sales for all the companies involved in this business. The world demand decreased by 12 per cent.

From 1989 onwards the market for golf equipment also declined, first in the USA and then in Europe. The world demand decreased by 5 per cent between 1989 and 1990 and 10 per cent between 1990 and 1991; the market was reaching maturity and suffering from the world economic crisis. Additionally, between spring 1989 and spring 1990 *both* the US dollar and the yen lost value compared to the French franc (respectively − 12 per cent and − 24 per cent). Very few experts predicted this simultaneous weakness of the two main currencies. More than two-thirds of Salomon's sales were in US dollars or the yen, and the company was not well insured against this risk (especially on the yen which was seen as relatively stable). The consequence was a loss of FFr.170 million.

At that time Salomon had to continue with its ski project, which was costly but was not yet generating any cash. The worldwide extension of the distribution network of the golf division had to be achieved (creation of subsidiaries in Sweden and Canada). The price of Salomon shares slumped from FFr.3,400 to FFr.1,400. Michel Barthod retired, the new chief executive Jean-François Gautier and Georges Salomon made quick radical decisions. Two new diversification projects were postponed: golf balls and tennis rackets. Fixed costs were reduced by FFr.300 million (especially overheads). The number of employees was reduced by approximately 500, mainly among the 'cadres': management, functional and technical staff (from 2,831 persons in March 1990 to 2,346 in March 1991). More resources were shared between the businesses of the winter sport equipment *direction*.

The ski project, however, did not suffer from rationalization: the market test was undertaken in Switzerland in 1989–90, and the entry into the world market took place as planned in 1990–91. Also in 1990 the top management decided to launch a new product line – hiking shoes – that did not require high development or manufacturing investments.

### The recovery: skis, hiking shoes and what else?

Figures 12.1 and 12.2 and Tables 12.1 and 12.2 show that Salomon's recovery was quick, quicker than that of most competitors in winter sports equipment. Fortunately winter 1990–91 had been wonderful (i.e. cold, plenty of snow, etc.), the retailers sold their extra inventories and the following year the market started to grow again. However, the economic recession (especially in North America) resulted in a continuing decrease in demand for golf equipment. The new ski and the new hiking shoes were successful. Thus, altogether, optimism flourished again and the desire to win was stronger than ever. The number of employees increased by 180 to 2,526.

The total world market for skis amounted to FFr.5.5 billion in 1989–90 (of a total of FFr.12 billion for all winter sports equipment). Rossignol and its subsidiary Dynastar had a 26 per cent market share, Atomic (Austria) 12 per cent, Head (Austria) 11 per cent, Fischer (Austria) 8 per cent, and Elan (Yugoslavia) 7 per cent, of the total number of pairs (i.e. 5.75 million). The remaining 36 per cent were manufactured by some 80 small firms using small-scale production processes.

Salomon was aiming at the up-market segment first. The skis launched in the Swiss market in 1989–90 were priced above FFr.3,000 a pair (which was more than twice the average price) and the product range was narrow (three models: 1S for giant Slalom, 2S for slalom and 3S for super slalom). The Swiss were among the most demanding skiers in the world, they had high purchasing power and all the main manufacturers were present in the Swiss market. A thousand pairs were sold and the customers were interviewed in order to receive feedback and improve. Salomon offered its ski to the French junior ski team, and the year after to junior ski teams in other countries. Actually the champions already had contracts with other manufacturers and new entrants had to wait for the renewal of contracts.

The composite material of Salomon's ski gave an excellent weight/rigidity ratio and lighter skis. The gradual profile of the edges reduced friction and lateral shocks, a new distribution of weight along the ski reduced the vibrations. However, according to many experts, the real advantage of Salomon was in the automatization of the manufacturing process while preserving regular high quality.

In order to match the characteristics of the new ski, a new system of references was defined: the power reference system based on skier's weight, ability and fighting spirit (replacing the normal system based on the skier's size and abilities).

At the beginning of 1990 the Rumilly plant had 160 employees including Salomon people and newcomers: technicians in composite materials and young graduates with double experience (for instance technical *and* marketing, commercial *and* sports). The whole manufacture was completed by Salomon in its highly protected plant. The three skis were launched in autumn 1990 in all the main markets, but through specialized retail chains. About 75,000 pairs were sold, representing a turnover of FFr.160 million. In 1991–2 four more models were added to the product range and 135,000 pairs were sold. At the end of 1992 the sales for the 1992–3 season were estimated at around 270,000 pairs, that is to say 20 per cent of the up-market segment, and 4 per cent of the total world market. The objectives were as follows: 380,000 pairs in 1993–4 (with four series in the up- and mid-market segments), and 1 million pairs a year at the end of the 1990s.

A line of hiking shoes was developed in 1990 and sales began in 1991, the investment amounting to FFr.10 million. The market for hiking shoes was fragmented and multi-domestic: a leader in one country was unknown in a neighbouring country. The top management of Salomon aimed to be among the four brands which were sold internationally. As stated by Jean-François Gautier in an interview given to *La Revue des Entreprises* (*CNPF*, no. 549):

> Salomon looks for universality . . . We wanted to change the image of the traditional hiker with big heavy shoes and a stiff look. Today new people come to hiking as it is a way to get closer to nature. So we created light shoes with a special internal tightener that we invented, so that the foot does not slide aside.

In 1992–3 the estimated sales were around FFr.56 million, and Salomon already had a 4.4 per cent share of the world market.

At the beginning of 1993 the Salomon ski won its first two gold medals at the Morioka World Championships with Carole Merle and Urs Lehmann.

## NOTES

1  © R. Calori 1995
   This case study has been written as a basis for class discussion rather than to illustrate effective or ineffective managerial or administrative behaviour.
2  The accounting periods run from March to March – given the seasonal winter peak of activity.

# Chapter 13

# JVC: the VHS success story[1]

*Martyn Pitt*

## EDITORS' OVERVIEW

This case study explores the impact of technological innovation on
corporate strategy. It also explores styles of leadership in promoting and
implementing technological innovation. The case focuses on the development of two competing home video-cassette recorder (VCR) formats,
Betamax and VHS, and their respective Japanese proponents, Sony and
JVC, the latter a comparatively small subsidiary of the giant Matsushita
Electric. Their approaches can be contrasted with the other influential
players of the era, Ampex and RCA of the USA, and Philips of Holland.

Having described the Sony and JVC approaches, supplemented by
background information about the technology and the firms in Appendices, the case outlines industry developments until 1988 when Sony
finally accepted the dominance of VHS over Betamax and converted its
production to VHS machines. The text notes the ongoing role of
product innovation, including the introduction of new miniature formats
leading to the camcorder.

The case also notes the importance of complementary products in the
widespread acceptance of VCRs, including the emergence of pre-recorded
video-cassettes for films and educational materials, for sale and rental.
Sony apparently recognized the potential of this complementary 'software' to the sale of VCR hardware, and tried to stimulate its production
at an early stage, but its senior executives evidently did not see this as a
commercial opportunity for Sony, which may help explain the later
acquisition of CBS Records and Columbia Pictures.

A variety of issues are raised. There is the principal issue of strategy
selection. The technological innovation literature has characterized the
options as 'technology push' versus 'demand pull', echoed more recently
in the corporate strategy literature in terms of 'competence driven' as
opposed to 'position/opportunity driven' and between 'first mover' and
'early follower'. The reader can reflect on the strategies of the various
players in the emergence of the VCR industry, and whether simplistic

strategy labels are really appropriate. For example, is it realistic to characterize Sony as a first mover, driven principally by the desire to enhance its technological prowess, with JVC the market-oriented, early follower? Perhaps a better argument is that the main protagonists pursued essentially the *same* strategy, albeit with markedly different success in the details of implementation plans and timing.

Much has been said in the strategy literature about the significance of organizational learning and experience, encoded in notions of *competence trajectory* and *experience curve*. According to these concepts, success should accrue to the firm that effectively pioneers new products and markets, provided that it continues to *learn* from its experiences. One aspect of this is the capacity of the learning firm to 'bundle' a variety of technologies into new configurations, leading to new products and new diversification possibilities. The evidence in the VCR and related industry sectors is worthy of discussion.

These considerations confront us squarely with the question of *appropriating the returns* to innovative efforts. Here the facts are ambiguous. A superficial analysis would suggest that Sony failed to achieve adequate financial returns compared with JVC. But how are we to explain that JVC's technical success generated large financial returns for Matsushita which, like RCA, Sony and Philips, developed its own VCR format, ultimately to no avail? Indeed, some factions in Matsushita were openly hostile to tape-based systems, preferring to support the development of a disc system, as RCA did.[2] More recently, three Korean firms have emerged and seem well set to dominate the less technically sophisticated, high volume end of the VCR market. Is long-run sustainability of a technology-based position therefore a myth?

What should technologically advanced firms do to enhance their prospects of due rewards? How significant are technical standards and market research in their competitive strategy? One can also ask to what extent the global perspective of the main Japanese players was fundamentally more appropriate than the geographically constrained strategies of the American and European players. Likewise, how important was it to integrate marketing and distribution strategies with production and technology strategies?

A significant issue that ties all these considerations together is the role of leadership, not just at the top, but leadership of project teams, including idea championing, the pursuit of parallel research tracks, technology 'shoot-outs', and informal, non-sanctioned activities in so-called 'skunkworks'. Was top management more enlightened at Sony than at JVC? Or was it the other way round? Or were the really shrewd leaders to be found at Matsushita? How big a part did visionary, creative thinking play in each firm?

## Discussion questions

- Contrast Sony's strategy with that of JVC, Matsushita, Philips, Ampex and RCA. Which strategy constitutes the greatest success, and which the greatest failure? On what basis do you reach these conclusions?
- Is the main criticism of Sony's strategy that it was reckless, or that it should have switched to VHS much sooner – when it became obvious that Betamax was likely to be swept aside by VHS? Indeed, for how long is it reasonable to expect a firm to sustain a competitive advantage in the face of clever and resourceful competitors?
- Who were the strategic leaders in JVC and Sony? Discuss their roles and what each contributed. How different were their approaches (i) from each other and (ii) from that of Matsushita? In hindsight should *top managers* in each firm have behaved differently?
- Are JVC and Sony better companies for having experienced the VHS/Betamax episode? What have they learned? What might they have failed to learn? Who among the key individuals learned most?
- Was Matsushita correct to maintain an arm's-length relationship with JVC over VHS development? Would it not have been better to pool resources across the various divisions of the corporation?
- How might Ampex, RCA and Philips have competed more effectively with the Japanese companies?

## List of named characters

Masaru Ibuka, chairman of the Sony Corporation
Nobutoshi Kihara, head of Sony R&D
Kazuo Iwama, Sony R&D engineer for VCRs
Akio Morita, Sony chief executive
Konosuke Matsushita, founder and chairman of Matsushita, JVC's parent company
Kenjiro Takayanagi, JVC's founder and chief executive
Shizuo Takano, team leader, JVC VHS video project team
Yuma Shiraishi, senior engineer, JVC VHS video project team
Kokichi Matsuno, CEO of JVC after 1975

## Keywords

First-mover strategy; technology strategy; international strategy; product innovation; design standards; visionary leadership; collaboration/partnership; appropriability; attention to detail

## INTRODUCTION

The dream of permanently capturing images and sounds is probably as old as *Homo sapiens*. But the innovative, ubiquitous and life-enriching product development we know as the domestic video-cassette recorder (VCR) emerged as recently as the mid-1970s.

Two Japanese firms, the Sony Corporation and JVC, were prime movers in VCR development for home use, together with Philips of Holland. Radio Corporation of America (RCA) might also have been a influential force in the industry, but opted out. It is a matter of record that the design standard promoted by the small, least well-known company, JVC, known as 'Video Home System' or VHS was the long-run commercial winner. How did this happen?

This case study documents VCR development and market introduction. In particular it contrasts the strategies of Sony and JVC. For the interested reader there are brief accounts of the development of recording techniques and the pioneering work of the Ampex Corporation in professional video-tape recording (VTR) applications in Appendix 1 and Appendix 2 respectively. Early developments in home video technology including the conception of a *cassette*-based video-recorder (VCR) are outlined in Appendix 3.

## THE SONY APPROACH TO DEVELOPING A CONSUMER VCR[3]

Sony's innovative first-to-market track record in consumer electronics is now legendary (see Appendix 4 for a brief account of Sony's early history and style). The development of the VTR and later VCR was therefore a natural route for it.

As early as 1951, when Sony was still a very insignificant firm, Chairman Masaru Ibuka and a small technical team made a prototype fixed head VTR. Ibuka realized it was unlikely to be an attractive commercial proposition for many years, yet low-key developments continued until 1958 when serious work began by a team led by Nobutoshi Kihara and Kazuo Iwama (who had worked closely with Ibuka on the development of transistor applications).

This team created the transistorized PV100 in 1962, a professional machine that sold well to medical companies, educational institutions and airlines for in-flight entertainment. A second machine, the 1965 CV 2000, was conceived as a consumer device, but it was still too large and expensive for home use.

When Philips introduced the Compact Audio Cassette in 1964 it was clear that an integrated tape cassette had potential for the VTR too. Sony's 1969 VCR prototype called the U-Matic offered several significant advances. In addition to the cassette itself, it incorporated patented design innovations including the magnetic tape loading and transport mechanism and a rotating, helical-scan head.[4]

Whilst U-Matic was being developed, Sony engineers maintained informal links with counterparts in competing firms. At a trade show in Osaka in December 1970 members of three firms, Sony, Matsushita and JVC, met to review their respective progress in the development of colour VCRs based on three-quarter inch wide magnetic tape. All were experiencing technical difficulties, but the U-Matic prototype with a playing time of one hour seemed the most promising.

Prompted by recent announcements from the US firms CBS and RCA of intent to launch disc-based systems, the three Japanese firms signed a cross-licensing agreement that allowed each to apply the current and future patented VCR technologies of the others without the need for royalty payments. In fact Sony explored licensing with other Japanese electronics firms too, and it announced publicly that seven manufacturers had agreed in principle to adopt the Sony format. Though leading US consumer electronics firms like RCA saw this agreement presaging a rapid cost reduction of VCRs, they did not participate for fear of anti-trust implications.

Whilst in theory the tripartite agreement was even-handed, it seems that in fact Sony extended its know-how to the others to induce them to adopt U-Matic as the *de facto* standard. In the event, each firm continued with its own development, and collaboration in what Sony called 'the spirit of the cross-licensing agreement' effectively ceased in 1971, though rights under the agreement persisted.

The U-Matic design soon became a standard in worldwide broadcasting, especially for electronic news gathering (ENG), and also found many industrial, professional and education/training applications. It underpinned Sony's growing dominance of professional TV and video equipment markets. But the mass consumer market still eluded Ibuka. At the prevailing price of the various offerings available in 1971/2 (equivalent to around $US1,600) the U-Matic did not prove acceptable to many domestic users and Sony alone made modest profits from consumer sales at that time.

The drive to develop a domestic video-recorder was spurred by the almost evangelistic determination of Masaru Ibuka to create a mass market product. According to Dr Nobutoshi Kihara, head of R&D:

> Mr Ibuka would often come in with the 'seed' of an idea and ask [us] to try it out. After the first VTR prototype had been demonstrated Ibuka said, we want to make commercial video-recorders, can you develop one that will sell for 2 million yen [$US5,500]? When that had

been done he said, now can we make a colour recorder for the home at 200,000 yen?

As Ibuka recalled:

> We invented the one head machine. Ampex had studied the rotating head . . . we developed our own system. Many [Sony] engineers wanted to imitate the Ampex machine and make a good business in the broadcast field. I strongly ordered that we would make a $500 dollar home machine.

According to Ibuka's long-time business colleague and Sony chief executive, Akio Morita:

> Ibuka was never satisfied. He wanted a truly small unit with a very handy cassette. He returned to the office one day from a trip to the United States, and he called together the video development group. He emphasized that the home video-tape recorder was the most crucial project in hand and that the size of the unit was crucial. He reached into his pocket, took out a paperback book he had bought at the airport in New York, and placed it on the table. 'This is the size I need for the cassette,' he said. 'This is your target. I want at least one hour of programme time on a cassette that size.' That was the challenge that created the original Betamax system.

By 1974 Sony had advanced greatly in the development of the Betamax format using a compact, half-inch VCR tape system evolved from U-Matic technology. Again it sought support from other manufacturers. In June 1974 a four-man technical team from the US company RCA visited Japan to see the Betamax prototype. They were so impressed that RCA drastically curtailed its own VCR development in favour of disc technologies.[5]

Sony also contacted Matsushita and JVC to persuade them to adopt the Betamax standard. In this it failed, for after a single meeting in autumn 1974 JVC project engineers declined further contacts. However, Konosuke Matsushita, the founding father and chairman of JVC's parent company, *did* accept an invitation in January 1975 to inspect the new Betamax production facility, which had a capacity of 10,000 units per month. He was reportedly most impressed by the technical ingenuity of the product and the substantial investment Sony had made, but he did not countermand the decision of JVC's R&D engineers to continue development independently.[6] As Ibuka later regretfully claimed: 'All the relevant [Betamax] technologies were invented by us. We asked [them] to join us in that standard. But they had a licence to operate with our original patent. So they denied us.'[7]

Not daunted, Sony opted for a pre-emptive strike, launching the one-hour Betamax in Japan in 1975 and in the American market in April of 1976, as a combined video plus TV package priced at $US2,300 retail. In Japan it supplied, unusually, not just its 1,500 dedicated Sony stores but 12,000 other selected retailers. In the USA it concentrated on specialist electrical retailers. Although Betamax was much cheaper than previous VTR designs, Sony's initial strategy was to price Betamax high to present a quality image and offer retailers good profits. Yet within 18 months of the Betamax launch in both countries Sony was offering a stand-alone recorder for $US1,300 retail (against an estimated ex-factory selling price of $US 850–900) as it faced competition from VHS.

The take-off of Betamax was encouraging rather than explosive. Research suggests that most viewers used these early machines for time-shifting their TV viewing, for fast-forwarding over commercial breaks, and in some cases for replaying 'adult' and underground pornographic material that rapidly began to circulate in the USA.

By the end of 1975 Sony had sold about 45,000 Betamax VCRs in Japan. A year later it had delivered a further 100,000 + to the Japanese trade and a similar number to the USA, of which some 70,000 had sold. In 1977 (the first full year of competing VHS sales), Japanese deliveries of Betamax VCRs reached about 215,000, yielding the format some 60 per cent local market share. By the end of 1977 the worldwide installed base of Betamax VCRs was around 500,000 units and video equipment of all kinds generated some $US400 million revenue (14 per cent of its total) for Sony that year.

Encouraged both by its reception in the domestic market and mindful of VHS competition, according to Morita, Sony had decided by this time to 'bet its future on the VCR'. This meant entering new retail territory (for Sony), metropolitan area discount stores in Japan, where it gained an initial VCR share of 80 per cent, albeit with retail prices eroding fast.

## JVC'S PARALLEL DEVELOPMENT OF VHS[8]

By 1953 the Japan Victor Company (JVC) was a wholly-owned, though largely autonomous subsidiary of the giant Matsushita Electric Company. At that time, JVC's founder and chief executive Kenjiro Takayanagi turned his attention to video-recording machines. As Sony and Matsushita did, JVC set up a video project team, led by an enthusiastic young engineer, Shizuo Takano. This team created marketable products, but JVC failed to benefit financially from VTR developments in the late 1950s and early 1960s.

Meanwhile, design standards among the various competing VTR interests in Matsushita failed to converge. This impressed on Takano's team the importance of internationally acceptable product standards. So they maintained informal links with other interested parties, leading to JVC's participation in the 1970 cross-licensing agreement.

In 1971, still uncertain of how strong future demand for VCRs would be, JVC management established a separate Video Products Division to ring-fence the activity. Sales of JVC's three-quarter inch VCR were mediocre in competition with U-Matic and provided inadequate investment funds for new R&D. Indeed, after 1972 it was far from clear to senior corporate executives in Matsushita and JVC that VCRs had any commercial future in consumer markets and they opted to concentrate R&D effort elsewhere, notably on a form of video disc.

The combined number of JVC and Matsushita engineers working on magnetic VCR technology declined from ninety to ten, not all of whom were dedicated solely to VCRs. At times members of the JVC team were required to be field salesmen and repair engineers. These events were desperately disappointing for Takano and his colleague Yuma Shiraishi, who remained the nucleus of the VCR team at JVC. But still they persevered, for as Takano later explained:

> Many opinion leaders said that video is never going to make it. Headquarters in many companies did not have much interest in any sort of video any longer. But I had personal friends in many companies with whom I shared the dream that video was going to be a good thing, going to change people's lives. We kept in touch, we discussed our research. Since headquarters in each company didn't pay much attention we were able to pretty much do what we wanted to do.

Shiraishi elaborated:

> When we were a large group doing R&D on VCR at the main laboratories, we had constantly been told to meet such-and-such goals within such-and-such period, because we were going to have an announcement on such-and-such a date. There was constant pressure on us. And, of course, top management always had deep interest and concern about us. Then they had lots to tell us, lots to drive us. When we moved into the Video Products Division, we were an invisible team. Nobody told us to do anything, we didn't have any pressure, no top management had any complaints – because they didn't know we were doing things like this . . . We did have a hard time finding the money, but all in all, it was a good environment [for research].

The 1973 oil shock accelerated Japanese inflation and JVC made windfall profits by clearing out its substantial stocks of obsolescent three-quarter-inch VCRs at prices competitors were unwilling or unable to match. This provided a financial cushion that supported low-key VCR development in the Video Products Division. Between 1971 and 1976 the small team evolved no less than five prototypes for the video home system (or VHS) at which their efforts were firmly directed. The prevailing 'underground' wisdom in the industry was that half-inch tape cassettes were the way to go. But as Takano recalled:

> Looking back on all the failures we decided to start out from scratch. All work of the past was forgotten. We began to realize there might be some kind of conditions that had to be incorporated into a home-use machine we hadn't thought of before.

They asked themselves what users, manufacturers, retailers, and repairers would really expect of a domestic VCR. They identified a variety of key requirements. Specifically, they thought it would have to fulfil the following criteria:

- Connect to an ordinary TV set and yield broadcast quality sound and vision when playing back recorded material. Ideally, it should also connect to a video camera.
- Use a widely accepted design standard of tape cassette.
- Record for two hours, long enough for uninterrupted showing of a typical full-length movie.
- Be easy for the home user to operate and be affordable.
- Hence, be a low-cost, modular design, for ease of manufacture and servicing.

If these criteria were met, they believed, VHS would be capable of being a mass medium for transmitting information and culture. This almost visionary ambition helps explain why the team believed so passionately in what they were doing.

In late 1974 when VHS prototypes were well advanced, though not production ready, Takano received Sony's invitation to inspect the Betamax design. He and Shiraishi visited Sony's Tokyo headquarters. They quickly realized that Sony was not prepared to compromise on the specifications of a new half-inch format and they left the meeting tactfully. To their relief, the Sony prototype though technically impressive, was by no means a *tour de force*. Most significantly they felt, it still used a one-hour cassette, influenced presumably by the U-Matic precedent. JVC's two-hour tape cassette was clearly going to outperform a one-hour Sony alternative, and hence be very attractive to users. Shiraishi explained:

> Sony was working faster than we were, which might explain why they didn't examine more closely whether the cassette should play for one hour or two. But our first VCR was much lighter than Sony's first VCR – thirteen kilos compared to twenty one – and it fulfilled a goal that was very important to the companies who adopted our format: it was much easier to manufacture.

Takano was now convinced that the VHS standard could succeed in the market-place, though the risk was high:

> Big companies, much bigger giants were doing video developments. Not only myself, but everybody in our division, two hundred and fifty people, felt threatened. It was such a bold decision to go with our own system in direct competition with those giants. But we had such a wonderful product! One day, I called the managers in our division into one room. I asked them how they felt about doing the project, if they are prepared to commit suicide with me. We may not succeed, I told them, but if everybody agrees, then we go. I said, if there is anybody who feels uneasy about it, please say so; you can leave. One member of the team departed. Everybody else agreed. At that moment, I felt the greatest satisfaction. Without that moment, I don't think VHS could have succeeded.

Sometime later, Konosuke Matsushita himself visited JVC's Yokohama plant, having already seen the Sony prototype. He watched Takano's demonstration of the VHS recorder in silence. When it was over, he smiled, leaned over and pressed his cheek against the recorder. He said simply: 'Its marvellous. You have made something very nice.'

The JVC engineers took this to mean that the VHS system was to go ahead. Their attention now turned to marketing. JVC's current factory had the capacity to produce at most 20,000 units a year, a small number if VHS proved really successful. In addition JVC had only a modest network of company-owned retail outlets in Japan and though it would have been logical to enlist the manufacturing and marketing support of Matsushita, JVC's executives doubted that there was enough political support in the parent company to resolve these difficulties quickly.

The JVC solution was to seek collaboration with as many external partners as it could persuade to form a *de facto* anti-Sony alliance by adopting the VHS standard. To this end JVC offered other producers open access to its technology and generous licensing terms. In addition to Matsushita, JVC approached Hitachi, Mitsubishi, Sharp, Sanyo and Toshiba. The first three of these five soon signed up. Meanwhile, Matsushita pressed on with a market-ready alternative design called VX2000.

Kokichi Matsuno who became CEO of JVC in 1975 stressed the need for JVC staff to be 'very polite and gentle' and 'to understand what your business partner is thinking'. When dealing with other firms JVC representatives had to moderate their passionate advocacy of the VHS standard with an appropriate degree of apparent humility – if anyone had a better design then let that prevail. As Takano said:

We never tried to monopolise the technology we developed. If (it) was good, then we believed we should share it (with) companies that would maintain certain standards our format requires. Our basic policy was to spread the information as well as spread the technology and the format. The market is large enough to hold everybody. Japan does not have to monopolise the video market or video production. One single company does not have to monopolise the whole profit.

By mid-1976 Sony products were on sale worldwide. Matsushita had still not endorsed VHS, and Toshiba and Sanyo had committed themselves to Betamax, which JVC staff privately blamed on Matsushita's apparent indifference to VHS. Toshiba and Sanyo launched two-hour Beta models and Sanyo was soon supplying the US retail chain Sears Roebuck. On the other hand, Hitachi, which had been rebuffed by Sony when it sought a sourcing agreement for Betamax equipment in 1974, had made a deal with JVC in January 1976 for VHS supplies.

In June MITI[9] representatives convened a meeting with JVC and Sony executives, ostensibly to establish once and for all whether these key players could agree a common standard. From JVC's perspective it was a thinly disguised attempt to pressure JVC to abandon the VHS standard in favour of Betamax. But with the stakes high and support for both formats, neither side would give way. Thus MITI conceded gracefully, if reluctantly, that the market-place could decide the outcome.

JVC's VHS recorders went on retail sale in Japan in October 1976 and it began supplying Hitachi and Sharp in late 1976 and early 1977 respectively. Thereafter Takano and his team participated in a travelling road show to extol the virtues of VHS to potential European partners. Philips of Holland had demonstrated its own prototype VCR to other parties including RCA back in 1970. Failure to establish this as the international standard had not deterred Philips and it rejected outright JVC's 1977 approach. Grundig and AEG-Telefunken of West Germany, Bang & Olufsen, ITT and Marantz had also joined the Philips alliance. Still, JVC lined up Thomson in France and Thorn–EMI in Britain and AEG–Telefunken also expressed interest.

In Japan an estimated 30–35,000 VHS units were sold to consumers by the end of 1976, mostly to well-to-do professionals and 'gadget-freaks'. After the initial rush of enthusiasm, sales almost died in early 1977 and retail stocks escalated. JVC's foresight in offering a video-camera at the launch came to the rescue, because it enabled its loyal and imaginative retailers to demonstrate the creative and event recording potential of the system. The initial importance of tied retailers was vital – one source estimated that 77 per cent of Japanese sales were via manufacturer-owned retail outlets.[10] In this way JVC extended the appeal of VHS to a broad range of consumers, resulting in 1977 Japanese market sales of about 140,000. Thus JVC initially resisted pressures to cut prices in the home market battle with Sony, though Takano quickly realized the need to upgrade specifications and add new features.

JVC entered the US market in January 1977 and Europe a year later. Sony tried to maintain its premium price position and reached a marketing agreement in March 1977 to supply Beta VCRs to the Zenith Corporation (after RCA the leading domestic US-branded manufacturer of television sets). But Sony was then overtaken by events. In April 1977 RCA changed its mind about VCRs and approached JVC to market the latter's products under the RCA brand name. Because JVC lacked adequate production capacity Matsushita became RCA's supplier. RCA, however, insisted on a *four*-hour machine (with a 24-hour timer) capable of recording an entire live ball game. Even so, RCA restricted its initial order to 40,000 units. Soon after its August 1977 launch at $US1,000, this figure was increased to 60,000.[11] Magnavox followed with a Matsushita-sourced de luxe VHS four-hour machine at $US1,085.[12]

For its autumn 1977 US marketing campaign Sony introduced a revised two-hour Beta format machine priced initially at $US1,300 retail versus the $US1,280 of JVC. In response to the RCA launch Sony reduced the retail list price of its machine to $US1,085. In the pre-Christmas 1977 period a dramatic price war ensued among US retailers with VHS prices posted as low as $US800 against a trade price of $US750. As in Japan a year earlier, the market almost died in the new year and in the short run had to be resuscitated by aggressive and imaginative marketing campaigns.[13]

## MARKET AND COMPETITIVE DEVELOPMENTS FROM 1978

Matsushita abandoned its VX2000 format in January 1977 under pressure from Japanese retailers who complained of its clumsy cassette and inferior picture quality. During 1978 this switch propelled VHS to about half the Japanese market, while Betamax's share fell to 40 per cent (seven units in every ten of which were supplied by Sony), the remainder being U-Matic and other formats.

The US VCR market entered a rapid growth phase in the second half of 1978 and ended the year a similar size to the Japanese market. In the USA, VHS was now outselling Betamax in a ratio of 5:3, with other formats under 10 per cent. 1978 was also VHS's first year in Europe where it achieved some 38 per cent market penetration, over half of its sales being in Britain where Thorn exploited its TV rental base to enable consumers to rent rather than purchase what was widely seen as an attractive, but expensive and unreliable device. Betamax, by contrast, made

*Table 13.1* Japanese VCR production and export performance 1975–85*
(thousand units)

| Year | Production | Domestic shipments | Exports | | | |
|------|-----------|--------------------|---------|-----|--------|----------|
| | | | Total | USA | Europe | Elsewhere |
| 1975 | 119 | 49 | 70 | 70 | — | — |
| 1976 | 288 | 149 | 139 | 104 | 23 | 12 |
| 1977 | 762 | 360 | 402 | 343 | 33 | 26 |
| 1978 | 1,470 | 400 | 973 | 588 | 275 | 110 |
| 1979 | 2,199 | 480 | 1,671 | 761 | 555 | 355 |
| 1980 | 4,441 | 970 | 3,444 | 1,090 | 1,448 | 906 |
| 1981 | 9,498 | 1,548 | 7,355 | 2,533 | 3,265 | 1,557 |
| 1982 | 13,134 | 2,344 | 10,661 | 2,871 | 5,559 | 2,231 |
| 1983 | 18,217 | 3,659 | 15,237 | 6,203 | 5,716 | 3,318 |
| 1984 | 27,124 | 4,271 | 22,071 | 11,896 | 3,752 | 6,423 |
| 1985 | 28,538 | 4,006 | 25,475 | 15,922 | 3,261 | 6,292 |

* *Source*: EIA of Japan, *Japan Electronics Almanac, Business Japan* (various publications)

a slow start in Europe and had under 10 per cent of the 1978 market.

Including domestic deliveries, Japanese VHS suppliers shipped an estimated 840,000 units in 1978 compared with around 530,000 Betamax units by Sony and its supporters. Sales and production figures for the increasingly dominant Japanese manufacturers are shown in Table 13.1. From the late 1970s competition among manufacturers centred on rapid expansion of production capacity and in the early 1980s Japanese firms had the lion's share of VCR production.

Philips with its obsolescent 1972 design watched its hitherto dominant share of the continental European market crumble to 50 per cent in 1978 (40 per cent in the UK). In 1979 it opened a $US230 million, 700,000 unit capacity VCR plant in Vienna for the sophisticated new V2000 model, a design also adopted by Grundig, Bang & Olufsen, Marantz and ITT, but not Telefunken. However, the V2000 proved difficult to manufacture; its tape transport mechanism in particular was said to be over-engineered. It was costly, selling at a 20–30 per cent premium over nearest Japanese rivals. By the time the new Philips plant reached half capacity operation the European market was already worth over 2.5 million units per annum.

Betamax's Japanese market share was pinned back to 33 per cent in 1980 and declined rapidly thereafter. By 1981 VHS was outselling Betamax in the USA by almost four to one, with RCA-branded products having over 25 per cent of the market. Betamax retained some 40 per cent of the UK market in 1981 largely at the expense of the Philips

V2000 as VHS advanced, and held 25 per cent until 1983, given heavy advertising and R&D expenditure. (Sony's UK share actually grew between 1977 and 1980.)

In October 1982 the French government tried to restrict Japanese VCR imports by insisting on customs clearance through a single inland inspection point. Philips and Grundig combined forces to file anti-dumping lawsuits against the leading Japanese exporters. In reply the Japanese government set a voluntary export limit of 4.6 million units to Europe for 1983. Some Japanese firms started European assembly plants and agreed to achieve 45 per cent local value added by the end of 1985.

VHS format VCRs accounted for between two-thirds and three-quarters of most European markets in 1983, with Betamax typically below 20 per cent. The Philips V2000 format enjoyed around 20 per cent of the West German and Italian markets, but only 2 per cent in the UK. Compatible tapes were relatively hard to find, and it had a reputation for unreliability – one estimate was that 80 per cent of the early models had to be returned to the maker for repair. Later versions were much enhanced, but so also were VHS and Beta models. V2000's potential was never fully realized and in 1984 Philips discontinued its manufacture and adopted VHS. This withdrawal reportedly cost Philips as much as $US400 million, though its share of the total Europe market later recovered to a respectable 10 per cent.

Sony, by contrast, persisted with Betamax. Though its professional U-Matic machines continued to have a good following, Betamax's share of the world market for domestic VCRs declined progressively. According to its annual reports Sony's video revenues increased until 1982 when they accounted for 43 per cent of total. Thereafter the proportion declined steadily to about one-third in 1987 when its share of the world VCR market was less than 5 per cent. Betamax now had only 7 per cent of the Japanese market and 1 per cent of the US market. Sony threw in the towel and adopted VHS in 1988.

Back in the spring of 1979 over 800,000 US homes already had a VCR installed, albeit under 1 per cent of homes. By the end of 1981 this figure had doubled and the VHS format was found in some two-thirds of the VCRs in US and UK homes (Table 13.2). By mid-1985 VCR penetration of the US market had reached one home in five (one in three in Japan). In Japan the VHS proportion of the installed base was not quite as high as in the USA at the equivalent time, but the trend was similar.

Despite or perhaps because of its open approach to the licensing of VHS, JVC retained a large share of the world market (about 20 per cent by value) throughout the mid-1980s, when its VCR activities generated some $US2.4 billion or two-thirds of its total revenues, with Matsushita deriving an even greater amount through its National Panasonic brand.

*Table 13.2* VHS penetration of the US and UK markets 1977–81*

| Year | US market | | UK market | |
|------|-----------|--|-----------|--|
| | VHS share % | Cumulative % | VHS share % | Cumulative % |
| 1977 | 37 | 26 | nil | nil |
| 1978 | 60 | 45 | 80 + | 70 |
| 1979 | 65 | 57 | 65 | 70 |
| 1980 | 70 | 63 | 61 | 64 |
| 1981 | 80 | 70 | 63 | 63* |

*Source*: Author's estimates based on the various sources cited in the text
*Note*: * The annual and cumulative figures dropped as Sony entered the market
from 1978. But by 1981 VHS share was again rising, leading to 94 per cent
share in 1985 and an estimated cumulate share of about 75 per cent.

For example, in fiscal year 1983 Matsushita sales of video products accounted for over 1400 billion yen, some 36 per cent of its turnover.

By 1985 the Japanese industry was producing VCRs at the rate of over 28 million per annum.[14] However, the Korean firms Samsung, Gold Star and Daewoo were progressively building market share with low cost, fairly basic machines. Korean production by this time had reached over 4 million units per annum, of which 3 million were VHS.

By the late 1980s the installed base of video-recorders exceeded 200 million, of which 90 per cent according to JVC were VHS format. The USA alone had over 70 million and VCR penetration of US homes was estimated at 65 per cent or more, greater than for black and white TV sets, with some homes having two or even three VCRs. Remarkably, this market was still absorbing a staggering 15 to 16 million units a year including portable units. However, market value appeared to peak as early as 1985 as Japanese ex-factory unit prices fell from over 240,000 yen in 1975 to around 58,000 yen in 1986 (Table 13.3). On the evidence of export versus other prices, however, allegations of dumping appear dubious.

## THE IMPORTANCE OF CONTINUING PRODUCT INNOVATION

The domestic video-recorder was enabled by a range of technical innovations over the years. Advances in the miniaturization of electronic circuitry and in the design of servo motors enabled the Betamax and VHS formats to be realized. Likewise, tape manufacturers achieved substantial improvements. Enhanced coating technology enabled improvement in picture quality, whilst much stronger, thinner substrate

Table 13.3 Price progression of Japanese
VCR output 1975–86 (thousand
yen)

| Year | All production | Export shipments |
|------|---------------|------------------|
| 1975 | 240 | na |
| 1976 | 198 | 223 |
| 1977 | 165 | 164 |
| 1978 | 139 | 130 |
| 1979 | 135 | 133 |
| 1980 | 127 | 129 |
| 1981 | 114 | 116 |
| 1982 | 98 | 101 |
| 1983 | 83 | 83 |
| 1984 | 77 | na |
| 1985 | 67 | na |
| 1986 | 58 | na |

Source: As Table 13.2

polymers allowed for much extended playing times in the same compact cassette.[15] In 1979 a five-hour Betamax cassette became available, countered by a six-hour VHS tape, and an eight-hour version in 1982.

The industry showed great ingenuity in the continued enhancement of product specifications as competition intensified. Seven-day programming was a VHS facility from 1979, rising to fifteen days by 1982, quickly matched by Betamax. Other convenience features such as freeze frame, fast and slow motion, were also available on high-end VHS machines from the late 1970s. Though JVC was the initiator of the basic innovations (like programming) that consumers quickly appreciated, Sony made the pace with high speed scanning, clean freeze frame, picture in picture, Nicam stereo (1986) and later, high definition TV compatible machines.

In 1983 the concept of a miniature video-recording format was proposed, based on a slim 8mm tape cassette (Video-8). By 1985 some 127 companies were said to have accepted the format.[16] In early 1985 Sony became the first company to introduce a product using the new format: a miniature video-camera containing a tiny VCR (which became known generically as a camcorder). It offered ninety minutes of recording. Sony sold 100,000 units in 1985. In 1986 it introduced the HandyCam, which offered similar performance in an even smaller package. Sony offered a package priced at $US1,800 retail and spent $US10 million promoting it in 1986.

Since Video-8 was incompatible with VHS, Matsushita and JVC were reluctant to endorse it. In 1987 they introduced VHS-C, an alternative

Table 13.4 Sales of video tapes in the USA 1980–87 (million units)

| Year | Pre-recorded | | | Blank | | |
|------|------|------|-------|------|------|-------|
| | VHS | Beta | Total | VHS | Beta | Total |
| 1980 | 2.0 | 1.1 | 3.1 | 12.9 | 6.1 | 19.0 |
| 1981 | 3.5 | 1.6 | 5.1 | 20.5 | 7.9 | 28.4 |
| 1982 | 4.6 | 2.0 | 6.6 | 27.4 | 11.2 | 38.6 |
| 1983 | 7.0 | 2.6 | 9.6 | 65.9 | 212 | 87.1 |
| 1984 | 14.8 | 4.9 | 19.7 | 122.0 | 35.9 | 157.9 |
| 1985 | 35.7 | 7.4 | 43.1 | 231.4 | 43.0 | 274.4 |
| 1986 | 58.2 | 6.7 | 64.9 | 312.8 | 34.2 | 347.0 |
| 1987 | 62.7 | 5.9 | 68.6 | 314.8 | 23.1 | 337.9 |

Source: B. Klopfenstein, in M. R. Levy (ed.) The VCR Age (Newbury Park, Calif.: Sage, 1993), taken from industry sources

micro format that could be replayed on standard VHS machines with an inexpensive adaptor. Later they added an enhanced VHS-H version which they claimed offered video quality truly comparable with the full-size cassettes. Again, there were proponents of both formats: Aiwa, Fuji, Kyocera and Sanyo lined up with Video-8, Hitachi, Minolta, Mitsubishi, Sharp and Toshiba with VHS-C. However, Matsushita made both VHS-C products for sale under its own brands and as original equipment supplier for others, whilst supplying Kodak and other US firms with Video-8 machines for sale in the USA.

## THE IMPORTANCE OF COMPLEMENTARY PRODUCTS[17]

VCR purchase would presumably not have advanced so rapidly if users had not found VCRs useful and versatile, so a full appreciation of their impact requires some consideration of how patterns of use evolved and affected subsequent demand.

Sony began promoting its products largely on the ability to time shift TV viewing. Industry statistics (Table 13.4) show that from 1980 each VCR sold in the USA typically generated sales of around two dozen blank cassettes and four to five pre-recorded cassettes. This suggests some purchases of copyright material, but more recording of off-air material, and possibly longer-term storage, despite the infringement of copyright this practice usually involves. The latter was a concern to legislators from the late 1970s, but they have done little about it. For several years Sony was the subject of litigation in the USA by Universal Studios who argued that its VCRs breached prevailing copyright provisions. Sony finally won this action in the Supreme Court in 1984.

Initially few pre-recorded tapes were on general release. From the start Sony set itself the target of 1,000 pre-recorded titles on Betamax, hoping to persuade the Hollywood film studios to distribute their movies on this medium. Despite the possibility of using established distribution outlets, the film makers were reluctant for a number of reasons:

1 The Beta format was not yet well established – VHS tape was on the horizon, to say nothing of a variety of incipient video disc formats.
2 They found it hard to predict if home viewing would adversely affect cinema attendances.
3 They thought the expected cost of a pre-recorded cassette would be too high to interest a mass audience.

In 1978 and 1979 many of the available videos tended to be of low quality, produced by small entrepreneurial film makers, and three-quarters of all pre-recorded tapes at that time were estimated to be 'adult'. By 1980 the average retail selling price of a pre-recorded cassette in the USA was $US69 for VHS and $US62 for Beta equivalent. By 1987 these prices had fallen to $US35 and $US33 respectively.[18] Curiously, the pattern of video usage differed markedly across the world, at least in the early years. One survey of VCR usage in the USA put the playback of pre-recorded tapes at 50 per cent of usage, compared with 75 per cent in Europe and only 5 per cent in Japan.

In retrospect, RCA's active endorsement of the VHS format can be seen as a turning point, since it redirected its plans for developing a large catalogue of pre-recorded Selecta Vision discs from a wide variety of sources towards the VHS format. What few observers (including RCA itself) predicted, however, was the rapid emergence of the video tape rental phenomenon, as thousands of independent outlets and chains like Fotomat in the USA systematically exploited the growing interest in short-term rentals for as little as a two dollars a cassette. By 1981 the rental market was worth as much as $US800 million and 'adult' movies accounted for well under half of this. Interest in pre-recorded tapes also drove the rental phenomenon in Europe, especially in Britain. By contrast, third party cassette rentals did not start in Japan until April 1983.

More recently, as well as re-releasing old movies Hollywood has found it profitable to release new movies ever more promptly following cinema premiere. Though movie attendances may have suffered for a time, the combined total of cinema and home viewing has increased the popularity of movies considerably. In addition, many third party producers of informative and educational materials have entered and developed the market in new ways.[19]

The seemingly unstoppable momentum of VHS in America meant that even by 1980 most industry observers were convinced that VHS would dominate the future installed base of video home entertainment equipment. So it proved. Arguably, providers and distributors of hardware and software had a common interest in standardizing the medium, since production in multiple formats increases costs and inventory management problems. However, most commentators agree that software producers responded to and therefore reinforced, rather than created the emerging dominance of the VHS format.

## CONCLUDING REMARKS

The VHS/Betamax contest was a fight to the death by two virtually equal, but incompatible formats. In promoting Betamax, Sony evidently created an awareness of VCRs from which VHS subsequently benefited. The fierce competition between the formats, many commentators believe, accelerated total VCR sales.

As MITI foresaw, market forces decided there was room for only one successful format. Product performance was apparently not the crucial factor in the outcome, as independent tests found little difference between Betamax and VHS in, for example, picture and sound quality. It is true, however, that JVC was quicker than Sony to add features that consumers could immediately see the value of, such as longer recording, extended delay timers, etc.

For Sony, growth through first moving has always been important. Its growth between 1960 and 1984 has been rapid, absolutely and in comparison with other leading VCR-producing firms (Table 13.5). Morita has been quoted as saying 'Sometimes face is more important that profit.'[20] Sony still holds a dominant position in the professional and broadcast markets and since adopting VHS it has reasserted itself in consumer video. None the less, its video experiences influenced its more recent decision to acquire sound recording and film studios in Hollywood to control software sources. Despite reverses, Sony has arguably done much better than Philips, RCA and the many other US and European consumer electronics manufacturers who have comprehensively lost out to Japanese firms.

Whilst JVC has done well out of VHS, its video-disc venture was not successful. Meanwhile, Matsushita, JVC's parent company, had grown larger than RCA by the late 1970s and ranked alongside GE and ITT of America, Philips of Holland and Siemens of Germany as one of the largest producers of electrical goods (and one of the top fifty corporations by size). Its success has been attributed to its emphasis on the following:

Table 13.5 Key financial data on the leading VCR firms, 1960, 1970, 1980 and 1984 ($US million)

| Year | Matsushita | Sony | RCA | Ampex |
|---|---|---|---|---|
| **Sales revenues** | | | | |
| 1960/1* | 256 | 52 | 1,495 | 68 |
| 1970 | 2,588 | 414 | 3,326 | 296 |
| 1980 | 13,690 | 4,231 | 8,011 | 469 |
| 1984 | 24,890 | 6,702 | 10,112 | na |
| **Net profits** | | | | |
| 1960/1* | 29 | 2 | 35 | 4 |
| 1970 | 196 | 28 | 92 | 14 |
| 1980 | 585 | 325 | 315 | 35 |
| 1984 | 1,214 | 344 | 341 | na |
| **Total assets employed** | | | | |
| 1960/1* | 195 | 57 | 815 | 51 |
| 1970 | 2,040 | 445 | 2,936 | 386 |
| 1980 | 11,636 | 4,158 | 7,148 | 351 |
| 1984 | 21,499 | 6,827 | 8,221 | na |

Source: Annual reports etc. as presented in R. Lurie and D. Yoffie, World VTR Industry (Boston, Mass.: Harvard Business School, 1987)
Note: * Fiscal 1960 data for all firms except Sony which is 1961

1 Product quality and reliability.
2 Marketing competence (strong brands, heavy advertising, control of distribution channels).
3 Production skills achieving low unit cost through careful design for manufacturing.[21]

These strengths have secured dominant positions in many markets via economies of scale and scope. Matsushita has not pursued a strategy of technological leadership, being content to let competitors make the initial breakthrough, which its own technologists and production engineers then elaborate. The VHS story epitomizes this strategy.

## NOTES

1 © M. Pitt 1995
   This case has been written as a basis for class discussion rather than to illustrate effective or ineffective managerial administrative behaviour. It has been prepared from a variety of published sources, as indicated, and from personal observations.
2 See M. Graham, The Business of Research: RCA and the VideoDisc (Cambridge: Cambridge University Press, 1988) for a fascinating account of technology development.

3 This section draws on Akio Morita's quasi-autobiography *Made in Japan*, (Morita *et al.*, London: Collins, 1987) and on J. B. Quinn 'Sony Corporation', in Quinn *et al.*, *The Strategy Process*, 1st edn (London: Prentice-Hall, 1988).

4 The combined read/write vision head rotated at an angle to the direction of movement of the tape, creating a complex scanning pattern. Thus, it was possible to maintain a high relative tape to head speed whilst further reducing the bulk of tape needed for a given recording time.

5 See Appendix 3 for a fuller explanation.

6 Reported in *Clash: Sony vs. Matsushita* (Tokyo: Nihon Keizai Shimbun, 1979).

7 On the historical evidence the phrase 'configuration of technologies' might be more accurate. Also, B. Klopfenstein (in Chapter 2 of M. R. Levy (ed.) *The VCR Age*. (Newbury Park, Calif.: Sage, 1993)) credits Toshiba and JVC with the first helical scan mechanisms in 1959.

8 This section draws on Chapter 2 of P. R. Nayak and J. M. Ketteringham, *Breakthroughs* (London: Mercury Books/W. H. Allen, 1987) and R. T. Pascale and A. G. Athos, *The Art of Japanese Management* (New York: Simon and Schuster, 1981).

9 The powerful Japanese Ministry of International Trade and Industry.

10 UK Price Commission, *Prices, Costs and Margins in the Distribution of VTRs and their Accessories* (London: HMSO, 1979).

11 RCA's ambivalence is illustrated by the executive in charge of marketing VHS recorders in the USA, who said that in 1974 'We had looked at Betamax because that's all we had to look at. They were first on the market. But we didn't see a product that would capture the minds of the American consumer. And yet, instinctively . . . we've always believed in home recording . . . possibilities' (M. Graham, *The Business of Research: RCA and the VideoDisc* (Cambridge: Cambridge University Press, 1988)).

12 Magnavox had also been interested in marketing a video-disc system based on RCA technology. By 1981 it was affiliated with North American Philips to make and market a laser-based system called Discovision based on Dutch patents.

13 Price cutting was more aggressive and sustained in the USA than in Japan.

14 For comparison, Japanese colour TV output had reached 10 million in 1978 from almost nothing in 1965.

15 Whereas the original Ampex machine with a two-inch wide tape required 750 square feet of magnetic surface per hour of playback, and the U-Matic needed 70, Betamax required only 20 and VHS 16.

16 R. Lurie and D. Yoffie, *World VTR Industry* (Boston, Mass.: Harvard Business School, 1987).

17 Data in this and the preceding section derive from various sources, quoted in P. Grindley and R. McBryde, 'Video cassette recorders: the value of co-operation', in P. Grindley (ed.) *Standards, Business Strategy and Policy: A Casebook* (London: London Business School, Centre for Business Strategy, 1992), Chapter 2, 17–40: Klopfenstein op. cit., Lurie and Yoffie op. cit., UK Price Commission op. cit.

18 The average 1980 price of a blank VHS cassette was $US13 (Beta, $US10.40), falling to $US3.50 by 1987 (Beta, $US3.24).

19 Such as the British firm Video Arts founded by John Cleese and others to produce attractive training films, which made him a multi-millionaire when he sold it in 1989.

20 *Sunday Times*, 22 January 1978.

21 Pascale and Athos op. cit.

## APPENDIX 1: EARLY DEVELOPMENTS IN MAGNETIC TAPE RECORDING

Many of the basic technologies for recording sound and vision have been known for over a century. Louis Daguerre in France created the first practical photographic imaging process in 1839. Kodak introduced the roll film in 1889 and by 1895 in Paris the Lumière brothers had projected the first silent movie on film. In 1880 Ayrton and Perry in Britain proposed an array of photoelectric cells as a means to convert visual images into electric signals, but this was technically infeasible until charged-coupled solid state devices were developed in the 1980s.

The American Thomas Edison made the first mechanical sound recording on a grooved metal cylinder in 1877, evolving into the familiar phonograph disc. The British TV pioneer John Logie Baird experimented with image recording on waxed phonograph discs in 1927.

The Dane Valdemar Poulsen demonstrated magnetic sound recording using piano wire in 1898, though the commercial development of sound recording occurred only after the introduction of the thermionic amplifier valve in the 1920s.

The British Broadcasting Corporation began recording radio programmes in the early 1930s with a Blattnerphone, a massive machine which employed huge rotating reels of steel tape. Recording was achieved by transporting the tape very quickly across a static recording head which encoded data on the tape in the form of a magnetic field. Repeating the procedure enabled the data to be decoded by a similar playback head. The German Magnetophon of 1935 innovated by using a tape made of magnetic oxide-coated paper (and later plastic) as the recording medium.

After the Second World War German recording technology was appropriated by the USA, and R&D into magnetic tape recording accelerated, notably by RCA and Ampex. By the early 1950s audio tape recorders were commonplace for broadcast and professional use, though the equipment was bulky. To achieve reasonable sound quality, designers depended on high linear tape-to-head speed, necessitating two spools of tape up to 12 inches in diameter, one either side of the record and replay heads.

Sound quality was also constrained by the comparatively inferior materials and magnetic tape coating technologies of the day. Accordingly, a number of leading corporations including among others 3M, DuPont, TDK and Sony began to invest substantial sums in the development of enhanced magnetic tapes.

The invention of the transistor at the Bell Laboratories of AT&T between late 1947 and 1951 (for which William Shockley received a

Nobel prize) and the integrated circuit independently by Kilby and Noyce in 1959 also made significant contributions to the subsequent quality, reliability and miniaturization of recording equipment.

## APPENDIX 2: THE EMERGENCE OF BROADCAST/ PROFESSIONAL VIDEO-RECORDERS IN THE 1950S[1]

### Ampex Corporation and Radio Corporation of America (RCA)

In 1951 more than 11 million US households had a TV set and this number was set to double every two to three years for the next decade or so. This put great pressure on the US TV broadcast authorities to increase programming output, which at that time could only be broadcast live. Hence the broadcasters – including the RCA subsidiary NBC – actively promoted video-recorder research and development.

The design configuration of audio-recorders, however, was problematic when applied to the recording of video images since the latter would require a very high rate of data transfer between tape and sensing head, equivalent to a linear tape-to-head speed more than 100 times greater than for audio. An early RCA prototype on this principle demonstrated its impracticality.

In 1955 a six-man team at Ampex Corporation[2] demonstrated the first practical audio-visual tape recorder (VTR). It had four heads (quadruplex) and used a two-inch wide tape. Sound was recorded conventionally, but video was recorded by a rotating head whose axis was parallel to the tape movement, hence the term transverse scanning. Patents were immediately applied for.

Despite a cautious demand forecast the Ampex Board decide to proceed with the first, very expensive ($US60–75,000) VR1000 production machine, the size of a juke box. At a sales convention in 1956 Ampex received orders from broadcasters around the world for 100 VR1000s which were used in US black and white TV broadcasting from late 1956. Broadcasters could now routinely achieve time-lapse, obviating the need to broadcast live programmes simultaneously across the various US time zones. By the end of 1960 Ampex had sold an estimated 900 machines, a third outside the US, three-quarters of all VTRs in use. Ampex sales had risen to $US70 million ($US10 million in 1956). Over the next decade the Ampex VR1000 was introduced into broadcasting studios around the world and remained the standard for almost twenty years, even though it was a demanding machine to maintain at peak performance.

RCA engaged – unsuccessfully – in VTR development from 1951. By the early 1960s it was making VTRs under licence from Ampex (in exchange for allowing Ampex access to its colour TV patent know-how) and it had captured most of of the broadcast/professional market not directly served by Ampex.

## VTR developments in Japan and West Europe

TV broadcasting started in Japan in 1953, using US technology and broadcast standards. By 1957 over half of Japanese homes had a TV set. By 1959 the Japanese public broadcasting corporation NHK was in the forefront of VTR practice and already deployed three Ampex VR1000 video-recorders. In late 1958 it showed the VR1000 to a variety of local electronics manufacturers to prompt them to manufacture an equivalent product.

Encouraged by MITI, Sony, Matsushita and its JVC subsidiary, and others set about emulating the Ampex machine. Within three and a half months of first seeing it, Sony developed a working prototype with assistance from NHK technicians. It was bigger, more costly and used more tape per minute than the Ampex machine. Sony entered a cross-licensing arrangement with Ampex whereby, in exchange for use of Ampex patents, Sony assisted the latter with developing transistorized circuitry. Ampex terminated this arrangement after two years over alleged non-payment of due royalties.

Sony's first commercial machine, the PV100, was a compact two-inch reel-to-reel machine, of lower quality than Ampex, which in 1962 sold to professional customers in Japan for the yen equivalent of a quarter of the Ampex price. It gained a large share of the Japanese market although Ampex soon introduced a similar machine for non-broadcast professional use about 10 per cent cheaper than Sony. The leading electronics firm Matsushita and its subsidiary JVC took some five years to introduce separate VTRs. Theirs was a small, two-head design using two-inch tape. It was neither compatible with the Ampex machine nor commercially successful.

In Britain the BBC and the Independent Television Companies were early users of Ampex machines. No significant commercial developments in the design and manufacture of VTRs took place in the UK, however. Across Europe a number of incompatible black and white (and later colour) broadcast standards hindered professional VTR development, though a number of companies including Philips, Grundig and Telefunken of Germany were all actively involved in TV and related technologies.

## NOTES

1 These notes draw *inter alia* on Graham op. cit., Lurie and Yoffie op. cit., Morita *et al.* op. cit. and Quinn op. cit.
2 Including Ray Dolby whose later patented noise reduction techniques converted the Philips audio compact cassette mechanism into a true hi-fi medium in the 1970s.

## APPENDIX 3: EARLY DEVELOPMENTS IN HOME VIDEO

As many as thirty firms in the USA, Europe and Japan engaged in VCR development during the 1960s. The US firms began with a significant advantage in respect of prior expertise, and market power in TV and broadcast markets.

### North America

Encouraged by its success in professional markets, the Ampex Corporation began a substantial expansion drive in consumer and professional electronic products. It set up five divisions to produce a range of professional and domestic recorders, computer memory devices and magnetic tape. This strategy had an unpromising start, since the firm lost $US4 million in 1961. Still, it designed a wide range of up-market consumer audio products and in 1964 it entered a joint venture with Toshiba of Japan to mass-produce recorders and computer tape drives.

By 1965 it was distributing its products through 800 stores in the USA and claimed 50 per cent of its target market segments. It also launched the VR7000 black and white VTR onto the consumer market. However, this machine was successful only among professional and industrial users and sales flattened after only two years in the light of reliability problems and competing products, with only 500 units sold to consumers.[1]

Research commissioned by Ampex in 1968 showed that consumers wanted lower-priced, longer-playing, easier to use machines, primarily for home programming. In 1970 Ampex demonstrated its Instavideo system to meet their needs. It was a simple, lightweight machine priced at $US1,000, able to record and playback in black and white and colour. For an extra $US500 consumers could buy a compatible colour camera.

Because Ampex did not have the necessary skills or facilities for mass-producing Instavideo it was natural to hand this task to its joint venture company. Production of Instavideo proved problematic and combined with over-ambitious expansion plans, Ampex lost $US12 million in 1971 and $US90 million in 1972. A new management team abandoned Instavideo and retreated to its core professional markets. By the late 1970s the new helical scan Ampex VTR machines had became standard broadcast equipment. Ampex was taken over in 1980.

In the mid-1960s RCA was earning substantial revenues from licensing its colour TV patents, but forecasts suggested that domestic colour TV sales would saturate within a decade. Already virtually all homes had a TV and many had several, at least one being colour. RCA began to see home video as a new and attractive growth prospect. Its pre-eminent position in a variety of fundamental and applied fields of electronics research enabled it to follow a number of different research tracks using tapes and discs, using both magnetic and optical (lasers, holography) recording techniques.

RCA's Holotape prototypes were shown publicly in 1969, but poor imaging and reliability severely embarrassed the firm. From that point many of RCA's top executives and influential researchers believed that magnetic tape was technically inadequate for video recording. This led R&D progressively away from tape towards disc-based technologies.

Concurrent US developments reinforced this decision. NBC's rival broadcast company CBS introduced a video home system in 1970. The EVR system used a high resolution photographic film cartridge (players were made by Motorola) offered at $US800. There were manufacturing problems and EVR was abandoned after a year owing to poor consumer take up, CBS losing more than $US35 million. In 1972 another US system, Cartrivision magnetic tape recording/playback, was launched by a start-up company as an integrated TV/recording console, at a package price of over $US1,000. Cartridge TV Inc. went bankrupt in July 1973.

RCA believed consumers would want pre-recorded materials. They saw that control of NBC gave RCA the opportunity to market a wide repertoire of pre-recorded video disks using NBC programming, provided they could devise a suitable playback device. Because RCA owned Victor phonograph records, senior executives also had great confidence in the vinyl disc medium. None the less, one faction in RCA's Consumer Electronics Division remained committed to tape recording and low-key VCR development continued until 1974, largely against the contingency of unresolvable technical difficulties emerging with SelectaVision.[2] Until 1974 RCA was reluctant to accept Sony's claim that time-shifted viewing of off-air TV recordings would be important.

Creating a disc system, however, proved anything but straightforward for RCA. Problems arose with excessive disc and stylus wear, and the design, reliability and cost of the players. The RCA SelectaVision disc system was ultimately launched in 1981 (in the depths of a recession) well after home VCR systems had become widely accepted. Despite massive first year advertising – equivalent to $US200 per player sold – and dramatic price cutting, it flopped so badly that it was scrapped in 1984 at a cumulative cost to RCA of $US600 million.[3]

## Europe and Japan

In 1964 the highly innovative Philips Company launched the first one-inch tape VTR aimed mainly at the professional closed circuit TV market. This was followed a year later by Sony's first half-inch compact reel-to-reel design. These machines demonstrated the potential for

*Table 13.6* Early price progression in the VTR industry

| Company | Model | User target* | Tape width (inches) | Intro. date | Price in constant $US 1967 |
|---------|-------|--------------|---------------------|-------------|------------------------------|
| Ampex | VR1000 | B | 2 | 1956 | 60,000 |
| Sony | PV100 | I/P | 2 | 1962 | 13,000 |
| Ampex | VR1500 | I/P | 2 | 1962 | 12,000 |
| Philips | EL3400 | I/P | 1 | 1964 | 3,500 |
| Sony | CV2000 | I/P | .5 | 1965 | 600 |
| Sony | UMatic | I/P | .75 | 1971 | 1,100 |
| Philips | N1500 | I/P | .5 | 1972 | 1,150 |
| Sony | Betamax | C | .5 | 1975 | 850 |
| JVC | VHS | C | .5 | 1976 | 790 |
| Philips | VR2000 | C | .5 | 1979 | 520 |

*Source*: Adapted from J. B. Quinn, 'Sony Corporation', in Quinn *et al., The Strategy Process*, 1st edn (London: Prentice Hall, 1988)
*Notes*: * B  broadcast
        I/P  industrial and professional
        C  consumer

dramatic cost reductions and pointed the way to smaller, simpler designs for consumer use. Substantial technical problems remained to be solved, including inconsistent picture quality owing to misaligned tape/head tracking, which was critical if a tape recorded on one machine was replayed on another. Poor reliability of the hardware was also a continuing concern.

The first professional device to use a proprietary cassette, based on three-quarter inch tape, was the Sony U-Matic launched in 1971, matched by the non-compatible Philips N1500 using a half-inch tape. The 1975 Sony Betamax, based on a half-inch tape and priced at $US1,300 retail, was the first colour VCR to be generally affordable by consumers. Marketing efforts concentrated almost at once on the wealthy US market. Expressed in constant dollar prices at 1967 levels (see Table 13.6), the price of state-of-art video-recorders fell in little more than a decade from $US60,000 (Ampex Quad) to $US600 (Sony CV 2000).

## NOTES

1 Klopfenstein op. cit.
2 Graham op. cit.
3 Philips introduced a nominally similar 12-inch format LaserVision disc system using a non-contact laser pickup with digital data encoding that anticipated the now ubiquitous audio compact disc. Commercially, it fared little better than SelectaVision, though CDi seems set to do better in the 1990s.

## APPENDIX 4: BACKGROUND NOTES ON THE MAIN VCR PROTAGONISTS

### JVC and Matsushita

Konosuke Matsushita founded the firm that bears his name in 1918. By the mid-1930s the firm was selling everything from light bulbs to industrial equipment. By the 1950s it had grown to be the biggest manufacturer and retailer of electrical products in Japan. Its consumer product ranges included rice cookers, television sets and white goods and these were sold under brand names like National, Panasonic, Technics and Quasar. Matsushita had some 21,000 stores dedicated to its various brands and its products were featured in 12,000 others. Its policy was never to take substantial risks with new technology, rather to wait until a new product category was becoming well established and then to exploit it ruthlessly through efficient mass production and distribution.

To this end Matsushita had over the years made various acquisitions and entered a variety of pragmatic national and international licensing agreements, reflected in an extensive and divisionalized organizational structure. In 1951 it acquired a 50 per cent stake in the Japan Victor Company (JVC). JVC became a wholly-owned subsidiary two years later, though it remained largely autonomous within Matsushita.

Since the 1930s JVC had operated under licence from the Victor Talking Machines Company, a subsidiary of RCA, to make and market phonograph records and players in Japan, led by its founder and TV experimenter Kenjiro Takayanagi. Later JVC diversified into television manufacture, and though Takayanagi failed to achieve the personal recognition as a TV pioneer to which he aspired, the firm was commercially successful. By 1960 it held almost 60 per cent of the domestic market for TV receivers.

### The Sony Corporation[1]

Sony emerged in 1946 from the rubble of war-ravaged Japan as the Tokyo Telecommunications Research Laboratory (TTK), founded by university scientist Masaru Ibuka. His team of eight was soon joined by a graduate physicist, Akio Morita. For several years they survived by making electronic instruments and communications equipment for the occupying US military.

Earlier in their respective careers Ibuka and Morita had both experimented with audio wire recording. TTK might well have developed such a machine, but for Ibuka's failure to negotiate a suitable supply of high precision wire. Then TTK 'discovered' an American Wilcox-Gay tape recorder which Ibuka immediately wanted to copy. The main obstacle, according to Morita, was Mr Hasegawa, an accountant employed by Morita's father, himself a successful businessman, to keep the young TTK men on the straight and narrow:

> Ibuka and I were so excited by the new concept of the tape recorder (as a consumer product) and so convinced it was right for us that we decided to gang up on Hasegawa and make him see the light. We invited him to dinner at a black market restaurant, where we had a magnificent feast complete with beer, which was a rare commodity then. We told him all about the virtues of the tape recorder and how it would revolutionise an industry and how we could get in on this new field early, that we could beat all the slow-moving competition of the giant companies if we started immediately ... he approved our project on a full stomach right then and there and we were on our way.

Despite having to make their own magnetic tapes because none were available to them in Japan at that time, TTK launched its first audio tape recorder in 1949. It weighed 75 lbs and was priced around $US500, equivalent to almost three years' wages for a typical Japanese college graduate. It didn't sell! Morita revised their assumptions about the market and sold a number of machines to professional users in the Japanese law courts and in schools and colleges. Subsequently TTK concentrated on reducing the bulk and cost of its recorders and exploited a patented technical advance in circuit design by licensing it to other firms in Japan.

It also capitalized on the newly invented transistor, by producing battery-powered miniature radios with which in the late 1950s Morita opened up the American market on behalf of the now renamed Sony Corporation. To do this Ibuka and Morita purchased a $US25,000 user licence from the US Western Electric, to be paid for out of future earnings. In so doing they incurred the wrath of MITI which for months refused even in principle to sanction the outflow of capital payments from Japan.

In parallel with its development of professional and consumer audio and video recording products, Sony continued to develop magnetic recording tapes, becoming a leading producer in the 1960s. In 1959 it introduced a miniature solid state black and white TV. Small sets were desirable in cramped Japanese homes but Morita predicted, correctly, that US families would also buy a small portable set in addition to their main TV. Then, dissatisfied with US design standards for colour TVs, Sony engineers invented the single gun colour picture tube (Trinitron) which led in the mid-1960s to the launch of the first miniature Sony CTV. It was priced at $US400, roughly the same as a full-size black and white cabinet model. The US manufacturers largely ignored this market and Sony had little competition for a considerable time.

These experiences illustrate the core of Sony philosophy. Ibuka and Morita sought to innovate and be self-reliant in product and process technologies. They were keen to enhance existing products via miniaturization and to improve specifications progressively over time. They wanted to bring new products quickly to market and trusted their judgement when pioneering new markets. Sony presented its products as innovative, premium quality and priced them accordingly. This approach was especially true of markets outside Japan, which Sony penetrated at a much earlier stage than its bigger Japanese competitors.

From the start Ibuka and Morita determined that Sony would be a brand widely recognized by consumers and they refused to supply US firms with products under the latters' own names, as other Japanese firms were doing. Thus Morita recalled a 1955 conversation with a Bulova purchasing executive:

> Fifty years ago your brand name must have been just as unknown as ours is today. I am here with a new product, and I am now taking the first step for the next fifty years of my company. Fifty years from now I promise you that our name will be just as famous as your company name is today.

Ibuka fostered a flexible, entrepreneurial, and comparatively non-hierarchical culture in the firm. Development teams normally comprised six to eight people. Decision-making was decidedly untypical of the slow, consensual approach favoured by most Japanese firms of that era. Important decisions were generally made directly by Ibuka and Morita, though Dr Kihara was a contributor to R&D decisions. Indeed, many of Sony's most significant patents were registered by Kihara, of whom it was later said in 1982:

> Kihara was in charge of what kind of developments would be pursued, what systems to use. At Sony development moves fast. We make quick – but not rash – decisions. Kihara believes there are only a few people directly involved in a new technology who have adequate knowledge about that technology. With new products one must create a new market. Not many people know how these new markets will develop, what a product can do, how well it will function, how it could be used by customers.

## NOTE

1  This section draws on Morita *et al.* op. cit. and on Quinn op. cit.

# Chapter 14

# The Samsung Corporation: commitment to change in a global leader[1]

*Peter T. Golder and Chong Ju Choi*

**EDITORS' OVERVIEW**[1]

South Korea has transformed itself from one of the world's poorest countries to one of three leading economic players in North East Asia, the others being Taiwan and Japan. It has done so largely as a result of manufacturing goods for export to developed countries around the world. Many of the products that South Korean firms sell in the West are manufactured under original equipment manufacturing (OEM) conditions, that is, made to be sold under the brand name of the purchasing company. In the last ten years, however, South Korean companies have increasingly been selling their products under their own brand names. The Samsung Corporation is one of these firms. What makes it truly exceptional is that in so doing it has managed to become one of the world's leading manufacturers of semiconductor devices.

Many large international enterprises are faced with problems that are in one way or another related to management of change. Change variously takes the form of increasing R&D costs attributable largely to the complexity of high-technology products, increasingly international competition, and the problem of managing diverse business operations characteristic of the so-called conglomerate firm. These are problems to which the South Korean *Chaebols* such as the Samsung Corporation are by no means immune.

This case study examines the rise of Samsung and makes a comparison with its strongest domestic rival, Lucky Goldstar. It focuses in particular on the radical changes undertaken within Samsung in the last three years. Not only has Samsung embarked on a new approach to internationalizing its businesses, it has also been busy implementing new organizational and management strategies that aim to enhance its productivity. Additionally, Samsung is now placing great emphasis on quality as the basis for competitive advantage, and is seeking fundamentally to alter the perceptions of the firm's managers from the very top downwards. This programme of radical change stems from what has become known in Samsung as Chairman Lee Kun-Hee's 1991 Frankfurt 'burning bridges' declaration.

The case enables one to consider the leadership problems of managing large and complex business organizations. Samsung is complex in many ways, notably in terms of the large number of countries in which it operates production plants and markets its wide product range. It is also complex in terms of its relations with governments, both at home and around the world. Lee Kun-Hee decided that one way to control the managerial task was to refocus the corporation on selected high growth sectors in which the firm has or can develop world standard competences and to divest itself of low growth and peripheral activities. However, in his own estimation, part of the problem was a cumbersome bureaucratic structure in which too many key decisions were taken at a senior level instead of being devolved. Just one result of this was a failure to respond to local conditions around the world.

Accordingly, he set in train a series of radical organizational changes that were both substantive and highly symbolic in their significance. To take just one example, he decreed that working hours would be amended to give employees more time outside the firm to spend with their families and for self-improvement study. These changes have been quite extraordinary in their vision, boldness and high cost. Yet though it would be premature to say that they have definitively succeeded, the evidence to date is that they are succeeding. Samsung appears to be on track to achieve its goal of becoming one of the largest high technology corporations in the world by the turn of the century.

## Discussion questions

- Why did the chairman feel it was necessary to articulate a programme of revolutionary change in 1991? Could a similar result not have been achieved by other means?
- What leadership qualities does Lee Kun-Hee possess? Could he have initiated a similar change process in a company with a more dispersed share holding?
- What strategic managerial lessons does this case offer firms in Japan, in the USA, and in Europe?
- Are the critical factors for global success the same irrespective of the home base, or does Samsung possess specific advantages by virtue of its South Korean base?
- Will Samsung maintain its leading position in semiconductors? What threats and opportunities are inherent in this sector?
- Is the diversification into automobile manufacture a sound strategic move? How should it be put into effect if it is to secure a global platform for growth for Samsung? What risks does it entail?

## List of named characters

Lee Kun–Hee, current chairman of Samsung

## Keywords

Leadership; focus and divestment; diversification; global strategy; creativity and innovativeness; radical change; decentralization; staff motivation

# INTRODUCTION

Asian countries have gained great economic power over the last few decades. Japan, South Korea and Taiwan, the North East Asian countries, have managed to achieve economic prosperity almost equal to that of western countries. Hong Kong and Singapore represent special cases: while Singapore geographically belongs to South East Asia and Hong Kong returns to China in 1997, in terms of economic performance they are part of North East Asia. Both 'city-states' are former British colonies, so they represent a familiar 'hub' for western firms in the process of entering other, less familiar Asian territory.

In 1994 when the western world was slowly emerging from recession, Asian markets were booming. Industrialists could see that China presents great economic potential although its political environment leaves many questions unanswered, making the prospects for foreign direct investments risky.

South Korea and Japan exhibit similar patterns of economic policy and development. Japan's famous MITI (Ministry of International Trade and Industry) promoted a policy of manufacturing for export in the late 1950s, whilst South Korea embarked on a similar path in the 1960s. Both countries also established a similar enterprise structure: in Japan the *Zaibatsus* which were supplanted after 1945 by the *Keiretsus*, and the *Chaebols* in South Korea. In both countries many of these organizations have succeeded to the point where they have become large multinational conglomerates. Samsung Corporation is one such.

The Japanese *Keiretsu* system is well known for the way many trading firms and banks are linked via complex cross-share holdings and across industry sectors. The system confers great economic strength and stability on its members and it poses significant entry barriers to outsiders. South Korea's counterparts, the *Chaebols*, are in the process of gaining the same reputation. Their economic strength and the lack of foreign competitors able to compete in the semi-closed South Korean economy have created an image of dominance and toughness for South Korean conglomerates. Like their Japanese counterparts, they manufacture everything from chemicals, to electronics to vehicles. Taiwan, in contrast, has engaged in a very different economic policy, where promoting small and medium-sized firms has been considered the key to success. Taiwanese firms pursue niche strategies, such as the manufacture of computer mother boards.

The pressure to globalize in world markets poses a challenge to both forms of economic strategy. Moreover, the success of these different approaches to achieving global presence in all the Triad consumer markets (Asia, Europe and the USA) is seen as vital for the long-term development of business enterprises in these Asian nations.

## THE SOUTH KOREAN BUSINESS LANDSCAPE

South Korea was one of the world's poorest countries in the 1950s. However, over the last forty years the nation has managed to achieve phenomenal economic growth coupled with a growing international presence of South Korean products in world markets, despite several political setbacks. Part of this success is attributable to the country's industrial policy which aimed largely to emulate Japan's co-ordinated promotional export manufacturing policy.

The South Korean economy experienced great turbulence during the early 1960s. When former president Park Chung-Hee took power in 1961 through a military *coup d'état* many rich people were charged with tax fraud and illicit accumulation of wealth. As a result, they had to make large contributions to the state before being allowed to continue their business activities. However, the military regime of the early 1960s also proclaimed economic development as a national goal. During the 1960s the South Korean government targeted key industries and assigned them to certain firms, thereby granting them a *de facto* monopoly at home.

These co-ordinated policies were tied to achieving a minimum level of exports in a given period of time. If a firm was unable to reach its stated export target for that period, the government would decrease the amount of subsidies for the next period, thereby punishing the firm. Conversely, when a firm was able to export more than the actual target, the government would reward the firm with extra subsidies for the next period. This control mechanism ensured that only profitable and effective firms ultimately became genuine world players, able to serve all Triad markets simultaneously. These export-promotion policies permitted successful firms to diversify into various areas, thereby laying the foundation of today's conglomerates.

When another military regime took power in the 1980s, many large companies had to make severe adjustments to their strategic business units. In the case of Samsung, the company had to divest its radio and TV operations. In the late 1980s South Korea was still undergoing drastic industrial restructuring. Although by this time the government had refrained from imposing too many restrictive obligations on its enterprises, it still maintained a *de facto* technological barrier to firms entering industrial sectors. Some of the key technologies for the machinery, car and electronics industries still had to be imported from the USA and Japan, with a notable exception in respect of the Samsung Electronics Corporation and its semiconductor undertakings. Reliance on foreign technology and know-how gave the government a continuing control mechanism by allowing the ministries in charge to grant (or deny) a *Chaebol* entry into a new and often much desired industry.

The latest example in the quest to enter new business sectors is the case of the Samsung Corporation entering the motor car industry. The government was for a long time reluctant to grant the largest South Korean *Chaebol* permission to engage in automobile manufacturing, though it eventually agreed, subject to conditions.

## AN OVERVIEW OF THE SOUTH KOREAN ELECTRONICS INDUSTRY

Some of the most prominent South Korean *Chaebols* are heavily engaged in the production of computer components, mainly semiconductors. Lucky Goldstar and the Samsung Electronics Corporation, the star performer of approximately thirty companies in the Samsung empire, are among the most prominent companies engaged in the electronics industry worldwide.

These South Korean electronics firms followed very similar patterns of international development. Lucky Goldstar was established in 1958; Samsung Electronics Corporation was founded eleven years later on condition that it would export the majority of its products for the first few years. By setting up strategic alliances, Samsung managed to acquire sufficient knowledge to enter the semiconductor memory chip (DRAM) market successfully.

When the Samsung Corporation was founded its management decision making and control style were dominated by a small family clan. At the time, the economic environment was quite stable as a result of the strongly protected domestic market. Moreover, there were only two influential players in the electronics business: Lucky Goldstar and Daewoo.

The South Korean consumer electronics firm increased exports rapidly by using sales and distribution agents. In this way Samsung was able to boost its exports to 70 per cent of its total production, although virtually all of these were shipped to the USA on an OEM[3] basis, driving down the market share and profits of US and later Japanese producers.

In the late 1970s the South Korean electronics firms started to build their own foreign operations, mainly marketing networks. They started to sell products under their own brand names, although the proportion of branded products versus OEM products was less than 30 per cent. They also started to expand into other developed countries such as the UK and Spain. Samsung and Lucky Goldstar continued to enjoy a duopoly position in their protected home market. However, the South Korean electronics industry, as a result of its globalization efforts, was now starting to feel the need for global integration of its operations.

In the early 1980s direct foreign investments of the South Korean *Chaebols* were extended to build production plants in some of the

developed western countries. Some of these decisions need to be understood as political investments rather than exploitation of direct economic
opportunities in these countries at the time. The principal investment
targets were in the European Union and the USA, which also made up
the lion's share of the *Chaebols'* customer markets. The same period
was also characterized by a 50 per cent increase in the ratio of branded
products to OEM products exported.

For Samsung, the various trade wars between South Korea and other
parts of the world, along with the perceived need for further internationalization strategies, forced the company to adopt a more bureaucratic
control system, shifting away from the autocratic, family clan-dominated
system that had prevailed since the foundation of the company. Lucky
Goldstar, however, in part still maintains its clan control structure.

The latest stage in the process of establishing local presence in the
global environment is characterized by the firms' efforts to built manufacturing sites all around the world, not just in developed countries. In the
late 1980s countries such as China, Thailand and Mexico started to
attract the South Korean *Chaebols*. This stage is characterized by intensified global market competition and the beginning of greater liberalization
of the South Korean market. The need to control business-related
uncertainty including technological advances, global market presence
and political instability – coupled with the ongoing process of global
integration – emphasized the need for more suitable control mechanisms.
Thus Samsung and others adopted a global product division structure to
replace the international structure that predominated in the mid-1980s.

## GLOBALIZATION OF THE SAMSUNG CORPORATION

Samsung, which means three stars, is widely considered to be the most
successful South Korean *Chaebol*. The Samsung Corporation comprises
some thirty companies (with about fifty subsidiaries) in various lines of
business. Of these, Samsung Electronics Corporation is the outstanding
performer, having emerged as the world's number one semiconductor
manufacturer in terms of volume. In 1992, Samsung's DRAM[4] business
soared 35 per cent, to $US1.2 billion.[5] This marks the first time that a
South Korean company had outperformed a Japanese semiconductor
manufacturer. Moreover, the South Koreans are now in a position simultaneously to match Japanese quality and deliver their products at a lower
price.

A comparison between Samsung Electronics Corporation and its
competitor Lucky Goldstar is instructive. Figure 14.1 and Table 14.1
illustrate the phenomenal success of Samsung. In the twenty years to
1993 Samsung has outperformed its competitor in terms of sales growth,
one of the most important criteria for South Korean firms, by a factor of

*Table 14.1* The growth of Samsung Electronics Corporation and Lucky Goldstar (billion Won, exchange rate 800 Won/$US)

|       | Samsung | | | Goldstar | | |
|-------|--------|--------|-------|--------|--------|-------|
|       | Assets | Profits | Sales | Assets | Profits | Sales |
| 1974  | 10.0   | 0.6    | 13.4  | 21.5   | 2.0    | 31.5  |
| 1976  | 38.0   | 1.4    | 41.0  | 58.9   | 2.6    | 69.2  |
| 1978  | 112.4  | 4.4    | 159.1 | 140.0  | 5.7    | 170.7 |
| 1980  | 255.8  | (5.5)  | 233.6 | 257.6  | (9.1)  | 253.0 |
| 1982  | 387.4  | 5.1    | 426.4 | 355.1  | 9.6    | 454.3 |
| 1984  | 607.7  | 25.1   | 1351.6| 718.0  | 10.5   | 1295.6|
| 1986  | 872.7  | 31.6   | 1958.9| 1124.1 | 20.7   | 1539.6|
| 1988  | 2462.0 | 101.8  | 3028.3| 2228.6 | 18.2   | 2825.3|
| 1990  | 4057.2 | 73.0   | 4511.7| 2614.6 | 33.3   | 2984.0|
| 1992  | 6326.6 | 72.4   | 6102.7| 3436.7 | 26.5   | 3787.4|
| 1993  | 6659.4 | 154.6  | 8154.8| 3652.1 | 65.6   | 4323.5|

*Source*: Y. H. Kim and N. Campbell 'The internationalisation process and control style of MNCs: the case of Korean electronics companies', First Conference on East Asia, EU Business, Birmingham, 4–6 January 1995; annual reports and various company documents

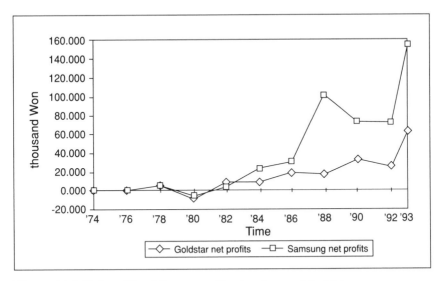

*Figure 14.1* Net profits of Samsung Electronics and Goldstar

almost 4.5 times. A similar ratio also holds for the growth of assets. Although Samsung was half the size of Goldstar in 1974, it was able to overtake Goldstar in 1984 in both sales and profits and by 1988 Samsung had outgrown Goldstar in terms of assets too. One of the reasons for the exceptional growth of Samsung Electronics Corporation relative to Goldstar is that since its foundation Goldstar has maintained its family clan control style, whereas Samsung adopted a professionalized bureaucratic control style along its evolutionary path.[6]

By 1993 the Samsung Corporation as a group was ranked the world's 14th largest industrial conglomerate with total sales of $US55 billion and 105th in profits with $US374.2 million.[7] It had started to establish production facilities all around the world. Some industries are exposed to pressures for globalization much sooner than others. The high technology sector of the electronics industries in which Samsung Corporation is engaged, namely semiconductors, is one of these, arguably for the following reasons:

• The very high capital investment costs of setting up state-of-the-art facilities.
• The high risks involved, both technological and commercial.
• Its oligopolistic industry structure – relatively few, but powerful competing firms.

In addition to strictly business-driven aspects of direct foreign investment there were political reasons to establish foreign operations, as the case of Europe clearly illustrates.

Samsung Corporation's UK operations were established as far back as 1969. The firm's European operations also include a Spanish production site where the company manufactures TVs and VCRs and a jointly operated plant with Texas Instruments Inc. in Portugal. One of the reasons for the early move into Europe was the array of actual and potential economic sanctions that the European Community presents to non-Community members, including anti-dumping measures, import quotas and taxes. However, for Samsung the decision to enter the European Community was not just political; the growing importance of the Triad markets and increasing competition from South European countries, mainly based on the low labour costs, made it seem virtually an imperative for the South Korean *Chaebol* to establish a local presence within the European Community.

Samsung's preference for establishing its main European operations in the UK rather than mainland Europe include the following reported reasons:

• Infrastructure and UK government support.

- Labour productivity and competitive wage rates as a result of the UK's decision to opt out of the Social Charter.[8]
- Greater cultural overlaps between the Koreans and the British, notably the Koreans' familiarity with the English language.[9]

Samsung decided to build its new manufacturing plant in Cleveland, North East England. The decision was also influenced by the proximity of Cleveland to Scotland's 'Silicon Glen', one of Europe's most prominent high technology centres, where a large number of potential customers for Samsung's semiconductor products are located. This commitment to Britain is further supported by Samsung's announcement that it will move its European headquarters from Frankfurt, Germany, to London.

Furthermore, in its attempts to become a global player, Samsung's presence is also required in the other two Triad markets: the USA and Asia. Owing to its origins it has long been a leading force in Asian markets, nevertheless, the company is establishing new manufacturing facilities in China and Thailand where wage levels are still much lower than in South Korea. Moreover, both countries represent a large potential consumer base which requires localized strategies and the setting up of local distribution channels.

## RADICAL CHANGE IN THE SAMSUNG CORPORATION

It can be argued that consumers have undoubtedly benefited in two ways from Samsung's move into western markets in general and semiconductors in particular. First, increased competition has driven down costs and prices of components and ultimately finished products. Second, fierce competition has led to higher performance and ultimately better value for money products.

However, in the late 1980s Samsung's consumer electronics products still suffered from a comparatively poor image because of high defect rates. Moreover, the group had not yet established its brand label as a world class product, partly because it still manufactured over 30 per cent of its products under OEM conditions. Its lack of reputation as a quality company was further constrained by the fact that it remained largely dependent on foreign key technologies. Although the company was able to demonstrate one of the first working 16 megabit DRAM chips, it still lacked technological know-how in many core activities including chemicals, machinery and car manufacturing

The current chairman, Lee Kun-Hee, took charge in 1987 after the death of his father, the founder of Samsung. Then Samsung was a widely diversified group with business interests ranging from electronics to nutrition. According to Lee Kun-Hee, despite having become the world's fifth largest electronics corporation, the rest of the group aside from the semiconductor business was not catching up fast enough with leading competitors such as Sony, General Electric and Philips.

Accordingly, Lee Kun-Hee imposed drastic changes on the conglomerate. He began with his 'Frankfurt declaration' in which he sought to create perceptions of a crisis in the firm, by articulating and spreading the belief that Samsung simply could not stand still. Thus, through his 'burning bridges' strategy, he aimed to create momentum for substantial changes, the initiation of which marked the beginning of the 'reengineering' process currently underway in the Corporation.[10] 'Burning bridges' signalled to the entire organization that the only way to go was forward and it has forced the company into making radical commitments to the ambitious globalization programmes personally advocated by Lee Kun-Hee.

It needs to be stressed, here, that Samsung is not only undergoing a restructuring process but also pursuing a radical strategy to make the *Chaebol* one of the world's biggest corporations, that is, one of the very top players in the global electronics industries. Samsung is giving equal weight to restructuring its internal processes and hierarchical structures and to the way its external relations are managed. These radical changes involve simultaneous implementation of the firm's globalization programme and its reorganization of internal hierarchical structures. The process involves essentially (i) divestment of peripheral strategic business units and (ii) delayering, empowerment and cultural change.

### Divestment and refocusing of business activities

Samsung has experienced three large-scale reorganization exercises since 1991. The current organizational restructuring follows the introduction of management reforms in 1994 to promote autonomy among the group's main business areas of chemicals, electronics, machinery, trading and finance.

Samsung and other large South Korean *Chaebols* are aware that their rampant diversification efforts of the mid-1980s actually turned out to be an obstacle in achieving global competitiveness. Thus, Lee Kun-Hee has since declared that the Samsung group needs to concentrate on a few core industries to achieve success abroad: the real future of the company lies in specialization.[11] This implies substantial divestments and restructuring programmes as listed in Figure 14.2. These efforts attempt to consolidate its operations by cutting the number of subsidiaries from fifty to twenty-four through mergers and disposals and they reinforce the conglomerate's intention to focus on core industries and thereby make itself more effective and efficient.

- Ten subsidiaries will be merged. The Samsung Corporation, the group's trading arm will take over several construction units, including Samsung Engineering and Construction, Samsung Engineering and Samtech, and Cheil Industries, the textile company.
- Samsung Heavy Industries, which specializes in transport equipment and construction machinery, will absorb Samsung Aerospace, Samsung Forklift and Samsung Kloeckner Machinery.
- The Samsung General Chemicals group, the conglomerate's petrochemicals unit, will be merged with the recently acquired South Korea Fertiliser and Chemicals.
- Yonpo Leisures will be merged with the property group Joong-ang Development, while Kwangjoo Electronics will be absorbed by Samsung Electronics. Samsung Watches will change its name to Samsung Precision with additional activities of the semiconductor manufacturing equipment being added to this unit.
- Very labour-intensive subsidiaries, mainly in the textile, food and service sector, will be sold due to their profitability being eroded by the higher wages now prevailing in South Korea.
- Other companies that will be sold include Cheil Food & Chemical, Cheil Synthetics, Hicreation, Cheil-Bozell Advertising, Daekyung Building, Korea-Alaska Development, Cheil Frozen Food, Chonsun Hotel, Taejon Station Business, Cheil Futures, Samsung Emerson, Korea Information Group in electronics, Shin-etsu-silicone Korea, Cheil Ciba-Geigy, and Daehan Precision; the country's main newspaper *Joong-ang Daily* will also be sold by the year 2000.

*Figure 14.2* The new face of the Samsung Corporation

Source: J. Burton, *Financial Times* 28 October 1994: 28; 3 December 1994: 9; 8 December 1994: 5; 6 December 1994: 28

In this respect, Samsung claims that its current reorganization also meets the government's goals for the reform of South Korean's leading conglomerates, including business specialisation and the dilution of family ownership. The most controversial aspect of this strategy, however, is Samsung's effort to establish its own passenger car business, where the company plans to manufacture approximately 200,000 per year until the end of the century, after which time production will be significantly increased. Since the recent liberalization and privatization efforts of the government, the *Chaebols* have gained more freedom. Yet the government granted permission for Samsung to enter the auto industry only under restrictive conditions, such as a promise that 55 per cent of the cars it makes will be exported, thus avoiding any disturbances of the already saturated South Korean car market. Still, perhaps mindful of the enormous potential of emerging markets in Asia, this reluctant decision by the government has only reinforced the company's determination to restructure around its defined core areas of business activity.

## Delayering, empowerment and cultural change

In 1993 Lee Kun-Hee introduced wide-ranging management reforms that promote individual responsibilities among Samsung's management cadre. Formerly the group was known for its hierarchical structure and was heavily influenced by Japanese management practices.

The balance between centralization and decentralization in a corporate environment is often problematic. The approach of the Samsung Corporation is clearly to separate the firm's globalization strategy from the corporate headquarters, which continues to manage the strategic business unit portfolio by making investment and divestment decisions. However, at the strategic business unit level, management teams are now empowered to make decisions at a local level.

In addition to the need to adopt global organization and work practices, there are other fundamental problems that the chairman felt had to be addressed if Samsung was to become a top global player. Lee Kun-Hee complained that many employees had so far been reluctant to acknowledge the gap that exists between the firm and its world leading competitors. Likewise, Samsung managers had not yet fully understood the impact of a rapidly changing and highly competitive global environment.

In an attempt to narrow the gap in outlook between Samsung's management and that of its competitors, the *Chaebol* embarked on increased R&D spending in order to sustain its leading edge position, and it is also trying to educate its workforce into adopting a radical outlook. According to the message of the Frankfurt Declaration, 'Quality first, no matter what', the company has embarked on various total quality management (TQM) programmes to alter managerial perceptions. Some of these very costly programmes are as follows:

- The 7 to 4 Programme – Since July 1993, the chairman has required employees to work from 7 a.m. to 4 p.m. This is disturbing in a country where typical office hours are from 9 a.m. to 8 p.m. Lee Kun-Hee's intention is to make people aware of the changes he requires from his employees by literally altering their working (and hence living) arrangements. Fundamentally, the change aims to increase the productivity of individuals, whilst also allowing time for self-improvement courses.
- The Regional Specialist Programme – The idea of this programme is to build a more globally-informed management cadre. This is being achieved in a rather unusual way: each year 400 executives are picked and sent abroad for one year with about $US50,000 to spend, no questions asked. When they return, they are expected to have a sound understanding of the culture and language of the host country they

| Strategic issue | Old strategy | New strategy |
|---|---|---|
| Authority | Centralized/top-down | Decentralized/more individual |
| Product Quality | Moderate/ low priority | The best/high priority |
| Human Resources | Low priority | High priority/new emphasis on learning and empowerment |
| Reputation/branding | Poor/low priority | High/much higher profile |
| Strategic portfolio | Large/diversified | Smaller/focused on core competences |

*Figure 14.3*   Samsung's strategies for change

have lived in. After a few years back in South Korea, they will return to their country of specialization to promote Samsung's products and services.

- The Techno-Valleys Programme – The purpose of this programme is to allow 'problem-makers' to raise their voice and come up with innovative new ideas. One small group originated a new concept for selling TVs in Mexico: Samsung has now introduced a TV that constantly carries a sponsor's logo at the top of the screen, allowing the company to sell its commercialized product at a 30 per cent discount compared with its competitors.

The extent of Samsung's strategies for radical change are summarized in Figure 14.3.

## SUMMARY AND CONCLUSIONS

The Samsung Corporation has undergone – and continues to undergo – radical changes initiated by the chairman, Lee Kun–Hee. The firm has embarked on a new approach to globalizing its businesses, and implementing new management strategies to solve the problem of large excessively diversified business conglomerates. The other South Korean *Chaebols* are also facing these problems.

Radical change at the Samsung Corporation involves underpinning the firm's globalization efforts by refocusing on core business areas. Specific changes involve substantial divestments and new investments in areas such as automobiles. Despite the fact that the South Korean government now exerts less control over the large *Chaebols*, Samsung's recent move into the automobile sector shows that there are still some government-created barriers to entry. Evidently, entry into such protected, profitable markets is easier for large corporations, which have more bargaining power with the government.

The question of whether to engage in new technology alliances remains a vital issue of competitive strategy. On the one hand, especially in intensive R&D markets, there is typically a shift *away* from strategic alliances towards a more oligopolistic market structure as licensees become more competent and licensers are increasingly wary of conceding their technological lead. On the other hand, despite successful alliances, South Korean corporations are still relatively dependent on the technical equipment of US and Japanese machine manufacturers, for instance in the production of advanced microchips. Thus the Samsung chairman still considers it vital for the long-term success of the firm to set up new strategic technical and commercial alliances in selected key areas. This will be allied to the encouragement and rewarding of special task forces to promote technological innovativeness in the firm, narrowing the knowledge gap that still exists between it and some competitors in the high technology sectors in which Samsung operates.

Furthermore, Samsung has embarked on various programmes of internal restructuring and culture change. The Regional Specialist Programme, aimed at creating insights into local market conditions, is set to alter the cultural perceptions of a large number of senior managers. Coupled with other learning activities, it demonstrates that Samsung is seeking to empower managers much more widely throughout the organization than ever before. Indeed, the transfer of responsibility to lower levels of management is now a key characteristic of Samsung's drive to become one of the world's biggest, high quality product suppliers. Camaraderie and the total and credible commitment to change made by the senior management – exemplified in the Chairman's Frankfurt declaration of the 'burning bridges' strategy – are keys to the successful ongoing change at Samsung. The fact that the Samsung corporation has been forced by its chairman to respond to a crisis imposed upon it without actually experiencing a real (financial) disaster is not unique, though it is extremely unusual in a corporation of this size.

The early results of this approach are found in the company's financial performance for 1993. Its turnover reached $US54 billion with core technology businesses accounting for about 42 per cent, up from 26 per cent in 1991. The group plans to achieve sales of $US200 billion by the year 2000 with core businesses accounting for approximately 75 per cent. Samsung Electronics' contribution in 1993 accounts for approximately one-fifth of the conglomerate's total turnover.

Although it is too early to assess the long-term value of Samsung's newly implemented strategies, the company hopes it is now in a position to maintain momentum and extend across a broad front the technological competence it presently enjoys in its semiconductor operations. The articulation of Lee Kun–Hee's ambitious vision and the resulting drive for change are putting South Korea's largest conglomerate into a good position to become one of the world's biggest economic players in the twenty-first century.

## NOTES

1 The editors of this volume gratefully acknowledge Peter Golder and Chong Choi's contribution to drafting these notes.
2 © Peter T. Golder and Chong J. Choi 1995
This case study has been written as a basis for class discussion rather than to illustrate effective or ineffective managerial or administrative behaviour.
3 Original equipment manufacturing.
4 Dynamic random access memory chips.
5 L. Nakarmi and N. Gross, 'Masters of the clean room – how Samsung upstaged Japan to become No. 1 in DRAMs', *Business Week*, 27 September 1994, pp. 68–9.
6 Y. H. Kim and N. Campbell, 'The internationalisation process and control style of MNCs: the case of Korean electronics companies', First Conference on East Asia, EU Business, Birmingham, 4–6 January 1995.
7 *Fortune Magazine*, 1994.
8 *Financial Times*, 18 October 1994: 12.
9 C. J. Choi, 'Leadership and change in the Samsung Corporation', *Long Range Planning*, June 1995.
10 The term 'reengineering' is borrowed from M. Hammer, 'Reengineering work: don't automate, obliterate', *Harvard Business Review*, July/August, 1990 and M. Hammer and J. Champy, *Reengineering the Corporation: A Manifesto For Business Revolution*, (London: Nicholas Brealy, 1993), though the changes at Samsung are perhaps more radical in form and scope than these sources envision.
11 L. Nakarmi, N. Gross and R. Hof, 'Samsung: Lee Kun-Hee's management revolution', *Business Week*, 28 February 1992: 34–7.

# Managing complexity and international organizations

# Chapter 15

# Benetton: the global network company

*Gianni Lorenzoni*

## EDITORS' OVERVIEW

The name of Benetton needs little introduction. What started in 1965 as a small knitwear factory in Ponzano, Italy, has developed into a fashion clothing company which today operates in over fifty countries worldwide. Throughout its life, there has been considerable continuity in the top management of the firm, with founder Luciano Benetton, his sister and two brothers still very active in its affairs.

The reader may be aware of a number of case studies about Benetton, mostly written at arm's length by US authors who became aware of the company only when it began to operate in the USA in 1980. Our case is written by an eminent Italian professor who has studied Benetton closely over a long period. Although written more recently, it focuses on the situation in late 1984 at the time the company had confronted the comparative failure of its US venture. In response Luciano Benetton adopted a characteristically bold strategy of accelerating expansion in the USA, drawing on the financial and organizational reserves of the parent company accrued over the preceding six years, which saw an almost tenfold increase in sales revenue as Benetton increased its international presence to the extent that overseas sales rose from 2 per cent to 55 per cent of total.

How was the Benetton success achieved? This case provides answers partly by reviewing the principal management functions and systems in and around the firm. These are both distinctive and consistent over time. However, one should also consider the managerial style or culture of the firm and how that has travelled beyond its Italian roots. Also, one should be mindful of the driving entrepreneurial personality of Luciano Benetton himself, the contribution of other family members, as well as the commitment of managers, agents and retailers at all levels throughout the firm. In sum they constitute a coherent and well-integrated formula that has so evidently proved effective and highly problematic for potential competitors to emulate.

This case study covers the following principal functional areas:

- Product management – creating and managing the seasonal sample collections, and how they are merchandised at point of sale.
- Marketing – in particular, establishing and controlling the dense network of retail outlets in Italy and abroad, both Benetton-owned and operated, and franchised, via the role of loyal sales representatives/agents, many of whom rely entirely on commission payments.
- Manufacturing and logistics – notably the distinctive Benetton approach to subcontracting, the communication of sales demand from retail stores back to the Ponzano 'nerve centre', thence to the factories, and the technological upgrading of production and distribution processes and facilities.
- Finance and control – private ownership and cash repatriation outside of the banking system.

It traces the emergence of the firm and how it created new markets – in essence mass fashion for the young. In retrospect the timing of the company's launch was impeccable: in the mid-1960s young people throughout Europe had, for the first time, enough discretionary income and sense of independence from the older generations to be assertive in their behaviour and dress code. The brash and vivid Benetton colours were distinctive and differentiated the firm from bland and less style-conscious competitors. For this, Giuliana Benetton can take much of the credit, seeming to have an unfailing sense of what will appeal to the young all around the world.

Definitely not to be forgotten is the driving entrepreneurial behaviour of the charismatic Luciano Benetton, who believed in a vision of the future and placed it as the centre-piece of an innovative company strategy. Profits were arguably not the fundamental motivation so much as the means to achieve the idea. Right from the start Benetton challenged industry norms, though Luciano – ever the pragmatist – was willing to learn from others, and to adopt what he felt was appropriate to his business.

Thus he visited the reputable Scottish woollen manufacturers at an early stage and his firm used re-engineered discarded machinery. Benetton's subsequent achievements in garment manufacturing were substantial, particularly in its early use of (often quite small) subcontractors. Benetton would enter long-term, flexible relationships based on trust rather than legal contracts, often underpinned with cross-holdings of equity. It opted for industrial rather than craft production methods and adopted the practice of piece dyeing 'grey' garments after the popularity of specific colours had been established. Born of necessity, flexible and economical use of resources has remained a chief characteristic of the firm that, allied to heavy reinvestment of profits, quickened the pace of expansion without becoming ridden with debt.

However, it can be argued that Benetton's electrifying growth was truly enabled by its dynamic and innovative management of marketing and distribution channels. Thus it established small company-owned shops, and made a virtue of necessity by creating the impression of being lively, colourful, fashionable, and exciting. It chose staff for their youth and enthusiasm, looked favourably on management buyouts, and appointed franchisees and agents on the basis of trust without contracts. In addition, as it grew it began to use information technology to speed the feedback of information from the outlets on trends and finances.

Can the success continue? As of 1984 success in the US market is still elusive. As the scale of its operations continues to grow, logistical problems will also multiply and may give rise to problems for which there are only costly and perhaps problematic solutions. Informality in its style of working may have to give way to greater formality and discipline, which may affect enthusiasm and commitment. Looking further ahead, will other competitors be able to emulate Benetton's success, not least in the European single market?

## Discussion questions

* Identify and evaluate the core competences Benetton has developed and exploited to achieve such dramatic growth.
* How has Benetton made a strategic virtue of complexity? Is its success attributable to specific advantages or to the effect of various factors working in combination?
* What internal problems may require management attention in the foreseeable future? What external problems could inhibit the growth of Benetton in the 1990s?
* How successful is Benetton in financial terms? Are there any areas of possible concern?
* What are the ways in which a leading competitor might effectively contest the markets Benetton has realized? What are Benetton's competitive vulnerabilities, if any?

## List of named characters

Luciano Benetton, founder and chief executive
Giuliana Benetton, co-founder and fashion director
Carlo Benetton, production director
Gilberto Benetton, finance director
Daniela Poggi, a retail manager
Mr Aluffi, contracts manager

G. L. and R. V., sales agents/representatives
Pier Alfonso Orsi, head of finance and control
Mr Palmieri, new managing director
Giorgio Cantagalli, personnel manager

## Keywords

Core competences; flexibility and responsiveness; continuous upgrading; networks (of trust: subcontractors and franchised outlets); managing fashion; sustaining growth; entrepreneurial vision; creating a new formula

## THE BUSINESS IDEA

Benetton of Ponzano Veneto (Italy) is a multinational company which operates in over fifty countries, selling 30 million articles of clothing through 2,600 outlets. The group has 1,650 direct employees, at its nine plants (seven in Italy and two abroad). In total, it had a turnover of $US300 million in 1983.

The Benetton venture began in 1965 with a plant at Ponzano Veneto to produce knitwear. It has always been a family-run business of three brothers and one sister. The driving force behind the group was, and still is, Luciano Benetton, now 49 years old, whose background is unusual as he has little formal education and began working at an early age. He was a sales representative in textiles and clothing products for local craftsmen. Outside interests include a passion for sport (especially canoeing and basketball) but as he says, 'I was never the best, even though I was always the captain' (*Capital*, September 1983). Giuliana, his sister, used to make knitwear items at home which she designed in bright and unusual colours. When Luciano saw these he was certain that he could sell them, and so the Benetton business began. In the early days, Luciano was the technician in his sister's business, where he was adapting a dry-cleaning machine to fulling. Luciano and Giuliana's brothers soon joined the business: Gilberto is now responsible for finance, and Carlo in charge of production.

In a recent magazine interview, Luciano Benetton explained why he started up his business:

> I never asked myself why I set up in business and I have no idea what could push me into doing it. The only motivation for me which has no value is the money ... I was sure of succeeding right from the beginning This is a typical entrepreneurial attitude – to be not surprised at success once you are convinced of the validity of your own plan.

> (*Capital*, September 1983)

Benetton's products were different from the other products on the market as the company used bright, unusual colours and aimed at the youth market. Alongside this marketing strategy, the Benettons' intention was to have constant product renewal by making small changes to the old designs. Luciano Benetton has said, 'I had enough sensitivity to guess that fashion is an important component, but one that can be exploited in greater depth.' In contrast, one competitor has argued that 'Benetton doesn't sell a product, he sells a colour!'

Other aspects of the strategy adopted by Benetton were also completely different from domestic competitors. In terms of manufacturing, he adapted fashion to allow industrial-scale production. In terms of retailing, the aim was to eliminate middle-men and find a new kind of outlet. He believed that conventional clothes shops were unsuitable for fashion-oriented casual wear, especially as most traditional Italian shop-keepers thought it was difficult to make a living from knitwear sales. More often than not, they sold other products and occasionally sold knitwear products as a sideline.

## The company's development

After three years, in early 1968, Benetton opened two experimental outlets: 40 square yards of floor space in Belluno (population 34,000) and another in Cortina (a holiday resort). The manager of the Belluno outlet was a partner of Benetton. The range of goods was narrow – brightly coloured sweaters aimed at the youth market – and the design of the sales point (simple, but bright and cheerful) was intended to reinforce the product image. The shops sold exclusively Benetton prod-ucts under the 'My market' trade name (this name was chosen so as not to compromise the Benetton name at this experimental phase). The first outlets were small, but their results were excellent.

In 1969, the company opened a new outlet in the university town of Padua (population 200,000; 50,000 students). It was an important test for the Benetton formula because of the diverse social and geo-graphical backgrounds of the Padua population. After the success of this shop, the Benetton management realized that the formula worked and a more ambitious expansion programme was embarked upon. The number of applications from aspiring franchise holders increased as the success of the first branches was consolidated. This did not lead to unrestrained expansion: as one of the people collaborating in the Padua project asserted, 'The company moved with great cau-tion, carefully selecting the applicants, or directly choosing its own candidates.'

> The incubation of the idea lasted for five or six years. I thought about it for a long time so that I had clear ideas on how to put into practice the basic idea when I launched myself into business. However, it is true that at the beginning, we were able to work in peace and anonymity, always being able to surprise the competition by keeping a card up our sleeves. This is our particular characteristic, not to put all our cards immediately on the table . . . I still remember clearly that five or ten years after having started the business, the competitors still hadn't understood what we were doing.
>
> (Luciano Benetton, quoted in *Capital*, September 1983)

The expansion in the number of shops was impressive: by 1975, there were some 300 shops in Italy and a few abroad; by 1978 there were

*Table 15.1*  Benetton turnover for the main product lines (billion lire)

|        | 1981 (%)    | 1982 (%)    | 1983 (%)    |
|--------|-------------|-------------|-------------|
| Wool   | 193 (52.2)  | 193 (52.2)  | 215 (47.8)  |
| Jeans  | 114 (31.1)  | 137 (34.3)  | 157 (35.5)  |
| Cotton |  62 (16.7)  |  70 (17.5)  |  95 (16.7)  |

1,000; in 1981, 1,600; and some 2,000 in 1983. Although the product range in the early years was limited to women's knitwear (using carded wool), it underwent substantial changes in the 1970s when cotton products, jeans and pants were introduced to supplement the line of woollen goods (see Table 15.1). Over time, the Benetton range of products has taken on a 'combined products' image which should be bought together, or which can be added to a base product.

Although the first non-Italian shop was opened in 1969, the problem of the foreign market was not really tackled until 1973. In 1978, foreign sales were about 10 per cent of turnover, but by 1983 had increased to 55 per cent. The few shops abroad in the early 1970s grew in number to 100 in 1979, 300 in 1980, 1000 in 1982, and 1,300 in 1983. In 1979 Benetton International Holding was founded to incorporate all the subsidiary companies. Further expansion took place: in 1980 the company bought a 50 per cent share in Fiorucci, a competitor with a turnover of $US50 million.

## THE SAMPLE COLLECTION

The company prepares two sample collections a year; one for the autumn/winter season, the other for the spring/summer season. (See Appendix 4 for more details about Benetton's operational system.) The sample collection is a result of collaboration between the design office and the marketing staff. The design office works on its own creative lines. The marketing staff perform several functions: preliminary selection, communicating with different groups, such as sales representatives and shopkeepers, and checking prices.

Giuliana Benetton still works in the creative part of the business. She still looks at garments and materials, and turns these into Benetton products. Through his contacts, Luciano also brings home many ideas which are then put into incubation.

In general, a non-hierarchical system seems to have developed which allows a continuous informal exchange of information. If an acceptable garment arrives (it does not matter from where) that is not in the sample collection, then a Fashion Flash is issued to bring the garment to the attention of all relevant parties. In some cases, the Fashion Flash article might be put into production immediately.

The company has seventy-one representatives/agents worldwide. Each agent is responsible for a region and maintains contacts with the outlets in that region. The sample collections are presented to the agents who then present the models using videotapes or fashion shows. Within a month of the presentation, the agent collects the orders from the Benetton shops.

> In this phase, the vertical contacts are intense. The aim is to make the most important articles emerge from the sample collection through an information network which signals the pre-chosen articles. At the same time, the system tries to single out the winning products.
>
> (Luciano Benetton)

A good example of this is in knitwear. From the 400 garments which form a sample collection, about one-fifth will be discarded. This is because they are either not selected, or do not reach the minimum volume of orders required for a production run.

> We have become a world-wide company and the sample collection has to be wide and diverse; but we must be selective at the same time. The smallest orders are rejected, and we propose alternatives . . . We see it as a favour for those who make mistakes. We let these buyers know that they aren't in line with the others, so a certain order is inadvisable.
>
> (Luciano Benetton)

At this point, the sales campaign is closed and the production programmes are designed in terms of both quantity and sequence. The work pattern solves the problems of assortment in the shops and the correct production mix.

> The shopkeeper buys garments in ten different colours. People usually only want three of these. It's impossible to foresee which of these colours will sell out. But the season lasts for four months – our task is to supply the preferred colours for the whole period. By doing this, we gain a vitally important competitive advantage.
>
> (Luciano Benetton)

Benetton has perfected a mechanism which concentrates on the three winning colours, as well as adaptation to these colours. Although orders are good on a quantitative basis, in reality, the articles are prepared and left undyed. The articles are dyed much later because even though a particular article of knitwear is assigned to a specific client, the client can modify the colour of the article in the period between placing the order and the dyeing process. Hence, the client may profit from early indications of changing fashion trends.

> The preparation of undyed knitwear articles and the capacity to redefine the assortment just on the basis of colour are perhaps the most important ideas in the Benetton formula, also for its promotional aspects.
>
> (Luciano Benetton)

An informal but efficient system of cross-checked indications help the identification of colour trends. Three main sources are used:

- 'Pilot' shops, which tend to show fashion trends forming at an earlier stage than other shops.
- Marketing staff, who make the connection between sales and production.
- Agents.

Of course, re-orders occur to take into account unforeseen demand and purchases of articles which were launched after the sample collection (the *pronta-moda*). These are produced in smaller numbers and are intended as a contingency strategy when trends may change. Although the *pronta-moda* causes imbalances in production, they are seen to be necessary. The collection requires rapid revisions three months after the launch of the sample collection. This allows Benetton's producers to work in real time as much as possible and allows them to take into account changes in fashion until the last minute before manufacturing takes place. This limited revision of the product range is very important in completing product strategy. Luciano sees it as a kind of feather in the Benetton cap as 'it reinforces our image, and at the same time the articles have a very rapid turnover'.

The sample collection has to take into account the manufacturing plant, to allow efficient production: as one manager says, 'The sales effort is important ... but we have to make sure that we present a sample collection that we are capable of producing.' The most common problem for the Benetton manufacturers is trying to satisfy the demand for articles which are not available in the shops. Benetton have several ways of dealing with this. First, there is often room for manoeuvre because of late dyeing which allows changes in the order to be made. Second, orders can be substituted from another client who may have less need of one article or a different seasonal cycle. When this happens, most of the work is carried out through agents, so that the agent does not feel bypassed or excluded. And third, Benetton telephones 'pilot' shops to get indications of what will be popular, and in this way a production run can start before it has reached the 'minimum order' size. Until a few years ago, the Benetton brothers personally telephoned the most sensitive shops to keep in touch with fashion trends.

These different channels require a very complex information system. For some years the company has been developing an information network to connect all the key points of the system. All of the agents are connected to one another and they are able to launch a series of enquiries using the network, as well as control the progress of sales points, orders, etc. The sales points are also linked to the network and the most recent addition to the network is the 'cash register project'. This memorizes day-by-day data on sales, and every 24 hours transmits the data to a central computer.

## THE MANUFACTURING SYSTEM

At the end of 1983, the group had nine plants (two abroad) and about 1,700 employees. However, the retail side of the business is not seen by Luciano Benetton as the most important: 'the network of shops was only an attempt to eliminate the filter between us and the consumer which paid off'. The Benetton family still sees itself as 'basically, manufacturers [who] have put fashion on an industrial level' when most of Italian fashion is still at the level of the artisan.

Each process in the manufacturing system receives different levels of company involvement. Almost all final producers in the clothing industry employ subcontractors for the manufacturing phase. The design of garments is maintained by the company, as is the distribution of the finished goods. Since the dyeing and finishing phases have always been considered strategically important, they have been carefully supervised by the company. But the 'hi-tech' weaving phase has been partially contracted out.

Particular emphasis on production has always distinguished the historical development of Benetton. In 1962 Luciano was sent to Scotland to visit some wool manufacturing plants. At this time, the Scots used rudimentary machines with wooden arms which beat the raw wool in water to full and soften the wool. In the early days, Benetton limited itself to copying the Scottish system, practically softening the wool by hand for the first samples of lambswool in 1965. Luciano remembers not being able to dry the samples with a centrifuge so 'we tied them round a stick and swung them rapidly around in the air' (from an interview in *Capital*). Machines arrived later, but Benetton started the fulling process 'ten years before anyone else in Italy'.

During the most rapid growth period, the company implemented a policy of diversifying the locations of the manufacturing units (see Figure 15.1). While the plants at Cusignana, Fontane and Resana are very near Ponzano, the other two are about 150 miles away. Some of the plants were already well equipped and in working order when acquired but others needed to be reorganized.

| Ponzano | | | |
|---|---|---|---|
| Research and design | | Marketing | |
| Patents | | Purchasing | |
| Production planning | | Production | |
| Administration | | Office staff | 170 |
| Finance | | Workers | 350 |
| **Cusignana 1** | | **Resana** | |
| Production | | Production | |
| Warehouse | | Office staff | 2/3 |
| Office staff | 3 | Workers | 120 |
| Workers | 120 | | |
| **Cusignana 2** | | **Monzambano** | |
| Production | | Production | |
| Office staff | 2 | Office staff | 3/4 |
| Workers | 100 | Workers | 100/120 |
| **Fontane** | | **Reggio Emilia** | |
| Production | | Production | |
| Office staff | 3 | Office staff | 2 |
| Workers | 100 | Workers | 50/60 |

*Figure 15.1* Benetton plants and employees

In the Cusignana plants where jeans and casual wear are produced, CAD systems for the design and cutting of material have been installed. As with the rest of the company, the experimental mentality is dominant at the plant level. Technical up-dating has been continuous and Luciano Benetton believes that the mechanical plant should not create problems but resolve them: 'We have never surrendered in the face of technical difficulties.' There are many problems to overcome: changes in the product range (and hence the technology required); variations in demand; as well as the commercial growth of the company. This commercial success creates problems for the productive process, as the entire production staff has always had to deal with the 'commercial hare' demanding adjustments in the shortest possible time. In the years of the greatest growth in turnover (1980–81), it was impossible to deliver more than 60 per cent of orders.

Part of the Benetton 'legend' is the purchase of old machinery which was then adapted to new uses. This was true of the hosiery machinery, which was purchased as scrap-metal and re-utilized to produce knitwear on the suggestion of an employee.

We bought these machines as scrap-metal because nobody wanted stockings with seams any more. We paid one million lire. We used 90 per cent of it, changing only the part which weaves.

(Luciano Benetton)

The conversion cost was 4 million; hence a total of 5 million lire (about $US3,000) was spent on a machine which in those days cost 50 million lire. However, this method of purchasing machinery has not continued: in 1982, the company made fixed investments of more than 30 billion lire to improve plant technology.

The plants begin production runs only when all of the orders from the outlets have arrived to allow standardization in production. According to one plant manager, 'We have to perfect a system which utilizes the plant to the full. We must maintain continuity of production even when there are fluctuations and discontinuity in the type of product requested.' Hence, there is no warehouse for the finished product (excluding some minor cases), as the finished product is already allocated to one of the various outlets, and warehousing is only for goods awaiting delivery.

The use of outside suppliers is held to be fundamentally important by Benetton because fashion changes annually and the outsider can be an excellent guarantee of product flexibility.

All plants must try to maintain a degree of flexibility as sample-based sales amount to only 80 per cent of the total. The remainder consist of the important *pronto-moda* (up-dating of current fashions), and re-orders, where a good relationship between production, marketing, and stock control is vital. Consequently, the Benetton family stresses that control of sales points allows it to optimize its overall activity.

**Subcontracting**

The growth in Benetton sales in 1980 and 1981 led to a considerable growth in both the level of production and the number of sales points. During this period, production could not keep up with demand and as Luciano Benetton argues, 'To absorb the whole of this growth within the company would have been foolish' (from an interview on *Panorama*, 1 August 1983).

In Benetton, decentralization has passed through various phases in the use of subcontractors. It was the company itself that encouraged the birth of subcontracting activity although, at the start, the intermediary phases were difficult to contract out. Mr Aluffi of Benetton argues that the formula of using outside labour was Benetton's own. It was invented as far back as 1966 and it has changed gradually with the evolution of the company. At the beginning, it affected purely manual labour, such as work on the seams that were left unfinished by the machine and had to be completed by hand, or they would have opened up during the first wash. In those days the company made 500 pieces a day (nowadays 36,000 a day) and had problems convincing the workforce to work on Sundays (the two-or three-shift cycle hadn't been adopted yet). Therefore,

Giuliana and Aluffi decided to give a pack of woollens to the girls every evening. This was to be brought back the next day after being finished with the help of the family and payment was made on a piece-rate basis. This helped Benetton to avoid taking on another 50 workers.

When production reached very high levels, the company asked the mothers of the girls who worked in the factories to form groups and set themselves up in business. The unions opposed this on the grounds that it was 'domestic labour' (or 'cottage work'). As Aluffi says, 'It was in overcoming this problem that we found ourselves able to increase the size of the company by using subcontractors in various manufacturing phases.' Nowadays Benetton relies on over 200 contractors for externally decentralized manufacturing operations. Most of them are within 50 miles of Ponzano Veneto. These contractors differ greatly in size: many are small businesses of 10 to 20 people, but some exceed even 100 people. It's not unusual for the Benetton family to have an equity interest in the principal contractors.

In recent years, levels of decentralization have varied according to the activities into which the company has diversified: 50 per cent of knitting is contracted out (but knitting that requires specialist machinery is usually done internally), cutting and assembling are mainly done externally, all dyeing is done internally, and finishing, ironing and packaging are mainly done externally. In the production of jeans, cutting is done internally, finishing is contracted out, and quality control is internal.

Some contractors handle only a single stage in the production cycle (e.g. knitting, or cutting and assembling); other, larger, subcontractors take on two or three stages, often subcontracting one of the stages to smaller businesses.

According to Benetton managers in charge of procurement, the professional background of subcontractors is quite varied, and previous experience in the textile industry is not a main factor in selection of subcontractors: 'We usually have a better relationship with people coming from outside the textile industry. They are more willing to agree to the "Benetton system" of trust and readiness to give Benetton first priority.'

## THE OUTLETS

The best ambassadors of the formula are first of all the representatives, then the shops' personnel and finally the clients: there is a chain that begins with us and goes all the way down to our clients abroad. I haven't invented anything. I listened to people, and I understood them.

With this simple phrase Luciano Benetton summarized the essential guidelines of the *metafranchising* system on which the incredible expansion of the company is based, especially its strong presence in the retail trade where 2,500 Benetton outlets sell exclusively Benetton products. What the company has put into practice is not the traditional franchising mechanism.

Part of the Benetton legend is the care taken in the selection of its outlets, their managers and their image. The outlets are situated in the 'front line', i.e. the most heavily frequented shopping locations. In Milan, there is one in the Via Montenapoleone, in New York there are five in Madison Avenue, and in London and Paris the shops are located in key shopping centres. Luciano Benetton has said that in many cases, years have been allowed to pass in order to be able to open in the right place. The concentration of the outlets in specific parts of the city is deliberate and this has contributed to the company's image.

The outlets are selected by the sales representatives, who act as a link between the company and the outlet's owners. The sales representatives receive 4 per cent commission on the factory sales of goods sold. A Benetton representative explained the economics of a typical outlet:

> We are in the fashion business, so we prudently reckon that only 75 per cent of the merchandise bought by each outlet will be sold at the normal 85 per cent mark-up. The remaining 25 per cent will be sold at a loss – let's say about 20 per cent less than cost. It's a matter of arithmetic to calculate a turnover of 160 lire for every 100 lire of merchandise bought. Labour costs, rent and utilities represent about 9.5 and 7 per cent of the turnover respectively. This breakdown gives a gross margin of 14 per cent of the turnover.
>
> The investment needed to open a new shop is about 280 million lire, and the average turnover about 600 million lire per year. These figures give a pay-back period of about three years.

Over a period of time, individual outlets have required considerable investment and have involved various commercial partners, including Benetton itself. From the beginning, Benetton opened its outlets in association with retailers because it was believed that the traditional shop represented an obstacle to the diffusion of casual products.

> One's own shop, or a partner's shop, is a component in a simple mechanism. The traditional shopkeeper didn't accept the idea of our product and made us lose time. If I asked for an appointment to show the sample collection, they would give me one after 25 days.
>
> The old-style shopkeeper would never have allowed the manufacturer to guide the underlying choices of the sample collection, the reordering, and the image of the shop. Our problem was to conquer the consumer – the traditional shopkeeper acted as a kind of brake so we

cut him out. Instead, we involved a kind of retailer who the day before may have been a florist or a shop assistant. What was important was the right spirit to work in a Benetton shop.

The choice of partner is held to be of particular importance, both at the level of representative/agent and at the shop level. Choosing the right person guarantees results. I spent a lot of time in studying this choice but the results have paid me back.

(Luciano Benetton)

The Benetton shops are partly company property and partly franchises, even though this is not a particularly apt term to describe specific cases. According to Benetton management, the company holds only a minority shareholding of its 2,500 outlets. Only twenty shops are completely company-owned, none of which are in Italy, and recently there has been a tendency to sell these shops to the various partners. As Luciano Benetton argues, 'We are interested in manufacturing, we are not interested in investing in outlets.' The shops follow the main Benetton line: they sell only Benetton products; prices are fixed at the same level in all locations, as are the sales policy and the aesthetic image.

In answer to those who argue that the retailer is in a state of complete subjugation, certain points should be noted. The central idea was to find partners with whom a 'long-term association could be built, and at the same time an association that is capable of growing'. The retailer has always held at least 51 per cent of the investment capital in the sales point; and Benetton demands no royalties and there is no hierarchical relationship, neither between agents and retailers, nor between companies and retailers. Benetton argues that this method allows the relationship to pass from one of diffidence to one of trust ('I gave him 51 per cent.'). It is a common opinion that the manufacturing process should work at its best, and, in parallel, develop harmoniously with the market, thus 'the shops must be made sensitive to this problem'.

The rules that have been created for the shopkeepers are not an abuse of their rights. There is no alternative if one wants to put into practice a mechanism which was inspired by a specific desire to simplify. From this point of view, the 'Benetton shop' is a component in a simple machinery. Great effort has been made to make the whole organization aware of it: 'This is not a franchise system, the term is out of place, we don't ask for royalties, we have no contracts.' This feature also singles out Benetton from any other franchising organization. That there is no love lost for paperwork and lawyers is constantly repeated; they are of little use in handling contracts with the outlets. It should be emphasized that the relationship between the shops and Benetton is completely free, the former can break this relationship whenever they wish.

**The sales representatives**

There are fifteen sales representatives in Italy and eighteen abroad. They work on a fixed commission on sales in their zone and they are in direct contract with the clients and the outlets. They work in close contact with the Benetton marketing staff and are an important link in the chain.

The story of G. L., who is a sales representative in central Italy, is an example of the role the representatives played in the growth of the company.

> We arrived at Benetton having had other experiences as sales representatives; here, the term takes on a completely different meaning from the conventional one. I was a representative for 20 companies, then, after six months I decided to choose Benetton alone.

Benetton is a company which involves its agents in many problems that demand absolute focus and specialization.

> We came from different backgrounds. Luciano needed people who understood the message he wanted to send out. First of all, he taught all his representatives how to market – before we used to sell, not market. The difference is substantial, but it is simple because the mechanism was simple. We enjoyed tackling something new and we had a strong desire to do something.

According to G. L., the traditional sales representative tries to sell without worrying about after sales attention, while the Benetton representative evaluates the sample collection, tests it out with the clients, makes fine adjustments with marketing, and follows it day by day.

> We go to the shop, follow the image, if something isn't going right in the sales point or in turnover we get to know about it in real time . . . Every Monday I have the sales performance of the previous week . . . The number one enemy of the manufacturer is the wholesaler – his interests are mean and trivial, he doesn't understand industry's problems. Benetton invented a formula which suited him, but it suited the retailer too.
>
> As a basis there must be a good collection. Lots of people make good products, maybe better than ours, but we sell the most.
>
> There can be mistakes in the choice of articles from the sample collection on the part of individual shops; that's not important, it's more important that these mistakes can be checked, that you can correct your aim without correcting productive programmes. The possibility to stock undyed articles and to have time margins to choose colours allows us in part to correct our aim.

The mechanism by which fashion trends are spotted and by which errors are corrected is important. In this process, the mass of clients, the marketing staff at headquarters, and the representatives all intervene in a series of cross-checking and horizontal, vertical and lateral filters.

> We send messages between one another – such as 'I've re-ordered the blue waistcoat' – but you can't be careful all of the time, and something might slip by. The important thing is that someone lets you know ... Each one of us has a small network and the most significant signals get sent to Ponzano, and from Ponzano messages arrive ... We are a team, there is affinity among us.

## The development of the outlets

As R. V., another sales representative from one of the most competitive areas, says:

> I was made a representative in September, and in July of the following year I had opened five of my own shops. I am taking risks with Benetton because these shops are 100 per cent mine. I can offer advice to clients from my own personal experience. If I advise them to stock blue, they can see that I have it in my own shops. Some even say to me, 'You decide.'
>
> I see what Benetton did; my employees see what I am doing, and they open shops too. One of my employees, a smart one, opened three shops, and in two of these he gave 50 per cent to the shop assistant.
>
> In the period of great growth, if I had a tried and proven retailer and we singled out a shop to open, we went into business together – Benetton, the retailer and I. Later, if things went well, we sold the retailer the entire holding but at the opening price, we have no speculative intention.

The shops are organized in clusters and one person may be in charge of several shops, even as many as twenty. 'There are some retailers who are a great point of strength, who have grown considerably ... They could stop now and retire even though they are young, but they have Benetton in their hearts.'

The development of the outlets has been encouraged by the sales representatives, who know the investments and know who has risked opening a shop, and do not abandon them.

> We are Benetton agents and we are at the disposal of the shop. We work Saturdays, and we work 12 hours a day.
>
> We have taken risks with people, and then we have helped them – we don't remain inert. We've always aimed for young people; there are plenty of them who are prepared to work; my oldest collaborator is 26 years old. This is just as valid for my representative organization as it is for the outlets.

When it has been the case to invest abroad, the sales representatives and outlets repeated the experience that Benetton had had in Italy. We laid our money on the energy of young people, or on people who know how to lead the pack.

## The influence on the outlets

If I give signals, especially in some countries abroad, I run the risk of being followed in a pedestrian manner; the same is true in Italy. In every message, there is always the risk of it being standardized, so I prefer to put things in another way: 'I'd do it like this, but you do it better.' This is a way of standardizing the basic points, but still leaving room for and stimulating personal initiative.

(Luciano Benetton)

The initiatives or the hunches of the outlets influence general manoeuvres and fine adjustments. If there is a 'top of the class', he helps the others, because they follow him. At headquarters, a lot of attention is paid to these 'top of the class' because they help to select the sample collection, they send the advance information, they contribute to triggering the mechanism which guides this organization.

On the other hand, there are some fixed merchandising policies for all Benetton shops. The end of season sales are among these. The opening date is the same for all shops, the duration is three weeks, the prices and the mark-ups are standardized. At the end of the sales, the shops are emptied and re-stocked. On the 2nd and 3rd of September, and the 5th and 6th of February, the new collections are displayed.

For about one month, nobody else has their whole collection on display, they all arrive late because retailers have had to combine various orders from various manufacturers, and the latter are nearly always late.

In that month it is possible to see how the market will go. The shops have no warehouses and tend to display the greatest possible amount of goods. 'From this point of view we have innovated in warehousing and in running inventory. We aren't dictatorial, but we cannot consider other conditions as far as this is concerned.' This mechanism of relationships, this almost daily relationship between representative and outlets offers a series of important signals which allows intervention in those shops in difficulty. The representative is influential, he is listened to, and he is asked for advice. In this way, insolvencies are more or less eliminated.

G. L. concludes,

I am responsible for 87 shops, some of them are mine. I grew with

Benetton and without it I would have remained a traditional sales representative. Luciano could sell anything. He has taught us everything, perhaps with his metaphors about relay races and bicycle racing.

Also the people further down the organizational chain are an important part of the Benetton machine. Daniela Poggi's experience is emblematic:

'I first joined Benetton in 1974, when I was 19. I had previously worked in other shops and already knew the trade, how to sell, dress windows, etc. The owner of the outlet which I was responsible for (who also owned other Benetton shops) taught me how to run it. Above all, he taught me how to use my head rather than my hands, and how to delegate, to instruct others and not do everything by myself . . .

Our shops are small and always crowded, they must always be in perfect shape, clean and orderly . . . These are just simple things but they must be done well. It's necessary to use your head, otherwise we couldn't manage. I learnt a lot and also trained new shop assistants for the other outlets . . . and together with my growing expertise, my personality grew, my ambitions became greater and I decided to start up on my own.

I told the owner of the shop about my plans and he offered me the opportunity to become the supervisor of a number of new outlets which he wanted to open in a nearby county . . . I became the manager of these eight outlets and subsequently I bought myself into them. Obviously, the nature of my work has changed. I make the purchases for all the shops, but the shop managers and shop assistants are deeply involved too . . . they take part and get enthusiastic. I want them to be aware of what we are doing; they have to know what we are ordering because this keeps them informed and allows them to answer customers enquiries correctly. I am particularly careful about how they serve the customers, and how they keep the shop in order . . . I don't want jerks . . .

Our assistants must know how to deal with young people, they have to know how to dress the window, and whoever dresses the window has to be able to play about with different colours and combinations. These things must be done simply, since it is the simple thing which is the most effective.

Benetton girls have a certain *savoir-faire*. They have to be on the ball . . . If they are sure of the work they are doing, if they like it, they will keep with the latest trends, read fashion magazines. This is the only way to give the shop the right image.

I keep an eye on the shops, and if it's necessary, I intervene, especially in the difficult periods. There's always a lot of work and if some problem crops up, I try to solve it. I am a 'Benettonian'. I've grown up, both professionally and personally here at Benetton, and Benetton has grown up with me . . . the products, materials, and the shops have all improved.

Before the end of the interview, Daniela pulled out a sheet of paper and rubbing her brow said:

Look, at the moment our problem is whether to bet on the grey or the blue; I've already ordered the articles; they are already finished and stocked undyed in the warehouse. My batch is going to be dyed in three weeks and now I have to decide whether to stick with 140 or go for 016, whether to put a cross here or there. The other shops have the same problem too, but being part of the Benetton team helps us to resolve it.

## FAILURE IN THE USA

In 1980 Benetton established some experimental outlets in the USA and by 1984 the company had eighty-two US outlets. However, it was having problems in translating its distinctive European formula into success in the American market.

In Europe, Benetton products are distributed through small specialized outlets, so when the company began selling in the USA a similar pattern of distribution was followed. Alongside this form of outlet, and in contrast to its European practice, the company also rented space in department stores. However, Benetton believed that the sales managers in the department stores were unable to provide the same back-up as European sales personnel who can advise on co-ordinated products sold together, rather than just a single article of clothing. In the specialized outlets in the USA, the management still could not understand the European sales concept of co-ordination to produce multiple sales. The retailing problem was further heightened by the increased costs of selling in the US market where transportation adds 7 per cent to costs and a further 20 per cent (on average) is imposed by customs duties. Hence, Benetton is at a disadvantage compared with US domestic manufacturers – who have no customs duties – and newly industrialized countries – as Benetton products incur high labour costs.

Benetton's success depends on exporting a 'European look' to the USA, with a strong fashion emphasis. Benetton management had to ask many questions about its future in the US market. What would be the reaction of the US market? Would Benetton be able to promote its 'style' through the 250 outlets that the company planned to have created by the end of 1984 (reaching 400 in 1985), with its own particular brand of franchising? Would it be able to train shop assistants and managers capable of handling its formula? What effect would the lack of local manufacturing plants have on its stocks and abilities to handle re-orders and colour flexibility which are an important aspect of its competitive edge? To what extent will the typical small European outlet be a successful retail model in the USA?

## MERCHANDISING

'Mr Benetton is the greatest marketing man in Europe,' one employee said, and great attention has been paid both in building the range and creating the image. A distinctive characteristic of the Benetton shops is the open display of all articles, like a supermarket, with great emphasis on grouping the articles together by colour. The outlets are all relatively small, usually about 50–60 square yards. This characteristic has been important, especially at the beginning. According to one of the marketing staff, 'Because a small shop always seems full – you can hardly get in – it is good advertising.' The outlets offer a full range of casual clothing. Each outlet sells on average 9–10,000 pieces per annum at an average price of \$US30–40 in Europe. There are some exceptions: the outlet in Brompton Road in London sells 100,000 pieces a year; and in the USA, prices are pushed up by transport and custom duties.

A vital role is played by the shop assistants: the company has placed great emphasis on training to pass on its image to potential customers. New assistants undergo a training period in a shop, being taught how to serve customers by giving advice in a discrete and informal manner. This is very important for the youth market and for the sales policy as a whole which aims primarily at the female consumer. The sales policy attempts to sell not just one article but a 'combination' of articles. This policy is facilitated by having no counters separating goods from customers and the goods are displayed within easy reach. Shopfitting plays an important part in the Benetton image, as does the display and the window. In the last few years direct and indirect advertising expenditure has been considerably increased, the latter through sports sponsorship of basketball, motor racing, yachting and rugby.

The shops have also had other effects on working arrangements and the global development of activity.

This new relationship with the retailers brings the advantage of being able to have disposable cash at the end of every working day. The traditional shopkeeper would have reacted to this and confirmed his own autonomy, paying quarterly as is the custom in the sector. Our retailer was willing to pay cash. In this way we could cut out the banks.

Credit institutions and traditional shopkeepers are traditional structures
– one can eventually work with them, but they cannot be allies.

(Gilberto Benetton)

The financial manager argues that the willingness to pay cash within
short periods on the part of Benetton's retailers has had important
effects on the financing of growth. This is not just in the short term but
also and more importantly, on the willingness to invest. Once selected,
the retailers themselves invested their resources in new shops, laying
their money out on future growth, financing it, and taking risks.
However, this characteristic of financing is not a primary objective, but
is considered a by-product of the formula.

The Benetton collection is the first to come out on the market and the
shops can offer their new articles before their competitors. Defining the
product range requires thorough research and considerable investment
to create a winning mix. The marketing staff assert with pride that
'many wait for us to begin their season'.

The basic philosophy of the outlets has never been changed although
it has undergone some adjustments. The individual shops are helped by
the representatives during the starting up and conversion phases. The
reduction of the gross margins has stimulated the reduction of shopfitting and maintenance costs. Yet it should also be noted that success
has not led to a stagnation of ideas, and experiments still continue
about different types of shop from the traditional one.

## FINANCE AND CONTROL

Pier Alfonso Orsi, a 41-year-old with experience in diversified groups,
joined Benetton in 1984 to take charge of finance and control. 'At
Benetton, the first problem I dealt with was to start a monthly reporting
system which was able to keep the company under control.'

Financing customers is seen by Orsi as the most important financial
problem at the moment. Benetton has two seasonal peaks and a huge
number of accounts receivable in April and October, and these debts are
financed by bank overdrafts. Several sources agree that the ninety-day
average collection is long; the collection period starts from the beginning
of the season not from delivery. The manager of logistics states that
Benetton's policy is not to have an inventory of finished products.
Therefore, as soon as products come out from the manufacturing
process or are received from subcontractors, the various batches are
delivered to the outlets. In order to pursue this policy, the company
calculates from the collection period and not from the date of a theoretical triggering of the season.

Our investments are mainly working capital . . . the structure of our costs enables us to have a high Debt/Sales and Debt/Equity ratio . . . Our return on net assets is higher than our financing cost, I think this isn't a typical case in the Italian economy.

(Pier Alfonso Orsi)

The specific type of relationship which exists between Benetton and the outlets, especially at the beginning of the company's history, had a relevant impact on finance. People have told us that Benetton retailers favoured the growth process with their willingness to anticipate payments. Luciano Benetton has pointed out that the conventional retailer's attitude towards manufacturers is more or less 'This is my shop, I bought your products, you should appreciate my choice, and I'll pay you in due course' (quoted in *Capital*). But the new Benetton retailer was willing to accept an earlier payment if he had cash. Insiders consider this ability to bypass the bankers as a fundamental element in the growth of Benetton, but not a priority: again, it is considered an effect of the Benetton formula as a whole.

Benetton is still a privately held company, but the new managing director, Mr Palmieri, maintains that in future the company should consider the possibility of becoming public in order to finance its own growth.

## DEVELOPMENT OF THE ORGANIZATION

This company is a miracle: there is no organizational chart; it isn't clear who does what. It was created on a non-industrial framework. Compared to the experiences that I've had in other more structured companies, it seems everything holds together by chance, and yet we turn over more than 500 billion lire a year.

This assertion by the new personnel manager, Giorgio Cantagalli, summarizes various aspects of the company which, at first glance, seem contradictory.

From 1980 onward, the extremely rapid growth was not matched by a similar growth in the professional profile; the company resorted to headhunting especially for top managers. The personnel manager says that rapid growth easily creates vacuums and some places are difficult to fill, arguing that taking on outsiders is not always practical and has its limits, in particular it leads to demoralization among middle management. During its growth the company's employees were co-operative and this contributed to the overcoming of many obstacles created by growth. However, it must be asked, 'How long can it last?' There is a danger of reaching the threshold of one's own competence. Yet, Benetton is still growing. This is true not only for internal personnel but also for subcontractors and outlets. The mentality of the founders in this regard is well summed up by this statement from Luciano Benetton:

As a growing entrepreneur, you mustn't be a missionary for too long. Once the basic idea has been worked out, you have to involve other people. It's essential to transmit your idea, get the group to accept it, in order to work together as a team.

Another organizational paradigm seems to be the search for simplification. Benetton refused to sign franchise contracts because the contracts the lawyers drew up were 'too complicated'; efforts are made to discover the most simple relationship possible with the client.

We put 30 million articles into 2,500 shops, but we manage to maintain the simplest possible relationship because each of our clients has on average four or five sales points, and so there are only 500 orders. Simplicity is strength, and what is simple is useful when you've become big. I asked myself whether this effort to simplify has a levelling effect, stopping us thinking; it is certain, however, that it makes it easier to transmit and make people learn.

Even during the period of most rapid growth, between 1980 and 1982, the number of employees increased proportionally less than turnover; the company increased its purchases and increased its subcontracting. In the same period it sold hundreds of shops to the 'franchisees'.

In addition to this attention to simplicity, there has been a great capacity to involve the people who work in the organization, putting trust in them and letting them grow. The most frequently used expression that crops up in various interviews referring to relations between Luciano Benetton and his staff is 'charisma'. One employee says, 'We know his faults, but people do what he wants', whilst another argues, 'I've tried to explain to you how things work here. But you should go to Mr Luciano; he'd explain the same thing much more simply, and much more clearly. We've learned to work in this way.' Also, in its recent entry to the US market, the company has confirmed this tendency to count on individuals, putting trust in them, taking risks with them. It is said that various offers by large investors to acquire the rights and the know-how of the Benetton system have been turned down.

## THE FUTURE

The market is now saturated in Italy, but in Europe there are still many openings. However, the signals seem to suggest a special interest in other countries: the USA, Latin America and Japan. Growth in Europe was achieved with the same partners as growth in Italy. Will it be the same for the USA and Japan? Will the fashion content, so important in the basic formula, have the same effect on other countries? Is the Benetton formula exportable, considering the distance of the markets and the lack of a well-oiled mechanism such as that of production-marketing-shop?

In Italy and Europe the sector was highly fragmented, and the competition weak and inexperienced; the same cannot be said for the competition in the USA and Japan. But in Europe the competition is also becoming more aggressive: in Italy many companies are trying to copy the Benetton formula.

> It is all right to have one good idea. The difficult thing is to adapt it, to keep it up to date. In Benetton we are always looking for new solutions. We are even ready to endanger what we have already achieved ... 20 years ago we began by-passing the traditional shop-keeper and the department store and today maybe we ourselves are becoming 'traditional'.
>
> (Luciano Benetton, quoted in *Capital*)

## NOTE

1 Parts of this study were written in 1984, other parts in 1988. Grateful thanks to Charles Baden-Fuller and Ronnie McBryde for their assistance.

© Gianni Lorenzoni 1984, 1988

This case study has been written as a basis for class discussion rather than to illustrate effective or ineffective managerial or administrative behaviour.

## APPENDIX 1: THE KNITWEAR INDUSTRY

The knitwear industry is generally considered by experts as 'mature', with stable or declining consumption, facing tough competition from new industrialized countries (NICs), and with a drop in employment levels. At the European level, however, competition is highly differentiated, as manufacturers in different countries have reacted differently to this onset of maturity. There are few entry and mobility barriers with which to overcome the competition based on cheap labour from NICs. Many European companies have chosen subcontractors in Africa and the Far East and limit their activity to design and marketing. Some countries have planned the dismantlement of the industry, shifting activity to NICs, as has happened in Japan where trading companies have played a leading role in this transfer.

The knitwear industry in Italy has always been highly fragmented, and most plants have fewer than ten workers. Many of these plants work as subcontractors, and the presence of converters, whose function is limited simply to design, image promotion of the brand, and distribution, is widespread.

Among EEC countries, Italian knitwear accounts for about two-thirds of total production. The companies are mainly located in a few monosectoral districts, such as Capri, where knitwear is the prevalent, if not the only, activity.

Unlike trends in other European countries, the knitwear industry in Italy is actually increasing in number of companies and reducing in number of employees per company. Census data confirms this tendency for the decade 1971–81: in 1971 there were 21,802 units and 165,034 employees while in 1981 the number of units reached 30,641 and employees increased to only 178,334.

Benetton is the industry leader in Italy with a market share of about 4 per cent.

*Table 15.2* Knitwear–hosiery

| Country | Employees | | Companies | | Production (tons) | | Foreign trade balance (tons) | |
|---|---|---|---|---|---|---|---|---|
| | 1981 | 81/76** | 1981 | 81/76** | 1981 | 81/76** | 1981 | 81/76** |
| West Germany | 74,507 | − 20.4 | 616 | − 44 | 139,500* | − 9.6 | − 92,457 | + 53.1 |
| France | 71,565 | − 18.6 | 673 | − 12.6 | 89,131 | − 14 | − 49,700 | + 46.8 |
| United Kingdom | 93,800 | − 22.5 | 342 | − 6 | 116,204 | − 40 | − 24,718 | + 101.2 |
| Italy | 154,500 | + 0.3 | 20,000 | + 2.6 | 295,000 | + 10.3 | + 112,454 | + 19.9 |

*Note:* *1980 ** percentage change

*Table 15.3* Knitwear–hosiery

| Country | Employees/firm | | Prod/employees (tons) | | Trade balance/ production | |
|---|---|---|---|---|---|---|
| | 1981 | 81/76** | 1981 | 81/76** | 1981 | 81/76** |
| West Germany | 121 | + 42 | 1.74 | + 5.4 | − 0.68* | + 74 |
| France | 106.4 | − 6.9 | 1.24 | + 5.1 | − 0.56 | + 75 |
| United Kingdom | 274.3 | + 32.3 | 1.24 | − 22.5 | − 0.20 | − 68 |
| Italy | 7.7 | − 2.2 | 1.91 | + 6.7 | + 0.38 | + 0.8 |

*Note:* *1980 ** percentage change

*Table 15.4* External knitwear, Italy

| | 1970 | 1975 | 1980 | 1982 |
|---|---|---|---|---|
| **Millions of pieces** | | | | |
| Production | 317.3 | 421.5 | 611.4 | 588.0 |
| Export | 156.6 | 220.2 | 241.5 | 239.1 |
| Home consumption | 165.2 | 290.1 | 385.8 | 366.1 |
| **Billion lire** | | | | |
| Production | 683.5 | 1,117.1 | 3,388.4 | 4,740.0 |
| Export | 370.0 | 649.3 | 1,597.2 | 2,228.3 |
| Home consumption | 325.3 | 490.3 | 1,899.0 | 2,650.2 |

*Table 15.5* Italian knitwear production statistics

| Plant size | **Hosiery & knitwear (Italy)** | | **Knitwear (Italy 1981)** | |
|---|---|---|---|---|
| | No. of plants | Total employees | No. of plants | Total employees |
| up to 10 | 26,560 | 57,360 | 24,600 | 51,852 |
| 11 to 100 | 3,885 | 81,776 | 3,467 | 72,584 |
| 101 to 500 | 188 | 33,835 | 156 | 27,009 |
| 501 to 1000 | 7 | 4,302 | 5 | 2,963 |
| over 1000 | 1 | 1,061 | 1 | 1,061 |

## APPENDIX 2: A) BENETTON GROUP CONSOLIDATED BALANCE SHEETS (31 DECEMBER 1984 AND 1983) (Million Lire)

*Table 15.6* Consolidated balance sheets

|  |  | *1984* | *1983* |
|---|---|---|---|
| Assets | *Current assets* | | |
|  | Cash | 19,109 | 14,478 |
|  | Marketable securities | 41,059 | 24,712 |
|  | *Accounts receivable* | | |
|  | Trade receivables | 253,211 | 220,401 |
|  | Other | 11,221 | 11,966 |
|  | Less: allowance for doubtful acounts | (8,752) | (5,183) |
|  |  | **315,848** | **266,374** |
|  | Inventories | 100,438 | 92,840 |
|  | Prepayments | 4,869 | 4,019 |
|  | Total current assets | **421,155** | **363,233** |
|  | *Investments and other non-current assets* | | |
|  | Investments and loans to affiliates | 4,699 | 5,030 |
|  | Guarantees deposits | 680 | 898 |
|  |  | **5,379** | **5,928** |
|  | *Fixed assets* | | |
|  | Land and buildings | 68,848 | 52,828 |
|  | Plant, machinery and equipment | 64,494 | 37,705 |
|  | Vehicles and aircraft | 14,170 | 16,602 |
|  | Office equipment and furniture and leasehold improvements | 6,727 | 6,375 |
|  | Construction in progress and advances for fixed assets | | 27,561 |
|  |  | **154,239** | **141,071** |
|  | Less: accumulated depreciation | (66,323) | (46,748) |
|  | **Net fixed assets** | **87,916** | **94,323** |
|  | *Intangible assets* | | |
|  | Licenses and trademarks | 8,292 | 9,091 |
|  | Deferred charges | 2,902 | 3,881 |
|  |  | **11,194** | **12,972** |
|  |  | **525,644** | **476,456** |

*Table 15.6 cont.*

| | | 1984 | 1983 |
|---|---|---|---|
| Liabilities and stockholders' equity | *Current liabilities* | | |
| | Bank overdrafts | 94,458 | 98,099 |
| | Current portion of long-term loans | 24,455 | 26,004 |
| | Accounts payable | 150,574 | 122,460 |
| | Other payables and accruals | 21,017 | 18,377 |
| | Accrual for exchange losses | 1,731 | 2,022 |
| | Reserve for income taxes | 23,874 | 5,095 |
| | **Total current liabilities** | **316,109** | **272,057** |
| | *Long-term liabilities* | | |
| | Long-term loans, net of current portion | 64,924 | 81,018 |
| | Reserve for severance indemnities | 6,886 | 5,886 |
| | | **71,810** | **86,904** |
| | Capital gains roll-over reserve | **635** | **904** |
| | Minority interest in consolidated subsidiaries | — | **2,121** |
| | *Stockholders' equity* | | |
| | Capital stock | 8,000 | 8,000 |
| | Surplus from spinoff and monetary revaluation of assets | 81,557 | 81,557 |
| | Other reserve and prior years' retained earnings | 11,481 | 12,811 |
| | Net income from the year | 37,180 | 13,230 |
| | | **138,218** | **115,598** |
| | Less: treasury stock | (1,128) | (1,128) |
| | | **137,090** | **114,470** |
| | | **525,644** | **476,456** |

## B) BENETTON GROUP CONSOLIDATED INCOME STATEMENT (31 DECEMBER 1984 AND 1983) (Million Lire)

*Table 15.7* Consolidated income statement

|  |  | 1984 | 1983 |
|---|---|---|---|
| Revenues | Net sales | 711,323 | 559,815 |
|  | Other revenues | 2,693 | 2,374 |
| Cost of sales | Materials and net change in inventories | 252,721 | 195,111 |
|  | Labour and related costs | 29,622 | 26,018 |
|  | Outworkers services | 170,046 | 141,597 |
|  | Depreciation | 6,613 | 14,960 |
|  | Other costs | 16,808 | 15,577 |
|  |  | **475,810** | **393,263** |
|  | **Gross profit** | **238,206** | **168,926** |
| Selling general | Labour and related costs | 22,126 | 22,732 |
| and administrative | Distribution | 22,909 | 23,422 |
| expenses | Sales commissions | 30,408 | 23,240 |
|  | Advertising and promotion | 20,436 | 14,367 |
|  | Depreciation | 16,213 | 8,064 |
|  | Other costs and expenses | 31,558 | 26,908 |
|  |  | **143,650** | **118,733** |
|  | **Income from operations** | **94,556** | **50,193** |
| Other (income) | Interest income | (11,432) | (8,330) |
| expenses | Interest expense | 41,992 | 37,233 |
|  | Other (income) expense, net | (945) | 1,037 |
|  |  | **29,615** | **29,940** |
|  | **Income before taxes and minority interest** | **64,941** | **20,253** |
| Income taxes |  | 30,782 | 8,588 |
|  | **Income before minority interest** | **34,159** | **11,665** |
| Income from minority interests |  | 3,021 | 1,565 |
| **Net income for the year** |  | **37,180** | **13,230** |

# APPENDIX 3: BENETTON GROUP COMPANIES INCLUDED IN CONSOLIDATION (31 DECEMBER 1984)

*Table 15.8* Benetton Group companies included in consolidation (31 December 1984)

| Name | Location | Currency | Capital stock | % owned |
|---|---|---|---|---|
| **Parent company** | | | | |
| Invep SpA | Ponzano Veneto (Treviso) | L. | 8,000,000,000 | |
| **Italian subsidiaries** | | | | |
| Benetton SpA | Ponzano Veneto (Treviso) | L. | 31,000,000,000 | 99.99 |
| Benetton Lana SpA | Ponzano Veneto (Treviso) | L. | 24,700,000,000 | 100.00 |
| Benetton Jeans SpA | Cusignana di Giavera del Montello (Treviso) | L. | 15,600,000,000 | 100.00 |
| Benetton Cotone SpA | Fontane de Villorba (Treviso) | L. | 3,200,000,000 | 100.00 |
| Industrie Benetton SpA | Ponzano Veneto (Treviso) | L. | 200,000,000 | 99.00 |
| In Factor SpA | Milan | L. | 2,000,000,000 | 60.00 |
| Fiorucci SpA | S. Donato Milanese (Milan) | L. | 2,500,000,000 | 49.00 |
| Fiormil Srl | Milan | L. | 20,000,000 | 48.02 |
| Edma Srl | Bari | L. | 30,000,000 | 48.02 |
| Azzurro Srl | Brescia | L. | 90,000,000 | 48.51 |
| Immobiliare Paolo & Maria Srl | S. Donato Milanese (Milan) | L. | 20,000,000 | 48.51 |
| **Foreign subsidiaries** | | | | |
| Benetton International Holding SA | Luxembourg | SFr. | 23,000,000 | 100.00 |
| Benetton SARL | Paris | FFr. | 11,536,000 | 65.33 |
| Cobenza SARL | Paris | FFr. | 1,100,000 | 82.66 |
| Hoben SARL | Paris | FFr. | 1,000,000 | 97.92 |
| Nota Bene France SA | Toulon | FFr. | 250,000 | 100.00 |
| Stuttben GmbH | Stuttgart | DM | 900,000 | 100.00 |
| Ber-Ben Textilhandels GmbH | Berlin | DM | 500,000 | 100.00 |
| Benetton SA | Brussels | BFr. | 41,500,000 | 81.60 |
| Benetton (UK) Ltd | London | £ | 1,150,000 | 100.00 |
| Tabando Ltd | Hawick | £ | 500,000 | 100.00 |
| Benetton SA | Barcelona | pta. | 50,000,000 | 100.00 |
| Benetton Japan KK | Tokyo | ¥ | 25,000,000 | 100.00 |
| Benetton Services Corporation | New York | $US | 550,000 | 100.00 |
| Benetton International Holding NV | Utrecht | fl. | 1,000,000 | 100.00 |
| Claridge Clothing SA | Fribourg | SFr. | 200,000 | 95.00 |
| Benetton do Brasil SA | St Paul | Cz | 25,000,000 | 100.00 |
| Fiorucci International Holding SA | Luxembourg | SFr. | 1,000,000 | 49.00 |
| Fiorucci Inc. | New York | $US | 200,000 | 49.00 |
| Fioparis SA | Paris | FFr. | 100,000 | 42.28 |
| Fiore SARL | Paris | FFr. | 100,000 | 39.20 |

## APPENDIX 4: OPERATIONAL SYSTEM

*Table 15.9* Operational system

**Spring/summer collection**

| | M | J | J | A | S | O | N | D | J | F | M | A | M | J | J | A | S | O | N | D |
|---|---|---|---|---|---|---|---|---|---|---|---|---|---|---|---|---|---|---|---|---|
| Samples display | * | * | * | | | | | | | ● | | | | | | | | | | |
| Raw material orders | * | * | * | * | | | | | | * | | | | | | | | | | |
| Raw material delivery | * | * | * | * | * | * | * | | * | | | | | | | | | | | |
| Deliveries from suppliers | | | * | * | * | * | * | * | * | | | | | | | | | | | |
| Payments | | | | | * | * | * | * | * | * | * | * | * | | | | | | | |
| Manufacturing | * | * | * | * | * | * | * | * | * | * | * | | | | | | | | | |
| Deliveries and invoicing | | | | | | | * | * | * | * | * | * | * | | | | | | | |
| Revenues | | | | | | | | | | * | * | * | * | * | * | * | | | | |
| Commissions to agents | | | | | | | | | | | * | | | * | | * | | | | |

**Autumn/winter collection**

| | M | J | J | A | S | O | N | D | J | F | M | A | M | J | J | A | S | O | N | D |
|---|---|---|---|---|---|---|---|---|---|---|---|---|---|---|---|---|---|---|---|---|
| Samples display | | | | | * | * | * | * | | ● | | | | | | | | | | |
| Raw material orders | | | | | * | * | * | * | | * | | | | | | | | | | |
| Raw material delivery | | | | | | | * | * | * | * | * | * | * | | | | | | | |
| Deliveries from suppliers | | | | | | | | * | * | * | * | * | * | | | | | | | |
| Payments | | | | | | | | | | | * | * | * | * | * | * | * | * | * | * |
| Manufacturing | | | | | | | | | * | * | * | * | * | * | * | | | | | |
| Deliveries and invoicing | | | | | | | | | | | * | * | * | * | * | * | * | | | |
| Revenues | | | | | | | | | | | | | | * | * | * | * | * | * | |
| Commissions to agents | | | | | | | | | | | | | | | | | | | | * |

*Source:* Benetton

*Note:* ● Flash collection

# APPENDIX 5: MANUFACTURING UNIT LOCATION

*Figure 15.2* Manufacturing unit location

## APPENDIX 6: BENETTON SALES
**Sales** (billion lire)
Table *15.10* Benetton sales

| Year | Abroad | % | Italy | Total |
|---|---|---|---|---|
| 1978 | 1.3 | (2) | 64.6 | 65.7 |
| 1979 | 10.3 | (10) | 92.6 | 102.9 |
| 1980 | 50.8 | (26) | 144.6 | 195.4 |
| 1981 | 115.7 | (36) | 205.9 | 321.6 |
| 1982 | 176.1 | (44) | 224.2 | 400.3 |
| 1983 | 256.4 | (54) | 218.4 | 474.8 |
| 1984 | 342.1 | (55) | 279.9 | 622.0 |

**Production mix (%)**

| Year | Wool | Cotton | Jeans | Sales (billion) |
|---|---|---|---|---|
| 1976 | 53 | 13 | 34 | 40 |
| 1977 | 54 | 17 | 29 | 63.5 |
| 1978 | 51 | 17 | 32 | 65.7 |
| 1979 | 48 | 22 | 30 | 102.9 |
| 1980 | 46 | 25 | 29 | 195.4 |
| 1981 | 49 | 24 | 27 | 321.6 |
| 1982 | 47 | 25 | 27 | 400.3 |
| 1983 | 42 | 28 | 30 | 474.8 |
| 1984 | 43 | 27 | 30 | 622 |

**Exports (billion Lire)**

| | 1982 | | 1983 | | 1984 | |
|---|---|---|---|---|---|---|
| | L. | % | L. | % | L. | % |
| France | 69.6 | 39.5 | 83.3 | 32.5 | 83.1 | 24.3 |
| West Germany | 40.0 | 22.7 | 67.2 | 26.2 | 84.8 | 24.8 |
| UK | 14.1 | 8.0 | 24.6 | 9.6 | 34.6 | 10.1 |
| Switzerland | 16.4 | 9.3 | 18.5 | 7.2 | 19.8 | 5.8 |
| Austria | — | — | 11.5 | 4.5 | 11.6 | 3.4 |
| USA | — | — | 12.3 | 4.8 | 52.7 | 15.4 |
| Spain | — | — | — | — | 7.3 | 2.1 |
| Other countries | 36.0 | 20.5 | 39.0 | 15.2 | 48.2 | 14.1 |
| Total | 176.1 | 100.0 | 256.4 | 100.0 | 342.1 | 100.0 |

# Chapter 16

# IKEA of Sweden: the global retailer[1]

## *Martyn Pitt*

### EDITORS' OVERVIEW

IKEA is one of the most innovative mass market home furnishing retailers in the world, as more than 100 million people in two dozen countries around the world can confirm. Although it is now 50 years old, it has achieved extraordinary growth in the last twenty years – a twelvefold increase in its stores, a fifteenfold increase in staff employed, and a fortyfold increase in sales revenue.

As it has grown, IKEA has evolved a variety of synergistic elements in its global approach. Whilst it can be argued that none of these is unique when viewed in isolation, in concert they have been integrated over the long term into a consistent and complex business formula for producing, distributing and retailing furniture and household goods essentially without parallel.

IKEA's approach has many aspects and it is worth exploring what these are and how they knit together. The case study considers corporate style and philosophy, sourcing, distribution and product policy, the approach to pricing and cost reduction, customer communication, and the in-store experience. It then examines how IKEA entered the UK market in 1987 and contrasts this with the firm's experiences in North America, closing with broader questions about the policy of standardization in future, of rejuvenation, and what will happen after the founder ceases to influence events.

The reader may wish to begin by reflecting on the nature of consumer demand for domestic (and office) furniture and buyer behaviour, and why IKEA has proved so attractive to consumers in so many countries. One can then consider the nature and significance of IKEA's distinctive competences and how these are leveraged for competitive advantage.

IKEA has pursued strategies that are clear and bold, but also paradoxical. For example, flexibility and market effectiveness have apparently not compromised operating efficiency. Is it feasible for others to emulate IKEA's approach? Few elements of its strategy (such as flat packing and sourcing from lowest cost countries) are hard to understand or impossible to copy. How big is the advantage conferred by first-moving on a *global* scale? Why has no other retail company been able or willing to expand in a similar way? Habitat of the UK has been notably less successful in its overseas ventures, for example. Marks & Spencer, a very effective UK retailer, has also found that overseas expansion is a difficult challenge. Is IKEA's success explained by its attention to detail or the 'architecture' of its relationships with suppliers, designers, governments, etc., held together by a powerful Swedish cultural 'glue'?[1]

What may impede future growth? Is it wise, for example, to diversify into supplying office furniture? How similar are the market needs and competences required? Does this reposition IKEA more directly in competition with well-entrenched players and if it does, how significant is this? Will IKEA be extremely reluctant to change any fundamentals of a winning formula? Will the risks be seen as simply too great? Might it experience the phenomenon of 'strategic drift', meaning that its approach gradually diverges from customer needs and industry best practice? Will IKEA's global competitiveness in future depend on combining greater variety with lower volume per merchandise line?

Finally IKEA's management has to consider the pressures and time-scale for change. Can rejuvenation be managed continuously and proactively as Ingvar Kamprad seems to believe or does it have to await the possibility of crisis?

**Discussion questions**

- What do you feel are the *key* components of IKEA's winning formula? Are some more important than others, and if so, why? How can they be *upgraded* in the future? How big a part have vision, detailed planning and luck contributed to the strategic development of the firm?
- Do you agree with the statement that IKEA is essentially a high volume, low cost approach?
- Should IKEA pursue strategies that are more country-centred? If so, what should it continue to do globally and what should it do locally?
- Is continued worldwide growth still the best strategy for IKEA or should senior managers put more emphasis on managing the business even better at its present size? What other strategic options may exist?
- What effects will Ingvar Kamprad's ultimate departure have?
- How might a leading retailer compete effectively with IKEA internationally and appropriate a substantial proportion of IKEA's current market share and financial returns?

## List of named characters

Ingvar Kamprad, founder and chairman of IKEA

Anders Moberg, president and chief executive

Rutger Andersson, Tord Bjorklund, Carina Carlsson, Niels Gammel-gaard, Knut and Marianne Hagberg, Tomas Jelinek, Lars Norinder and Erik Worts: all named product designers

Fred Andersson, worldwide head of product design and sourcing

Terence Conran, founder and former chairman of Habitat, acquired by IKEA in 1992

Goran Carstedt, chief executive, IKEA of USA

## Keywords

Strategic recipe/formula; culture; entrepreneurial vision; global strategy; cost reduction and low cost leadership; dominance; innovation in products and delivery systems; flexibility; growth and rejuvenation

## THE FORMATION AND EXTRAORDINARY GROWTH OF IKEA

The name IKEA was registered in 1943 in Sweden by Ingvar Kamprad, an ambitious 17-year-old keen to extend his commercial scope beyond the family farm in southern Sweden. The initials derive from his name, the first letters of the farm (Elmtaryd) and its location (Agunnaryd).

The firm began as a mail order activity, selling a diverse range of products including fish, seeds, magazines, pens and furniture. However, Kamprad was enthused with the idea of mass-produced, low cost, basic furniture to meet the post-war needs of young Swedes. He found that the Swedish furniture industry was a cartel that rejected his ideas and tried to prevent him trading. Thus in 1953 he set up a warehouse showroom in a disused factory in Almhult and negotiated supplies from independent producers in Sweden and also from Poland. A year later he employed fifteen people.

IKEA negotiated with new and more open-minded furniture suppliers. They took advantage of local supplies of inexpensive softwood such as pine and spruce and the pioneering work of the Swedish timber industry in wood-based materials such as plywood, block, particle and fibre boards, well suited to mass production methods when allied to the strong, waterproof adhesives developed in the 1950s.

The business grew rapidly. In less than a decade IKEA's turnover was 80 times greater than the typical furniture store, its productivity in terms of turnover per employee and per square metre was double, and its stockturn (at 3.2 times per annum) approximately 50 per cent higher.[3] In 1964 it opened a second store near Stockholm. It employed 250 staff and had a turnover of Skr.79 million. Over the next decade IKEA opened seven new stores in Scandinavia, each with an attractive, youthful, relaxed shopping environment. The business grew progressively, reaching a turnover of SKr.480 million in 1973.

Kamprad decided the time was right for rapid expansion across Europe. IKEA opened its first store outside Scandinavia in Zurich, Switzerland in 1973, quickly followed by Munich, West Germany. Thus by 1974 it had ten stores in five countries employing 1,500 people and achieved sales of SKr.616 million. Despite trade hostility in Germany similar to Kamprad's early experience in Sweden, IKEA opened ten stores there in its first five years. By 1984 it had sixty-six stores in seventeen countries with 8,300 workers. IKEA began to operate stores in Canada (1976), the USA (1985), the UK (1987), Poland and Hungary (1988) and Italy (1989). Today, although more than 80 per cent of sales still derive from Europe, it has some twenty-six stores in North America and a somewhat fewer number of mostly franchised retail operations scattered across the Middle East, South East Asia and Australasia.

# The IKEA expansion

| | Outlets | Countries | Co-workers | Turnover in NLG |
|---|---|---|---|---|
| 1954 | 1 | 1 | 15 | 2,200,000 |
| 1964 | 2 | 2 | 250 | 55,500,000 |
| 1974 | 10 | 5 | 1,500 | 372,900,000 |
| 1984 | 66 | 17 | 8,300 | 2,678,700,000 |
| 1994 | 120 (125*) | 25 (26*) | 26,600** | 8,350,000,000*** |

\* Refers to stores opening within the next 12 months
\*\* 26,600 co-workers are equivalent to 21,500 full-time
\*\*\* Corresponding to net sales of the IKEA Group of companies

1 NLG = $US 0.565, SEK 4.37

## Turnover (million NLG)

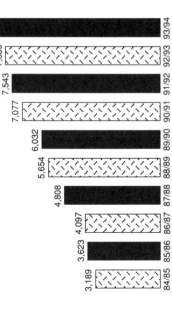

| 84/85 | 85/86 | 86/87 | 87/88 | 88/89 | 89/90 | 90/91 | 91/92 | 92/93 | 93/94 |
|---|---|---|---|---|---|---|---|---|---|
| 3,189 | 3,623 | 4,097 | 4,808 | 5,654 | 6,032 | 7,077 | 7,543 | 7,880 | 8,350 |

# Sales distribution

(Percentage of turnover)

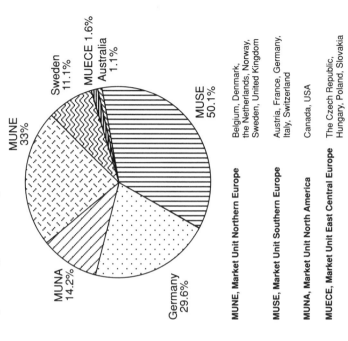

MUNE 33%

Sweden 11.1%

MUECE 1.6%

Australia 1.1%

MUSE 50.1%

MUNA 14.2%

Germany 29.6%

**MUNE, Market Unit Northern Europe** — Belgium, Denmark, the Netherlands, Norway, Sweden, United Kingdom

**MUSE, Market Unit Southern Europe** — Austria, France, Germany, Italy, Switzerland

**MUNA, Market Unit North America** — Canada, USA

**MUECE, Market Unit East Central Europe** — The Czech Republic, Hungary, Poland, Slovakia

*Figure 16.1* IKEA sales and distribution statistics
*Source:* IKEA publicity

# Number of visitors

in the stores belonging
to the IKEA Group

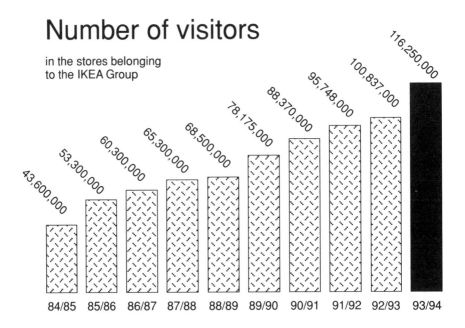

# Surface area

of the stores worldwide in sq. m.,
including adjacent warehouses and not
including distribution centres

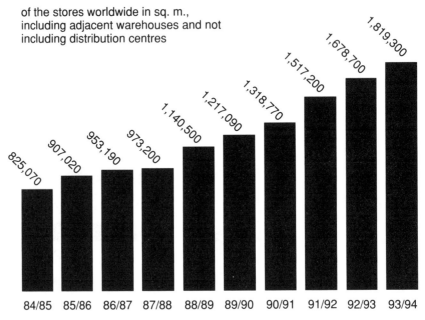

*Figure 16.2* IKEA retail stores statistics
*Source:* IKEA publicity

To facilitate expansion within the European Economic Community and to avoid high Swedish corporation taxes Kamprad vested ownership of IKEA in a Dutch charitable foundation controlled by the Kamprad family into which profits are channelled as royalties for the use of the IKEA concept and its trademarks. Its corporate management now operates out of modestly sized headquarters in Denmark.

Over the last ten years IKEA has averaged a remarkably consistent annual sales growth of 9 per cent. Despite its size it remains a private company. It maintains greater secrecy over its operating performance than a public limited liability corporation could do. Informed estimates put its net profit margins after tax consistently in the range of 6 per cent to 7.5 per cent of sales revenues. Growth has been financed through retained earnings without recourse to external equity or debt. In its financial year ending August 1994 IKEA employed some 26,600 people at 120 stores, covering over 1.8 million square metres in twenty-five countries. These stores were visited by 116 million people, generating sales turnover of 8.35 billion Dutch guilders (approximately $US4.5 billion). See Figures 16.1, 16.2 and Table 16.1 for growth patterns.

*Table 16.1* IKEA retail outlets 1994/95

|  | Year of first opening | Gross area (sq. m.) |
| --- | --- | --- |
| **Australia** | | |
| Sydney (Gordon) | 1975 | 2,100 |
| Sydney (Blacktown) | 1981 | 5,700 |
| Melbourne (Moorabbin) | 1986 | 7,000 |
| *Perth*** | *1986* | *5,200* |
| Brisbane (Springwood) | 1987 | 7,800 |
| Melbourne (Nunawading) | 1989 | 5,800 |
| Sydney (Moore Park) | 1991 | 4,100 |
| **Austria** | | |
| Vienna | 1977 | 26,200 |
| Graz | 1989 | 15,200 |
| Linz (Hard) | 1991 | 15,500 |
| **Belgium** | | |
| Brussels (Ternat) | 1984 | 15,100 |
| Brussels (Zaventem) | 1984 | 12,100 |
| Antwerp (Wilrijk) | 1985 | 14,600 |
| Liège (Hognoul) | 1985 | 13,000 |
| **Canada** | | |
| Vancouver | 1976 | 18,100 |
| Toronto | 1977 | 21,300 |
| Edmonton | 1978 | 10,400 |
| Calgary | 1979 | 6,300 |

| | | |
|---|---|---|
| Ottawa | 1979 | 9,200 |
| Quebec | 1982 | 10,000 |
| Montreal | 1982 | 16,400 |
| Toronto (Burlington) | 1991 | 17,000 |

**The Czech Republic**

| | | |
|---|---|---|
| Prague | 1991 | 10,700 |

**Denmark**

| | | |
|---|---|---|
| Copenhagen (Tåstrup) | 1969 | 37,000 |
| Århus | 1980 | 10,500 |
| Odense | 1985 | 1,400 |

**France**

| | | |
|---|---|---|
| Lyon | 1982 | 18,900 |
| Paris (Evry) | 1983 | 24,200 |
| Marseille (Vitrolles) | 1985 | 15,800 |
| Paris-Nord | 1986 | 24,900 |
| Lille (Lomme) | 1988 | 16,200 |
| Bordeaux | 1990 | 14,200 |
| Paris (Plaisir) | 1992 | 20,600 |
| Toulouse* | 1995 | 19,000 |

**Germany**

| | | |
|---|---|---|
| Munich (Eching) | 1974 | 25,300 |
| Cologne (Godorf) | 1975 | 23,000 |
| Dorsten | 1975 | 7,600 |
| Hannover (Grossburgwedel) | 1976 | 15,200 |
| Bremen (Stuhr) | 1976 | 13,200 |
| Frankfurt (Wallau) | 1977 | 25,900 |
| Dortmund (Kamen) | 1978 | 17,900 |
| Stuttgart | 1978 | 5,500 |
| Berlin (Spandau) | 1979 | 21,700 |
| Düsseldorf (Kaarst) | 1979 | 18,100 |
| Kassel | 1980 | 19,400 |
| Fürth | 1981 | 22,400 |
| Saarbrücken (Schwalbach-Bous) | 1981 | 6,200 |
| Freiburg | 1981 | 7,400 |
| Heidelberg (Walldorf) | 1981 | 20,300 |
| Löhne-Gohfeld | 1983 | 5,700 |
| Hamburg (Schnelsen) | 1989 | 24,000 |
| Leipzig | 1992 | 22,800 |
| Chemnitz | 1992 | 20,500 |
| Essen | 1993 | 23,500 |
| Berlin (Waltersdorf) | 1993 | 26,000 |
| Braunschweig | 1993 | 19,400 |

**Hong Kong**

| | | |
|---|---|---|
| *Tsimshatsui/Sun Plaza*** | *1975* | *2,100* |
| *Shatin*** | *1987* | *2,800* |
| *Tsuen Wan*** | *1992* | *1,500* |
| *Causeway Bay*** | *1993* | *3,700* |

**Hungary**

| | | |
|---|---|---|
| Budapest | 1990 | 12,600 |

**Iceland**
*Reykjavik** *                              *1981*        *9,200*

**Italy**
Milan (Cinisello Balsamo)                   1989          11,900
Turin                                       1990          14,600
Milan (Corsico)                             1992          21,300
Brescia                                     1992          12,700

**Kuwait**
*Kuwait City** *                            *1984*        *9,200*

**The Netherlands**
Rotterdam (Sliedrecht)                      1979          14,600
Amsterdam                                   1982          20,300
Duiven                                      1983          10,900
Eindhoven                                   1992          13,200
*Delft** *                                  *1992*        *19,500*
Heerlen*                                    1994          9,300

**Norway**
Oslo (Slependen)                            1963          19,600
Bergen                                      1984          10,700
Stavanger (Forus)                           1988          14,000

**Poland**
Warsaw                                      1990          5,900
Poznan                                      1991          6,600
Gdansk                                      1993          3,700
Warsaw (Janki)                              1993          13,600

**Saudi Arabia**
*Jeddah** *                                 *1983*        *17,500*
*Riyadh** *                                 *1993*        *16,600*

**Singapore**
*Singapore** *                              *1978*        *6,100*

**Slovakia**
Bratislava                                  1992          8,400

**Spain**
*Las Palmas (Gran Canaria)** *              *1980*        *6,900*
*Santa Cruz (Tenerife)** *                  *1983*        *6,600*
*Palma (Mallorca)** *                       *1992*        *7,500*

**Sweden**
Älmhult                                     1958          23,400
Stockholm (Skarholmen)                      1965          45,800
Sundsvall                                   1966          13,000
Malmö                                       1967          22,700
Gothenburg                                  1972          25,500
Linkoping                                   1977          18,200
Jonkoping                                   1981          7,500
Gavle                                       1981          12,600
Helsingborg                                 1982          14,400
Orebro                                      1982          13,100
Uppsala                                     1982          13,500

| | | |
|---|---|---|
| Vasterås | | |
| Stockholm (Jarfalla) | 1993 | 27,100 |
| **Switzerland** | | |
| Zurich (Spreitenbach) | 1973 | 27,200 |
| Lausanne (Aubonne) | 1979 | 18,300 |
| Lugano | 1991 | 10,400 |
| Zurich (Diethkon) | 1992 | 7,500 |
| **Taiwan** | | |
| *Taipei* ** | *1994* | *3,000* |
| **United Arab Emirates** | | |
| *Dubai* ** | *1991* | *7,100* |
| **United Kingdom** | | |
| Manchester (Warrington) | 1987 | 19,100 |
| London (Brent Park) | 1988 | 23,500 |
| Birmingham | 1991 | 17,600 |
| Newcastle | 1992 | 15,800 |
| London (Croydon) | 1992 | 22,000 |
| Leeds* | 1995 | 16,600 |
| **USA** | | |
| Philadelphia | 1985 | 15,100 |
| Washington (Woodbridge) | 1986 | 14,800 |
| Baltimore | 1988 | 19,400 |
| Pittsburgh | 1989 | 15,600 |
| New Jersey (Elizabeth) | 1990 | 24,900 |
| Los Angeles (Burbank) | 1990 | 22,100 |
| New York (Long Island) | 1991 | 21,000 |
| Los Angeles (Fontana) | 1992 | 14,200 |
| Los Angeles (Tustin) | 1992 | 13,500 |
| Los Angeles (City of Industry) | 1992 | 13,200 |
| Houston | 1992 | 14,400 |
| Los Angeles (Carson) | 1992 | 19,600 |
| *Seattle* ** | *1994* | *13,800* |

*Source:* IKEA publicity.
*Notes:* * Will be inaugurated after 1.9.94 and is not included in total figures.
** Outlets outside the IKEA Group. Gross area includes adjacent warehouses.

As it has grown, IKEA's managers have avoided any marked departure from the pioneering, core retail business concept: the provision of
affordable and varied home furnishings. The IKEA brand name has
achieved considerable prominence and is synonymous with its mass
merchandising concept the world over. None the less, there have been
extensions to the concept over time.

The 69-year-old Ingvar Kamprad, now living in Lausanne, Switzerland, may no longer be greatly involved in the detailed operations of the
firm, but as chairman of IKEA's Supervisory Board he has maintained a
strong interest in its continuing development and policy formulation. As

staff numbers have grown, he has keenly promoted distinctive values and culture in IKEA.

## THE IKEA APPROACH

### Corporate style and philosophy: 'A better everyday life for the majority of people'

The company has always promoted high ideals and standards and its philosophy is encapsulated in the above quotation from the charismatic and visionary Kamprad. He has articulated the corporate goal of helping customers in their quest for democracy and a healthy and rewarding lifestyle. This attitude evidently goes well beyond the generation of profits – which are seen as merely the means to these ends. Kamprad has strongly promoted the 'IKEA way' to employees with whom he has tried to maintain close contacts. To this end he still conducts annual managerial seminars personally.

Even today, many company 'legends' derive from and elaborate on Kamprad's personal style. To sustain a distinctive IKEA culture, Kamprad prepared an 11-page statement of guiding principles in 1976, entitled *Testament of a Furniture Dealer*. It contains statements such as 'an idea without a price tag is never acceptable', 'by daring to be different we find new ways', 'to assume responsibility has nothing to do with education or position' and 'to make mistakes is the privilege of the active person – only while asleep does one make no mistakes'. Core values in IKEA can be summarized as simplicity and economy, informality, modesty, reliability, enthusiasm, willingness to respect and help others, the exercise of creative problem-solving skills, the duty to challenge the *status quo* in the quest for efficiency, cost-consciousness and attention to detail.

IKEA's working practices are egalitarian even by western standards. Senior managers share secretaries and travel economy class. The office environment is informal, with open plan layouts. Staff are typically young (lower wages, more enthusiasm!) and dress in jeans and sweaters, addressing one another familiarly, for example using 'tu' rather than 'vous' in France, 'du' not 'Sie' in Germany. Terms and conditions of employment maintain high standards. Training is something of an obsession. When dealing with customers, staff are encouraged to be polite without being subservient or pushy, to regard them as partners whose long-term loyalty is valued and not taken for granted.

Swedish nationals occupy 90 per cent of senior managerial positions around the world in a conscious attempt to retain the IKEA ethos of doing business honestly and openly. Over three hundred managers have been assigned the task of being an 'IKEA ambassador', promoting

IKEA's philosophy and values by word of mouth and as role models in their functional duties. Though there is no overt discrimination in favour of Swedish nationals, as Anders Moberg, the current president and chief executive has said:

> I would advise any foreign employee who really wants to advance in this company to learn Swedish. They will then get a completely different feeling for our culture, our mood, our values. We encourage them to have as much contact with Sweden as possible, for instance by going there for their holidays.[4]

Anders Moberg was promoted to CEO in 1986 when he was only 35 years old. Many managers are younger than this, having assumed responsibility early in their careers because the company has been growing so rapidly. IKEA managers operate with autonomy and minimal interference from head office, a policy of 'freedom with responsibility'. As one explained:

> We try to have everyone who works for us believe that they have the freedom to do their job in the best way possible. It's almost impossible to push the philosophy down to the cashier level, but we try.[5]

Fast, flexible decision making is aided by a flat organization hierarchy, with only four levels between Moberg and IKEA's in-store staff.

To its clientele the company also promotes a classless, ethical image. It strives to offer a service of high integrity, expressed tangibly in its terms of trade and product policies including a written 'no-nonsense' guarantee of satisfaction. Local regulations on product safety are rigorously adhered to. For example, all upholstery and lighting equipment on sale in British stores conform to appropriate BSI standards for fire resistance and electrical safety.

On the environmental front, timber is sourced from sustainable sources, principally Scandinavian softwoods. Endangered hardwood species like teak and mahogany have been phased out in favour of varieties such as ash, beech, birch and elm whose use is restricted mainly to veneers on particleboard. More recently IKEA's range includes items such as dining chairs made from recyclable composite plastics which it promises to take back for recycling when ultimately discarded. It was also one of the first retailers to promote the benefits of low energy light bulbs.

However, low costs remain central to IKEA's philosophy, for only by offering good quality products at the lowest possible prices can it combine 'a better everyday life for the majority of people' with rapid growth. Containing costs is a constant battle calling for problem-solving skills of a high order. As Ingvar Kamprad has said: 'Expensive solutions to problems are often a sign of mediocrity. We have no interest in a

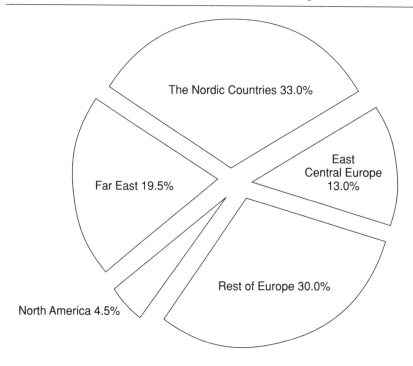

Number of active articles: 12,200
Number of suppliers: 2,300 in 67 countries
Number of distribution centres: 12

*Figure 16.3* IKEA: purchases 1994/5
Source: IKEA publicity

solution until we know what it costs.'[6] To this end IKEA has developed distinctive approaches to the design and sourcing of merchandise, as well as operating economically.

### Sourcing and product policy: 'High quality, low price. How does IKEA do it?'

'We do our bit. You do yours. Together we save money.' There are a number of complementary strands to IKEA's approach to sourcing and product policy.

IKEA relies on outside suppliers located around the world. Currently there are some 2,300 in 67 countries (Figure 16.3). For furniture alone, there are 1,500 suppliers in forty countries. Given the scale and dispersion of the IKEA supply chain, sourcing and logistics are keys to its efficiency, especially since a large percentage of its sales in each country derive from imports. Many products are transported in 'knocked down' flat packs for home assembly by the consumer.

In the early days IKEA's longer-established Swedish retail competitors threatened to boycott furniture producers that supplied IKEA. Thus it began to trade with smaller manufacturers, whether or not they had prior experience of the products IKEA needed. For example a ski maker was invited to make tables, a shirt maker chair cushions. Since many firms had limited resources IKEA became actively involved with them. It began to develop expertise in product design and engineering, in warehousing, and in purchasing raw materials and packaging at the most favourable prices. Additionally, it grew accustomed to supporting suppliers by making loans to fund specialized equipment, and contracting to take all of a manufacturer's output: 'We don't buy products, we buy production capacities.'[7]

What started as a necessity soon provided major competences and sources of advantage. IKEA continues its policy of long-term relationships with suppliers, working closely with them in a style often associated with large Japanese companies. It has a structure of first and second tier suppliers, the latter providing minor components such as doors, hinges, seat cushions, etc. for inclusion into the flat packs for shipment. Multiple sourcing of components is not unusual. Sometimes IKEA demands an exclusive arrangement with a supplier, other times it prefers the supplier not to become wholly dependent.

By the mid-1980s the proportion of purchases from the Nordic countries had fallen to about half and today it is down to one-third. Global sourcing has become a key aspect of IKEA's approach, although most furniture is produced for IKEA in Europe. IKEA began developing supplier relationships in Eastern Europe long before the break up of the Soviet sphere of influence. By value, its sources of supply in 1994 were Nordic countries 33 per cent, Eastern Europe 13 per cent, other European countries 30 per cent, North America 4.5 per cent, Far East 19.5 per cent.

Suppliers deliver products direct to IKEA's twelve regional distribution centres which in turn supply the stores in its four geographic operating regions: Scandinavia, Rest of Europe, North America and Rest of the World. Where severe supply difficulties arise, stores can seek supplies out of region. On the 3,000 items featured in its annual catalogues IKEA aims for a 95 per cent level of service. The risk of periodic stock outs has to be balanced against the extra cost of holding higher stocks.

Whilst stock outs and higher costs both hurt customer satisfaction, stock outs are more obviously noticeable, and statements in the catalogues clearly signal that occasional stock outs are part of the quid pro quo for low prices. Compared to traditional competitors, some of which have achieved stock turns as low as two to three times per annum, IKEA's inventory performance is very good. Estimates put target stocks at five to ten weeks' worth of expected sales, according to the nature of the line, with a further two to three weeks in transit.

Wherever feasible IKEA furniture is sold in flat-pack form, complete with necessary fixings and a simple illustrated guide that an average 10-year-old child can make sense of. Indeed, IKEA makes a great virtue of home assembly, symbolized by the anthropomorphic Allen key symbol on posters in every store.[8] Being able to dismantle furniture is also useful for the customer who later wishes to move bulky items from one room to another or from one house to another.

Whilst there is much continuity in IKEA's product range, it introduces new products regularly and eliminates slow sellers. At any one time as many as 20,000 product items have to be managed. Stores carry substantially the same merchandise lines, though there are variations from store to store within a country and more especially between countries. A typical store holds 10–12,000 lines, a large proportion of which are small household accessories sourced according to national reputations and skills, allied to lowest delivered cost.

A random selection of these products offered in 1994 included brightly coloured woollen Turkish rugs and cotton dhurries from India, Polish wooden storage fitments, glassware from the Czech Republic, earthenware drinking mugs from Romania, Taiwanese desk fittings and stainless steel cookware, Japanese china ornaments, Belgian fabrics, and German light bulbs.

The combination of standardization and flat packing could result in boring furniture. Unlike competitors such as UK-based MFI, IKEA has shunned utilitarian design. The majority of product designs originate with named Scandinavians including Rutger Andersson, Tord Bjorklund, Carina Carlsson, Niels Gammelgaard, Knut and Marianne Hagberg, Tomas Jelinek, Lars Norinder and Erik Worts. Their concepts are typically clean and unfussy, in muted colours that accord with the natural quality of the materials used, such as pine, cotton canvas, leather and ceramics. However, they also create strikingly elegant designs in chrome and black steel, glass and plastics. Less expensive lines made from particleboard are veneered and/or stained to achieve a variety of attractive effects, or simply lacquered in bold, primary colours, especially products for children. Where competitors emulate IKEA products, the firm normally prefers to upgrade designs rather than waste effort on expensive copyright lawsuits.

IKEA uses Swedish names for its products, even when these may seem bizarre to some audiences, for example the Smedvik dining suite, Folkabo and Pixbo armchairs, Edefors dining chair, Fritz and Bra wardrobes. IKEA's products are typically based on the metric sizes accepted in Sweden: thus for example, its beds and bed linen are more generously proportioned than those from most UK manufacturers.

Purchasing, product range development and distribution management are based at a centre in southern Sweden which has the umbrella title of 'wholesale' function, under Anders Moberg's direct control. Prototypes are made by some 200 designers and production engineers. Purchasers are selected for their hard-nosed, cost-conscious approach. Central staff who are virtually all Swedish tend to be more specialized than distribution and store managers and to change jobs less often.

IKEA rigorously tests furniture to demonstrate its integrity to withstand years of daily use. These tests assess safety, durability, comfort, material quality, workmanship and finish in ways appropriate to expected use. Tests are supervised by the independent Swedish Furniture Research Institute and items successfully passing the tests are awarded the *Mobelfakta* seal. This classes a product as either basic, high quality, or suitable for commercial use. Results are displayed in store on each item.

IKEA recognizes that many customers have young children and places special emphasis on furniture that is safe for the family. It also offers a range of safety accessories such as anchor brackets to prevent tall units toppling over, child-proof catches for drawers, cupboards and windows, self-adhesive bumpers for sharp corners on tables and cabinets, anti-slip floor strips, and safety gates for doorways and stairs.

## The approach to costs and pricing: 'No-one beats IKEA on price'

IKEA sets its prices each summer and publishes them in its August merchandise catalogue. It guarantees that prices will not change for a full twelve months, except for changes beyond corporate control, such as increases in sales or value added taxes. When an IKEA store finds it cannot offer a product at a substantial discount compared with local competitors, that product is unlikely to be stocked.

IKEA's prices compare very favourably with what consumers would pay for equivalent products elsewhere. Commentators have suggested that the firm aims to offer merchandise 30–40 per cent below the price of nearest competitors on a like for like basis. One example, a full height, free-standing solid pine wardrobe one metre wide, was available from IKEA UK in late 1994 for £279. This price was unchanged since August 1992 and guaranteed till August 1995. A similar offering (with somewhat less manufacturing content) from a well-known UK furniture retailer with over 100 stores, was concurrently available at a 'special' price of £375, against a stated 'normal' price of £449.

In recent times IKEA has been determined to reduce prices to consumers in the face of worldwide recession. In the UK it offered a 'lowest price challenge' whereby customers who buy an IKEA product and then find they could have bought a comparable product cheaper elsewhere can claim back the difference from IKEA and also a free meal in its restaurant. IKEA UK also promised to reduce the store price of that product for other customers.

By assuming complete responsibility for product design IKEA achieves low cost through careful attention to every detail of specification, method of construction and packaging. IKEA engineers work closely with chosen suppliers to realize cost savings in practice. A good illustration of cost control is the application of mass production methods to domestic furniture.

IKEA's subcontractors adopt modern, precision engineering methods, including the use of automated machinery with dimensionally stable manufactured materials, ensuring economies of scale and low cost per unit without compromising the appearance or the effectiveness of the product in use.

Precision manufacture creates components such as frames, panels and legs, with an accuracy measured in a parts of a millimetre. Because components are interchangeable, craft-based assembly methods – at the factory or elsewhere – are eliminated. Precision manufacture guarantees consistency, vital for flat-pack construction where simple butt joints have to be accurate, otherwise poor fit spoils the appearance. It also ensures that when assembled units stand next to each other they look well matched, even if bought at different times.

Crucially, these techniques enable IKEA to sell economical 'flat-pack' furniture with simple, but effective metal and plastic fixings, that customers can assemble at home. This enables component production to continue in high labour cost countries like Sweden and Denmark, close to European markets. Delivery to store in 'flat-pack' kits eliminates all the low skilled, but costly and hard to automate factory assembly tasks. It reduces transport costs – less distance, far less space per unit in a shipping container, and only basic, recyclable, packaging.

Precision also supports design modularity. The current range of IKEA kitchen furniture, for instance, is based on three cabinets, two floor standing and one wall mounted. Each has a fixed height and depth, and a range of widths based on 30, 40 and 50 cm modules and multiples thereof. Yet despite standardization, IKEA offers eight styles of floor standing cabinet in sixteen sizes, eight tall cabinets in ten sizes and eight wall cabinets in seventeen sizes. All are offered in thirteen different finishes with eight laminated work top options. So customers have a wide choice without cost penalty.

### Communicating with the customer: 'The key to success'

The company believes it is successful because it is flexible and customer-oriented. As worldwide product head, Fred Andersson has been quoted as saying: 'Unlike other companies, we are not fascinated with what we produce, we make what our customers want.'[9] And when customers complain, it is by no means unusual for the general manager of that country to telephone them in person to discuss the problem.

IKEA's clientele is for the most part under 45 years old, typically families with children. To maintain as wide an appeal as possible, the company deliberately avoids segmenting its markets using sophisticated demographic and psychographic techniques advocated by consumer marketing consultants. Instead, managers believe that good quality products at unbeatable prices are of universal appeal. Anders Moberg explained:

> We don't spend much money or time on studies. We use our eyes and go out and look, and say [we] will probably do quite well here . . . we may adapt, but quite often we stick to our opinions.[10]

IKEA strongly communicates to consumers the qualities positively associated with its Swedish origins. These include wholesomeness, trustworthiness, the absence of class divisions and, increasingly, sophistication and environmental awareness. The bold and simple IKEA corporate logo echoes the Swedish national colours of blue and yellow and is much in evidence in its stores and promotional literature.

An important message is fair dealing. On its regular merchandise IKEA offers a written 'no-nonsense' guarantee that if for any reason a customer is not 100 per cent satisfied with a purchase, a full refund is available within one month of purchase, provided that the item is returned as purchased. On some items such as floor coverings, a refund is available for up to three months.

IKEA's values are also evident in its principal promotional tool, the 300 + page, full-colour merchandise catalogue which is completely revised each year and available to all store visitors. In addition to some 3,000 regular merchandise lines, it details special promotional offers available during specified weeks through the coming year. It is also a source of useful information about how IKEA operates. It promotes the idea that customers are *partners* since they are required to assemble their purchases with the help of the famous little Allen key.

Some 45–50 million catalogues, costing around $US2, are printed and distributed around the world each year in a dozen different languages and twenty-five to thirty editions. Literally hundreds of thousands of households in the catchment area of a store will receive a catalogue each year. In this way IKEA hopes to encourage people to visit regularly, perhaps three or four times a year, and to become loyal customers.

Above the line advertising is not a major plank of IKEA's consumer marketing communications in all countries, though it is used in the early stages of a new store opening to gain awareness, and regularly in more sophisticated markets such as North America. Direct mail is also used to communicate with its increasingly significant business clientele.

### The in-store experience: 'Have a day out in Sweden. Visit IKEA'

IKEA operates vast stores of up to 45,000 square metres, with parking for up to 3,000 cars. To minimize operating costs they are sited out of town centres where land is inexpensive, typically on trading parks close to motorway junctions and somewhat remote from other stores. The Birmingham store in the UK, for example, is located off junction 9 of the M6, north of the city, in what was a derelict industrial site earmarked for redevelopment. The company received considerable encouragement to locate there, including new access roads linking the store directly to the motorway and to local conurbations.

Each store must attract visitors from a catchment radius of approximately 50 miles. IKEA promotes the in-store experience as 'more like a day out than a shopping trip', somewhere that competes well with other family entertainment venues. It tries hard to convey a sense of excitement and anticipation. Stores are 'designed to make buying furniture fun – for all the family'. First-time visitors are unlikely to feel they have had a thorough look around unless they spend at least half a day in the store. Even regular visitors find it difficult to leave without spending money, upwards of a £100 for a collection of relatively minor purchases is not unusual, whilst a large purchase will run into hundreds.

As IKEA expanded, new stores would vie with well-established ones by adding more merchandise departments and customer facilities. Thus, what has worked well is incorporated into what are now largely standardized architectures and layouts. Facilities now include a restaurant and snack bar, a specialty Swedish food store, toilets/rest rooms and a variety of child-minding facilities and play areas such as a video room, climbing frames, and a 'ballroom' for toddlers – a room with small climbing frames, filled to a depth of a half metre or so with brightly coloured plastic balls.

Stores are typically divided into three main selling areas, often on two levels. Product catalogues and tape measures are available at the store entrance. Smoking is forbidden, as are pets, though guide dogs for the visually impaired are welcome and there is good access for the wheelchair bound. Visitors proceed along a predetermined path through a series of simulated room displays or studios where domestic furniture and accessories are on show. Some present office furnishings.

Furniture items carry comprehensive information tags and are classed either as red tag 'full service' items or blue tag 'self-serve' items. Stores employ sales assistants sparingly because IKEA takes the view that they are not only expensive, but can also be irritating to visitors who prefer to browse in peace. To be visible, store personnel wear a standard uniform, such as red T shirts and blue trousers.[11] When asked, an assistant offers information about a product and checks stock availability via a computer terminal in the display area. If the customer decides to buy a red tag item the assistant generates an invoice from the terminal without delay and gives the customer a copy for later payment.

When visitors finally return to their starting point they have seen as many as seventy-five separate displays, though short cuts are possible. They find themselves near the restaurant where such delicacies as Swedish meatballs with lingonberry sauce and Danish pastries are on offer. Alternatively, they go to the second display area featuring smaller household fixtures, fittings and accessories. This is like an indoor, traditional market, ordered into merchandise categories, for example kitchen equipment, bathroom fittings, china and crockery, fabrics and window furnishings, carpets and other flooring materials, wallpapers and paints, toys, small storage units, lighting, prints and picture frames, plants – the list is almost endless. Again, the store layout discourages visitors from missing any display. Whilst some goods require service, for example cutting fabrics to length, most are blue tag items for the customer to put into a large trolley or a distinctive yellow shoulder carrier.

The third area of the store is the warehouse. Larger blue tag items are found here, their locations recorded on the tags attached to display items in the studio layouts. Again the customer self-serves, calling for assistance only if an item is too high to reach on the high rise racking. The concept of self-service in the warehouse began the day the Stockholm store was opened. Staff were overwhelmed with the number of customers, so the manager allowed them into the warehouse to select their purchases. This worked so well that it became a feature of all subsequent store designs.

Customers exit the warehouse via wide aisle, supermarket type checkouts. They pay for purchases by cash or credit card. Red tag items are collected at a special collection area. Bulky items go on a trolley to be wheeled to the loading bay where customers load their cars under cover. Car roof racks can be borrowed without charge and for those without a suitable vehicle, there is an extra-cost home delivery service. Typically, there is no mail order facility, though a proportion of goods are sold this way in North America.

Subject to minor variations to meet local regulations and preferences, stores have long opening hours. In the UK, for example, stores generally open between 10 a.m. and 8 p.m. on weekdays, Saturdays 9 a.m. till 6 or 7 p.m., Sundays 11 a.m. to 5 p.m.

## IKEA'S DEVELOPMENT IN THE UK: 'WELCOME TO IKEA'

IKEA's 1987 UK entry strategy provides an instructive model of patient, deliberate planning. Given its progress in Europe, IKEA entered the British market late, though there were reasons. Most obviously, throughout the 1970s and early 1980s the firm had been growing fast elsewhere, stretching its resources to the limit, and other markets were seen as more attractive.

The typical British consumer was markedly reluctant to spend as much on home furnishings as German, French or Swedish counterparts. They had conservative tastes, too. During the 1960s and 1970s only the Habitat chain, founded by design guru Sir Terence Conran, and up-market independents succeeded in promoting Scandinavian style. However, Habitat fell on hard times as its core 1960s/1970s supporters aged and were not replaced by sufficient numbers of young professional people setting up first homes.

For IKEA strong competition from well-established mass market retailers was also a deterrent. These included furniture multiples with big purchasing power, including MFI with a similar, less sophisticated format, Times Furnishing, Courts, Maples, Cantors, DFS and department store chains such as Debenhams, House of Fraser and the Co-ops. Moreover, flat-pack furniture as originally pioneered in the UK by MFI had an excruciating reputation for unattractive appearance and low quality.

The economic buoyancy of the mid-1980s encouraged people to move house, a trigger for spending on the home. Some national companies, including MFI with its *Hygena* brand and Magnet, were now selling more attractive engineered furniture for the kitchen and bathroom. Younger, open-minded consumers saw that modern construction offered acceptable appearance and quality if well executed. Moreover, traditional furniture from branded manufacturers was so expensive that it was increasingly out of reach of most people. Niche market groups like Casa Fina were offering more stylish design, and many, quite up-market, independent stores were moving to a semi-warehouse format.

IKEA managers sensed the British middle market was now receptive to honestly made engineered furniture throughout the home, if it offered good value rather than merely being cheap. Thus their merchandise would receive an open-minded examination in Britain, and once seen, would have wide appeal. IKEA located its first superstore at junction 9 of the M62, halfway between Liverpool and Manchester. More than five million people live within 20 miles. The second store was opened at Brent Park in sight of Wembley stadium, north west London, in 1988, when plans for another ten stores were announced. Stores followed in Birmingham in 1991, Gateshead in the north of England and Croydon, south of London, in 1992. The new store openings excited considerable interest. On their first day the Warrington and Birmingham stores created 10-mile traffic jams on access routes. IKEA rapidly established high awareness levels in the UK, and by 1994 few UK car owners had not visited an IKEA store at least once.

Excepting Gateshead, each current site has over three million people living within a 20-mile radius and over five million less than an hour away. Future sites will have rather less potential, the most obvious probably including Edinburgh/Glasgow, Leeds/Sheffield, Bristol/Cardiff, Essex, Reading/Slough, the Sussex/Kent border and the triangle defined by Leicester, Northampton and Cambridge. In 1992, in a largely opportunistic move, IKEA acquired the Habitat chains in Britain and France and set out to redevelop them as synergistic, stand-alone, niche market players.

Publicly IKEA has been satisfied with UK trading results to date. However, it was clearly a difficult period between 1990 and 1993, with the UK deep in recession, minimal new house building, and the pre-owned housing market severely depressed. Competition in self-assembly furniture intensified from new sources, notably the leading DIY chains, Texas Homecare, Great Mills and B&Q, and unexpectedly from the BAT-owned Argos catalogue store chain. The Co-op Retail Society launched a new out of town superstore format called HomeWorld, whilst Marks & Spencer also increased its commitment to selling quality furniture from its large out-of-town stores and via mail order.

A consequence of increased competition is that IKEA has had to compete hard on price. The 1993/4 catalogue actually cut prices on many lines, whilst more costly lines meeting price resistance were discontinued. An experiment to offer 'heirloom' quality furniture under the Stockholm name at Brent Park and Croydon was terminated after only two years. There has been greater attention to pruning slow-selling lines since 1992, perhaps associated with a new UK managing director. As of 1994 IKEA UK Ltd has had three chief executives, all Swedish, each presenting a more formal, businesslike image to the public than his predecessor.

In 1994 IKANO Financial Services, based in Nottingham, launched an IKEA credit card, mirroring a Marks & Spencer move of some years earlier. The firm also announced a comprehensive, free home interior design service for consumers planning to refurnish a complete room or the entire home.

## IKEA IN NORTH AMERICA: 'SELL THE SAME PRODUCT IN HOUSTON AND HELSINGBORG!'

IKEA entered the Canadian market in 1976 by licensing a franchisee. In 1979 the latter was failing and IKEA took over and turned it round over the next three years, under a management team of two Canadians and two Swedes. By 1986 the operation had nine stores, 75,000 square metres of selling space, a turnover of Canadian $106 million and net profits of 5 per cent of sales. Mail order accounted for some 7 per cent of sales.

Growth had exceeded expectations, but given the long supply lines, up to 300 lines could be out of stock at any one time. For fast-moving lines management developed local supply arrangements with some thirty Canadian firms until in 1985, when the first IKEA store opened in the USA, 21 per cent of Canadian sales by value were locally sourced.

The first US store was 15,700 square metres (169,000 square feet) on the outskirts of Philadelphia, the second a year later at Washington. Ingvar Kamprad personally decided the time was right for US entry. Combined store turnover in 1986 was $US77 million. The company was confident it would repeat European experience and break into profit after two to three years with three to four stores. By 1990 it had stores at Baltimore and Pittsburg, and Los Angeles on the west coast. Six more were planned within three years. But in 1989 IKEA experienced serious competition from Sears, a West Coast imitator called Stor, and IDOMO in Canada, all offering look-alike products. It was also clear that too many US consumers left IKEA stores without buying.

With Kamprad solidly behind the US venture, there was no question of retreat. Anders Moberg personally spent much of his time in the USA during 1989–90 talking to customers: 'We were behaving like all Europeans, as exporters, which meant we were not really in the country.'

The team diagnosed specific problems, notably that many products were simply too small for American tastes. This included everything from beds to storage cupboards to drinking glasses. Customers also complained of long queues and frequent stock outs. To compound its difficulties, by 1991 the US dollar had fallen from SKr.8.6 to 5.8, so IKEA was in no position to undercut local imitators with products still sourced from Europe.

Moberg and Kamprad decided to give new US chief executive Goran Carstedt more autonomy than his European counterparts. Thereafter, IKEA diligently persevered to overcome its problems. In December 1991 it purchased Stor, and its four stores in greater Los Angeles. By 1994 some 45 per cent of its furniture sold in the USA was produced locally. Designs had been resized (in inches) to suit American tastes, and prices were reduced three years running. Store layouts were also redesigned, and check-out delays reduced by 20 per cent. In addition to a more generous returns policy, US IKEA now offers a next-day delivery service and mail order. Since 1990 sales have tripled to $US480 million and operations broke into profit in 1992. It recently opened its thirteenth store, in Seattle, with two more in prospect.

## OFFICE FURNISHINGS: 'SEE IKEA AT WORK IN THE OFFICE TOO'

IKEA has sold higher quality flat-pack furniture suitable for office use since the 1960s. In the 1970s it extended its business range to appeal to restaurant, conference and hotel furnishers. Today, most IKEA stores offer an 'IKEA at work' package, appealing to small and medium-sized businesses. But it was only in 1982 that a business group was set up to offer IKEA FAKTURA or 'contract service', extending conventional 30-day credit terms to an agreed credit limit for suitable business customers.

Although the service generates a considerable proportion of some stores' sales, it is still presented in a low key fashion. For example, though office furnishings are displayed in a dedicated area of the store, only a handful of staff has particular responsibility for this merchandise, and the business customer does not have a special entrance.

This may be expected to change, as both IKEA and its business clientele realize that each has much to offer the other. However, there may be organizational difficulties in accommodating the needs and expectations of demanding business customers in what is essentially a consumer format. Worse, it could create divisions within the firm leading to divisive 'us-and-them' attitudes affecting its coherent operating ethos.

## IKEA'S GLOBAL FUTURE: 'EXPRESS YOUR OWN PERSONALITY'

In the space of fifty years IKEA has grown from a provincial Swedish company to a global player in the provision of stylish, value for money furnishings and accessories for home and office. In 1994 sales from its owned and operated stores broke down thus: Sweden 11.1 per cent; Germany 29.6 per cent; Rest of northern Europe 21.9 per cent; Rest of southern Europe 20.5 per cent; Eastern Europe 1.6 per cent; Australia 1.1 per cent; North America 14.2 per cent.

Despite obvious and marked differences of taste in its many markets, IKEA's management has relentlessly pursued a strategy that in respect of low cost, homogeneous organization culture and external image, product policy, sourcing and distribution, and retail format, manifests greater standardization of approach than almost any other multinational.

Paradoxes abound: despite its Swedish credentials – winning many friends and loyal customers – a large proportion of its sales derive from products never having been within a thousand miles of Sweden; only a company that sets such high value on personal initiative and responsibility could allow the ideas and drive of one individual to have so much influence; only in North America has it tailored its approach specifically to local consumers.

A variety of strategic questions currently exercise IKEA's senior management. First, how can it reduce administrative costs from a 1991/2 peak of 37.5 per cent of revenues back to the historical level of 30 per cent? Anders Moberg introduced a formal planning and budgeting process in 1988. Corporate three-year plans were to be the norm and cost-benefit was to supersede cost-consciousness. Yet in 1992 Moberg abolished internal budgets: 'We realised that our business planning system was getting too heavy; we can use the time saved for doing other things better.'[12] Now he requires each regional operation only to keep within an agreed and declining ratio of costs to sales revenue.

Second, how can IKEA improve the somewhat problematic quality of its East European suppliers? In some cases it has taken an equity stake. This question is not unconnected to Ingvar Kamprad's desire to expand in Eastern Europe and the former Soviet Union, involving a strategy for counter trading in the absence of convertible currencies. As one executive recalled: 'Our entire East European strategy was mapped out by Ingvar on a small paper napkin – we call it his Picasso – and for the past few years we have just built on and expanded that vision.'[13]

Third, there is the vexed question of continued long-term growth. IKEA has managed new store development very effectively using project teams before installing an ongoing retail management structure. Experience shows that a new store increases its sales for perhaps five years, then tends to plateau in real terms. This means growth has to come from continued new store openings. In addition to East Europe, IKEA has plans for ten stores in mainland China where it already has a developing supply network. Some executives have expressed concern that the firm may simply overextend its finite resources.

Linked to this, is the broader question of how to rejuvenate. Kamprad has always encouraged internal, amicable rivalry between individual stores and between territories. More recently, acquisitions such as Stor in the USA and Habitat in Europe have offered the prospect of separately managed performance benchmarks; similarly, IKEA now has fifteen franchise stores (versus 108 wholly owned) forming a separate operating unit. These are in the Middle East, Hong Kong, Spain and in the USA – Seattle is one example. For IKEA retail executives to justify new owned and operated stores in their territory they must convince top management that they can do a better job than a franchisee.

Although single-minded adherence to the value for money formula has served IKEA well, the US experience suggests that excessive standardization has to be questioned and may need modification in future. Otherwise, resourceful competitors could succeed with more responsive forms of low cost strategy. Conversely, to decentralize product design and sourcing functions to address the needs of local communities would surely result in some loss of global economy through increased variety in products and trading formats.

Finally, there is the question of life after Kamprad, who has buttressed an extraordinary, idiosyncratic culture (some managers would say ideology) in which expansionism and parsimony are unusual partners. Will this change and if so how – if, for example, future controlling interests wish to grow by seeking to diversify or to become a public corporation?

## NOTES

1 R. Normann and R. Ramirez have argued that IKEA is not so much a retailer as the central star in a constellation of services wherein customers are suppliers of time and effort, whilst suppliers are also customers for its business and technical expertise ('From value chain to value constellation: designing an interactive strategy', *Harvard Business Review*, 71(4), 1993: 65–77).

2 © M. Pitt 1995.
This case study has been written as a basis for class discussion rather than to illustrate effective or ineffective managerial or administrative behaviour. It has been prepared from a variety of published sources, as indicated, and from personal observations.

3 R. Martenson, Doctoral dissertation (Gothenberg, 1981) quoted in C. A. Bartlett and A. Nanda, *Ingvar Kamprad and IKEA* (Boston, Mass.: Harvard Business School, 1990, 1992).

4 Quoted from an unnamed published source by Bartlett and Nanda op. cit.

5 P. Beamish and P. Killing, *IKEA-Sears*, (London, Ontario: University of Western Ontario, 1988).

6 Ingvar Kamprad, 20 December 1976.

7 Bartlett and Nanda op. cit.

8 Some products, notably upholstered furniture, are made to special order only. Fabric swatches are prominently displayed in store and the customer is asked to wait no more than five weeks from placing the order.

9 Beamish and Killing, op. cit.

10 *The Economist*, 19 November 1994: 83–4.

11 In North America part-time assistants have in the past worn yellow shirts with the legend 'Temporary help – please don't ask me any hard questions'! Curiously, some 'IKEAns' think the concept of wearing a uniform is very 'un-IKEA' in spirit (M. Salzer, 'Identity Across Borders: A Study in the IKEA-World', Linköping, Sweden: Linköping University doctoral dissertation.

12 *The Economist*, op. cit.

13 Bartlett and Nanda, op. cit.

# Chapter 17

# The alliance of Motorola and Citibank: creating a global cash management system[1,2]

## *Chris Holland and Geoff Lockett*

### EDITORS' OVERVIEW

Motorola and Citibank are two highly successful US companies operating on a global stage, in electronics components/assemblies and in banking respectively. The subject of this case study is their strategic alliance in order to manage the massive cash flows between Motorola subsidiary companies and suppliers around the world. The evolution of this joint strategy is described, together with its rationale, its benefits and the issues that have had to be addressed. Additionally, more general issues of co-operative strategy and the associated use of information systems (IS) are considered. The reader obtains insights into why this alliance was justified and is successful, not least through the complementarity of the partners' resources and capabilities.

The case describes how Motorola first developed an in-house system for centralizing its foreign currency transactions. It began in 1976 with internal transfer payments, then slowly after 1980 external suppliers were included in the system. The system derives from the straightforward concept of cumulating supply and demand for various currencies world-wide, period by period, thereby requiring to exchange only net amounts, called currency netting. Coincidentally, Citibank was engaged from 1975 in developing expertise in supplying EDI (electronic data interchange) payments services to manufacturing companies. By 1989, the start of the alliance, both firms had reached a sufficient level of technical competence that communication between equals was possible and technical difficulties were manageable.

The case shows in some detail how information systems have played a critical role in the rapid processing and movement of large volumes of currency transaction data over long distances. Innovating in the modern global organization can take many forms and in this instance we see clearly the importance of painstaking attention to detail in one specific area of Motorola's business. We see also how, by engaging in a patient, long-term alliance, Citibank has carved out a new business activity based on upgraded banking competences.

The financial gains from the alliance are substantial for Motorola. Reducing unnecessary cash flows and foreign exchange transactions via centrally controlled currency netting, thereby saving on bank and exchange charges is estimated to save some $US6.5 million per annum. The reduction in complication, manpower requirements, enhanced supplier satisfaction and expansion potential give further definite, if hard to quantify, benefits.

The case study sheds light on other, non-technical organizational factors which contributed to the successful implementation of the strategic alliance. Both companies possessed similar cultures, a shared global perspective of business and they developed a high level of mutual trust. Paradoxically, the movement towards centralization of international payments within Motorola's treasury department arose from the initiative of the London offices of these two companies, enabled by the significant degree of decentralization existing in both these global corporations.

Notwithstanding the importance of information systems in this alliance, it is worth noting that it would have been stillborn or ineffective without substantial contributions from key individuals in both organizations, who through their effective communication skills were able to champion the alliance and thus influence the direction the process subsequently took.

Indeed the real significance of this case may be that it provides an exemplary model of strategic alliance between two organizations whose complementary skills and resources were harnessed for an innovative, but very specific purpose offering mutual benefit. As such it may have implications for other companies with global operations, where the established expertise in the strategic application of information technology (IT) of one firm can be exploited as a competitive advantage by the other to their mutual benefit, with the shared gains being both financial and the upgrading of respective core competences.

### Discussion questions

- Why was a global strategic alliance an appropriate strategy in this case? What were the principal factors that made the alliance successful? Why might they be difficult for others to copy?
- Why and how does this cash management system relate to broader issues of corporate strategy?
- By what alternative means could Motorola have pursued its objectives?

- How can the firms develop the alliance further? What kinds of problems could arise?
- To what extent are the alliance strategies of Motorola and Citibank *planned*, i.e. designed in advance, as opposed to *emergent*, i.e. the general pattern of activity becomes discernible only over a period of time? What are the implications?

## List of named characters

Jean Michel-Richard, Motorola European treasury manager
Ian Blackman, Citibank manager, Global Payments Division
Brian Bledsoe, manager, Motorola EDI Centre, Phoenix

## Keywords

Strategic alliance; competences; complementarity/upgrading; strategic use of IT; centralization/decentralization; idea championing; attention to detail; global operations

## INTRODUCTION

The subject of this case study is a strategic alliance between two global companies. It is concerned with the specific strategies of Motorola and Citibank and also with the general issues of co-operative strategy and the associated use of information systems. The purpose of the partnership is to manage cash flows between Motorola companies and their suppliers on a worldwide basis. There are several factors which explain the formation of this arrangement; strategic, technological and managerial. The strategic motivations of both companies are presented in the form of key strategic events listed in chronological order and in recent quotes by managers actively involved in the development of strategy and information systems.

The original nature of the strategies and associated organizational designs and novel use of information systems to manage a complex business process have several important implications for banking and manufacturing. It is shown that information systems play a critical role in supporting the alliance because IT allows the secure processing and fast movement of high volumes of payments data over large distances. However, use of the appropriate computer software, hardware and networks is a necessary but not sufficient condition for success. Other organizational factors played a significant role in ensuring the successful implementation. In particular, similar cultures and a shared global perspective of business, and a high level of trust between the two organizations, facilitated the implementation. Another important contribution was made by key individuals in both organizations who were effective communicators and could influence the direction within their own companies.

### Motorola

Motorola is one of the world's leading providers of wireless communications, semiconductors and advanced electronic systems and services. Its organizational structure is such that the separate companies within the Motorola group act autonomously and therefore trade with each other, often across national boundaries. However, the globalization trends in business are making co-operation a general rule and the businesses are having to work together even more closely.

Motorola's total quality management (TQM) strategy is illustrated by the general emphasis on quality in the Motorola statement of key initiatives:

1 Six Sigma Quality.
2 Total cycle time reduction.
3 Product and manufacturing leadership.

4 Profit improvement.
5 Participative management within and co-operation between
  organizations.

For Motorola these strategic objectives are not platitudes, they are a way of life in which business excellence is clearly seen in its approach to manufacturing. Because of its logistical nature, manufacturing, distribution and marketing strategies are being co-ordinated on a global scale. This necessitates that systems play a key part in the delivery of these strategies. It is only by the use of global computer networks that large volumes of data can be moved across great distances almost instantaneously, thereby negating the impact of geographic dispersion.

Motorola realized the importance of computer networks to co-ordinate organizational activity very early on and has now developed tremendous expertise in managing global networks and systems. It was an early adopter of EDI and used it as a method of delivering its quality expectations to trading partners. The recent revolutionary methods of quality improvement which have been to the fore in western businesses – such as TQM – found a welcome home in Motorola; it has achieved the Malcolm Baldridge award for its quality performance. Quality is now its guiding light and affects all relationships both within the company and with external suppliers. Measured quality reports are the standard way of communicating between the organizations – it applies to all aspects of the business, as is shown by the typical output from the EDI centre in Phoenix (see Figure 17.1). Motorola's aim for better and better quality is an ongoing process and it is clearly exemplified by the remarks of manager Brian Bledsoe who works in the EDI centre in Phoenix:

> The best of EDI implementations are done in conjunction with TQM. EDI is just a tool. Take our MRP application. Each day we electronically give them a 'delivery' forecast. It tells them what inventory they have used each day, the highest and lowest stocks allowed and what they have in stock. We don't send out an order and leave it up to the suppliers to maintain their inventories in the supply chain. We also measure them on a quality rating which includes how many times they have overstocked.
>
> All this has been done with continuous slow incremental improvements. It doesn't happen overnight – it's just hard work developing close relationships. We don't need invoices, we can pay on receipt using the contract price. Sometimes there is a 'paradigm shift' but this is possible because of the long-term close co-operation. You have to behave like this in today's business. With EDI there are no secrets and your competitors know what you are doing. Now we all contribute to the standards, we cannot have a strategic advantage in that

# Six Sigma Quality
# Geis Van Availability
# 1992-1993

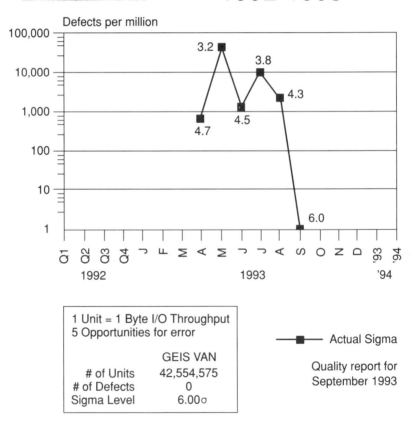

*Figure 17.1* Illustration of Six Sigma Quality Application

area. However, we can make sure that our processes are fully laid down. We can continue to drive out errors and improve quality. We have contributed some of our ideas to EDIFACT and they have become part of DELFOR – we gave it to the world. But we see this as a positive move because you cannot have secrets with EDI. However, it's like giving someone a gun without the bullets.

Competitors become aware of Motorola's EDI activities through common representation on the EDI standards boards and also by communication with common trading partners who exchange specific types of EDI messages with Motorola.

## Cash management

In parallel with the developments in manufacturing, the installed computer networks were used to handle problems of cash management. It seemed a natural progression and was complementary to the management of product flows. The ideas for the system were derived from the UK by the treasury manager who is located in Slough (near London). Slough is the chosen site for Motorola's European treasury group which controls the global netting service. Given the greater open windows in the UK for trading, it is fairly common for the finance centres of global companies to be located in West Europe. The recent tremendous improvements in telecommunications now make it even easier to implement global systems. The climate surrounding the project is outlined by Jean Michel-Richard, treasury manager at Motorola European Treasury, London.

The project has relied on close co-operation and trust between myself and Ian, Citibank's manager in charge of the project. We were both asking our organizations to commit considerable resources to obtain benefits from a project with a long lead time and that was highly visible within both organizations. It did help that EDI was seen as an appropriate technology to use. There was initial resistance to change from my management and I needed to justify the system. It took one year to convince my superiors (mainly in Chicago) through a series of presentations, conferences, discussion documents and I also needed to gain the support of end-users, worldwide. Once the internal implementation issues had been resolved the emphasis was changed to focus on Citibank, who needed to be convinced that our volume of payments and transactions justified a new approach, new standards and new systems. The project was hard work but it forced me to understand my environment and convinced me that I was heading the right way. I would do it again.

## THE EVOLUTION OF THE STRATEGY

The evolution of Motorola's cash management strategy has taken place over a period of sixteen years. During this time there have been substantial changes in information technology, strategic direction and focus while the system has been growing. The original objective was to improve cash management within the group using existing Motorola-controlled computer networks. A currency netting system was applied to transactions between Motorola companies to achieve cost savings by reducing both cash flows and the amount of foreign exchange deals effected for international payments. This concept is now being extended to include suppliers and involves the extensive use of value added networks (VANs) and suppliers to improve the management of the financial aspects of supplier relationships as well as to increase the benefits of reduced cash flows and foreign exchange savings already achieved.

### Evolution and growth

The success of the system is due to many factors and has some similarities with other large-scale information systems which are used to gain competitive advantages.[3] It has been driven by a clear vision – the electronic handling of money and the associated simplifications that this brings. However, in common with other large and successful systems it has evolved over a considerable period of time.

Table 17.1 details the evolution of Motorola's cash management strategy starting with the implementation of an internal global electronic mail system to the inclusion of external suppliers into the netting system.

> It seemed to be a logical evolution. The idea was there, all we needed was the IS technology to make it happen. Both Motorola and Citibank have long experience in global thinking which was a critical factor for success.

The main systems implemented by Citibank on the Motorola project are shown in Table 17.2.

> The technical issues were simple to resolve and did not provide a hinderance to the implementation. This was due to a common under-standing of the objectives of the project between the two companies and their high level of technical expertise and existing IT infrastruc-tures. The main issue that currently needs to be managed within both companies is to maintain the momentum and visibility of the project to ensure as large a portion of Motorola's third party cross-border payments are moved to the centralized system.

*Table 17.1* Evolution of Motorola's cash management strategy

| Year | Strategic focus | Activities | Information technology |
|---|---|---|---|
| 1976 | Reduce cash flows and foreign exchange requirements | Implement currency netting system for Motorola companies | Internal e-mail system using COBOL |
| 1980 | Include external suppliers into currency netting process | | |
| 1989 | Start of strategic alliance with Citibank | European treasury management function moved to London and connected to Citibank | Combine internal global system with external leased lines and value added networks to connect with Citibank and suppliers |
| 1992 | Increase level of financial integration with suppliers | Send remittance advice direct to suppliers | Development of EDIFACT standards for remittance advices |

Third party companies benefit from this system in several ways. Operational benefits are accrued by receiving payments faster and they also gain advance remittance advice, which improves their cash management because uncertainty over future cash flows is reduced. Connecting financially though is just one element of an integrative relationship with Motorola which also includes electronic links for logistics and e-mail in many cases. The financial link has been implemented in the context of a close business relationship which encompasses many other exchanges of information including social links and the sharing of knowledge.

It should be remembered that Citibank has been developing global computing banking systems for a long time. Like Motorola its success in this field has given it confidence to continue substantial strategic developments in cash management payment systems. Both organizations take a global strategic stance and have a clear vision of the way they wish to develop. Table 17.3 shows the growth in cash flows between Motorola companies from 1983 to 1991 and also the increasing number of companies which participate in the system.

The payments settled column is the sum of the accounts payable of all

*Table 17.2* Evolution of Citibank's cash payment product strategy

| Year | Strategic focus | Activities | Information technology |
|---|---|---|---|
| 1975 | Gain experience in EDI payments services | Implement pilot EDI payments link for a manufacturing company | Development of standards and use of networks |
| 1989 | Strategic alliance with Motorola to develop an EDI service for payments to their suppliers | Global interface with Motorola to collect payment orders | EDIFACT standards and IBM's worldwide data network used to share data with Motorola |
| 1990 | Develop relationship | Develop IT interface with Motorola using a variety of networks | Host-to host application with Motorola to collect extended remittance advices for cheque payments. Authentication and data encryption techniques developed |
| 1991 | Product innovation and improvement | Direct downloading of payments data from customers' information systems to Citibank's EDI service | Software interfacing and development of message standards for payment details |
| 1992 | Enhance payments service | Send remittance advice to suppliers | Single file received from Motorola containing all payment types |

netting companies. The net cash flow in 1991 was $US2,400 million which is a reduction of almost $US2,380 million. The foreign exchange with banks is the total value of currencies bought and sold. Without netting, it is expected that the figure for 1991 would have been $US4.3 billion, which represents a reduction of $US3 billion worth of foreign exchange transactions which equates to a direct annual saving of approximately $US6.5 million on foreign transactions alone.

There are approximately 2,500 transactions per month. At the moment, only a small number of suppliers are receiving remittance advice electronically but it is planned to have the great majority of suppliers linked in

*Table 17.3* Growth of Motorola's cash management netting system

| Year | Payments settled ($US million) | Foreign exchange with banks ($US million) | Number of Motorola participants |
|------|--------------------------------|--------------------------------------------|----------------------------------|
| 1983 | 600   | 229   | 38  |
| 1984 | 800   | 361   | 51  |
| 1985 | 1,100 | 391   | 53  |
| 1986 | 1,300 | 432   | 57  |
| 1987 | 1,800 | 415   | 65  |
| 1988 | 2,700 | 510   | 76  |
| 1989 | 3,000 | 650   | 85  |
| 1990 | 3,391 | 1,100 | 103 |
| 1991 | 4,780 | 1,281 | 106 |

this way in the next five years. Growth in the number of suppliers is expected to increase rapidly as the system gradually becomes seamless. Other improvements are to the information technology links between Motorola companies and the treasury function. Most of the data are entered manually at each factory. In these cases aggregate payment data only are recorded. Several of the leading edge users have direct interfaces to the centre which enable treasury management to pull transaction and vendor files directly off the systems. This improves the accuracy of the data and is less of an administrative load on the factories. Most semiconductors factories worldwide now have an interface in place which feeds payments directly from the local accounts payable system into the netting system.

A strong business vision coupled with the IT platforms of Motorola and Citibank has made it possible to implement a global cash management system which benefits both Motorola and its suppliers. This has been achieved through gradual innovations and is characterized by a learning process which allows the organizations to become accustomed to technical and organizational change and shift the strategy focus from an initial cost saving initiative to one that now yields significant strategic advantage. The information systems are being used to tie together the financial processes of Motorola companies and their suppliers by integrating the cash supply chain of Motorola, Citibank, suppliers' banks and suppliers. Although it looks complicated it is simply using EDI to its fullest extent. There are now no technical reasons why cross-border payments should not be made quickly and to a specified time. Motorola's cross-border payment system informs all companies on the Tuesday of each week what their exact cash position will be on the Thursday. This case represents a move towards just-in-time (JIT) money that will bring the banks into line with manufacturing organizations. An electronic revolution in banking may eventually occur.

Motorola has benefited considerably from an internal organizational change coupled with a business network redesign in its banking relationships. The potential for development though is limited to the extent of its business network unless it were to offer its financial expertise in cash management to other global organizations which have similar international flows of currencies. For Citibank this innovative project could be expanded in several ways. If there is a move towards JIT cash flows, which seems likely at the moment because of regulatory pressures and the increased capability of IT systems, then it will be at the vanguard of such developments and should be in a position to gain a large market share of such payments systems. This is especially important when one considers that a main source of revenue for banks in the past was from interest. In the future it appears that interest revenue will shrink and banks will earn money from processing payments and adding value to this activity by offering services such as advanced cash management facilities.

The handling of information is no longer seen as a barrier to innovation and change in the cash management strategy. Both Motorola and Citibank have internal global networks which allow them to transfer data relatively easily between any sites. The system also has many additional advantages, for example it allows managers to use applications which are located physically in another country. Treasury management is currently based in London but it could be anywhere on the network. The treasury management function is effectively location-independent. Europe has been chosen as a centre because of its time zone position, Motorola's strong manufacturing presence in Europe and accessibility to London's financial markets.

## SYSTEM DETAILS

Once every week all foreign currency transactions between Motorola companies are managed with a single payment or invoice from the centre to each Motorola company. Supplier payments and the associated netting of currencies is carried out on a weekly basis because of the volumes and frequencies of international payments. Essentially it is a compromise between having a large enough volume of payments to achieve significant reductions in cash flows and foreign exchange while also ensuring that supplier payments occur on a regular basis and in a reasonable time frame. National currencies are handled by the separate Motorola companies and are not part of the scheme. At 9 a.m. Tuesday data are collected from all netting users. These consist of a transaction file and vendor data. The netting system is then locked for about fifteen

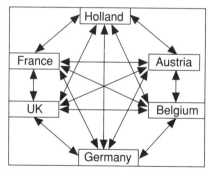

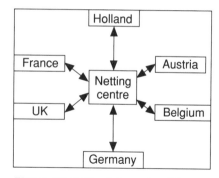

*Figure 17.2* The old system for managing payments between Motorola companies

*Figure 17.3* The internal netting system

minutes to achieve a clean cut-off point. Less than one hour later the total accounts payable and receivable are known by the treasury management centre. Each Motorola company is then advised by electronic mail whether it will receive a payment or is required to pay the centre. All transactions are conducted in local currencies so a German company receives or makes a payment to the centre in Deutschmarks for all its foreign currency transactions. The reduction in organizational complexity is illustrated in Figures 17.2 and 17.3. Prior to the netting system the old method for managing payments within Motorola is shown in Figure 17.2. The setting up of a netting centre reduces the organizational complexity because all the information flows and payments processes are handled centrally. Although conceptually and technically not very difficult, the implementation of a netting centre needs a paradigm shift for it to be successful.

The benefits arising from the internal netting system are a reduction in cash flows and the amount of foreign exchange deals. By moving from localized treasury management operations to one centralized team of dedicated staff, it is estimated that an annual financial saving (bank charges, foreign exchange) of about $US6.5 million per annum is achieved. However this does not include administrative savings gained from streamlining the operations, which obviously are more difficult to quantify. These have not been measured because the system is seen to be an outstanding success for the treasury management centre and all the companies. Each separate organization has taken the benefits in reduced costs. It was made possible because of a combination of factors. First is the foresight of the senior management. It had already committed itself to be at the forefront of IT and sees its use as giving it strategic advantage. The basic network was therefore already in place and once the scheme had been proposed its value was obvious to the participants – organizational resistance was low. It was also gradually introduced by building on successful stages of implementation. A few sites were chosen as prototypes initially. After these systems had become established and any operational difficulties resolved, the inclusion of other sites took place without difficulty.

Once the internal cash management was working smoothly Motorola then turned its attention to external relationships, that is, customers and suppliers. By this time it felt it had developed the necessary expertise to attempt this more difficult task. However, it is a far more complicated procedure in practice – not in concept – because of the involvement of a potentially large number of banks and their information systems. The way round this difficulty has been the co-operation with a complementary global banking company, Citibank, that had been considering the same problem. Its unique system of delivery fitted neatly with Motorola's system of collection – a clear example of synergy. The general aim for Motorola was fully to automate its netting system and communication platform with Citibank. This is the logical complementary development with EDI for supply chain logistics. Ian Blackman, a senior manager in Citibank's global payments division, describes the complementary role of Citibank:

> The savings in streamlining the overall process have provided large benefits in addition to the foreign exchange. The largest benefits are probably in the reduction in errors with the simplification of the process and better links with trading partners which have been facilitated by Citibank. The cost of loss of trust between trading partners due to errors in payments should not be underestimated particularly as resolving mistakes on payments can seriously detract from more important business-related discussions between the trading partners. The staff that are usually responsible for resolving payments errors are not always the best equipped to handle enquiries in foreign languages and to negotiate discussions with a chain of banks involved in the process.

The process for external netting and payments is presented in Figure 17.4 which depicts the information flows and geographic locations. In essence the system is very simple. Each week the clearing centre collects from each Motorola netting entity (factory) a transaction file detailing payments to suppliers and a vendor database via the mainframe in Chicago. The treasury function in London controls the netting system from the mainframe, collects the data by closing system access, proceeds with the foreign exchange transactions, initiates payment orders and finally advises Motorola companies of their net position.

After netting incomings with outgoings and combining common currencies, an approximate foreign exchange position is reached in which surplus currencies are sold and deficit currencies are bought. The

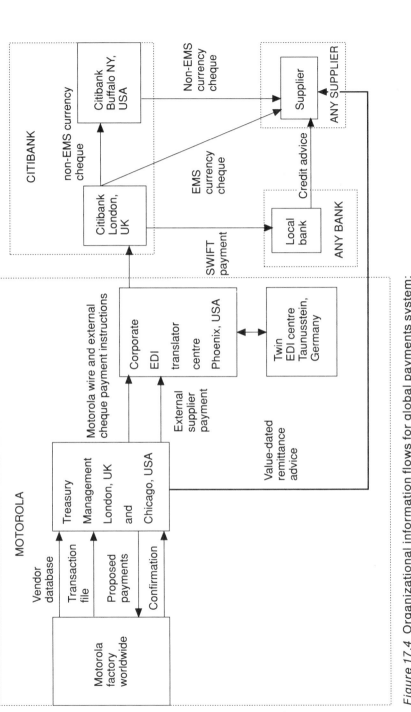

*Figure 17.4* Organizational information flows for global payments system: Motorola/Citibank

transaction value is approximately $US100 million per week. Two first tier banks and one from a pool of other banks are asked to quote for the foreign exchange dealings.

For external payments, better control is required because mistakes are more difficult and expensive to rectify. Therefore, before payment instructions are sent to Citibank each Motorola factory controller must sign electronically (on-line) all payments to external suppliers before the payments can proceed. The factory controller can amend or delete payments and retains all responsibility for the accuracy of the payment instructions. Costs of mistakes, principally unnecessary foreign exchange dealings, are borne by the individual netting entities. Therefore the central treasury function is in essence acting as an international bank.

There are three main classes of payment:

1 Electronic payments to Motorola companies.
2 Cheque payments for less than $US7,000 in value to external suppliers.
3 Electronic bank transfer payments over $US7,000 in value to external suppliers.

Payment orders (wire and cheques) are sent direct to Citibank London via the EDI corporate centre in Phoenix. Citibank then translates the EDIFACT messages into SWIFT (Society for Worldwide International Funds Transfer) and generates two types of file, wire transfer and cheque. Wire transfer payments use the SWIFT network. For cheque payments (less than $US7,000) Citibank uses 'Worldlink', an application developed by Citibank to generate cheques off-site. Citibank's cheque generation systems are located in Buffalo, New York for US dollar payments and London for all other currencies. If the cheque is payment for more than four invoices then the remittance advice is printed separately and sent with the cheque, each document referring to the other. Otherwise, remittance advice is printed directly onto the cheque. Payments to Motorola companies are all sent by bank transfers. (Motorola companies have already received by electronic message pre-notice advice of payments before the Thursday value date.)

External supplier payments are slightly more complex. Details of supplier payments and remittance advices are sent to the corporate EDI centre in Phoenix (Arizona) for translation into an EDIFACT format. This acts as an electronic gateway for all EDI messages from Motorola to its trading partners and vice versa. The payments details and EDIFACT standard remittance advices (PAYEXT) are then transmitted to Citibank London. SWIFT standards are used by Citibank to effect the payment through the international banking system and the remittance advice is sent separately and directly by Motorola to the supplier using a predefined VAN. Suppliers wished to receive a direct remittance advice which includes the value date of the payment rather than use the SWIFT network as a conduit for receiving this information.

The payments system uses a variety of different computer networks to support the sharing of data and software between Motorola companies, its trading partners, Citibank and other banks involved in the cash supply chain. Communication between Motorola companies and the Motorola central treasury management function is via an internal electronic mail system composed of three sub-systems covering the Central, Mountain and Pacific area time zones. Motorola's treasury management function uses a dial-up line to access Citibank's Global Telecommunications Network. The corporate EDI centre is connected to Citibank London via a VAN, which is also used to transmit remittance data to suppliers. Data security is ensured through the use of data encryption techniques and contingency/recovery plans are built into the system by mirroring all the activities of the Phoenix corporate EDI centre in Taunusstein, Germany. Citibank uses its own global network to transfer payment details between its branches and the SWIFT network to communicate with other banks to effect electronic bank transfer payments. A variety of different VANs are used to communicate the remittance advice to Motorola's suppliers. These are chosen by the suppliers and include AT&T, GEIS, Istel's INS and IBM's IIN.

## IMPLEMENTATION ISSUES

The high level of technical competency in both organizations meant that there were few technical difficulties with the project. However, there were several organizational issues that needed to be overcome for the project to progress beyond the concept stage. The traditional relationship between international treasuries and banks is often adversarial and primarily price-driven. It is common for US treasuries to tender their international business on a regular basis. Payment services are viewed as a commodity with a high level of service as given. In this context it was difficult for the US treasury group in Motorola to appreciate the difficulties and relatively high cost of moving funds across borders in Europe because of the relative simplicity and low cost of moving funds across the USA.

The largest delays in the project were in obtaining the intial buy-in within the Motorola organization. One generic issue here is that it is often very difficult for a project manager within a large multinational to identify for a project such as international payments all of the relevant decision makers that can impact on a large cross-section of the organization. In summary the momentum and visibility of the project were maintained only as a result of the efforts of key individuals in both companies who co-operated with each other and developed a relationship based on trust.

## KEY RESULTS

The key results are concerned with cash supply chains, financial relationships in business markets and strategy evolution. It can be seen that cash flows are being brought into line with product flows. The co-ordinating mechanisms to achieve this centre around the transparency of information from the transaction file and vendor database of the payer through to the supplier. It has been achieved largely through co-operation between a global manufacturer, a global bank and suppliers to Motorola.

The payments systems described in this study would be very difficult to implement with a group of national banks or with adversarial-style supplier relationships. It depends critically on organizations which expect to work closely with each other, i.e. they have a strong basis for trust and share common needs.

Motorola's cash management strategy has evolved over a long period of time, has delivered significant cost savings and is now being exploited strategically in the enhancement of supplier relationships. The cost savings are direct financial savings associated with reduced foreign exchange dealings and administrative savings associated with the streamlining of the treasury function which are perhaps worth considerably more but are difficult to measure accurately.

Co-operation between Motorola and Citibank has enabled a better payment system to be developed. It is therefore difficult to separate out individual firm strategies as Motorola and Citibank each benefit from the other's resources and expertise. This can be described as a co-operative strategy to streamline the cash supply chain from customer to supplier. Both organizations see themselves in global terms and provide worldwide services. They speak in a similar language.

Information systems form the backbone of the cash management strategy but any problems being encountered now are organizational rather than technical. The technology is not presenting significant problems and the limiting factor on implementation is the ability of the organization to learn and adapt to new treasury management ideas. Central to the implementation are resources for education and training for Motorola companies and their suppliers.

## NOTES

1 © C. Holland and G. Lockett 1995

This case study has been written as a basis for class discussion rather than to illustrate effective or ineffective managerial or administrative behaviour.

2  For a glossary of terms and acronyms used in this case study, see Appendix 1.

3  J. E. Short and N. Venkatraman, (1992) 'Beyond Business Process Redesign: redefining Baxter's business network', *Sloan Management Review*, Fall, 34(1), 7–21.

## APPENDIX 1: GLOSSARY OF TERMS AND ACRONYMS

| | |
|---|---|
| EDI: | electronic data interchange; the exchange of information across organizational boundaries using information technology. |
| IOS: | inter-organizational system; shared information system between two or more organizations. |
| TQM: | total quality management; a management philosophy which focuses on ensuring that all business processes are designed to ensure that quality is built into the end product/service rather than a more traditional approach of inspecting the output of a business process such as a production system. |
| Six Sigma Quality: | a statistical technique often used in conjunction with TQM philosophy which measures the number of failures per population of a product or service. The objective is to measure and continuously improve the performance of a product or management activity so that the number of faults per million is over six standard deviations from the norm which equates to approximately three to four or less product/process failures per million, which is effectively zero faults. |
| MRP: | manufacturing resource planning |
| SWIFT: | Society for Worldwide International Funds Transfer |
| EDIFACT: | European Standards Organization for EDI |
| DELFOR: | delivery forecast data standard |
| GEIS: | general electric information systems |
| VAN: | value added network |
| PAYEXT: | extended payment message which includes payment details and remittance advice |

# Chapter 18

# Honda Motors: a complex, paradoxical approach to growth

*Andrew Mair*

## EDITORS' OVERVIEW[1]

Honda is one of the great success stories of the post-war Japanese economy. Established in 1948, since the 1970s Honda has been widely recognized as a pioneering Japanese manufacturer and as one of the world's leading motor industry companies. Honda was the first Japanese manufacturer to make its products in Europe, when its Belgian motor-cycle factory opened in 1963. Honda became the first Japanese firm to manufacture automobiles in North America when it opened its Ohio assembly plant in 1982. Honda took the risk of entering into a long and complex relationship during the 1980s with a European company universally considered to be one of the least capable automobile manufacturers in the West, British Leyland (now Rover Group).

In the global automobile industry, Honda's achievements on the technology front are well recognized, ranging from its cutting-edge low pollution and low fuel consumption engine technologies to its achievement in powering World Champion Formula 1 racing cars for six years in a row during the 1980s. In 1989 the company's founder, Soichiro Honda, became the first Japanese to be accepted into Detroit's symbolic Automotive Industry Hall of Fame.

It is perhaps not surprising that examples of strategic management practice at Honda became widely quoted in the management literature during the 1980s. An undoubtedly successful firm was attracting the attention it deserved. But was that success a result of good management or was it due to a series of fortunate coincidences?[2] One problem with the way Honda has been analysed in the management literature is that its management innovations have been treated as a series of isolated stories frequently described in only a few sentences, and seemingly brought forth to justify or legitimate this or that new theory.

Is there anything more fundamental, more deep-seated, that underlies Honda's recognized proclivity for innovative and pioneering management strategies? This case study suggests that there is.

## Dualist puzzle solving: a method for innovative strategic thinking?

Underlying Honda's innovative strategic management, it is claimed, lies a process called 'dualist puzzle solving'. To see how it seems to work, consider the dozens of dichotomous categories that pervade management thinking and permeate all aspects and functions. There are dichotomies in buyer-supplier relations (e.g. vertical integration and market relationships), work organization (e.g. efficient and humane), product development processes (e.g. sequential and simultaneous development), and business strategy (e.g. cost and differentiation), to name but a few.

Why are these dichotomies important? Strangely, although we can come up with lists of them, few western managers consider them to be of any significance. And yet if we were to consider them as paradoxes or *puzzles that implicitly require to be solved*, we would discover a novel method for developing new ideas about traditional management problems.

The traditional, ingrained and implicit solution to dualist puzzles in the West has been twofold:

1  Assume a trade-off between them: hence, to take the example of the group-individual dichotomy, to gain the advantages of individualism it is necessary to sacrifice some of the benefits of the group, and vice versa.

2  Conceive of change management in terms of switching from one dichotomized – and mutually exclusive – pole to the other. Any attempt to sit in the middle, (trying to keep elements of both group- and individual-oriented organizational forms, for instance) has been thought of as 'muddling through', ending up with 'the worst of both worlds'.

If these ways of thinking seem self-evidently true to many in the West, to Honda they do not. The case study examines Honda's very different way of thinking.

## An example: 'right-first-time' or 'build in quality'

To illustrate the Honda approach, let us look at a very significant instance of the thought process that characterizes dualist puzzle solving and observe how it works. This example is well understood in Japan (it was not invented by Honda) and has also increasingly been accepted by many western managers in recent years.

Western management thinking has traditionally assumed trade-offs between product quality, cost and delivery: high quality cost more and took longer; low cost meant low quality too; fast delivery cost more and risked low quality. But the Japanese-developed 'right-first-time' principle inherent in the 'just-in-time' production system has revealed that there are better solutions to these dualist puzzles. By focusing on how to 'build in quality' to products rather than 'test in quality' afterwards, it is possible to reduce costs (less waste and downtime) and to rationalize production with minimal stocks, hence reducing delivery lead times too.

This example involves a strategic approach to manufacturing, and it has widespread ramifications for marketing, product positioning and competitive strategy. Yet significant as the example is, it has been taken up almost in isolation in the West. Few realize that it represents just one example of a wholly different way of strategic thinking rather than a solution to one particular management problem. There are many more dualist puzzles waiting to be discovered and solved, thereby providing innovative impetus to strategic thinking across the range of management functions. This case study of Honda lets the reader explore some of these dualisms and evaluate their implications.

## Discussion questions

- How would you characterize Honda's strategy in the world car market? How successful has Honda been?
- Is there a single 'model' of approach that Honda seems to apply to resolve implicit dualist puzzles, or does it adopt different paths to innovative solutions?
- Does the case provide evidence that the Japanese think explicitly in terms of dichotomies and how to resolve dualist puzzles? Or, does it merely impose a 'western intellectual framework' to interpret Honda's practice? Would the latter be justified to communicate the ideas to a western audience? Indeed, is this what Honda itself has done?
- Discuss the application of this approach to other well-known dichotomies in strategic management processes, for example, planning versus implementation; positioning approaches versus capabilities approaches; rational versus emergent strategies; top-down versus bottom-up strategies; the role of context versus the role of choice in strategy formulation and decision-making; low cost strategies versus differentiation strategies.

## List of named characters[3]

Soichiro Honda, founded company 1948; retired 1973
Takeo Fujisawa, joined company 1949, in effect business manager, leaving Soichiro Honda free to concentrate on engineering and product strategy; retired 1973
Kiyoshi Kawashima, joined company 1947, before it was officially

formed; ran works motor racing teams in 1960s; company president, 1973–83

Tadashi Kume, joined company 1953; ran works motor racing teams in 1960s; principal engineer in design and development of Life and Civic models; company president, 1983–90

Nobuhiko Kawamoto, joined company 1963; consecutively chief engineer, director and president of Honda R&D, 1970–91; company president and CEO, 1991–

**Keywords**

Global strategy; technology strategy; new product development; managing complexity; paradoxical thinking; dualist puzzle solving; supply chain architecture; work organization; structures and culture

By following a corporate policy that stresses originality and innovation in every facet of its operations – from product development and manufacturing to marketing – Honda has striven to attain its goal of satisfying its customers.

*(Honda Annual Report*, 1994: i)

## NOBUHIKO KAWAMOTO'S REFORMS

Shortly after taking office as company president in 1991, Nobuhiko Kawamoto introduced significant reforms to the top management structure of the Honda Motor Co., the Japan-based manufacturer of cars, motorcycles and power products like lawnmowers and small boat engines.

Since the 1973 retirement of the joint company founders, inventive engineer Soichiro Honda and financial mastermind Takeo Fujisawa, during their company's 25th anniversary year, Honda had become well known in the business world for the collective decision-making process utilized by its top executives, a process in which few of them seemed to have clear individual responsibilities. The collective process was symbolized in the physical layout of the Honda headquarters 'board room', in which none of the executives had their own offices, but instead shared an open space where there were not only individual desks but also various areas for them to meet, sit and talk together.

There was no doubt that Kawamoto's new ideas were significant. He established a clear hierarchy at executive level, with two leading executives joining him to form an innermost leadership circle. He also announced that executives could have private offices if they so wished. Moreover, Honda's global management structure was reorganized with clear and direct lines of responsibility to the top management group.

Kawamoto's reforms made front page news in the western business press. The *Wall Street Journal* ran the headline 'Just as U.S. Firms Try Japanese Management, Honda is Centralizing: Kawamoto Finds "Teamwork" Is No Longer Enough To Boost Market Share: Coming Soon: Private Offices'.[5] *Fortune* followed suit, with 'A U.S.-Style Shakeup at Honda: CEO Kawamoto has abandoned consensus management for American-looking organization charts. Result: Communications and decision-making are getting faster'.[6] As far as strategic decision making was concerned, the clear impression given was that Honda's penchants for *groupism* and *horizontal communication* were on the way out, with *individualism* and *vertical structure* the order of the new day. Apparently a Japanese company with a particularly Japanese management style had now decided that a western style was superior after all.

But was this interpretation valid? Was Honda a firm whose strategic management decision making switched from a collectivist mode to an individualist mode? In fact, the true picture is rather different, and the view presented in the western business press is, arguably, uninformed.

The joint board room had actually been set up in the mid-1960s by Takeo Fujisawa, who saw it as an adjunct structure to Soichiro Honda's highly individualistic style, a means of encouraging executives to talk about problems and solutions with each other, and to prepare younger managers for the day the founders would retire. In other words, the organizational structure to promote collective decision making existed *alongside* the individualist Honda (who is said once to have hit an engineer over the head with a spanner to drive home a point!).

Kawamoto's changes were only one of a series of periodic reorganizations at Honda. When Honda and Fujisawa retired in 1973, new president Kiyoshi Kawashima shifted Honda further towards a collective decision-making mode with the wide-ranging committee structure that he set up. When Tadashi Kume in turn succeeded Kawashima as president in 1983, he too instituted his own changes. Thus each new president has deliberately sent a shock wave of reorganization (of interrelationships as much as of people) through the firm. Indeed Kawamoto was by no means dispensing with collective decision making; what he was doing was injecting a strong dose of individual responsibility into the existing framework.

Kawamoto's changes are best interpreted less as a switch to a new type of structure, as the western press had it, from one pole of a dichotomy to another, than as a change in emphasis. A useful way to visualize this process is to think of the organization as a sailing ship sailing on a narrow tack against the wind, progressing in a zig-zag fashion, first towards individualism and vertical structure, then back towards collectivism and horizontal structure, then back again. All the while, the ship moves forward despite sailing against the wind, as each tack builds on the achievements of the last, despite the apparently dramatic changes of direction (Figure 18.1).

## HONDA'S STRATEGIC SUCCESSES

Honda's approach to the individual–group dichotomy in the strategic decision-making process is exemplary of Honda's approach to strategic problems. Indeed Honda is well known in the literature on strategic management for its capacity to innovate and surprise. A number of stories illustrating the innovative strategies behind Honda's rise to global prominence in the 1970s and 1980s have been told and retold in the management literature, and they well illustrate Honda's considerable achievements:

- When faced with great difficulty making inroads into the North

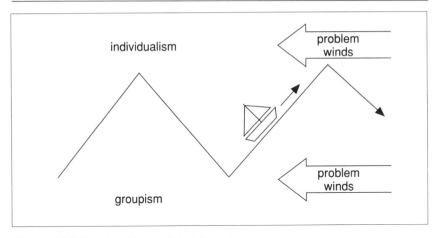

*Figure 18.1* The 'tacking ship' vision of progress

American motorcycle market it was accident and idiosyncrasy rather than long-term planning that catalysed the success of Honda mopeds in the USA.

- Honda redefined the American motorcycle market in the early 1960s with its 'You meet the nicest people on a Honda' marketing campaign.
- When faced with rival Kawasaki's plans to compete in the Japanese motorcycle market during the 1970s Honda accelerated its new product development plans and launched so many new products that it swamped the competition.
- When faced with American proposals in the early 1970s to curb polluting emissions from automobiles, Honda engineers created the radical new 'CVCC' internal combustion engine which easily met the new guidelines, even as the 'Big Three' US producers, General Motors, Ford and Chrysler, were claiming that the new standards were impossible to meet.
- Honda has built up 'core competencies' in engine design and manufacture which are leveraged into competitive advantage across the focused range of products that Honda manufactures and sells: motorcycles, cars and power products like lawnmowers and small boat engines.
- Honda has developed parallel 'core capabilities', business processes which enable it to meet customer demands as exactly as possible.
- Honda's 'SED' (Sales–Engineering–Development) simultaneous development process for new products has allowed it to cut new automobile development time to two to three years and to regularly replace its models every four years, compared with North American and European norms of eight to ten years.

| 1946 | Soichiro Honda sets up Honda Technical Research Institute in Hamamatsu, producing auxiliary engines for bicycles, and later, machine tools |
|------|---|
| 1948 | Company renamed Honda Motor Co. Ltd. First production Honda vehicle, 90cc B-type motorcycle |
| 1952 | Exports begin (to Philippines) |
| 1954 | Soichiro Honda visits European car manufacturers. First exports (of 200cc K-type 'Juno' scooter) to USA |
| 1955 | Honda becomes largest Japanese motorcycle manufacturer |
| 1959 | American Honda Motor Co. Inc. [sales subsidiary] established |
| 1961 | European Honda GmbH (now Honda Deutschland GmbH) [sales subsidiary] established in Hamburg |
| 1962 | NV Honda Motor SA (now Honda Belgium NV) established to assemble and sell mopeds in Europe (production begins 1963) [the first manufacturing facility opened by any Japanese company in the West] |
| 1963 | T360 lightweight truck and S360 sports car, first Honda 4-wheeled vehicles, go on sale |
| 1965 | Honda UK Ltd [sales subsidiary] established in London |
| 1968 | First exports of N360 and N600 microcars. Cumulative motorcycle production passes 10 million |
| 1971 | CVCC low emission automobile engine announced |
| 1972 | First generation Civic automobile introduced |
| 1973 | Soichiro Honda and Takeo Fujisawa retire to become Supreme Advisors |
| 1976 | First generation Accord announced. Civic production reaches 1 million after four years |
| 1977 | IAP Industriale SpA (now Honda Italia Industriale SpA) established in Italy [subsidiary to manufacture motorcycles] |
| 1978 | Honda of America Manufacturing Inc. set up to make motorcycles in the USA (production begins 1979). Cumulative production of motorcycles exceeds 30 million. Cumulative car production exceeds 5 million. |
| 1979 | Company signs technical collaboration with British Leyland, [now Rover Group], covering BL production of Triumph Acclaim car (production in the United Kingdom begins 1981) [first of several joint car developments between the firms lasting until late 1990s] |
| 1982 | European Head Office established in Belgium. Honda of America begins car production |
| 1984 | Plans to double Honda of America car manufacturing capacity to 300,000 units/year. Honda Research of America (now Honda R&D North America) established |
| 1985 | Plans announced to double car production in Canada from 40,000 to 80,000 cars/year |
| 1986 | Honda of America begins engine manufacture |
| 1988 | Plans accounced for second US car assembly plant. VTEC variable valve timing system principle announced. Plans announced to build R&D centre in Europe |
| 1989 | Soichiro Honda inducted into America's Automotive Hall of Fame [as first Japanese]; Honda Accord becomes best-selling automobile model in the USA |
| 1990 | Agreement with Rover under which Honda acquires minority shareholding in Rover. Accord Aerodeck becomes the first American-built car model to be exported both to Japan and to Europe |
| 1992 | European production of Honda Accord begins at Swindon, United Kingdom |
| 1994 | Honda unwinds formal relationship with Rover as BMW purchases Rover from its parent company; announcement of further investments in North America to take annual production capacity from 600,000 to 800,000 by 1999, with 150,000 of these vehicles exported |

*Figure 18.2* Significant milestones in Honda's development
*Source: Honda European Information Handbook*, 1991–2 and Honda Annual Reports

**Product range**

|  | Annual unit sales ('000s) | Percentage of sales by value |
|---|---|---|
| Motorcycles | 4,169 | 14.2 |
| Automobiles | 1,753 | 78.5 |
| Power products* | 1,714 | 7.3 |

Note: * General purpose engines, tillers, portable generators, outboard motors, lawnmowers, etc.

**Focus on internal combustion engines**
Honda produced just under 8 million internal combustion engines world-wide in 1992–3, or about 30,000 per day.

**Regional sales breakdown by value (percentage)**

| Japan | 33 |
|---|---|
| North America | 43 |
| Europe | 11 |
| Others | 13 |

**Factories**
Honda has a wide international production network, with 83 production facilities in forty countries.

**Employees**
Honda directly employs 91,300 people, approximately one-third of them in Japan.

*Figure 18.3* Snapshot of Honda activities, 1994
*Source:* Honda Annual Report 1993–4

These creative and innovative actions and processes have enabled Honda's rapid growth to global presence (Figures 18.2, 18.3 and Table 18.1). By the late 1980s, only twenty-five years after the firm entered the automobile industry, the 'industry of industries', Honda had become one of the world's top ten producers. Indeed, automobile production had come to dominate Honda's activities, responsible for nearly four-fifths of its turnover. By the early 1990s Honda also stood head and shoulders above other leading automobile producers in international sales (with 73 per cent of its sales by volume outside its home market region), and stood third behind Ford and General Motors (with their long-standing European presence) in international production, with a still-growing 38 per cent of its manufacturing output by volume outside its home market region (Table 18.2). Across its range of products, Honda now has 83 production facilities in forty countries.

In Japan, Honda remains a relatively small player, with market share

Table 18.1 Growth of Honda's worldwide automobile production 1960–95

| Year | Automobiles/light trucks ('000 units) |
|---|---|
| 1960 | 0 |
| 1965 | 52 |
| 1970 | 393 |
| 1975 | 414 |
| 1980 | 957 |
| 1985 | 1,363 |
| 1990 | 1,928 |
| 1995* | 1,797 |

Source: Honda Annual Reports, Japan Automobile Manufacturers Association
Note: * Honda projection

consistently under 10 per cent, on a par with Mazda and Mitsubishi, not far ahead of Daihatsu and Suzuki. But from a global perspective, Honda's early and rapid internationalization, first of sales during the 1970s, then of production during the 1980s, propelled the company spectacularly out of the ranks of mid-sized Japanese automobile producers to a status alongside Toyota and Nissan as one of the global Japanese 'Big Three' automobile producers. And Honda is now significantly more international than either Toyota or Nissan in both sales and production. Continued growth of sales and production during the first half of the 1990s was hindered – as in the early 1970s – by world recession. But the geographical spread of Honda's activities meant that, unlike most of its Japanese competitors, the firm was able to sustain profitability right through the post-'bubble economy' slump in the Japanese economy during the early 1990s (Table 18.3).

## DUALIST PUZZLE SOLVING AT HONDA

What, however, underlies and propels the individual strategic achievements and Honda's rapid growth to global presence? The answer, it appears, is that Honda has systematically implemented a dualist puzzle-solving approach to resolving some of the great dilemmas of twentieth-century management.

The word 'dualist' refers to the traditional dichotomous categories used in the West as an underlying framework to think about management. Thus in the case of Kawamoto's reforms, there is, first, the collective (or group) versus the individual, and second, vertical structure and horizontal structure. 'Puzzle solving' in this context refers to an approach in which the two poles are somehow (and that is the puzzle) reconciled with each other.

Table 18.2 Honda in global context

| Firm | 1992 Production | Geographical division of production (%) | | | | Geographical division of sales (%) | | | |
|---|---|---|---|---|---|---|---|---|---|
| | | North America | Europe | Japan | Others | North America | Europe | Japan | Others |
| Ford | 4,109 | 48.1 | 36.0 | — | 15.8 | 48.3 | 36.8 | 0.1 | 14.8 |
| General Motors | 5,053 | 57.9 | 33.6 | — | 8.5 | 63.1 | 33.0 | 0.1 | 3.9 |
| Honda | 1,721 | 32.7 | 1.9 | 62.0 | 3.4 | 49.6 | 10.2 | 27.1 | 13.1 |
| Nissan | 2,316 | 12.7 | 7.7 | 75.6 | 4.0 | 23.3 | 18.7 | 38.2 | 19.7 |
| Toyota | 4,097 | 10.1 | — | 77.4 | 12.5 | 20.3 | 8.2 | 38.4 | 33.0 |
| Volkswagen/Audi | 3,291 | 5.3 | 84.4 | — | 10.3 | 7.8 | 71.7 | 1.3 | 19.2 |
| Fiat | 2,001 | — | 73.7 | — | 26.3 | 0.2 | 80.1 | 0.2 | 19.5 |
| Renault | 1,761 | — | 90.2 | — | 9.8 | — | 81.3 | 0.1 | 18.6 |
| PSA (Peugeot) | 1,842 | — | 98.4 | — | 1.6 | — | 89.1 | 0.3 | 10.5 |
| BMW | 598 | — | 100.0 | — | — | 11.7 | 73.9 | 4.8 | 9.6 |
| Mercedes-Benz | 542 | — | 100.0 | — | — | 12.3 | 75.6 | 5.5 | 6.6 |

Source: Adapted from calculations by Marie-Claude Bélis-Bergouignan, Gérard Bordenave and Yannick Lung, 'Les stratégies globales: une mise en perspective des trajectoires des constructeurs automobiles', paper presented to the Second International Meeting of GERPISA-International, Paris, June 1994.

*Table 18.3* Honda's recent financial performance

| Fiscal year* | Net sales + other revenue (¥bn) | Net income as a proportion of sales (%) | Research and development (¥bn) |
|---|---|---|---|
| 1985 | 2,740 | 4.7 | 114 |
| 1986 | 3,009 | 4.9 | 135 |
| 1987 | 2,961 | 2.8 | 150 |
| 1988 | 3,229 | 3.1 | 164 |
| 1989 | 3,489 | 2.8 | 184 |
| 1990 | 3,853 | 2.1 | 186 |
| 1991 | 4,302 | 1.8 | 194 |
| 1992 | 4,391 | 1.4 | 192 |
| 1993 | 4,132 | 0.9 | 199 |
| 1994 | 3,863 | 0.6 | 189 |

*Note:* *Ends 28 February up to 1987, 31 March from 1988. Fiscal year therefore includes 9 or 10 months of previous calendar year. Figures for 1988 are author's estimate for comparative purposes, based on 12/13 of previous 13 months.

All yen conversions are at then-current exchange rates. During the above period, the value of the US dollar declined from 251 yen in February 1985 to 103 yen in March 1994. During the same period, Honda's unit automobile sales in North America remained roughly constant, proportionately, at approximately half of worldwide Honda sales.

The way in which Kawamoto 'changed tacks' from a group-based to an individual-based trajectory (not structure) is a classic example of dualist puzzle solving, Honda-style. Honda's strategic thinking rejects the typical western simple trade-off and emphatically rejects the typical western idea that failure to select clearly one or the other pole leads to indecision. Honda's solution to the group–individual dichotomy and the horizontal–vertical dichotomy is to progress flexibly with a 'tacking' motion along a well-defined and fairly narrow path. In other words, the puzzle solution sought is always one which incorporates 'the best of both worlds' (Figure 18.4).

The refusal to accept static trade-offs, and the rejection of any obligation to choose one pole or the other, lie behind many of Honda's strategic innovations.[7] The process can be seen at work across a wide range of activities at Honda, and constitute the hallmark of its strategic innovation.

## Organizational process: competition and the individual

Let us take a closer look at how the individual–group dichotomy is played out at Honda. Honda has a remarkable penchant for praising the successes of individual employees and for encouraging a sense of competi-

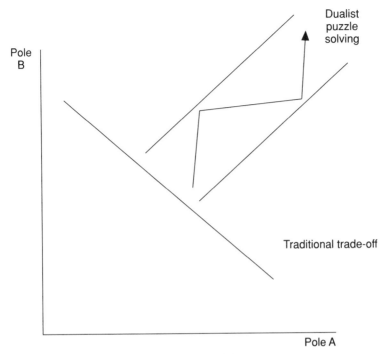

*Figure 18.4* Visualizing dualist puzzle solving

tion among them. Company-wide quality circle (called NH Circles; for New, Now, Next Honda) competitions have focused on the achievements of individual people (albeit, characteristically, working in small groups). Within Honda R&D, the subsidiary company that develops Honda products, competitive and individual-based basic research activities deliberately foster individual inventiveness. The competitive nature of employee suggestion schemes at Honda's North American operations, with awards given to annual 'winners', also fosters individualism.

In similar vein, individual managers remain closely associated with the projects and products for which they have been responsible; Tadashi Kume was lauded as the principal engineer behind the Life and Civic automobiles. Kawamoto has been known as 'Mr NSX' after the aluminium-bodied super-sports car Honda developed in the late 1980s, and he was also associated with Honda's 1980's successes on the Grand Prix racing circuit.

What is most interesting, however, is that individualism and competition are not stressed *over and above* loyalty and co-operation: each 'pole' within the individual–group dichotomy is a tendency that 'has its place' in a way that maximizes the contribution each can make, while minimizing any negative impacts of overemphasis on either individual or group. Hence alongside the stress on individual achievement can be observed the promotion of group processes: collective decision-making, in the corporate board room for instance; team working, the tight and disciplined co-operation of the various people involved in F-1 racing being communicated as a model of behaviour for all employees; and interdepartmental co-operation in the product development process, which is organized into highly co-operative 'SED' (Sales–Engineering–Development) teams that are explicitly differentiated from the individualist and competitive character of the basic research process.

## Organizational structure

A classic dichotomy in organizational structures is between vertical and horizontal structures. Recently many consultants have been advising large companies to dispense with vertical, hierarchical structures in favour of process-oriented horizontal linkages. Indeed a driving force behind reform of organizational structure at Honda has been the avoidance of 'big business disease'. In the Honda view, when a company grows bigger and adopts overly-rigid vertical structures of organizational control, it can lose the small-firm vitality and the horizontal linkages and communication that are so vital to innovation and dynamism.

At Honda there are regular drives to battle 'big business disease'. But significantly, these take place within, rather than replacing, a strongly hierarchical structural framework. Thus after he became Honda President in 1983, Tadashi Kume launched a series of initiatives to prevent bureaucratic structures from hardening. These included round-table meetings between executives and first-line supervisors to cut across layers of vertical hierarchy, regular round-table meetings between executives and middle-level managers, and the encouragement of 'diagonal' linkages whereby manufacturing managers, for instance, held discussions to share viewpoints with front-line sales staff.

In similar vein, strategic thinking about the career paths of individuals has been woven into organizational thinking to keep structure flexible and innovative. Honda's 'expert' system, developed during the 1950s and 1960s, allows technical experts to be promoted in a clearly vertical fashion without having to enter the ranks of management, on the grounds that the latter would be a sure-fire route to poor lower-level management since many technical experts desire promotion but do not actually want to manage other people. Moreover, managers can follow diagonal promotion paths (simultaneous vertical and horizontal moves). An example is the marketing manager who was put in charge of expanding one of Honda's North American factories in the late 1980s. One advantage Honda gained from this appointment was that manufacturing and engineering staff were obliged to be very clear about what they were doing and began to question taken-for-granted procedures.

Honda has pursued web-like organizational forms mixing group and individual processes, vertical and horizontal structures, and formal and informal relationships and positions to the point that it is wellnigh impossible for anyone entering the firm from outside to understand precisely what Honda's organizational structure is.

## Is Honda a 'Japanese' firm?

One dichotomy pervasive in the western management literature is the grand division between western firms and management methods, on the one hand, and Japanese firms and methods on the other hand. Many management theorists and practitioners have held to the idea that Japanese firms are fundamentally different from western firms: whether in organizational structures, company cultures, labour relations, inter-firm relationships, manufacturing systems, work organization, or marketing strategies. Analysts created a 'Japanese model' of management diametrically opposed, in classic dualist fashion, to the western model. Their argument was that adherence to this Japanese model explained much of Japan's economic successes during the 1970s and 1980s (Figure 18.5).

It may therefore seem strange even to pose the question of whether Honda can be considered a 'Japanese' firm. But remember that only one-third of Honda's turnover now derives from Japan, and the company runs over eighty manufacturing facilities throughout the world, nearly all of them outside Japan. The crux of the issue, however, is whether Honda is actually managed in a 'Japanese' way. Many assume that it must be, given its roots in a country with a particularly strong and unique culture. And yet Japanese analysts agree that Honda does not easily fit the 'Japanese model'. In Japan Honda has deliberately set out to counter what it views as negative traits of 'Japanese-ness'. It deliberately stresses decentralized management structures, praises the achievements of individuals, makes merit the key to promotion, and awards responsibility to younger employees: all this in a Japanese society founded on centralization, collective decision making and responsibility, status and seniority, and respect for elders. The point to grasp is that Honda has struggled to overcome the innovation-deadening impacts of these cultural forces. Soichiro Honda himself has been the model, portrayed as exemplary of an individualist who cared nothing for the position of his supposed 'betters', deliberately crossed status barriers, and promoted younger individuals across seniority levels. The result is that in Japan Honda is commonly viewed as a peculiarly 'un-Japanese' firm.

Thus Honda has injected so-called western attributes into the way it

| 'Western' model | 'Japanese' model |
|---|---|
| **Overall description** | |
| Mass | Lean |
| Mass | Flexible |
| Standardized | Flexible |
| Fordist | Post-Fordist |
| **Work process** | |
| Taylorist | Post-Taylorist |
| Do workers | Think workers |
| Unskilled | Polyvalent |
| **Production organization and logistics** | |
| Large-lot production | Small-lot production |
| Just-in-case | Just-in-time |
| Push system | Pull system |
| **Organization** | |
| Vertical | Horizontal |
| Fragmented duties | Broad duties |
| Individual as responsible | Group as responsible |
| **Labour relations** | |
| Job control focus | Employment conditions focus |
| Cross-company unions | Enterprise unions |
| Hire and fire | Job-for-life |
| **Industry organization** | |
| Separated firms | *Keiretsu* families |
| Distant inter-firm relations | Close inter-firm relations |

*Figure 18.5* The 'Japanese management model' seen as diametrically opposed to the 'western management model'

functions, which co-exist with the 'Japanese' features that employees bring with them – the results of their upbringing in Japan – as they enter the firm. Rather than pursuing a 'Japanese model' distinct from a 'western model', the big picture reveals Honda's innovation to be its simultaneous incorporation of both models so as to work consciously and deliberately with elements of each: precisely what we saw earlier in Kawamoto's reforms.

## Product strategy: guiding the technology development process

A recognized source of competitive advantage for Honda has been its 'core competence' in the advanced internal combustion engines which power the whole range of its products. But Honda's product strength goes far deeper: a dualist puzzle-solving approach characterizes both the *mental process* of technology research and the *philosophy* behind the actual product designs. The technology and design features of Honda products are the embodiments of successful dualist puzzle solutions which deliver direct and immediate competitive advantage.

The classic example of Honda's technology is the CVCC (compound vortex controlled combustion) engine, designed during the 1969–71 period. Indeed the CVCC engine is used within the firm to represent and communicate Honda's approach to technology. The compromise tackled and overcome by the CVCC engine was widely accepted in the world's automobile industry, namely a trade-off among the various pollutants emitted from internal combustion engines. According to the traditional view, attempts to reduce emissions of one chemical inevitably led to increases in others. The only way out of the dilemma, it was believed, was to add a process (e.g. catalytic conversion) to clean up the pollutants after combustion.

Honda engineers proceeded from the assumption that it would be more rational not to create pollutants in the first place than to have to clean them up. The CVCC engine design therefore denied the taken-for-granted compromises. The technical solution was to place two connected combustion chambers in each cylinder. A fuel-thin mixture of fuel and air was injected into a main combustion chamber. A fuel-rich mixture was injected into a smaller chamber where the spark plug was located. When the spark ignited the mixture, combustion spread from the smaller to the main chamber, with the result that the fuel and oxygen burned more completely, and with less fuel used, compared to a conventional engine. Each of these characteristics helped reduce a different pollutant, resulting in an engine in which the old trade-offs were overcome (Figure 18.6).

The thinking embodied in the VTEC (variable valve timing and lift electronic control) family of engines that Honda first introduced in 1989 derives from a similar approach. The conventional dualism and associated trade-off tackled by the VTEC engines was fuel economy versus engine power; to improve fuel economy meant losing power. However, in the VTEC engine the innovative variable valves (the mechanisms which let fuel and air in and out of the combustion chamber), in conjunction with the electronically controlled fuel injection system, control the ratio of fuel to air according to driving conditions. In normal mode, a fuel-thin mixture provides fuel economy. But at high engine speeds with the driver's foot pressed hard on the accelerator a fuel-richer mixture provides significantly more power. Figure 18.7 illustrates both the performance–economy trade-off of Honda's conventional engines, and the dualist puzzle-solving leap achieved by VTEC engines in Honda Accord automobiles.

While in product terms Honda is perhaps best known for its technologically innovative engines, refusal to accept taken-for-granted trade-offs characterizes all aspects of Honda's strategic approach to technological

**Regular engine**
- Supply of a denser mixture of air and fuel decreases NOx but increases CO and HC.
- Supply of a thinner mixture of air and fuel decreases CO and HC but increases NOx.
- As the mixture grows thinner, NOx and CO will decrease but the engine may die.

**Sources of pollutants**
- The higher the temperature of the gas in the cylinder, the greater the amount of NOx emitted.
- The more quickly the temperature of the gas in the cylinder falls in the process of expansion, the greater the amount of unignited fuel emitted as HC.
- The greater the amount of dense fuel supplied, the greater the amount of CO emitted due to incomplete combustion

**Merits of CVCC engine**
- Decrease in NOx by lowering the maximum combustion temperature.
- Decrease in HC by prolonging the time the temperature of oxidation is maintained.
- Decrease in CO by supplying very thin mixed gas so as to make sufficient oxygen available.

*Figure 18.6* How the CVCC engine simultaneously reduced pollutants in a way previously thought impossible
*Source*: Setsuo Mito, *The Honda Book of Management: A Leadership Philosophy for High Industrial Success* (London: Kogan Page, 1990)

change. This is well illustrated in the revealing language used by a Honda engineer describing an apparently mundane technological advance made by Honda R&D at its North American operations (see Figure 18.8).

## Designing automobiles

In addition to its technologically innovative products, Honda's product development process is respected within the automobile industry for its sheer speed. During the 1970s and 1980s Honda led the Japanese automobile industry's drive to reduce development lead times: today automobiles are being manufactured only two years after launch of their development process. Until recently five to six years or longer was the norm in the West, and few manufacturers achieve better than three to four years.

Honda's speed has been attained in two ways. The first is its organizational approach to the product development process, based on the SED teams mentioned above. The SED teams work together on projects from start to finish, in contrast to the traditional sequential development

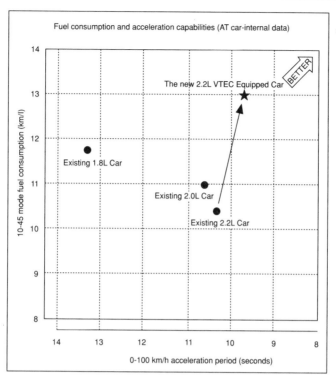

*Figure 18.7* The VTEC engine compared to the conventional fuel consumption–acceleration trade-off in the Honda Accord
*Source: Japan Autotech Report* (1993) 175: 23

process utilized in the West where each function makes its specialized input in turn (marketing, design, product engineering, production engineering and manufacturing).

The second is Honda's particular *model replacement* system. What is most significant about this system is the way it challenges an important dichotomy observed in the western automobile industry. This is between the 'complete model change', in which the whole design process starts from scratch with every component redesigned for a totally new automobile, and the 'facelift', in which only a small number of components are redesigned to give an older model a more modern image. As adherents of this dichotomous approach, for decades western automobile makers have made complete model changes perhaps every eight to ten years, and given facelifts to their models perhaps every two to four years.

Most Honda models are changed every four years. Thus new Honda Accords were introduced in 1981, 1985, 1989 and 1993, and new Civics in 1979, 1983, 1987 and 1991. Western automobile makers, wedded to

When it comes to weight reduction, the auto industry's appetite is insatiable. Honda is no exception.

As part of a corporate goal to reduce weight in its automobiles, Honda of America Manufacturing Inc. in Marysville, Ohio, is the first automaker in the United States to use a lightweight underbody coating, or sound deadener, with expanded polymeric microspheres supplied by Pierce & Stevens Corp. of Buffalo, N.Y.

Besides light weight, Honda sought several other attributes from any new underbody coating, including reduced volatile organic compound emissions and an improved durability standard.

Honda also wanted improved 'line-side workability' – the ease-of-use characteristics judged by those who work with the product on the production line.

In addition, the product could not require any modifications to the existing sound-deadener delivery and application systems.

It was a tall order, but according to Trish Peters, assistant manager of the Marysville plant's auto paint department, reformulations either meet all of Honda's standards or they aren't used at all.

'We aren't interested in trade-offs,' she said. 'We won't accept lesser performance in any aspect of a product to get improvement in some other aspect. Our sound-deadener suppliers – there are several – know this. They accepted our goals and came back to us with formulations that included polymeric microspheres – what we call "plastic balloons"' . . .

'We reduced the weight of the deadener by 30 to 40 percent,' said Lee Manville of the Marysville auto paint production staff. 'We got better adhesion of the product to the body surface and were able to reduce film build (the amount applied) while improving our durability standard' . . .

'We're satisfied with the performance of the reformulated sound deadener – for now,' said Peters. 'Honda has trained us not to make or accept assumptions about the performance of anything we use. Our department's goals – to improve existing materials and find new materials – are like our corporate goals to improve quality and drive down costs. They never end.'

*Figure 18.8* 'We aren't interested in trade-offs'
Source: Al Fleming, 'Honda switches to lighter underbody coating', *Automotive News*, 12 April 1993: 20.

their traditional approach, claimed that Honda was not 'properly' replacing models in these short cycles, but simply giving its models a cosmetic facelift.

Yet Honda's strategic approach to model replacement means that it does not face the same dichotomous choices. The process at Honda can be described schematically as follows.[8] Honda's model changes are neither complete changes nor mere facelifts. Instead, every four years, when a Honda model is 'officially' replaced, the components the driver can see or otherwise notice are replaced: the exterior body shape, the interior design, the lights. Then, also every four years with a two-year lag after the official model change, vital unseen components are changed, and new engines, gearboxes, braking systems, for instance, are introduced. The outcome is best described as a 'rolling' or 'iterative' model change programme with significant and regular changes to each model (and hence a regular boost to customer interest). The traditional distinction between complete change and facelift is dispensed with in favour of a smoother, more fluid and flexible approach. Manufacturing systems (for instance, sizes and shapes of machinery) and whole vehicle design configurations (for instance, sizes and shapes of components and the spaces they fit in) are pre-planned as far as possible to allow for the expected evolution of models and components.

This iterative process of model evolution is put into practice in three 'dimensions'. The first is over time, as described above. Thus the 1993 replacement for the Today model, sold in Japan, shared 40 per cent of its components with its predecessor. Second, it is practised laterally, in the development of parallel, 'sister' models for different market segments. The third dimension is geographical, in which models developed for different world markets are frequently spin-offs from existing models (neither entirely different, nor mere cosmetic changes). Hence both the Accord and Civic models that Honda was manufacturing in Europe in the mid-1990s were spin-offs, with significant engineering changes, from automobiles first manufactured for the Japanese market.

## Strategies for production and logistics: the assembly line

What philosophy guides how Honda actually makes its products? Honda has sought to combine the advantages inherent in what have normally been seen in the West as dichotomous and mutually exclusive production and logistics systems.

Honda first experimented with a 'free-flow' assembly line at its Kumamoto motorcycle plant on the Japanese island of Kyushu in the early 1980s. This system was an attempt to combine productive efficiency with human dignity. Efficiency and dignity have been treated as polar opposites in the traditional western strategy for manufacturing design which regarded the mind-numbing and alienating continuous assembly line, with its fragmentation of tasks carefully orchestrated by time-and-motion staff, as the epitome of efficiency, and viewed the efforts of the Swedish automobile manufacturers Volvo and Saab to develop more personally satisfying forms of 'group work' in the 1970s and 1980s as necessarily sacrificing efficiency.

Honda's free-flow assembly line, the first of its type in the Japanese motor industry, was based on a series of separate carriers upon which partially completed vehicles were placed (or hung). The carriers followed each other from work-station to work-station but their speed of movement was not controlled centrally as with the traditional chain-driven line. Advantages were sought in terms of efficiency *and* dignity. On the one hand both manual and automated assembly tasks could be undertaken more accurately since the separate carriers could stop at each work-station. Moreover, work could be completed satisfactorily before the carrier was sent on its way. On the other hand production workers could be given a sense of control over the production process since they could make the decision that the task had been executed properly and that the carrier should now move to the next work-station. The free-flow principle was later adopted for the new third automobile assembly line built at the Suzuka factory in the late 1980s, where Honda has continued to experiment with it.

## Production planning

Honda has also developed an innovative strategy for the planning of production, a strategy which exhibits characteristics of both the traditional dichotomous poles. One pole is 'large-lot mass production', in which manufacturing is organized so that thousands of identical or virtually identical products are made in a row, or series. This implies the use of dedicated machinery and, indeed, in the western automobile industry each factory frequently can make only a single automobile model, which is changed every few years. To many, the automobile industry is the epitome of large-lot mass production. In this system the goal is to reduce costs, achieved at the expense of product variety (the trade-off within the western mass production system).

At the other extreme is the 'flexible lot-of-one' production system said to characterize at least some firms in the Japanese automobile industry. In this system each assembly line can handle several different models with minimal if any changeover time, and the partly finished vehicles coming down the line are sequenced in 'lots of one', i.e. each vehicle is different from that preceding and following it (colours, options, engines, numbers of doors, models). The objective of this system is to permit far greater product variety (to the point of 'customized' products individually ordered). One drawback is the very complex logistics system needed to supply components to the assembly line in the correct order. In general terms, the Toyota-developed 'just-in-time' production and logistics system can be seen as a dualist puzzle solution permitting both product variety and productive efficiency.

Honda's own innovative strategy for production planning has been to develop a 'small batch' production system based around the key number 60 and its factors (30, 15, 12, etc.). Automobiles are sent down the assembly lines in batches in which each vehicle is exactly the same (including colour). Workers therefore execute exactly the same tasks for each batch. Components are delivered to the assembly line in batches (lot sizes, colours, optional extras) which exactly match the vehicles they will be fitted into. The objective is to combine the advantages of large-lot production (simpler logistics and quality control, less likelihood of error, easier to programme production schedules) and of small-lot production (ability to offer a wider range of products to consumers and greater worker involvement and satisfaction).

## Making production planning and product marketing coherent

This small batch production system is closely linked to Honda's strategy towards marketing and sales. Honda has tended not to offer its customers the spectacular breadth of choice developed by other Japanese automobile manufacturers during the Japanese 'bubble economy' of the late 1980s. Some firms expanded product variety so far that Japanese customers could choose among several dozen different steering wheels per model, a level of consumer choice which was soon recognized to have got out of hand. Honda's strategy emphasizes the high technology built into all its products and it was quick to offer features like advanced engines (though often available in only two sizes per model), anti-lock brakes, electric windows and sun-roofs as standard rather than optional extras, thus simplifying product variety within each model type.

In operations management, an important dichotomy distinguishes 'push'-based production planning and logistical systems from 'pull'-based systems. In the former, said to be typically western, production schedules for particular models are set out months in advance, and alignment of output levels with customer demand tends to focus on sales strategy (e.g. discounting may be necessary). In the latter, said to be typically Japanese, automobiles are only made to customer order.

Honda's approach to production planning is to operate a combination push-pull system. When planning at the annual scale, production levels of particular models can be varied up or down as a function of demand, because flexible equipment means that production lines can be used for various models (in gross terms, a pull system). When undertaking monthly planning, an 'un-Japanese' push system fixes the total mix of products and appropriate schedules several months in advance, based on market forecasts. Simultaneously a small-scale inventory pull system is utilized for everyday production planning, where it helps deal with unforeseen difficulties: if, for instance, there is a problem with a certain colour of paint in the paint shops, components makers may be alerted in a matter of hours that the production schedule has been altered and they will need to respond accordingly. The outcome at Honda is the simultaneous operation of pull- and push-based production planning systems rather than dominance of one type over the other.

**Relationships with components makers**

In the analysis of inter-firm relationships, in particular buyer–supplier relations in the components supply chain, a distinction is traditionally made in the West between vertical integration and market relationships (reflected in the 'make or buy?' decision). Honda's approach to relationships with its components suppliers transcends this dichotomy and others associated with supply chain management. In Japan Honda has only a handful of components makers that might be considered to belong to its supplier 'family', and is the only firm in the Japanese automobile industry not to organize its own 'suppliers association' as a forum for suppliers to meet and solve common problems. Honda does build long-term relationships with its suppliers, but these are not buttressed by the institutional mechanisms (cross-shareholding, 'family' relationships, supplier associations) often said to govern long-term relationships in Japan.

In North America, where a substantial network of more than eighty Japanese 'transplant' component makers has developed to supply Honda with components, Honda invested its own capital in a number of the early arrivals as a means of reducing the risk for its smaller Japanese partners. Other than this, formal linkages in North America are nonexistent. And yet in operational terms Honda intervenes directly in the 'internal' activities of its component makers when it believes this necessary. For a number of components Honda arranges the purchase of the raw materials, for example steel and aluminium, two or three tiers back along the supply chain, which will eventually find their way into Honda automobiles, gaining advantages in price and quality. Honda engineers also visit suppliers regularly, and may be stationed in their factories for a time if serious problems arise in components delivery and quality.

Thus relationships with component makers are based on complex combinations of close control and open, commercial relationships, creating a structure which defies the polar types in traditional views of buyer–supplier relations. The goal is clearly to solve the dualist puzzle to gain the advantages accruing from each polar type of organizing.

The same refusal to fit easily into traditional categories holds for the the number of supplier firms from which Honda sources each component. The traditional dichotomous choice between 'dual/multiple' sourcing strategy versus 'single' sourcing strategy is bypassed by Honda, where sourcing strategy is based on elements of both. Thus Honda sources a certain type of seat (the basic version, say) for its Accord model from supplier A, in single-sourcing fashion, and simultaneously sources a different type of seat (perhaps a high tech electronic version) from supplier B, also in single-sourcing fashion. The two suppliers are not in direct competition, yet Honda can subtly play them off (in dual-sourcing fashion) since each is aware of the other's existence and willingness to expand its market share when plans are made for the next Accord model change. Honda gains the advantage of both single sourcing (stable relationships with one supplier) and dual sourcing (an element of competition).

Honda's ability to find solutions even reaches into the geographical pattern of its relationships with component makers in North America. The traditional approach is to choose between purchasing from component makers located very long distances away, often to allow cheap labour sources in other regions and countries to be exploited (a feature of the 'western model'), and the spatially concentrated production system at Toyota City in Japan, where hundreds of supplier companies and nearly all Toyota's production capacity are concentrated into a few square kilometres, which is particularly advantageous for just-in-time logistics.

In North America, where Honda has greatly influenced the general location choices made by its Japanese component makers, the geographical pattern reflects both spatial dispersal and spatial concentration. In Ohio, where Honda's main manufacturing base has been constructed, there are now more than forty Japanese-owned firms making automobile components, nearly all of which supply Honda. Concentration within a two-hour travel-time permits just-in-time 'pull' logistics to be operated on a day-to-day basis. However, within Ohio the factories are dispersed to small town locations 10 to 20 miles apart; this way, their local labour markets are separated and the new investments and jobs they represent will not drive up local wages. Distant from Honda too, they can offer wages only half to two-thirds those paid at the automobile assembly plant. In other words, Honda's network of component makers is designed to combine the advantages of spatial concentration and spatial dispersal.

## CONCLUDING REMARKS

Honda's dualist puzzle-solving philosophy seems to permeate its strategic thinking, its functions and its operations: organizational process and structures; product technologies and designs; manufacturing systems; and relationships with component makers. With the internationalization of Honda operations it is now becoming possible to discern how Honda is tackling the puzzles implicit in the dichotomy between 'globalization' and 'localization' of organization and processes that has long influenced the development of multinational enterprises.[9]

In the traditional language of strategic management, we have been examining the resource side of the strategy equation. In the language of the recent literature, Honda possesses a key 'strategic competence' in its critical approach to the 'received wisdom' inherent in all functions of management. Understanding its creative approach to the dichotomous categories of the management world, its *dualist puzzle solving*, therefore presents us with precious insights into Honda's spectacular success in evolving from its foundation in 1948 to its status as one of the world's leading manufacturing companies.

It is Honda's refusal to accept taken-for-granted solutions that lies behind its strategic innovations. Innovative strategic thinking means dispensing with old certainties. The traditional 'mind-set' based on tolerating trade-offs and/or selection between mutually exclusive alternatives may provide a comforting framework, and is indeed enshrined in some areas of management, notably production and operations management and business/corporate strategic management. Comforting frameworks, however, do not challenge us to innovate and improve. Traditional approaches permit and legitimate strategic choices so that when we progress in one direction we regress in another, or we relentlessly pursue narrow objectives in the belief that we have to jettison other objectives which may 'contradict' them.

Regarding Honda's approach to dualist puzzle solving, many questions remain. Precisely how does Honda arrive at its problem solutions? Is there 'one best way' to solve each puzzle or are there multiple possible solutions? Has Honda found different, context-dependent, solutions in different parts of the world? Can we find examples in other companies, Japanese or western, that follow a similar approach in whole or in part? Above all, can we as managers study our own dualist puzzles and learn from Honda?

In the early 1990s Honda was experiencing similar competitive problems to other Japanese car makers, in the Japanese market especially. These problems seemed to have slowed its previous apparently inexorable growth. Yet Honda's success in globalizing its operations during the 1980s had provided critical resources (markets, production bases) which several of its competitors, Japanese and western, lacked. It does not seem unreasonable to predict that Honda will emerge with new and innovative surprises for the automobile industry and all management practitioners in the near future, outcomes of a paradoxical philosophy of strategy undergirded by advanced dualist puzzle-solving methods.

## NOTES

1  Overview written by Andrew Mair and the editors of this volume.
2  Perhaps the best-known study of Honda's decision making places a great deal of emphasis on the role of luck rather than good management at Honda (Richard T. Pascale, 'Perspectives on strategy: the real story behind Honda's success', *California Management Review*, 26(3), 1984: 47–72.

3 *Honda European Information Handbook*, 1991–2.
4 © A. Mair 1995.
  This case study has been written as a basis for class discussion rather than to illustrate effective or ineffective managerial or administrative behaviour.
5 Clay Chandler and Paul Ingrassia, *Wall Street Journal*, 4 November 1991: 1 and A10.
6 Alex Taylor III, *Fortune*, 20 December 1991.
7 Andrew Mair, *Honda's Global Local Corporation* (Basingstoke: Macmillan, 1994).
8 The evolution of each Honda model – Accord, Civic, Prelude, Legend, etc. – has followed a somewhat different path.
9 Andrew Mair, *Honda's Global Local Corporation* (Basingstoke: Macmillan, 1994). 'Honda's global flexifactory network', *International Journal of Operations and Production Management*, 14(3), 1994: 6–23; 'Strategic localization of the global corporation', paper presented to the annual conference of the British Academy of Management, Lancaster University, September 1994.